The Spirit of Montesquieu's *Persian Letters*

The Spirit of Montesquieu's *Persian Letters*

Edited by

Constantine Christos Vassiliou, Jeffrey Church, and Alin Fumurescu

LEXINGTON BOOKS
Lanham • Boulder • New York • London

Published by Lexington Books
An imprint of The Rowman & Littlefield Publishing Group, Inc.
4501 Forbes Boulevard, Suite 200, Lanham, Maryland 20706
www.rowman.com

86-90 Paul Street, London EC2A 4NE

British Library Cataloguing in Publication Information Available

Library of Congress Cataloging-in-Publication Data

Names: Vassiliou, Constantine Christos, editor. | Church, Jeffrey, 1978- editor. | Fumurescu, Alin, 1967- editor.
Title: The spirit of Montesquieu's Persian letters / edited by Constantine Vassiliou, Jeffrey Church, and Alin Fumurescu.
Description: Lanham : Lexington Books, [2023] | Includes bibliographical references and index.
Identifiers: LCCN 2022060883 (print) | LCCN 2022060884 (ebook) | ISBN 9781666913279 (cloth ; alk. paper) | ISBN 9781666913286 (ebook)
Subjects: LCSH: Montesquieu, Charles de Secondat, baron de, 1689-1755. Lettres persanes. | Montesquieu, Charles de Secondat, baron de, 1689-1755--Political and social views. | LCGFT: Literary criticism.
Classification: LCC PQ2011.L6 S75 2023 (print) | LCC PQ2011.L6 (ebook) | DDC 843/.5--dc23/eng/20230123
LC record available at https://lccn.loc.gov/2022060883
LC ebook record available at https://lccn.loc.gov/2022060884

Contents

Foreword

Helena Rosenblatt

The *Persian Letters* is one of the first bestsellers of the Enlightenment, if not *the* first. Published in 1721, it has amused, titillated, and provoked readers ever since. Montesquieu later commented that the *Letters* "were pleasant and gay and were found pleasing for that reason."[1] But they were clearly more than just pleasant and gay. They also asked profound and difficult questions, questions that are as relevant today as they were in the eighteenth century. Montesquieu left these questions largely unanswered, and in so doing, he invited his readers to try to answer them themselves—in other words, to think critically about themselves and their world. Above else, it is this invitation *to think* (and *to question*) that makes this book such an outstanding example of the Enlightenment.

Attacks on the Enlightenment have been an inextricable part of its history from the very beginning and continue today. One of the most common accusations in recent times has been that the *philosophes* had an unbounded faith in the powers of human reason. With newly acquired knowledge, they thought they could wipe away the past and build anew. Blind to diversity, their "universalist" and "rational" principles were in fact irremediably sexist, Eurocentric, and racist. Or so it has been said.

As this volume of essays makes perfectly clear, the *Persian Letters* shatters any such simplistic allegations. Montesquieu, an emblematic thinker of the Enlightenment, had no overweening confidence in man's ability to remake the world. On the contrary, one of the main themes of the novel is man's inability to change. Moreover, human beings, according to Montesquieu, are not driven by reason alone, and, in fact, reason itself is flawed.

There is little, if any, Eurocentrism in this novel. Montesquieu shows a keen interest in diverse traditions and superstitions, and his comparative perspective serves mostly to identify similarities between Persian and French cultures. The French believe in one virgin while the Persians believe in seven. French women wear one veil while the Persians wear four. Women are oppressed in both countries. In any case, Europeans in the novel are mostly portrayed as ridiculous—they are prey to their imaginations, and even their king holds fast to superstitions peddled by the pope. The head of the Catholic Church "sometimes makes the king believe that three is nothing but one, that the bread the person eats is not bread, or that wine one drinks is not wine, and a thousand other things of that sort" (Letter 24, 40). The reader is led to conclude that the French have little, if anything, to teach the Persians. All of this Montesquieu manages to convey with inimitable wit and humor.

Certainly, Montesquieu does not believe that reason alone can be counted on to change and improve the world. As several authors point out, the characters in Montesquieu's story are rather more governed by their passions and sentiments than by reason. In the seraglio, fears, jealousies, and forbidden sexual desires reign. In France, people are led astray by their imaginations. They believe in "peddlers of the wind" like John Law and "magicians" like the pope. But passions can also be good. The vanity of Parisian women drives the economy and provides work for the poor. Self-interest might also be good for the economy, but a constitution based on it would undoubtedly fail. Human nature is complicated, and life is full of contradictions. There is no reason to think that this will change any time soon. In some ways, the story Montesquieu tells is a tragedy, not a comedy.

The essays assembled in this volume marvelously convey the complexity and sophistication of the *Persian Letters*. Part I reminds us that we are dealing with a work of both literature and philosophy. By choosing the format of the novel, Montesquieu is able to deliver deep insights into human weaknesses and foibles with humor and wit. He identifies tensions and contradictions in human morals and manners, which is partly why the *Letters* invites multiple engagements and interpretations, even in the same reader. One quotation from the novel, provided by Céline Spector, stands out as a perfect response to the tendency to over-rationalize the Enlightenment and also explains why the novel format is so appropriate. Montesquieu has Usbek, the serious philosopher, say, "There are certain truths for which it is not easy to be persuaded, but which one must also be made to feel. Such are the truths of morality" (Letter 11).

Part II analyzes the *Persian Letters'* treatment of classic topics in political thought. An essay on international law shows Montesquieu's considerable doubts about universalist thinking and his recognition that human beings have difficulty in overcoming their cultural prejudices. Through comparison with the thought of Bodin, we are made to see Montesquieu's insightful decoupling of sovereignty and power, which illustrates his sensitivity to the psychosocial dynamics of life. Through a comparison with Hobbes we are made to see his sensitivity to the human need of recognition and honor. Montesquieu turns out to be quite the social psychologist.

Part III explores Montesquieu's views on commerce, which, as it turns out, are not as optimistic as has often been said. His views were darker and, again, more complicated. For example, he was acutely sensitive to the abuses of self-interest. We also learn of Montesquieu's keen interest in women's positive roles as motors of economic progress, but also of his realization that such "progress" meant accepting women's love of luxury, which could be morally harmful.

Finally, in part IV several authors invite us to think about who, if anyone, the hero is in the novel. In much previous scholarship, it has been Usbek, who often seems to express Montesquieu's own point of view. He is a philosopher and expresses enlightened ideas; for example, he is a proponent of international law and opposes empire. He believes in religious toleration and "mild government." As it turns out, however, Usbek is also a cruel despot who keeps his wives enslaved and rules them with an iron fist. He is so prideful and lacking in self-knowledge that he is not even aware of the contradiction. Where, then, is Montesquieu's own voice expressed? It is "everywhere and nowhere," and it is left for the reader to decide. One thing is clear: being enlightened does not necessarily mean that one is a good person or even that one is capable of improving. It can simply mean that one is a hypocrite.

Who, then, is the hero of the story? Perhaps it is Rica, because he is sociable and cosmopolitan and advocates for the emancipation of women. Yet Rica's ironic detachment and unwillingness or inability to act in the world also make him a flawed character. The person who comes closest to being a hero is actually Roxane, one of Usbek's wives, but she is enslaved, betrays her husband, and dies by suicide.

The concluding essays explore the anomalous relationship between the presentation and composition of the letters. What is Montesquieu's purpose in ordering them this way? There can be several reasons. This is only one of the countless riddles, contradictions, contrasts, and tensions in the *Persian Letters*, which is no doubt designed to convey the complexity of the human condition and the many obstacles to progress faced by modern men and women.

One can only agree with Stuart Warner's concluding remarks: the *Persian Letters* is an "exquisitely complicated book" that engages us to think deeply while we laugh.

NOTE

1. Montesquieu, "Mes pensées," in *Oeuvres complètes* (Paris: Bibliothèque de la Plèiade, 1956), 122.

PART I

The *Persian Letters* in the History of Political Theory

Chapter 1

Philosophizing the Passions

The Seraglio as Laboratory in the Persian Letters[1]

Céline Spector, translated by Catherine R. Power

"It is not by speechifying that despotism must be attacked, but by making clear that it tyrannizes the despot himself."[2]

Montesquieu is an essential link in the philosophical project to rehabilitate the passions and sentiment that began in the eighteenth century. He sought to avoid the oft-encountered pitfalls of the moralists. Debates about the passions should seek not only formal comprehension but the union of the soul and the body, which must involve the imagination. This is the reason for the rise to prominence of the novel: fiction is the ideal site for experimenting with the passions. The genre of fiction could uniquely be used to explain the relation between the physical and the moral; it allows the physical to find a place within morality.[3] Moreover, fiction must skillfully engage with the passions of its reader. This idea is expressed in the *Persian Letters* when Usbek responds to one of the interlocutors who had challenged him with this problem of the relations between passions, virtue, and happiness: "To fulfill what you prescribed for me, I did not believe I had to employ very abstract reasoning: there are certain truths for which it is not enough to be persuaded, but which one must also be made to feel. Such are truths of morality" (Letter 11, 18–19).

The contribution of the *Persian Letters* to this philosophical rehabilitation of the passions involves its use of Orientalist fictions.[4] Montesquieu's imagined seraglio serves as an experimental workshop in which to explore classic questions of practical philosophy: how are we to conceive of the nature of the passions in terms of their physiological and moral effects? Can reason and virtue tame them, or can they be swayed only by other passions? Montesquieu's conclusion is unequivocal: the fanatical repression of desires can lead only to perversion and revolution. Only "gentle" and nonviolent regulation of the passions can produce an enduring equilibrium. Fundamentalism to the command of the "Law" abolishing all liberty produces disorder—of which the despot himself proves victim. The lesson derives from the imagined lands of Islam and the effects of polygamy, but it implicitly applies equally to Christian nations, where the church rules as mistress over her convents and monasteries.

THE SERAGLIO AS LABORATORY

In the *Persian Letters*, Montesquieu oversees several philosophical experiments in order to observe, compare, and evaluate different models for regulating the passions. According to him, "life is nothing but a series of passions" that determine thoughts and actions.[5] His aim is nevertheless undogmatic: "We have scarcely ever more grossly deceived ourselves than when we have wanted to reduce men's feelings to a system."[6] This is why the seraglio can serve as a laboratory. It enables him to explore the effects of a despotic regime on human nature isolated from outside societal variables. This is where Montesquieu discovers the correlation between domestic, civic, and political servitude. He demonstrates that the passions' dynamics observed within the microcosm of the seraglio is analogous to the macrocosmic order of despotism itself. *The Spirit of the Laws* suggests that the seraglio can be conceived of as a laboratory. Montesquieu is proposing a thought experiment aimed at illustrating the despotic regime's need for domestic servitude. Montesquieu writes,

> Let us assume for a moment that the fickleness of spirit and indiscretions of our women, what pleases and displeases them, their passions, both great and small, were transferred to an Eastern government along with the activity and liberty they have among us: what father of a family could be tranquil for a moment? Suspects everywhere, enemies everywhere; the state would be shaken, one would see rivers of blood flowing.[7]

This scenario, imagined in *The Spirit of the Laws*, is actually the working hypothesis of the *Persian Letters*. Thanks to the medium of fiction, the reader is invited to question the value of the seraglio as a site for the privileging of male pleasure and female servitude within an environment where the force of the physical passions is such that "morality can do practically nothing."[8]

Nevertheless, one major distinction, too often overlooked, separates the two works. In *The Spirit of the Laws*, the seraglio's mechanism is fit to function. Montesquieu thinks that in southern countries, the violence of the passions annihilates the authority of morals and justifies the "cloistering" of wives. The seraglio appears to be the only disciplining instrument for women in places where exaggerated sensitivities lead to erotic mania and the eradication of all modesty. Two psychological laws define the relationship between physical and moral causes. The first suggests a correlation between climate and degree of vice—"As you move toward the countries of the south, you will believe you have moved away from morality itself";[9] the second, that the sequestering of wives is proportional with the purity of social mores. Imprisonment of the wives, the constant surveillance of eunuchs, and the rigorous discipline do seem to bear fruit: "In the various states of the East, the mores are purer as the enclosure of women is stricter."[10] In Oriental nations, where "a temptation is a fall . . . there must be bolted doors instead of precepts."[11]

Montesquieu suggests a different understanding in the *Persian Letters*.[12] Far from allowing wives to escape the temptations of vice, the seraglio is the modus operandi barring them from virtue; their enclosure is the mistress of all their perversions. The moral cause—the institution of the seraglio—no longer constrains the physical cause. The laws of the seraglio fail to inform social mores and make virtue reign over individuals purified of erotic pleonexia.[13] Montesquieu thus reveals the absurdity of fanatical virtue. The "sacred" is a pretext for constructing prisons in which "sacred" laws make women into martyrs. Usbek asks,

> What more would you do if you could leave that sacred place, which is for you a harsh prison, as it is to your companions a favorable asylum against the attacks of vice, a sacred temple in which your sex loses its weakness, and is invincible despite all the disadvantages of nature? What would you do if, left to yourself, you had only your love for me with which to defend yourself, which is so grievously offended, and your duty, which you have so shamefully betrayed? How holy are the morals of the country where you live, which draw you away from the outrages of the vilest slaves! You should thank me for the discomfort in which I make you life, since it is only due to that that you still deserve to live. (Letter 20, 35)

The demonstration brooks no exception; in the West just as in the East, religious and moral fundamentalism is destined for failure. Diderot picks up the theme in *La Religieuse*: where the libido's energy is powerful, the convent will only prove deadly, prone to cruelty and persecutions. Moreover, the oppressive order maintained by the iron glove of religion cannot endure. Liberty—of which sexual liberty is a major part—retains its subversive power.[14] Abolishing communication between the sexes always risks provoking rebellion. As the final return of Roxane reveals, despotism can be upended. Thought control cannot be total; slaves retain their taste for freedom. At the end of the book, the infidel Roxane rebels:

> How could you think that I was credulous enough to imagine that I existed in the world only in order to worship your every caprice, that while you permitted yourself everything, you had the right to torment all of my desires? No! I might have lived in servitude, but I have always been free. I have reformed your laws by those of nature, and my spirit has always remained independent. (Letter 161, 268)

Believing himself to be perceptive, Usbek the despot had been blind to the hatred his rule engendered. Determined to be a *philosophe*, he had been, in reality, "credulous," unable to understand the subversive power of desire.

TRANSFERENCE, SUBSTITUTION, SUBLIMATION

Montesquieu's experimentation within the laboratory of the seraglio reveals the inherent correlations between passion and three variables: a certain biological configuration, a psychophysiological disposition, and its object. The "Oriental novel" is a demonstration of the failure of the despotic regime to master the passions.

The Master

At first glance, the master appears to be the most fortunate of men. Inherently powerful, he is equally endowed with the means to satisfy all his passions—thanks to the plurality of wives at the service of his pleasure. Yet this omnipotence turns into impotence. Shortly after his departure from Persia, Usbek admits that he feels neither love nor desire for his wives, passion having in some way destroyed itself. In a word, the easy entitlement of despotism leads to disgust, not to joy.[15] Within the setting of fiction, we discover the moral truth recorded in Montesquieu's *Pensées* and in other theoretical pamphlets and voluptuous novels: a man can never know enduring, vigorous, and intense passion when he wears down his own machine and blunts his senses. From an abundance of violent joy is born the progressive desensitization of the pleasures.[16] As a result of polygamy, Usbek writes that "[l]ove, among us, induces neither trouble nor fury. It is a languid passion, which leaves our souls calm. The plurality of wives saves us from their empire; they temper the violence of our desires" (Letter 56, 92).

Not confining his satire to the Orient, Montesquieu's target is as much the ascetic apparatus of Christianity. A later letter clarifies that the desperate quest into the "desert" is equally in vain. Musing on the first hermits, tormented by their demons, Usbek writes thus to his brother, "*a santon, in the Monastery of Casbin,*"

> In vain we seek in the desert for a tranquil state. Temptations always follow us; our passions, represented by demons, still do not leave us; these monsters of the heart, these illusions of the mind, these vain phantoms of error and untruth, always appear before us in order to seduce us; they attack us even in our fasts and hair-shirts, that is to say, even in our very vigor. (Letter 93, 150)

The seraglio can impose temperance no better than the desert can. This is because the absence of love does not enable the master to extinguish all passion. Usbek's indifference is accompanied by "a secret jealousy that devours" him (Letter 6, 10), feeding his suspicions about the fidelity of his wives. Insensitivity transforms itself into fragile sensitivity. The fear of dispossession replaces the pleasure of possession, according to the mechanism uncovered in the *History of Jealousy*.[17] The despot's power is lost in the chasm that separates physical possession from moral possession, the hold on a body from the dominion over hearts. Within this chasm of freedom, the imagination runs wild, sustaining jealousy with all its doubts and anxieties.

The Eunuchs

The example of the eunuchs, pure guardians of the Law, confirms this ternary structure of passion, an interplay between biological determination, psychological elaboration, and an object of satisfaction or of substitution. The emasculated slaves experience the persistence of desire despite the loss of the organ. The disproportion between desire and aptitude does nothing but heighten desire. The letters of the eunuchs attest to the fact that appetite is not extinguished by one's inability to satisfy it.[18] The chief eunuch reveals his despair at being imprisoned in the places where constant temptation stokes his desire:

> Weary of serving in the most toilsome employment, I calculated sacrificing my passions to my repose and fortune. Unfortunate wretch that I was! My worried mind made me see the compensation, but not the loss. I hoped that I would be delivered from the blows of love by the impotence to satisfy it. Alas! *The effect of my passions was extinguished in me without extinguishing their cause*, and

far from being relieved from them, I found myself surrounded by objects that constantly excited them. (Letter 9, 14–15)

The eunuch's lived experience of the flesh is thus the dissociation of a cause—desire—and certain biological events. Passion is reducible neither to its biological expression nor to its somatic resonance. Passion overflows the organ. Just as Uzbek's concrete power translates into an impotence of desire, the impotence of the eunuch is accompanied by the decoupled power of desire. In his "Essai sur les causes qui peuvent affecter les esprits et les caractères," Montesquieu employs medical language to reveal the process by which sexual abstinence, by inducing a retention of semen, prompts a series of sad passions in the eunuch and the priest.[19] However, in the *Persian Letters*, the philosopher is above all interested in the libidinal economy's metamorphosis and the adoption of substitute satisfactions. Passion always finds other means of satisfying itself:

I have heard you say a thousand times that eunuchs feel a certain voluptuousness toward women that is unknown to us; *that nature compensates them for their loss*; that nature has some resources that make amends for the disadvantage of their condition; that one can indeed cease to feel; and in their condition, they operate, as it were, in a *third realm* of the senses, in which, so to speak, one is only changing pleasures. (Letter 53, 86)

However, this "*third realm*" that the despot invokes is a mystification. Indeed, all the complaints of the eunuchs, their rage and their despair, serve as proof that the third sex ignores the providential *compensation* through which nature indemnifies its own losses.[20] The substitutive economy can function only between distinct passions; as the intensity of one is assuaged, other passions move in to fill the "void" left by the first.[21]

The experimental method of the seraglio illustrates the various effects of substitution, of the transfer or sublimation between *libido sentiendi* and *libido dominandi*. The chief eunuch turns to his autobiography to explain how the decline in the intensity of erotic passion that comes with age provoked in him a sadistic augmentation of the lust for power. Frustration transforms itself into the vengeful pleasure of persecution. The pain of suffering becomes the pleasure in making others suffer, and the disillusionment of impotence finds its outlet in violence and abuses of power. Contemplating the wives, the eunuch writes,

Although I guard them for another, the pleasure of making myself obeyed gives me a secret joy. When I deprive them of everything, it seems to me that it is for me, and I always receive an *indirect satisfaction* from it. I find myself in the seraglio as in a small empire, and *my ambition, the only passion that remains in me,* is satisfied a little. (Letter 9, 15–16)

Alienated from himself and humanity, the eunuch embodies the Nietzschean figure of the slave—severed from his own ability, and in the absence of a God-Master—forcing women to conform to an ascetic ideal. The eunuch is the slave finding reactionary satisfaction in the "moral" frustration of the desire of others. The example of the Orient is paradigmatic. The author of the *Persian Letters* undoubtedly sought to popularize divine and profane love, and to illustrate Christianity's insult against human nature. In one of his youthful pamphlets, "Les prêtres dans le paganism," Montesquieu makes this same comparison of monks and priests with eunuchs.[22]

The Wives

The seraglio laboratory of Usbek's wives reveals, in the end, the correlations between frustrated aspirations and substitutive satisfactions, between the desire to please and the desire to dominate, between carnal lust and the will to power.[23] The revelation concerns the nature of passion itself in its relation to the object: desire pursues the representation of the good and judges as "good" all that which can be supplied to its satisfaction. All this happens as libidinal energy not bound to a single object finds its expression—be it via introversion into hysteria or via extroversion into the rage, the cruelty, and the delights of vengeance—but never in the durable submission to the Law. The setting for the *Persian Letters* reveals that nothing would suffice to reprimand the erotic frenzy of the wives, especially in the absence of the despot—neither the innocent diversions Usbek provides (the pleasures of music, countryside, of dance),[24] nor the moral law of purity and modesty inflexibly enforced by the eunuchs, nor even the precocious education of the seraglio intended to supplement the "might of reason" with the "meekness of habit."[25]

This is why the mechanisms of constraint, rigorous as they may be, have little efficacy. Behind the walls of the seraglio, the hatred of the eunuchs and the bulwark of the veils, the concupiscence of the wives is enchained in vain. The ruse permits not only the covert pleasures—adultery, homosexuality—but also phantasmal satisfactions enabling the frustrated wives to revel in the dreams and enchantments produced by the fire of the passions. Thus, in letter 62, Zélid confesses to her master that she derives more pleasure with imagination than the despot, who is always disappointed by a desire too easily fulfilled: "However, Usbek, do not imagine that your situation is happier than mine. I have tasted here a thousand pleasures unknown to you. My imagination has ceaselessly labored to make me know the value of them. I have lived, and you have only languished" (Letter 62, 101). Yet in describing the phantoms of her frustrated desires, Fatmé confesses to Usbek the impotence of unfulfillment: "How unhappy is a woman to have desires so violent, when she is deprived of those who alone can satisfy them" (Letter 7, 12).

The delights of imagination remain uncertain. That which the third wife, Zélis, deplores about her slave, Zélide, soon married to an impotent eunuch, applies equally to herself, doomed by destiny to a master without sufficient power: "And then! Always to dwell among images and phantoms! Living only in order to imagine! Always being close to pleasure and never having it! Languishing in the arms of an unfortunate wretch, and instead of responding to his sighs, only responding to his regrets!" (Letter 53, 86) This is the reason that wives suffer all the maladies associated with frustration: inertia, sadness, despair, but also hatred toward the master and the eunuchs that culminates in a desire for vengeance and a joy in cruel persecution.

Results from the system tried and tested in the seraglio laboratory are thus rigorously *dramatique*: humanity is denatured not by dominion of the passions, but by dominion of the Law, oriented toward the pleasure of a single person, which opposes the inclinations of all others with violence. Ironically, Usbek as philosopher would say the same thing with regard to the interdiction of wine: that the law designed "to render us more just, often serves only to render us more guilty," that the law should "treat man as a sentient being, rather than to treat him as a reasonable one," and that "the soul, united with the body, is ceaselessly tyrannized" (Letter 33, 54).[26] The philosopher-despot ought to understand that the economy of desire implemented in the seraglio is perverse and corrupt. From the ubiquity of mutilation to the necessity of constant recourse to punishment and the threat of death, life itself is negated by its powerlessness to produce and reproduce.[27]

ABSENT MASTER, HIDDEN GOD?

One question nevertheless remains. If the seraglio appears to be a laboratory characterized by its isolation and the absence of external disturbances, how is one to interpret the initial disturbance that sets the experiment in motion? The structure of the seraglio initially is effectively put in place by Usbek's departure to the West. The novel is presented as an observation of two overlapping variables: Usbek's extended absence and the rising disorder in the seraglio. Montesquieu is explicit about his project in his description of the design of the *Persian Letters*. The mechanism (the induced disturbance) reveals a real law, that "disorder in the Asian seraglio grows proportionally with the length of Usbek's absence, that is to say, *as fury increases and love diminishes*" ("Some Reflections," 269; emphasis added). The law states that competition between passions modulates in inverse proportion from one to the other. The master's absence coincides with the introduction of obstacles that lust must then overcome with strategy and subterfuge.

The seraglio experiment conducted in the absence of the despot reveals not only the disruption of a situation of initial equilibrium that throws the system into disorder and self-destruction, the final explosion of the seraglio, a veritable pressure cooker of overheated passions; it also reveals the development of the underlying turmoil of Usbek's form of pure despotism, his wives subjected as much by fear as by love. As *The Spirit of the Laws* explains, the very principle of despotic rule (fear) endlessly corrupts because it is, by its nature, corrupt. It endures only under exceptional circumstances—in this case, the passing benevolence of a despot toward his wives. Moreover, the experimental mechanism of the *Persian Letters* reveals the inversion of the normal and the pathological: that which one would believe to be pathological (a seraglio without a master, despotism without the despot) is in reality normal (in fact, the despot is always absent, delegating his power to his eunuchs or viziers).[28] The art of despotic rule manifests itself more purely to the extent that the master discharges himself from the daily life of the seraglio; the master is always absent.[29]

In this respect, the experimental mechanism of the *Persian Letters* explores the inevitable corruption of despotism. The passions can only be satisfied in oblique ways, through affectation and dissimulation. The master proves victim to the paradox of despotism: the more he controls, the less he rules. As the vice of tyranny is tightened, absolute power devolves into despotic power, and the passions, smothered but not extinguished, blaze back with all their fury, ultimately igniting revolution in the seraglio.

Herein rests the significance of the project linking fiction and philosophy: the novel is the laboratory of experimental philosophy. The thought experiment projected onto an exotic Other makes space for an investigation into the universal forms and general effects of the passions. Montesquieu's topic enables him to elucidate their nature, to discern their metamorphoses, and to understand their relations to the Law. Comparing the West to the East, a regime of free women to an alien and enslaving way of life, the scholar turns political: what he is proposing to the reader is not a science but a real *politics of the passions*, which would substitute the "violent remedies" of despotism with a "gentle and temperate regime" that regulates the passions and preserves political and civil liberty.

NOTES

1. This article is an abridged and amended version of my previous contribution titled "Le despotisme des passions dans les *Lettres persanes*," in *De Rabelais à Sade.*

L'analyse des passions dans le roman de l'âge classique, ed. C. Duflo and L. Ruiz (Saint-Etienne: Publications de l'Université de Saint-Etienne, 2003), 41–52.

2. Montesquieu, *My Thoughts*, trans. and ed. Henry C. Clark (Indianapolis: Liberty Fund, 2012), 1432: 413.

3. Ibid., 220: 93.

4. For a more in-depth analysis, see Céline Spector, *Montesquieu, les Lettres persanes* (Paris: Presses Universitaires de France, 1997).

5. Montesquieu, "Essai sur les causes qui peuvent affecter les esprits et les caractères," in *Œuvres complètes* (Paris: Gallimard, Bibliothèque de la Pléiade, 1951), II: 50; reprinted in *Œuvres et Ecrits divers*, I, in *Œuvres complètes*, vol. VIII, ed. P. Rétat (Oxford/Naples: Voltaire Foundation/Instituti Italiano per gli Studi Filosofici, 2003), 242.

6. Montesquieu, *My Thoughts*, 30: 9.

7. Montesquieu, *The Spirit of the Laws*, ed. and trans. Anne M. Cohler, Basia C. Miller, and Harold S. Stone (Cambridge: Cambridge University Press, 1989), book XVI.9, 270.

8. Ibid., XVI.8, 269.

9. Ibid., XIV.2, 234.

10. Ibid., XVI.9, 271.

11. Ibid., 16.8, 269.

12. Cf. C. Martin, "L'institution du sérail. Quelques réflexions sur le livre XVI de *L'Esprit des lois*," *Revue Montesquieu* 5 (2001): 41–57.

13. Cf. Jean Chardin, *Voyage de Paris à Ispahan* (Paris: La Découverte-Maspéro, 1983), pt. II, 59.

14. Michael A. Mosher, "The Judgmental Gaze of European Women: Gender, Sexuality, and the Critique of Republican Rule," *Political Theory* 22, no. 1 (February 1994): 25–44.

15. "It is not, Nessir, that I love them. I find myself, in this respect, in a state of insensibility that leaves me without desires. In the crowded seraglio where I have lived, *I anticipated love and destroyed love by love itself*" (Letter 6, 10; emphasis added).

16. Montesquieu, "Essai sur les causes qui peuvent affecter les esprits et les caractères," p. 50/242. Cf. also *My Thoughts*, 408: 155.

17. "If, in the uncertainty or fear of being unloved, we come to suspect someone of being loved, we feel a pain called jealousy." In Montesquieu, "History of Jealousy," *My Thoughts*, 509: 176. See also *My Thoughts*, 719: 217.

18. Cf. Diana J. Schaub, *Erotic Liberalism: Women and Revolution in Montesquieu's Persian Letters* (London: Rowman and Littlefield, 1995), 74, and Céline Spector, *Les Lettres persanes de Montesquieu*, ed. C. Martin (Paris: Presses Universitaires de France, 2013), 169–84.

19. Montesquieu, "Essai sur les causes qui peuvent affecter les esprits et les caractères," 49/241–42.

20. Cf. Letter 9. Moreover, an unnerved Zélis observes, "Never has a passion been more powerful and more heated than that of Cosrou, the white eunuch, for my slave Zélide" (Letter 53, 85).

21. Cf. Letter 56, where Usbek describes a passion for gambling in France, especially among women: "It is true that in their youth they scarcely devote themselves to it except as to favor a dearer passion; but as they grow older, their passion for gambling grows younger, *and this passion entirely fills the void left by others*" (91).

22. Cf. Montesquieu, "Some Fragments of a Work I Had Written on Priests under Paganism, Which I Have Tossed in the Fire," *My Thoughts*, 2004: 616.

23. Cf. Letter 3, "Zachi to Usbek": "I confess it to you, Usbek—an even more lively passion than ambition made me desire to please you. I saw myself insensibly becoming the mistress of your heart. . . . The triumph was completely mine, and the despair that of my rivals" (8).

24. " . . . amuse them by music, dances, and delicious drinks; persuade them to assemble often. If they want to go to the country, you may take them there." Letter 2, 6. N.b. Doctors and moralists were known to prescribe similar diversions during this period. (Cf. Denis Diderot, "Passions" (medicin) in *l'Encyclopédie de Diderot et d'Alembert*.)

25. As Zélis writes to Usbek, "With your daughter having reached the seventh year, I believed that it was time to have her enter into the interior apartments of the seraglio, and not wait until she was ten to entrust her to the black eunuchs. . . . Must everything be expected from the force of reason, and nothing from the gentleness of habit?" (Letter 62, 100).

26. As J. Goldzink states, in Usbek experience an internal conflict between "philosophe curieux" and "l'époux furieux"; *Montesquieu et les passions* (Paris: Presses universitaires de France, 2001), 25–29.

27. Cf. A. Grosrichard, *Structure du sérail. La fiction du despotisme asiatique dans l'Occident classique* (Paris: Seuil, 1979), 56.

28. Cf. Letter 64, on the seraglio in its pure state, and letter, 96, where the first eunuch articulates (complains about) the eunuchs' plight.

29. Grosrichard, *Structure du sérail*, 14.

BIBLIOGRAPHY

Chardin, J. 1983. *Voyage de Paris à Ispahan*. Paris: Le Découverte-Maspéro.

Courtois, J. 1999, January. "Comment Roxane devient philosophe. Romanesque de l'illisible et sexuation des concepts dans les Lettres persanes." *La Lecture littéraire* 3: 27–47.

Diderot, D. 1765. "Passions" *Encyclopédie ou Dictionnaire raisonné des sciences, des arts, et des métiers* 12: 142–46.

Goldzink, J. 2001. *Montesquieu et les passions*. Paris: Presses Universitaires de France.

Grosrichard, A. 1979. *Structure du sérail. La fiction du despotisme asiatique dans l'Occident classique*. Paris: Seuil.

Martin, C. 2001. "L'institution du sérail. Quelques réflexions sur le livre XVI de L'Esprit des lois." *Revue Montesquieu* 5: 41–57.

Montesquieu. 1951. *Oeuvres complètes*. Vol. II. Paris: Gallimard, Bibliothèque de la Pléiade.

————. 1989. *The Spirit of the Laws*. Edited and translated by Anne M. Cohler, Basia C. Miller, and Harold S. Stone. Cambridge: Cambridge University Press.

————. 2003. *Oeuvres complètes*. Oxford/Naples: Voltaire Foundation/Instituti Italiano per gli Studi Filosofici.

————. 2012. *My Thoughts*. Translated and edited by Henry C. Clark. Indianapolis: Liberty Fund.

Mosher, M. 1994, February. "The Judgmental Gaze of European Women: Gender, Sexuality, and the Critique of Republican Rule." *Political Theory* 22, no. 1: 25–44.

Schaub, D. J. 1995. *Erotic Liberalism: Woeman and Revolution in Montesquieu's Persian Letters*. London: Rowman and Littlefield.

Spector, C. 1997. *Montesquieu, les "Lettres persanes."* Paris: Presses Universitaires de France.

————. 2003. "Le despotisme des passions dans les *Lettres persanes*." In *De Rabelais à Sade. L'analyse des passions dans le roman de l'âge classique*, edited by C. Duflor and L. Ruiz. Saint-Etienne: Publications de l'Université de Saint-Etienne.

————. 2013. "Le despotisme des passions dans les *Lettres persanes*. In *Les lettres persanes de Montesquieu*, edited by C. Martin, 169–84. Paris: Presses Universitaires de France.

Chapter 2

Conflict in the *Persian Letters*

Pauline Kra

The world of the *Persian Letters* is one of conflict, contrast, and controversy between people, ideas, and institutions. Montesquieu pointed out the unity of the work by writing in "Some Reflections on *Persian Letters*" of the 1754 edition that philosophy, politics, and morals are joined to the novel by a secret chain. He also affirmed the eternal contrast between reality and perception, "that all charm consists in the eternal contrast between things as they really are and the singular, naïve, or bizarre way in which they are perceived" ("Some Reflections," 271). The aim of this paper is to explore the prevalence of the fundamental patterns of discord and to examine the sequences of letters in which they appear.

Several types of conflict are introduced in the very first Persian letter. The site of Kom contrasts religious pilgrimages with the voyage in quest of enlightenment. Religion is a subject of controversy and dispute in all the letters in which it appears. The conflicting expectations placed on women are suggested by the virgin mother of twelve prophets. Travel in pursuit of knowledge is contrasted with the pleasures of a peaceful life. Rica and Usbek are distinguished from other Persians, and their actions are a target of criticism. Provincialism is contrasted with opening to the world (Letter 1).[1]

Conflict between Usbek and the eunuchs, between Usbek and his wives, between the eunuchs and the women, and between the women themselves pervades the harem letters from beginning to end. Usbek's first letter to the eunuch introduces all the elements of conflict in the seraglio intrigue. The role assigned to the eunuch is an oxymoron of contradictory duties. He is the support of the wives and their executioner. He must act as either their master or their slave. In letters full of dissimulation, the women express passion for their husband but show profound resentment of their condition. Usbek invokes his love for them even in letters full of insults and threats.

15

Contrast and conflict are obvious in the story of the Troglodytes. The image of the vicious society includes every type of crime and corruption: revolt against authority, murder, theft, embezzlement, abduction, indifference to justice, refusal to pay for services. The harmony of the utopian society illustrates justice, cooperation, love, compassion, and unity, but even the utopia is confronted by foreign aggression and beginning of moral decline. Ecclesiastics are rejected as moral guides and their teachings are replaced by the lessons of history (Letters 10–14).

The chief eunuch's affectionate letter to Jaron, added in the supplement of 1754, separates the story of the Troglodytes from Usbek's exchange with the mullah, the rational discussion of morals from the irrational. It introduces the theme of religious intolerance, defilement contrasted with purification, polluted land inhabited by Christians contrasted with the land of the angels, travel that defiles contrasted with pilgrimage that purifies. It points out the conflict between the Prophet and Christians regarded as his enemies, between believers and unbelievers. The letter brings out also the complex psychology of the eunuch: feelings of affection concealed under a severe exterior (Letter 15). In the exchange of letters between Usbek and the mullah there is sharp contrast between the form of address used by the layman and the ecclesiastic. Usbek's invocation of the mullah is a series of hyperbolic oxymorons that mimic the praises of Ali inscribed in temples. To Usbek's exalted praise the mullah responds with equally intense contempt and humiliation. The debate about purity is a confrontation of reason with superstition. Usbek presents the rational argument that the notion of pollution stems from a subjective reaction of the senses. The mullah responds with an absurd narrative of the creation of impure animals in Noah's ark (Letters 16–18).

The description of the Ottoman Empire introduces the subject of decadence that results from bad government. The economy is destroyed by corrupt administrators. Christians and Jews are persecuted. Neglect of military training causes weakness, which Usbek predicts will lead to the defeat by a foreign power reported in letter 123 (Letter 19). The violent conditions and ominous prognosis for the Ottoman Empire are followed by the violence and threats of Usbek's first letters to his wives. His violent tone echoes the contempt and condemnation of the mullah. Zachi has been polluted by the crimes, regrets, despair, and impotence of a white eunuch. The letter to the eunuch continues the extraordinary violence of the one to Zachi: "And what are you but vile instruments, which I can break at my fancy . . . which breathe only so long as my happiness, my love, and even my jealousy need your baseness . . . if you set aside your duty, I shall regard your life like those insects I find under your feet" (Letter 21, 36). The letter from Jaron, added in the supplement of 1754, closes the first cycle of harem letters with an expression of hatred of eunuchs toward women (Letter 22).

Usbek's first letter from Europe portrays a flourishing city, Livorno, in contrast to the Ottoman Empire. The description of the condition of European women brings out both contrast and similarity to that of the Oriental. The women can look outside without being seen. They can go out with old women who guard them. They wear only one veil, while the Persian women wear four. The ironic statement that expresses the point of view of the Persian—"The women enjoy great liberty here" (Letter 23, 38)—introduces "the eternal contrast between things as they really are and the singular, naïve, or bizarre way in which they are perceived" ("Some Reflections," 271).

Rica's first letter from Paris continues to show the contrast and mentions all the major sources of discord in France. The letter presents French society as a scene of conflict, from the tumult on the street to pride, finances, religious beliefs, gender discrimination, court intrigues, and foreign wars. Multistory buildings are normal dwellings to the French but appear as several houses stacked on each other to the Persian. The rhythm with which people move on the street is extraordinary to him and leads to physical collision. The king draws his wealth not from mines but from the vanity of his subjects.

The conflict between reality and deception appears to Rica like a hallucination induced by two magicians: the king and the pope. The pope issues decrees to keep the people in the habit of believing. The French society is portrayed divided over the bull *Unigenitus*. There is conflict between the pope and people who refuse to accept the bull, between the prince who accepts it and the people who reject it. Women are at the head of the revolt that divides the court, the kingdom, and all the families. Women's revolt against the fact that the bull forbids them to read the scriptures continues the theme of the humiliation of European women that will be developed further in letter 141 (Letter 24). The pope is an ancient idol worshipped by habit. He is no longer feared but possesses enormous wealth. Bishops establish rules in public for which they grant dispensations in private. Theologians raise subjects of dispute: "There has never been a kingdom that has had as many civil wars as in that of Christ." The Inquisition violates all rules of justice. The letter ends with hyperbolic praise of Persian tolerance (Letter 29, 49).

Usbek's letter to Roxane shows the use of contrast for indoctrination. He gives her false assurances of happiness, security, and love in the seraglio, but the wedding night is described as a scene of violence. He seeks to justify the harsh discipline of the harem by comparing it to the freedom that leads French women to what he calls "brutal impudence." He attributes to Roxane actions described by Zachi and Fatmé: the use of precious essences and clothing, competition through dancing and song as expressions of love in contrast with the same behavior of French women, which is an outrage done to their husbands. He admits, however, in the end that the contrast is exaggerated, that continence is natural to women, that few commit the final infidelity, and that the severe harem regime is justified only by an exaggerated criterion of purity. What he says about the safety of the seraglio is the opposite of what he writes in letters to his friend Nessir, to whom he complains that he left his wives almost alone with cowards to protect them (Letters 6 and 27).

The contrast between perception and reality continues during Rica's visit to the theater, where he confuses the actors with the spectators. The inserted letter of the actress of the opera shows the deception practiced in relations between the sexes. She was abused by an abbé who promised to marry her while she was dressed in the white veil of a priestess of Diana. She hopes to improve her fortune in Persia, where she believes dancers are held in high regard (Letter 28). The curiosity of Parisians about Rica dressed as a Persian shows the incongruity between reality and fantasy (Letter 30). The counter-part of the surprise of Parisians at the sight of a Persian is Rhédi's astonish-ment upon his arrival to Venice, which he perceives as a city emerging from water. He mentions the wrath of the Prophet at the lack of fresh water to per-form the legal ablutions but is delighted to study a list of subjects that seems to announce the interests of Montesquieu during his travels. The concluding sentence, "I am coming out of the clouds that covered my eyes in the country of my birth," is connected in the following letter to the blind man's superior knowledge of Paris (Letters 31, 52; 32).

A series of comparisons brings out the contrast between European and Oriental mores. The use of wine is forbidden to Asian princes, but they use it to excess, while Christian princes drink in moderation. Europeans seek consolation in the works of Seneca, while Asians take beverages that cheer the mind by stimulating the body (Letter 33). The healthy way of life of Persian women, who do not drink wine, is compared to that of the French, and the gaiety of Frenchmen is contrasted with the gravity of Persians. The inserted speech of a European summarizes the harmful effect of the company of eunuchs on virtue and temperament (Letter 34). The conflict between Christianity and Islam is resolved ironically by similarity of practices and beliefs. As Usbek concludes, "Do what you will, the truth will break free and always pierce the shadows that surround it" (Letter 35, 57). A religious Muslim writing to a Jewish convert to Islam reports the extreme violence, upheavals, and conflict between forces of nature that occurred upon the birth of Muhammad and Jesus (Letter 39). The subject of the sequestration and nature of women is presented in the form of a debate between Asians and Europeans. A gallant philosopher is quoted saying that the power men assumed over women is tyranny: "But this is a veritable injustice. We employ every kind of means to destroy their courage. Our strengths would be equal if education were also equal" (Letter 38, 62). The respect women enjoyed in antiquity is contrasted with a koranic injunction that echoes the New

Testament (Letter 38). Funeral ceremonies and orations are found to contradict the reality they are supposed to represent (Letter 40).

A group of letters deal with conflict and competition in the social arena. The project to castrate a slave in the harem gives rise to expressions of hostility among different classes of slaves, the horror of the victim, and the clemency of the absolute master accompanied by threats (Letters 41, 42, and 43). The contempt the three estates have for each other is shown analogous to the feelings of superiority people have for their country (Letter 44). Self-confidence and delusion contrary to reality are illustrated by the alchemist (Letter 45). Religion is presented as a subject of dispute rather than observance. The practice of charity and humanity is declared to be more important than the observance of ceremonies that are invalidated by their diversity. In answer to Mirza's question in letter 10, the essence of religion is defined as living as a good citizen and a good father of family (Letter 46). The trip of the harem women to the countryside is in sharp contrast to Usbek's description of a gathering at a country estate where women associate freely with men. The Persian women travel covered by a cloud of black veils and cause the death of two innocents who happen to be on their way. Their own lives are endangered by the brutal intransigence of eunuchs during a storm. The French women, by contrast, receive attentions of men that range from a happy marriage to deception by a ladies' man. The social gathering is described as a battleground on which a series of characters strive to establish their credentials. Usbek concludes with a hyperbolic praise of the innocence of women in his homeland (Letter 48).

Different types of conflict arise from efforts to assert oneself in society. Rica expresses wrath at the capuchin monk who seeks protection for establishing an outpost of his order in Persia (Letter 49). He contrasts modesty with pride and despises a conceited man who boasts about himself (Letter 50). A humorous scene shows women in their desperate efforts to disguise their age (Letter 52). Rica overhears two men who form an alliance to support each other in the battle to gain reputation of wit (Letter 54). He describes the many ways in which crooks seek to cheat customers in Paris (Letter 58). Consummation of marriage on the day of the ceremony, marital jealousy, and gambling give rise to contrast between French and Persian customs and passions (Letter 55 and 56). The description of the French family court portrays matrimony as a domain of combat (Letter 86). The letter of the Russian woman who complains about not being beaten shows that domestic violence can be valued as a sign of status. Peter the Great is portrayed as a despot in conflict with his subjects and with the past as he strives to modernize his empire (Letter 51). Conversation among a group of people demonstrates deformation of reality by self-centered judgment: "If triangles were to make a god, they would give him three sides" (Letter 59, 96). A visit to a convent

reveals incongruity between ecclesiastic vows and practice, and between precepts and their interpretation (Letter 57). An ecclesiastic explains his friction
with people who refuse to accept practices and beliefs they expect him to
defend (Letter 61). The condition of Jews illustrates the sources of religious
intolerance and strife (Letter 60).

Zélis writes on the education of her daughter and the role of imagination
in her relation to Usbek. He is a captive of anxiety, while her imagination
makes her free (Letter 62). Rica portrays the contrast between the dissimulation of Persian women due to fear and the open behavior and badinage of the
French (Letter 63). The chief black eunuch reports the division, competition,
and strife between wives. He explains how women can be subjugated through
punishments and espionage (Letter 64). Usbek threatens to authorize the
violent methods advised by the eunuch (Letter 65). The story of Aphéridon
and Astarté presents a long series of obstacles to the happiness of incestuous
love and marriage: Islamic law, sale to a royal harem, jealousy of a superior,
marriage to a eunuch, conflict of religions, poverty, and slavery. Reciprocal
love of the couple and the kindness of an Armenian overcome the hardships
(Letter 67). The passion to write books is confronted with having nothing to
say (Letter 66).

Rica's visit to a magistrate begins a series of letters on justice and laws.
The judge's lack of interest in jurisprudence and his reliance on lawyers conflicts with the administration of justice (Letter 68). Usbek demonstrates that
God is endowed with contradictory attributes that are incompatible with his
justice (Letter 69). The brutal repudiation of a bride raises the question of the
evidence of virginity, to which Usbek replies that there are no reliable proofs
even though they are established in the scriptures as basis for condemnation
and absolution of girls. He wishes his daughter to be as pure as Fatima, the
virgin mother of twelve prophets (Letters 70 and 71).

A universal *décisionnaire* pretends to have knowledge unsupported by
facts (Letter 72). The Académie française issues decrees invalidated by usage
and competition (Letter 73). Insulting manners of the great in France are
contrasted with their politeness in Persia (Letter 74). Religion is once again
shown to be a subject of dispute as people reject practices and beliefs that
they expect ecclesiastics to defend. Conflict between religious conviction
and political expedient leads to the conclusion, "truth in one time, error in
another" (Letter 75, 124). A vigorous polemic is directed against laws that
punish suicide (Letter 76).

The satirical letter of a Frenchman on Spain decomposes the portrait of the
nation into a series of contradictions between behavior and common sense.
The suggested comments of a Spaniard on the French intimates the reciprocal nature of chauvinism (Letter 78). The subject of ways to avoid conflict
and to minimize its aftermath is introduced in Usbek's letter on the relation

of the stability of government and the severity of punishments (Letter 80). The Tartars created great empires but allowed their accomplishments to fade from memory (Letter 81). They contrast with the warriors at Invalides who preserve to the end of their life the image and devotion to military art in service of their country (Letter 84). The Tartars' indifference to glory is also the opposite of the endless agitation on the social scene of the "universal society" (Letter 87, 142). The controversy over the relationship of the justice and the existence of God is resolved by the inborn principle of justice in the heart of man (Letter 83). The exile of the most productive members of society caused by religious intolerance is contrasted with the positive emulation that results from multiplicity of religions (Letter 85).

There is similarity and contrast between the ways to achieve status in Persia and France. The two countries differ in the importance attached to glory and honor but are similar in the arbitrary nature of royal favor. Noble birth, virtue, and merit bring no distinction without the favor of the king in France. As Usbek writes to Rhédi, "Favor is the great divinity of the French" (Letter 88, 144). A Frenchman tells Usbek that in Persia reputation depends entirely on the favor of the prince: "Reputation and virtue there are regarded as imaginary if they are not accompanied by the prince's favor" (Letter 89, 145). Persian troops overcome fear of death with fear of punishments, while the French do it for glory (Letter 89). By demanding duels, honor comes into sharp conflict in France with laws that forbid them (Letter 90). An impostor ambassador offended the monarch he claimed to represent and the one he pretended to honor (Letter 91).

Several letters to ecclesiastics show how natural events are explained by supernatural intervention. Writing to his brother, who is a monk at a monastery of Casbin, at the same location where the capuchin monk wished to establish an outpost, Usbek rejects the Christian accounts of the struggles of the early anchorites with demons as allegorical representations of passions (Letter 93). In a letter to the same mullah whom he had invoked on the subject of purity, he deplores the defeat of the Turks as divine punishment for their infidelity (Letter 123). Rica explains how defeats attributed to supernatural causes can be explained by natural events (Letter 143). New scientific discoveries solve mysteries that in the scriptures are known only to God (Letter 97).

A comparison of monarchy with despotism and the British regime shows how political power depends on the manner of resolution of conflict. European monarchs limit their authority, while the immense power Oriental rulers exercise over their subjects causes instability. Since the least disgrace is punished by death, a Persian subject attacks the prince (Letters 102 and 103). In Britain, political power rests on gratitude and strength (Letter 104). The discussion of international law points out conditions in which armed conflict may be justified and the reparations necessary in its aftermath (Letters

94 and 95). In the debate on the good and evil that result from the progress of arts and science, Rhédi deplores the iniquity of slavery that resulted from the discovery of the compass. He mentions the effect of the development of gunpowder and the possible invention of weapons of mass destruction (Letter 105). Usbek replies categorically that if such weapons were discovered, they would never be used and would be buried with the unanimous consent of nations: "No: if a fatal invention came to be discovered, it would soon be prohibited by the law of nation, and the unanimous consent of nations would bury that discovery" (Letter 106, 171). He does not deny, however, that wars may continue in the future (Letter 106).

The death of Louis XIV introduces the conflict between people who seek to take advantage of the event. The king had tried to limit the authority of Philippe d'Orléans, but the regent reestablished the authority of the *parlements* to gain their support (Letter 92). The political and financial instability of the Regency gives many examples of the incongruity between reality and perception. The sudden reversals of fortune leave people astonished by the changes in their condition. The despicable character of the nouveaux riches prevents respect for wealth (Letter 98). There is incongruity between the attachment of the French to their fashions and the ease with which they change them. They seek to impose their usage in trivial matters like clothing and cuisine, but they adopt foreign laws (Letters 99 and 100).

Conflicts are shown to arise over insignificant matters and important concerns resolved by appeal to trivia. Women compete with ecclesiastics for influence at court and exercise their power through networks of connections (Letter 107). The efforts of a pretty woman are compared to those of a general preparing his troops for battle: she must appear neutral to rival suitors she betrays, overcome obstacles to parties, and above all give the impression of having fun (Letter 110). Journalists avoid conflict with authors by flattering them (Letter 108). Violent disputes over linguistic usage engage important institutions: the university of Paris over the pronunciation of letter Q, and the estates of Aragon and Catalogne over the language to be used in debates. As Rica writes, "It seems, my dear ***, that the heads of the greatest men shrink when they are assembled, and the more wise men there are in some place, the less wisdom that is there" (Letter 109). A humorous rendering of resistance to Mazarin shows how political conflict is linked to minor details and is remembered by them (Letter 111). In the series of letters on depopulation, humanity is shown to be threatened by natural disasters (Letter 113). Practices and institutions that promote population are contrasted with those that diminish it (Letters 114–22). Generous pensions to courtiers are blamed for the severe deprivation of the working people (Letter 124).

Subjective views of events and the contrast between the way things are and the way they are perceived appear in letters on the geometrician, legislators, journalists, and other contemporary professions. Oblivious to humor, architecture, gardens, battles, and natural disasters, the geometrician limits his interests to precise mathematical measurements. He denigrates the work of translators (Letter 128). Legislators are mediocre men, unfit for the greatness and majesty of their task. They use a foreign language to write laws that need to be understood. Paying attention to details, they neglect general principles. They keep useless Roman laws but do not preserve the most important paternal authority (Letter 129).[2] Journalists are criticized for their presumption, flattery, and discord in the treatment of affairs of state (Letter 130). People react to events according to their interests and temperament. A genealogist rejoices at the proliferation of the nouveaux riches. A fearful journalist predicts defeat in Languedoc, while a pessimistic philosopher notices a sunspot that could precipitate a cataclysm (Letter 132). Rhédi traces the role of conflict in the history of republics (Letter 131).

In the series of letters about Rica's visit to the library conflict appears as the subject of books and there is conflict also between the content of book and the inadequate manner in which it is treated. The series begins with the contrast between the head of the congregation who is not interested in books and the scholarly librarian who studies them (Letter 133). The scholar explains that the Bible is a battlefield where exegetes seek passages that support their views. "It is a battlefield in which enemy nations come together in many battles, in which they attack and skirmish in numerous ways" (Letter 134, 221). Grammarians, commenetators, and some philosophers lack common sense. Metaphysics, physics, and medicine exaggerate their subject (Letter 135). Books on European history relate the rise and fall of freedom and empires through conflict and flux (Letter 136). The letter on literature contrasts poetry with reason, Homer with other epic poets, the tranquility of pastoral poety with the agitation of courtiers, and novels with nature (Letter 137). The subject of books continues with an attack on the superstitious confidence in amulets made of passages from scriptures and on supernatural explanations of the outcome of battles. A satirical list of polemical works that provoke violent reactions is assembled by a doctor (Letter 143).

Rica observes the stubborn ways in which learned men defend their opinions or attack the ideas of others. He contrasts the modest men he admires with the proud men he condemns (Letter 144). The comparison continues with contrast between a man of superior intelligence who attracts enemies and a mediocre man who receives popular approval. A scholar relates the hostility to which he is exposed for having dissected a dog. Scholars used to be accused of magic and heresy. Historians are persecuted for writing the truth in contrast to those who disfigure the past. By publishing his book, a scholar gives rise to war with those who disagree with him (Letter 145).

The *Persian Letters* ends with a parallel between history and fiction, between the crisis that followed the collapse of system of John Law and the tragic revolt in Usbek's harem. Both outcomes are in contrast with the fiction inserted in letter 141, which is surrounded by the exile of the Parlement of Paris to Pontoise and an allegorical account of the system. The letter is remarkable by the complexity of its structure, with four levels of nesting and multiple images of harem in this world and the world to come. Rica writes to Usbek that he met a lady of the court worthy of a place of honor in the seraglio of the Persian monarch. She, on the other hand, finds life in a seraglio repugnant; she envies the happiness of the man and pities the women who must share him. She likes to read fiction and asks Rica to send her a Persian novel translated, like the Persian letters, from Persian to French. In Rica's tale, Zulema, a learned woman who knew by heart all the scriptures and understood all the commentaries, presides in the hall of a seraglio over what we would call today a consciousness-raising session. A woman asks if she believes that paradise exists only for men. Zulema replies that this is one of the opinions used to degrade women and that Jews maintain, on the authority of their sacred books, that women have no soul.[3] She promises her companions that virtuous women will receive the same rewards as men and will have harems full of slaves guarded by eunuchs for their pleasure.

Zulema tells her friends an Arab tale in which a tyrannically jealous man called Ibrahim has a harem of twelve beautiful wives whom he treats very harshly. His harem resembles that of Usbek as it is administered by the eunuch. The women are always locked up in their rooms, unable to speak to each other. One day, Anaïs, more courageous than the others, dares to tell Ibrahim that his wives are so unhappy that they are driven to desire a change. Instead of feeling pity for his wife, Ibrahim plunges a dagger in her chest. As she is dying, Anaïs promises revenge to her companions. In heaven she finds happiness in the company of fifty men kept in her seraglio. After eight days of varied and intense enjoyments, she retreats into an apartment of her palace to meditate about her condition and that of her friends. Montesquieu emphasizes the thoughtful character and courage of this woman, who, in the solitude imposed by her husband, has spent most of her life in meditation. To help her companions in the seraglio, she sends one of the celestial men to replace Ibrahim. The new regime established in the seraglio is a reform conceived by a female philosopher and realized according to her instructions. The authority in the seraglio is subject to the approval of the women. It is a republic in which the power of the master depends on the choice of the subjects. Under the new regime, there are no eunuchs and women are freer than those of Livorno, who wear only one veil and can look at men without being seen: "The new master observed a conduct so opposed to that of the other that it surprised every one of the neighbors. He dismissed all the eunuchs, making his home accessible to everyone. He did not even want his wives to be allowed to veil themselves. It was a singular thing to see them in banquets among men, as free as them" (Letter 141, 238). The new master does not deny himself any expense, spending profusely the wealth of the other one, who, upon his return, finds only his wives and thirty-six children.

The harem is a project Rica sends to Usbek to help him save his seraglio. Usbek, who is awaiting anxiously news from his wives, does not benefit from the Arab tale because letter 141, dated July 26, 1720, arrives too late. Usbek had sent violent orders to the eunuch Narsit in December 1718. He had written his last letters to Solim and his wives in October 1719. The seraglio revolt is reported in letters of March and May 1720. The contrast of the drama in Usbek's seraglio with the harem nested deep in the Arab tale is a promise of future liberation by way of reform. Montesquieu creates an environment in which he explores the multifaceted and conflicting, often humorously ironic attributes of the religious, political, economic, social, governmental, sexual, and moral issues dominating his time in France and internationally. Through the multiple examples of contrast, he teaches that there is choice. The many forms of conflict explored in the *Persian Letters* invite resolution through reason.

NOTES

1. The numbers of the letters are those of the edition of 1758.

2. In the first edition, letter 29 appeared as letter 77 among letters on laws.

3. Rica had raised this question in his first letter from Paris. Women's soul was a subject of debate based on Genesis 2:18 at the ecclesiastical council of Mâcon in 585.

BIBLIOGRAPHY

Montesquieu. *Persian Letters*. Edited by Stuart D. Warner. Translated by Stuart D. Warner and Stéphane Douard. South Bend, IN: St. Augustine's Press, 2017.

Chapter 3

Persian Letters in Time

Adhesive Past: Bright, Unstable Present: Divergent, Fragile Futures

Michael Mosher

PERSIAN LETTERS AS PIVOT

It has been a long time since my introduction to Judith Shklar's then-famous Enlightenment seminar, but I still remember being set back on my heels by the first assignment, Montesquieu's *Persian Letters*. Alan Gilbert was similarly swept away. He dropped out of the seminar to do an independent reading of the text with Shklar. Much later we published our parallel and differing accounts in *Political Theory*.[1]

Miho de Montesquieu, a contemporary descendent of the family, once asked me which of the renowned ancestor's books did I find most attractive. Without reflection I replied, the *Persian Letters*, although by then my published arguments were anchored in *The Spirit of the Laws*. I was simply being nostalgic about that first impact. This chapter is a creature of that same nostalgia, an experiment in which I rehearse my responses to readings of this book over many years. The focus on "my times" will track as well "Montesquieu's times"—the temporal orders at play in his works. Which past and which future established the problematic of the *Persian Letters* that led the author into the exceptionally different books of *Considerations on the Romans* and *The Spirit of the Laws*?

As a young graduate student, I felt the tides had shifted in moving to Harvard from Berkeley, the latter being the era of the free speech movement and of the Hannah Arendt/Sheldon Wolin–inflected Berkeley school of political theory. Usbek and Rica were somehow a pivot away from all that.

Later—in an encyclopedia article that channeled Leo Strauss's "What Is Political Philosophy?"—I tried to explain the pivot:

> Wolin carved out a heroic role for the political philosopher . . . who was preoc-
> cupied with threats to political autonomy and the loss of citizen capacity [that
> were] glimpsed in Machiavelli and republican thinkers and all but smothered, he
> thought, by social and organizational forces. . . . Being absorbed in the "social"
> augured the loss of political consciousness. It is possible to resist this argument.
> Montesquieu, the classic theorist of the role of society in politics, showed how
> the social "principles" of honor and virtue sustained rather than undermined
> political autonomy.[2]

Granted, assertions of autonomy in the *Persian Letters* were *mostly* either illusions or despotic desires. Even the casual reader notes that everywhere in the *Persian Letters* people are blind, except, naturally, in the institutions for the blind, where Rica finds the inmates playing cards (Letter 32). The incapacity to see is nearly the dominant theme. Usbek explains that "we are so blind that we do not know when we should grieve and when we should rejoice. We possess almost nothing but false sadness and false joy" (Letter 40).[3] Although Usbek thinks it is the task of an intellectual detached from illu-sions to point this out, it is the nature of his own blindness that is ultimately at stake. None of this was especially evident when I first read the *Letters*. Permit me to recall two pieces of writing that were then my touchstones: Paul Valery's haunting 1926 preface to *Persian Letters*, commended to me by Joe Paff, Wolin's teaching assistant and my mentor, and a chapter I later discov-ered from Marshall Berman's *Politics of Authenticity* (1970), which spied the origins of nineteenth-century political romanticism in the 1721 novel. One essay revealed the sad pessimism of the European who, in the aftermath of world war, saw in the *Letters* a mirror to 1920s malaise, prescient, it seems, in its intimations of unwanted futures. The other essay obviously exhibited the buoyant optimism and utopian political hopes of the American 1960s, hopes that would themselves be deflated in the coming decades.

For Valery, the very taste exhibited in the novel was "a sign of the end of the show."[4] It was on the surface an exhibit of epicurean pleasures situated between "order and disorder." It was also a prophecy:

> The institutions still stand. They are great and imposing. But without showing
> any visible alteration, their splendid presence is now nearly all they are . . . their
> future is secretly at an end. . . . Criticism and contempt weaken and empty them
> of all subsequent value. The body politic quietly loses its futurity.[5]

This was precisely the view of the doctoral thesis and first book of German conservative Reinhart Koselleck, who did so much to advance our awareness of temporal ghosts. He wanted to call his work *Dialectic of Enlightenment*, but that title had already been taken by Adorno and Horkheimer. In their strangely parallel works, we can see how twentieth-century thinkers from right and left saw dialectical reversals in the libertarian promises of the era of *lumière*. Valery's *Persian Letters* tracked Koselleck's warning that criticism of a certain sort engendered its own crises.[6]

Berman's argument was the flip side of this: optimistic, hopeful, and celebratory because (unlike Koselleck) he thought enlightenment and criticism created a better future. For him the *Persian Letters* "begins in exoticism and ends with revolution." The latter refers to Roxane's "harem" revolution/ rebellion against her husband Usbek, who was also a symbolic stand-in for the political tyrant.

For Berman the *Letters* pointed to a heroic 1789. The book, Berman writes, is "one of those rare works which contain within themselves the whole history of an epoch . . . [it] prefigures the course of European history in the eighteenth century." The later work of Montesquieu was dowdy and conservative. By contrast, in the *Persian Letters*, "we are here faced with a virtue that is profoundly revolutionary, whose deepest impulse is to overthrow a repressive status quo."[7] He did not linger on the figure of Roxane, but arguably she was cut out of the Berkeley school and Arendt-Wolin story about autonomous actors. She enacts a democratic revolution. Its failure, which Berman ignored, could be taken as a repudiation of expectations for autonomous action, reinforcement perhaps for Wolin's later pessimism. Democracy was only a "fugitive" phenomenon.

Despite the evident contrast in mood, the Valery-Berman claims were conceptually congruent. In 1721, in 1926, and in 1970, an epoch was ending, and the character of the future was now at stake. In addition, the sardonic wit of Valery seemed as drawn to the delights of disorder and anarchism as were the cheerful bromides of Berman.

DISTRACTED BY *ESPRIT/GEIST*

Of course, so was I so drawn. A year in Paris may have cured me of Berkeley anarchism. Ironically, in post-1968 France, 1970–1971, I discovered political authority and the state. That is to say, I started reading Hegel and the French Hegelians. I now understood how Montesquieu could write in 1753 to the exiled *parlement* judge, le president Durey de Meinières, that Meinières did not understand the appropriate role of the state:

> The safety of the state is the supreme law. . . . To say that you do not antici-
> pate the ruin of the state and that you will perish before it, is not a reason, for

your ruin counts for very little compared with that of the state. Think carefully about the state, examine things as they are; in comparison with the state, you are nothing.[8]

These sentiments appear in firm contrast to the opening of the *Persian Letters*. The old king (Louis XIV) is dead and the threat of despotic rule has been at least temporarily removed. Nevertheless, these admonitions to Meinières were consistent with Montesquieu's mature philosophy, in which the idea of legitimate constitutional monarchy—and of the modern regime—was tied to the Bodinian insistence that "the prince is the source of all political and civil power."[9] The famous intermediary bodies have their work cut out for them as official channels of resistance to monarchical power, but they shouldn't be imagined as a guerrilla force striking against an illegitimate executive. Together they were, as Montesquieu himself wrote, "the nature of monarchial government," which included its Bodinian foundation.

When I returned to the States, I suggested to Dita Shklar that the Montesquieu-Hegel trajectory might be a good thesis topic. She did not object. Later she wrote her own separate books about Hegel and Montesquieu, which was probably a more sensible division of labor.[10]

My work was not especially focused on the *Persian Letters*, however. Compared to the later work of Montesquieu and to any work by Hegel, there is nothing in the *Persian Letters* like this feeling for a social/political *esprit* (spirit/mentality) circulating through webs of law or for the shape shifting guises of *Geist* (spirit/mentality again) that might culminate in a rational state. The *Letters* is less a text in political philosophy or philosophy of history and more a series of reflections on moral psychology—a story of characters negotiating or failing to negotiate various terrains. Together they constitute a moral geography in which various kinds of disastrous relations are revealed among those who live either too far apart or too close together.

A tradition that stems from Montesquieu divides authority between state and society. Its successors include both allies and rivals: Rousseau, Hegel, Constant, Marx. The allies of Montesquieu have always been ambivalent about the character of authority. It is still a lively topic whatever one's partisan preferences. The theme of a choice between two camps runs through fellow Shklar seminar participant Paul Thomas's first book, *Karl Marx and the Anarchists*.[11] In a later generation, Jacob Levy's *Rationalism, Pluralism, and Freedom* found nourishment for an antistatist social plurality in Montesquieu against the "rationalist" claims of Hegel, whose spiritual descendants include apparently John Rawls.[12] I elided the differences between the two understandings of authority in "The Particulars of a Universal Politics: Hegel's Adaptation of Montesquieu's Typology,"[13] which channeled Michael Oakeshott's claim for Montesquieu and Hegel being allied thinkers for whom state authority meant citizens "joined in acknowledgement of the authority of a practice and not in respect of a common substantive purpose."[14] I was attracted by this description of liberal authority. Its defect was that it homogenized historical figures who were distinctive and concealed the pathologies of this idea of authority.

RETURN TO THE *PERSIAN LETTERS*

Fast forward to a summary of subsequent engagements with the book. To speak anachronistically (and, for some interpreters, erroneously), Montesquieu's "feminism" drew my attention. I began by noting that Usbek famously justified suicide with a Lockean argument designed to support rebellion, not suicide:

> Society is founded on mutual advantage. But when it becomes onerous to me, who should prevent me from renouncing it? (Letter 76, 125)

The argument parallels Usbek's commendation of the English, who believe that only mutual gratitude obliges and only a prince who pursues the happiness of the people should be obeyed. In the face of oppression, "nothing binds them; nothing ties them to the prince; and they return to their natural liberty" (Letter 104, 168).

Roxane adopted these Lockean liberal thoughts to her own purposes, the justification of revolution:

> I might have lived in servitude, but I have always been free. I have reformed your laws by those of nature, and my spirit has always remained independent. (Letter 161, 268)

This was the line that led me to Montesquieu's views on gender. *Political Theory* published the results, "The Judgmental Gaze of European Women: Gender, Sexuality and the Critique of Republican Rule," in 1994.[15] It was also a reply to a particular European woman, the person to whom I had falsely claimed that the *Letters* were the center of my attention. But in publishing this essay, the novel had once again grabbed my attention. In addition, the subtitle was a cookie crumb trail that led to the argument about forms of government in *The Spirit of the Laws*. A year later Diana Schaub published her own admirable interpretation of these issues in *Montesquieu's Erotic Liberalism*.[16]

In the aftermath of these studies, three more topics struck me as noteworthy. First, the novel lays down an outline to Montesquieu's views about empire, both pro and con, which were more fully developed in the

Considerations and *Laws*.[17] Second, I had previously ignored the Troglodyte letters, but did they hold the secret to Montesquieu's indecision about forms of government, as Michael Sonenscher argued? Third, I took up the issue of political economy. I wondered why Montesquieu so comprehensively and unambiguously condemned John Law's takeover of the Regency finances. Truth to tell, I disagreed with Montesquieu and felt closer to Voltaire's views on the topic. This last concern was the beginning of many conversations with Constantine Vassiliou in Rotterdam, Toronto, Vancouver, and now Houston.[18]

There was one other engagement with the text. A throwback to my old doctoral dissertation, it is found in a compact sentence I wrote for a book released in May 2021:

> Roxanne and Usbek were the doubled soul of the Enlightenment reader, simultaneously seeking to do good in revolt against tyrannical habits (Roxanne) and yet by the light of the same literature in doubt about whether there was anything good to do. (Usbek)[19]

I will unpack this sentence in due course, but for now let us turn to Montesquieu's time, the felt quality of past, present, and future in the *Persian Letters*.

PERSIAN LETTERS I—THE ADHESIVE PAST OF VALERY

Montesquieu painted on a vast canvas in all his books. The *Letters* articulated the nature of a political space measured by the distance of Persia from France. Time was a complicating factor in governing across such a distance. The commands of the prince (Usbek) in Paris directed to his realm in Ispahan took too much time to reach their destination in a "timely"—that is to say, effective—manner. The eunuchs (read: the neutered as colonial bureaucrats) were expected to carry out these distant orders, but given the difficulties of overcoming time and space, eunuchs became the real rulers. It was Montesquieu's first critique of empire as despotic form of government. The size or reach of empire defeated communication.

This book returns the reader to an Orientalist trope: the despotism of the East. At first the reader is misled. Usbek is the representative of the seeker escaping irrationality and superstation. He was indistinguishable from the enlightened European. In the shiny bright present of Paris, the old despotic king (Louis XIV) was gone and the succeeding era was busy parrying with wit and skepticism the tyrannical ideas of the past. Usbek was avatar of the universal appeal of these new ideas—as not only their champion but in his own right as an educator dialogically sensitive to the perspectives of diverse interlocutors.[20] However, when this hero should turn into villain, the adhesive past seemed to get stuck again in the present—despotic Ispahan and liberated Paris glued together, the Orientalist barrier between East and West turned illusion.

Usbek's enlightenment was a thing of the mind, not the heart. There was no balm for his obsessive emotions. Montesquieu introduced near the beginning of this vast movement of "enlightened" ideas what Adorno and Horkheimer wanted to say "dialectically" two centuries later. The empire of science—knowledge, enlightenment, truth—was capable of tyranny. For Montesquieu, however, this was a warning only about possibilities. For these later critics, it became foreordained necessity.

PERSIAN LETTERS II—THE MILITANT FUTURE OF BERMAN

In 1725 Montesquieu delivered an address to the Academy of Bordeaux "On the motives that ought to encourage us in the sciences."[21] It was, in effect, a supplement to Roxane's rebellion against despotism and a militant version of the *Persian Letters*, with all the lighthearted entertainment removed.

In this talk, Montesquieu asked how the sixteenth-century "Mexicans" and "Peruvians"—the "Americans"—could have resisted the Spanish conquistadors, those exemplars of the bad old past he had expected modernity to overcome. Here Montesquieu made the really extraordinary move. Survival and victory over the foreign invaders depended on modern philosophy and worldly social science. It relied not on the capacity of science to invent new weapons, but on its promise to reorient minds, a move that echoed Platonic antiquity: the turning of imprisoned souls toward the light of philosophy in the cave/city of false beliefs.

Montesquieu proposed a counterfactual history. Imagine that a century before the Spanish arrived on the shores of the Americas, the philosopher René Descartes had emigrated to become the teacher of the Amerindians. Descartes would have taught the Amerindians skepticism—how to throw doubt on what we believe in order to reconstruct belief on a worldly basis. For the young Montesquieu, this translated into materialism and skepticism about the gods. So instructed, no (native) American would have believed that the Spaniards, with their strange horses and beards, were irresistible gods. They were only mortal "machines." They could be worn out. The Amerindian nations could have starved the invaders or killed them on the beaches from a thousand hiding places. The proclaimed herald of "moderation"—which really is the theme of *The Spirit of the Laws*—here appears in tougher guise as the theorist of asymmetrical guerilla warfare.

There would be cultural loss on the side of the Mexicans and Peruvians. For Cartesian science to turn the minds of the Amerindians toward the light, it had to undermine traditions, religion, and culture: everything that had made them susceptible to illusions about their situation. It was unavoidable. Montesquieu's science pointed to "curing people of destructive prejudices," a line taken from the Discourse of 1725 and inserted into the preface to *The Spirit of the Laws*. It paralleled another remark from the preface: "It is not a matter of indifference that the people be enlightened."

The story of a European philosopher whose teachings led to the fantasy of a Mexican defeat of the still half-barbarian European conquerors was in effect a projection onto colonial frontiers of an internal European "struggle of enlightenment with superstition," Hegel's summary explanation for the causes of the French Revolution.[22]

THE BRIGHT UNSTABLE PRESENT

The temporal present of the *Persian Letters* was bright with possibilities but shadowed with doubts about the disastrous past. This past initially appeared to be receding rapidly, as the Parisian public, buoyed by new currents of thought, was ready to sail into the shining future. The speed of the retreat from the past could be rendered as spatial metaphor. It matched the distance from France to Persia, which, in a yearlong travel began Rica and Usbek's education into a new, apparently more rational world. By collapsing that distance (Usbek's meltdown, his wife's rebellion) Montesquieu gave away the game. Oriental despotism was not the main topic. The main topic was the continued nearness of despotism even on the shores of the European enlightenment, a theme nicely articulated by Vickie Sullivan's *Montesquieu and the Despotic Ideas of Europe*. Moreover, the reversal of enlightenment hero into despot put all schemes for change and improvement into doubt.[23]

Unlike other scenarios of modernization, Montesquieu's was not a story about a self-confident developmental state trying to usher in the future. Christopher Clark's *Time and Power: Visions of History in German Politics* illustrated what was involved by contrasting the developmental state thesis against its antithesis. In the Brandenburg-Prussia of Friedrich Wilhelm (1620–1888), the political elite felt "the present as a precarious threshold between a catastrophic past and an uncertain future," which it was the task of state officials to manage in resistance to local authorities. A present threatened by past and future captures as well the temporality of the *Persian Letters*, but significantly, in Montesquieu's text there is no reliance on state authority as pilot or guide to the future. The argument of the *Laws* is for negotiation/compromise between the crown and "intermediary bodies." The model is closer to the temporality of Frederick II, who replaced the developmental model of a "forwards-leaning historicity"[24] inaugurated by his great-grandfather and opted instead for a "neo-classical steady state temporality in which motifs of timelessness and cyclical repetition predominated and the state was no longer an engine of historical change."[25] Caution and pessimism had replaced optimism and self-confidence in the integrity of elites.

FINANCING *DOUX COMMERCE*

It is a central feature of the *Laws* but not really a theme in the *Letters*: *doux commerce*, or "soft," peaceful international trade and communication. *Doux commerce* projected a vision not unlike the much lamented post-1989 globalizing world economy. Commercial world war—the so-called Seven Years' War, from 1756–1763—was to threaten the prospects for Montesquieu's vision only eight years after the publication of *The Spirit of the Laws*. Similarly, national rivalries seem to have threatened the latest version of globalized *doux commerce*. In the *Persian Letters*, however, globalizing economy was far from a remedy to political instability, for the *Letters* focused on how *doux commerce* was financed.

The denouement of Usbek's seraglio coincided with Montesquieu's report on the instability and tyranny of the Regency financial "system," the ingenious scheme of Scottish economist and gambler John Law. Along with similar volatile schemes in England and Holland, Law's system led to Europe's first stock market crash in 1720. Usbek was a stand-in for Law, who, for Montesquieu, was the personification of enlightenment thinker as despotic actor. In the *Letters*, Law was a confidence man who sold bags of wind— paper money—in exchange for gold and exhorted bewildered audiences to enter into "the empire of imagination," which meant not an imaginative life, but an imaginary existence (Letter 146, 241).

Nevertheless, Voltaire thought John Law had saved France. Despite the bankruptcy, commerce had revived. Reducing debt and stimulating the economy were the two principal defenses of Law's reforms. In addition, the French could have benefited from a bank that consolidated the finances of the monarchy, but its failure to do so led to the unsustainable public debt that was one of the causes for the calling of the Estates General, which transformed itself into a National Assembly that stumbled into a French Revolution.

DIVERGENT FUTURES: FRAGILE MODERATION
OR REVOLUTION WITHOUT TRACTION

The world of the *Persian Letters* opened up onto two futures that were mutually exclusive. One opening was the hedged and qualified global compromises of *The Spirit of the Laws*. This relative retreat from forward-thinking, state-led development was most likely motivated by the memory of the stock market crash of 1720, which represented to Montesquieu the dangers inherent in the management of international finance. Sometimes enlightened intellects made things better, but sometimes they made things worse. The future Montesquieu projected in the *Laws* was utopian enough—*doux commerce* and all that—but it was a project of cautious moderation. The alternative—the heroic developmental state—required better moral characters than could be reasonably expected.

The other future of the *Persian Letters* Montesquieu rejected. It was what Berman saw potentially in the text: celebration of democratic revolution in the figure of Roxane. Arguably this is what Montesquieu also saw in his old fantasy story of Descartes among the Amerindians. There remains a question: Why shouldn't we take the harem rebellion as Berman did, as an intimation of the necessary democratic revolutions to come? There is something troubling about Usbek and Roxane. They were a couple united by coercion on one side and deceit on the other. I do not forget that Usbek really did have enlightened ideals—of the mind, not the heart. He was an educator of others, including Roxane, even if in the end he was a hypocrite, a conformist to patriarchal heritage, and a man enslaved to his passions. Worse still, his skepticism led him into nihilist disregard for others. I have so far quoted only the reasonable Lockean half of letter 76. This defense of suicide—which, as already recounted, doubles as a defense of rebellion—falls into a darker place when Usbek exults, "I can disturb all of nature as I please." He adds, "One man more or less in the world—what am I saying—that all men together, a hundred million heads like ours, are only a tenuous and minute atom" (Letter 76, 126).

The remedy for this chilling nihilism may simply be the heroine Roxane. Maybe, but think about Usbek and Roxane as a single, strangely complementary figure. In *Neveu de Rameau* (Rameau's Nephew), Diderot took up the model of the skeptical idealist torn between moderation and revolution.[26] It was a dialogue between Moi (me) and Lui (him). Lui was a Parisian bohemian who lived by his wits and believed in no one and in nothing. The narrator Moi attempted to defend principle and moderation but was overwhelmed by the skeptical arguments of Lui, who nevertheless was all along only a projection of the unwanted thoughts of Moi. Hegel adopted this dialogue as an explanation for how the moderate Enlightenment became revolutionary. Lui and Moi were the double sides of a single personality. Moi was the moderate Enlightenment, whose procedures for self-inspection led worryingly to the voice of Lui.

Diderot's prescient dialogue about the origins of revolutionary action remained unpublished in the eighteenth century, but consider the pair Usbek/Roxane as a predecessor description. Usbek was an intelligent representative of the skeptical Enlightenment who in the end believed in nothing. He was not a bohemian but a figure of authority—the skeptic as despot (Napoleon?)—and, despite his "enlightenment," given to bouts of irrational rage. His wife Roxane was the "Moi" of this narrative: a moderate except when pushed to the wall, when she rationally and methodically prepared a well-justified Lockean-like revolt, but for a rebellion/democracy that failed. It might not have failed had she borrowed not only Usbek's ideals but his nihilism about human lives in her pursuit of revolutionary means, but then as many subsequent histories of revolution have demonstrated, it would have failed in another way.

Roxanne and Usbek were the doubled soul of the Enlightenment reader, simultaneously seeking to do good in revolt against tyrannical habits (Roxanne) and yet by the light of the same literature in doubt whether there was anything good to do (Usbek).[27]

CONCLUSION

Despite the intellectual and comic pleasures of this Regency novel, it had no especially desirable future. (1) In the light of the moves made in *The Spirit of the Laws*, the *Letters* pointed to a vision of moderation, *doux commerce*, that was probably the best that could be expected but had to remain blind to the forces disrupting it: predatory war, colonial adventure, and so on. (2) Or it pointed to the skeptic's revolution where the ideals that might have inaugurated rebellion would have no traction, no way of morally anchoring the revolutionary means employed to establish a new world. Whether desirable or not, these two paths out of the novel managed to circulate through a lot of history in the following centuries.

Although my earliest readings of the *Persian Letters* are now remote memories, it appears that I never fundamentally departed from the trajectory established in my thinking through the incompatible but also strangely congruent perspectives of Paul Valery and Marshall Berman. Trajectories (Montesquieu

1721–, Valery 1926–, Berman 1970–) also show how they have betrayed their original impulses.

NOTES

1. Alan Gilbert, "'Internal Restlessness': Individuality and Community in Montesquieu," *Political Theory* 22, no. 1 (February 1994): 45–70; Michael Mosher, "The Judgmental Gaze of European Women: Gender, Sexuality, and the Critique of Republican Rule," *Political Theory* 22, no. 2 (February 1994): 25–44.

2. Michael Mosher, "Political Philosophy," in *Encyclopedia of Political Thought*, ed. Michael T. Gibbons, Diana Coole, Elisabeth Ellis, and Kennan Ferguson (Malden, MA: Wiley, 2014).

3. Montesquieu, *Persian Letters*, ed. Stuart D. Warner, trans. Stuart D. Warner and Stéphane Douard (South Bend, IN: St. Augustine's Press, 2017).

4. Paul Valery, "The Persian Letters," in *History and Politics*, trans. Denise Folliot and Jackson Mathews, Bollingen, Series XIV 10 (New York: Pantheon, 1962), 221.

5. Ibid., 219. For the French preface, see Paul Valery, *Varieté*, vol. I and II (Paris: Gallimard, 1978).

6. Reinhart Koselleck, *Critique and Crisis: Enlightenment and Pathogenesis of Modern Society* (1959; reprint, Cambridge, MA: MIT Press, 1988); Max Horkheimer and Theodor W. Adorno, *Dialectic of Enlightenment: Philosophical Fragments*, trans. Edmund Jephcott, ed. Gunselin Schmid Noerr (Stanford, CA: Stanford University Press, 2002).

7. Marshall Berman, *The Politics of Authenticity: Radical Individualism and the Emergence of Modern Society* (New York: Atheneum, 1970), 5, 44.

8. Michael Mosher, "Monarchy's Paradox: Honor in the Face of Sovereign Power," in *Montesquieu's Science of Politics: Essays on The Spirit of Laws*, eds. David Carrithers, Michael Mosher, and Paul Rahe (Lanham MD: Rowman and Littlefield, 2001), 196. See also Jean Erhard, *L'Esprit des Mots: Montesquieu en lui-même et parmi siens* (Geneva: Libraire Droz, 1998), 153.

9. Montesquieu, *The Spirit of the Laws*, trans. Anne Cohler, Basia Miller, and Harold Stone (Cambridge: Cambridge University Press, 1989), II.4.

10. Judith N. Shklar, *Freedom and Independence: A Study of the Political Ideas of Hegel's Phenomenology of Mind* (Cambridge: Cambridge University Press, 1976); Judith N. Shklar, *Montesquieu* (Oxford University Press, 1987); and my own Charles Taylor–inflected thesis, *The Spirit That Governs Cities: Modes of Human Association in the Writings of Montesquieu and Hegel* (PhD diss., Harvard University, December 1975).

11. Paul Thomas, *Karl Marx and the Anarchists* (London: Routledge and Kegan Paul, 1980).

12. Jacob T. Levy, *Rationalism, Pluralism, and Freedom* (Oxford: Oxford University Press, 2015); for the suggestion that Rawls was allied with Hegel, see 290, n. 7.

13. Michael Mosher, "The Particulars of a Universal Politics: Hegel's Adaptation of Montesquieu's Typology," *American Political Science Review* 78, no. 1 (March 1984): 179–88.

14. Michael Oakeshott, *On Human Conduct* (Oxford: Clarendon, 1975), 242.

15. Mosher, "The Judgmental Gaze of European Women," 25–44

16. Diana Schaub, *Montesquieu's Erotic Liberalism: Women and Revolution in Montesquieu's Persian Letters* (Lanham MD: Rowman and Littlefield, 1995).

17. Michael Mosher, "Montesquieu on Empire and Enlightenment," in *Empire and Modern Political Thought*, ed. Sankar Muthu (Cambridge: Cambridge University Press, 2012), 145–205; Michael Mosher, "Montesquieu on Conquest: Three Cartesian Heroes and Five Good Enough Empires," *Revue Montesquieu* 8 (2005–2006): 81–110.

18. On topics two and three, see Michael Sonenscher, *Before the Deluge: Public Debt, Inequality, and the Intellectual Origins of the French Revolution* (Princeton, NJ: Princeton University Press, 2007), especially chap. 2, "Montesquieu and the Idea of Monarchy."

19. Michael Mosher, "Democratic Crises, Revolutions and Civil Resistance: Revolutionary Imaginaries in an Era of Enlightenment, 1640–1799," in *A Cultural History of Democracy in the Age of Enlightenment*, vol. 4, ed. Michael Mosher and Anna Plassart (London: Bloomsbury, 2021), 175–200.

20. See Ryan Patrick Hanley, "Distance Learning: Political Education in the Persian Letters," *Review of Politics* 83, no. 4 (fall 2021): 533–54. I agree with the overall thesis, albeit by way of a slightly different angle of vision and as filtered through a different literature.

21. Montesquieu, "Discours sur les motifs," *Oeuvres Complètes de Montesquieu*, ed. Jean Erhard and Catherine Volpihac-Auger (Oxford: Voltaire Foundation; Napoli: Instituto Italiano; Roma: Instituto Enciclopedia Italiana; Paris: ens Éditions Classiques Garnier, 1988), vol. 8, 495–502; see also Montesquieu, *My Thoughts*, trans. and ed. Henry C. Clark (Indianapolis, IN: Liberty Fund, 2012), no. 1265, 338–40.

22. G. W. F. Hegel, *Phänomenologie des Geistes*, ed. Johannes Hoffmeister (Hamburg: Felix Meiner Verlag, 1952), 385–406; G. W. F. Hegel, *Phenomenology of Spirit*, trans. A. A. Miller (Oxford: Oxford University Press, 1977), 329–48.

23. Vickie B. Sullivan, *Montesquieu and the Despotic Ideas of Europe* (Chicago: University of Chicago Press, 2017). See my review, "Montesquieu and the Despotic Ideas of Europe: An Interpretation of the Spirit of the Laws," review of *Montesquieu and the Despotic Ideas of Europe*, by Vickie B. Sullivan, *Perspectives on Politics* 16, no. 3 (September 2018): 826–28.

24. Evident theoretically in Hegel and actually in Japan. See Michael Mosher, "Nihonteki Riso to Hegeru Seijiron [Japanese Ideals and Hegel's Political Argument]" in *Gendai Nihon no Paburiku Firosofi* [*Public Philosophy in Modern Japan*], ed. Naoshi Yamawaki (Tokyo: Shinseisha, 1998), 80–99.

25. Christopher Clark, *Time and Power: Visions of History in German Politics, from the Thirty Years' War to the Third Reich* (Princeton, NJ: Princeton University Press, 2019), 2. For two essays that explore the second of these eighteenth-century temporalities, see Michael Mosher, "What Montesquieu Taught—'Perfection Does

Not Concern Men or Things Universally,'" in *Montesquieu and His Legacy*, ed. Rebecca E. Kingston (Albany: State University of New York Press, 2009), 7–28; and Michael Mosher, "Free Trade, Free Speech, and Free Love: Monarchy from the Liberal Prospect in Mid-Eighteenth Century France," in *Monarchisms in the Age of Enlightenment: Liberty, Patriotism, and the Common Good*, ed. Hans Blom, John Christian Laursen, and Luisa Simonutti (Toronto: University of Toronto Press, 2007), 101–18.

26. Denis Diderot, *Rameau's Nephew*, trans. Jacques Barzun and Ralph H. Bowen (1956; reprint, Indianapolis, IN: Hackett, 2001)

27. Mosher, "Democratic Crises," 194.

BIBLIOGRAPHY

Berman, Marshall. *The Politics of Authenticity: Radical Individualism and the Emergence of Modern Society*. New York: Atheneum, 1970.

Clark, Christopher. *Time and Power: Visions of History in German Politics, from the Thirty Years' War to the Third Reich*. Princeton, NJ: Princeton University Press, 2019.

Diderot, Denis. *Rameau's Nephew*. Translated by Jacques Barzun and Ralph H. Bowen. 1956. Reprint, Indianapolis IN: Hackett, 2001.

Erhard, Jean. *L'Esprit des Mots: Montesquieu en lui-même et parmi siens*. Geneva: Libraire Droz, 1998.

Gilbert, Alan. "'Internal Restlessness': Individuality and Community in Montesquieu." *Political Theory* 22, no. 1 (February 1994): 45–70.

Hanley, Ryan Patrick. "Distance Learning: Political Education in the Persian Letters." *Review of Politics* 83, no. 4 (fall 2021): 533–54.

Hegel, G. W. F. *Phänomenologie des Geistes*. Edited by Johannes Hoffmeister. Hamburg: Felix Meiner Verlag, 1952.

———. *Phenomenology of Spirit*. Translated by A. A. Miller. Oxford: Oxford University Press, 1977.

Horkheimer, Max, and Theodor W. Adorno. *Dialectic of Enlightenment: Philosophical Fragments*. Translated by Edmund Jephcott. Edited by Gunselin Schmid Noerr. Stanford, CA: Stanford University Press, 2002.

Koselleck, Reinhart. *Critique and Crisis: Enlightenment and Pathogenesis of Modern Society*. 1959. Reprint, Cambridge, MA: MIT Press, 1988.

Levy, Jacob T. *Rationalism, Pluralism, and Freedom*. Oxford: Oxford University Press, 2015.

Montesquieu. "Discours sur les motifs." In *Oeuvres Complètes de Montesquieu*, volume 8. Edited by Jean Erhard and Catherine Volpihac-Auger. Oxford: Voltaire Foundation; Napoli: Instituto Italiano; Roma: Instituto Enciclopedia Italiana; Paris: ens Éditions Classiques Garnier, 1998.

———. *My Thoughts*. Translated and edited by Henry C. Clark. Indianapolis, IN: Liberty Fund, 2012.

———. *Persian Letters*. Edited by Stuart D. Warner. Translated by Stuart D. Warner and Stéphane Douard. South Bend, IN: St. Augustine's Press, 2017.

———. *The Spirit of the Laws*. Translated by Anne Cohler, Basia Miller, and Harold Stone. Cambridge: Cambridge University Press, 1989.

Mosher, Michael. "Democratic Crises, Revolutions and Civil Resistance: Revolutionary Imaginaries in an Era of Enlightenment, 1640–1799." In *A Cultural History of Democracy in the Age of Enlightenment*, volume 4, edited by Michael Mosher and Anna Plassart, 175–200. London: Bloomsbury, 2021.

———. "Free Trade, Free Speech, and Free Love: Monarchy from the Liberal Prospect in Mid-Eighteenth Century France." In *Monarchisms in the Age of Enlightenment: Liberty, Patriotism, and the Common Good*, edited by Hans Blom, John Christian Laursen, and Luisa Simonutti, 101–18. Toronto: University of Toronto Press, 2007.

———. "The Judgmental Gaze of European Women: Gender, Sexuality, and the Critique of Republican Rule." *Political Theory* 22, no. 2 (February 1994): 25–44.

———. "Monarchy's Paradox: Honor in the Face of Sovereign Power." In *Montesquieu's Science of Politics: Essays on The Spirit of Laws*, edited by David Carrithers, Michael Mosher, and Paul Rahe. Lanham MD: Rowman and Littlefield, 2001.

———. "Montesquieu and the Despotic Ideas of Europe: An Interpretation of the Spirit of the Laws," review of *Montesquieu and the Despotic Ideas of Europe*, by Vickie B. Sullivan. *Perspectives on Politics* 16, no. 3 (September 2018): 826–28.

———. "Montesquieu on Conquest: Three Cartesian Heroes and Five Good Enough Empires," *Revue Montesquieu* 8 (2005–2006): 81–110.

———. "Montesquieu on Empire and Enlightenment." In *Empire and Modern Political Thought*, edited by Sankar Muthu, 145–205. Cambridge: Cambridge University Press, 2012.

———. "Nihonteki Riso to Hegeru Seijiron [Japanese Ideals and Hegel's Political Argument]." In *Gendai Nihon no Paburiku Firosofi [Public Philosophy in Modern Japan]*, edited by Naoshi Yamawaki, 80–99. Tokyo: Shinseisha, 1998.

———. "The Particulars of a Universal Politics: Hegel's Adaptation of Montesquieu's Typology." *American Political Science Review* 78, no. 1 (March 1984): 179–88.

———. "Political Philosophy." In *Encyclopedia of Political Thought*, edited by Michael T. Gibbons, Diana Coole, Elisabeth Ellis, and Kennan Ferguson. Malden, MA: Wiley, 2014.

———. *The Spirit That Governs Cities: Modes of Human Association in the Writings of Montesquieu and Hegel*. PhD diss., Harvard University, December 1975.

———. "What Montesquieu Taught: 'Perfection Does Not Concern Men or Things Universally.'" In *Montesquieu and His Legacy*, edited by Rebecca E. Kingston, 7–28. Albany: State University of New York Press, 2009.

Oakeshott, Michael. *On Human Conduct*. Oxford: Clarendon, 1975.

Schaub, Diana. *Montesquieu's Erotic Liberalism: Women and Revolution in Montesquieu's Persian Letters*. Lanham, MD: Rowman and Littlefield, 1995.

Shklar, Judith N. *Freedom and Independence: A Study of the Political Ideas of Hegel's Phenomenology of Mind*. Cambridge: Cambridge University Press, 1976.
————. *Montesquieu*. Oxford: Oxford University Press, 1987.
Sonenscher, Michael. *Before the Deluge: Public Debt, Inequality, and the Intellectual Origins of the French Revolution*. Princeton, NJ: Princeton University Press, 2007.
Sullivan, Vickie B. *Montesquieu and the Despotic Ideas of Europe*. Chicago: University of Chicago Press, 2017.
Thomas, Paul. *Karl Marx and the Anarchists*. London: Routledge and Kegan Paul, 1980.
Valery, Paul. "The Persian Letters." In *History and Politics*, translated by Denise Folliot and Jackson Mathews. Bollingen, Series XIV 10. New York: Pantheon, 1962.
————. *Varieté*. Vol. I and II. Paris: Gallimard, 1978.

PART II

The *Persian Letters* on Nature and Convention in Politics

Chapter 4

Pitfalls of Abstract Ideals
Usbek on the Law of Nations

Andrea Radasanu

In *Persian Letters*, Usbek emerges as a champion of international law, based on his faith in natural justice that extends across national boundaries (Letters 94 and 95, 151–54). Interpreters tend to conclude that Montesquieu speaks through Usbek in this regard, relying heavily on letters 94 and 95 when supporting this view.[1] The assumption that Usbek is a stand-in for Montesquieu has a long history,[2] even with the character's clear shortcomings as a mouthpiece for Enlightenment ideals. While in *Persian Letters* Montesquieu says nothing strictly in his own name, later writings show concern about the prospects for international peace and are mostly at a real remove from Usbek's idealism. A comparison between Usbek's and Montesquieu's respective views on international relations allows us to tease out the limitations of Usbek's worldview. We begin to see that there isn't a problem only with Usbek's tyrannical role as master of a seraglio, but that his principles—especially with respect to the specific theme of international law—and his idealism are part of the problem of Usbek. Although Usbek echoes some of Montesquieu's opinions about the goodness of moderate government, among other subjects, the story of Usbek shines a light on Montesquieu's doubts regarding problematic universalizing trends within Enlightenment philosophy.

The nature and importance of the distance between creator and creation, Montesquieu and Usbek, is best understood by acknowledging the polyphonic aspects of *Persian Letters*. Usbek is one character among others, and his beliefs about morality and other topics appear in the context of many competing voices. Most relevantly, the work in its entirety is a meditation on travel, perspective, and the difficulty of transcending one's prejudices. A key theme of *Persian Letters* concerns the thorny problem of mistaking one's customs and ways for universally valid knowledge. The structure of the novel turns on several Persian travelers' experiences and their varying degrees of success in overcoming the narrowness of their own prejudices—all the while exposing the prejudices of the lands that are new to them and to which they bring a stranger's perspective for the (probably Western) reader. Usbek seems to be more serious than his companion Rica, who is often dismissed as more superficial, if wittier and more urbane, than Usbek.[3] Yet it is Rica who makes personal progress in overcoming his prejudices. Usbek's idealism with respect to international law, his insistence that natural law provides immutable moral laws, turns out to be an instance of mistaking his own prejudices for universal law. To the degree that anyone can shed their prejudices and adopt a point of view that is, if not objective, then cognizant of the multiplicity of mores, laws, and ways of life, it is Rica who foretells of whatever peace and mutual understanding may be available among humans and nations. Before proceeding to an analysis of Usbek and the discussion of the possibilities and limits of overcoming one's prejudices, we will first tease out Montesquieu's views on the law of nations as distinguished from Usbek's.

MONTESQUIEU AND HIS USBEK
ON THE LAW OF NATIONS

Montesquieu's treatment of war and peace has puzzled interpreters in ways that are relevant to disentangling Usbek's ideas on this issue from those of his author. In *The Spirit of the Laws*, Montesquieu seems to express buoyant hopefulness about progress in international relations with respect to a gentler right of nations and the logics of commerce.[4] Yet in this later work as well as the earlier writings on which this chapter focuses, it is difficult to miss a pronounced realist streak in Montesquieu's treatment of war and peace.[5] In *Reflections on Universal Monarchy in Europe*, written a decade after *Persian Letters*, Montesquieu offers a proto-Hegelian account of war: its moment had passed. Expensive and inconclusive, the interconnectedness of European nations meant that war had become an ineffective means for achieving true power and influence. While it might be tempting to interpret Montesquieu's statement that Europe is a nation made up of many parts as an expression of his cosmopolitan ethic, the trouble is that the nations that made up this interdependent network were not cognizant of these dynamics.[6] Indeed, whatever Montesquieu means by the ties that bound European nations together, he never proposes a European federation on the well-known model advanced by Abbé St. Pierre.[7]

Reflections, in short, presents the reader with the problem of war in Europe, not a rosy declaration that peace was simply on the horizon. In the wake of the latest Roman-inspired attempt to establish universal monarchy in the form of Louis XIV's ambitions, Europe found itself at a crossroads that it didn't fully appreciate. Montesquieu demurs for a moment on whether Louis XIV intended world domination, but then takes it for granted that he did just that.[8] But, for many reasons, the Sun King's ambitions were doomed to fail. The most important factors that caused this failure were structural: not even large and powerful states could increase their power through warfare. That said, even a great many defeats didn't sufficiently derail these sorts of ambitions. France's losses at Blenheim, Turin, Ramilles, Barcelona, Oudenarde, and Lille (all of which Montesquieu lists—pouring salt on wounded French pride) did not have the effect of significantly diminishing Louis XIV's power. When considering this impasse, Montesquieu's use of the term "stability" in describing the European situation doesn't read as an affirmation of a balance of power solution to curbing imperial ambitions.[9] In addition, Montesquieu offers no argument for extending international law, nor does he lay out a hopeful vision for the end of war as such. In fact, he brings up one of the advances in the law of nations as another hindrance to successful warfare: Namely, the interdiction against sacking cities (at least among European nations) meant that one had to capture fortified towns, a more expensive and difficult prospect than sacking them.[10]

The Europe of Montesquieu's day was dealing with a relationship to war and conquest as toxic and as futile as the Spanish conquest of the Americas, which led to impoverishment through the large-scale plunder of gold and silver and their resulting devaluation on the global market. The most serious symptom of the persisting desire for martial glory in Europe took the form of growing standing armies, or what Montesquieu called the "sickness of the times."[11] No one had a sufficient advantage that couldn't be imitated, yet European nations engaged in a bankrupting arms race. Montesquieu likened contemporary Europeans to Tartars: "We are poor even with the wealth and commerce of the whole world, and soon, because we have so many soldiers, we will have nothing other than soldiers, and we will be like Tartars."[12] Tartars make several important cameos in Montesquieu's writings, often as conquerors par excellence. While in many cases Tartars are relegated to exemplars of Asiatic despotism, there are interesting moments—like the one singled out above—in which they point to the barbarism of Europeans.[13] Another important example of this comes at the beginning of *Considerations on the Causes of the Greatness of the Romans and Their Decline*, where Montesquieu compares early Rome to Tartary. Twice in the first chapter of this work, which is a companion to *Reflections*,[14] Montesquieu equates early Rome to a Tartar city, which is to say a storehouse for plunder.[15] As Rome served as inspiration for subsequent European pursuits of universal

monarchy, Montesquieu here deflates the romantic or mythological founding
of Rome in the European imagination.

Tartars are featured in *Persian Letters* as either despotic or primitive conquerors (Letters 44, 66, and 131), but, most relevantly, they help set the stage
for Usbek's exposition of his views on the law of nations. Nagrum, Persian
envoy in Muscovy, provides a comical tribute to Tartars as universal conquerors: "This bellicose nation, occupied only with its present glory, certain
to vanquish at all times, never thought of distinguishing itself in the future
through the memory of its past conquests" (Letter 81, 134). For Nagrum, the
Tartars are the apex predators of world power, natural rulers who subjugated
the whole world, including Europe. This tribute reminds us, once more, of
the importance of always considering the polyphonic epistolary nature of the
work. Usbek doesn't deign to respond to this letter (or to Nagrum's first, letter 51), but his musings on the principles of universal justice begin soon after
Nagrum's homage to the Tartars (Letters 83 and 93).

Surely Montesquieu doesn't share Nagrum's point of view, but we mustn't
immediately conclude that he fully agrees with Usbek's rebuttal. It goes
without saying that Tartars do not reflect a model for emulation, nor are they
invincible conquerors of Europe. Montesquieu makes clear in *Reflections* that
they were no match for European fortifications and were all but eliminated
by the Russians.[16] The comedy of Nagrum's overblown praise of the Tartar
nation aside, his tribute to them offers the reader a reminder that the history
of the world is one of successive empires. Nagrum is the only official diplo-
mat who is featured in *Persian Letters*, which doesn't give the reader much
comfort that the development of permanent diplomatic ties among nations
represented a step toward better international relations.[17] Nagrum appreciates Russia insofar as it has common cause with Persia against Turkey but is
counting the days until he is permitted to return to Persia—which is something he has in common, ultimately, with Usbek. There is some dark humor
to Nagrum's circumstances: he is stuck in a country from which no one is
allowed to travel except the ruler, Peter the Great, whose harsh disposition
leads him to be absent and always seeking conquest. Clearly, not all travel and
diplomacy lead to more peaceful international relations.

It is worth recalling that some of Montesquieu's formulations regarding
relations among nations don't stray too far afield of the state of war that
Tartars represent. In book I of *The Spirit of the Laws*, "*le droit des gens*" is
a mitigation of the state of war that arises naturally among nations. Among
individuals, war is preceded by timidity and some sociability, but the fact
that individuals coalesce seamlessly into cohesive social groups points to the
naturalness of protonationalism spurred by in- and out-group dynamics.[18] The
content of the positive law of nations is founded on the principle that "the
various nations should do to one another in times of peace the most good

possible, and in times of war the least ill possible, without harming their true interests." He continues, "The object of war is victory; of victory, conquest, of conquest, preservation."[19] This principle bows to the primacy of one's own political community and presumes a landscape of international competition. If commerce is a solution to conflict, as it seems to be in book XX of *The Spirit of the Laws*, it is still within a competitive landscape in which nations jealously guard their own interests and even trample on those of others, especially when those nations are not European.[20]

Usbek, on the other hand, expresses optimism that international law provides the tools necessary to avoid anything approaching an international state of war. The exchange between Rhédi and Usbek on the consequences of technological innovations in war—an exchange, in other words, between two characters Montesquieu has created—provides an important wedge into how Montesquieu views the possibilities and limits of progress in international relations. In letter 105, Rhédi writes to Usbek about the detrimental effects of bombs and gunpowder. He associates the great destructiveness of bombs with the expansion of standing armies (as opposed to citizen armies), which represent instruments of oppression against the very people they are supposed to protect (Letter 105, 169). Gunpowder, Rhédi argues, means there is no respite from "injustice and violence" anywhere on earth. Usbek's angry response is a wholesale defense of modernity, arguing in favor of commerce, wealth, and science against Rhédi's more austere argument in favor of the naivete of simpler times (Letter 106). Rhédi, after all, not only takes aim at modern weaponry and the potential for further discoveries that will "furnish a quicker way to make men die and destroy entire peoples and nations," but also opposes the compass for causing great suffering to nations conquered because of advances in seafaring.

To the extent that Usbek takes the side of commerce and wealth, he does sound very much like Montesquieu himself. But, in a pattern that we will continue to see, Usbek doesn't quite express Montesquieu's view. In responding to Rhédi, Usbek admits to no drawbacks in modern warfare. He concludes that the advances in warfare technology make for quicker and more decisive war, and he credits gunpowder with less bloodshed due to the reduction of hand-to-hand combat (Letters 106, 171). In *Reflections*, as discussed, Montesquieu argues that technological advances in modernity spread in such a way that the first adopter has no significant advantage. In other words, he does *not* side with Usbek on the consequences of modern weaponry. Usbek's overly hopeful appraisal of the effects of powerful offensive weapons is joined by his claim that if an indiscriminately destructive weapon were to be invented, it would "soon be prohibited by the law of nations, and the unanimous consent of nations would bury that discovery" (Letter 106, 171).

This faith in the good sense of princes is consonant with Usbek's declaration that there is no difference between civil and international law, and that human beings as such have obligations to one another that transcend national boundaries (Letter 95). He goes even further, stating that he is confident that obligations among nations are clearer and more readily met than duties towards one's own compatriots (Letter 95, 152). Montesquieu is much more circumspect than Usbek regarding the prospects for perfect enlightenment—even when one's interests rather than obligations lead the way. He, however, sounds (or appears to sound) Usbekian in one important instance with respect to progress and the law of nations. In book X, chapter 3 of *The Spirit of the Laws*, Montesquieu croons that Europeans have conjured up a gentler right of conquest due to "contemporary" religion, mores, and philosophy. He trots out no fewer than four versions of natural law to support the case that nations ought to limit their aggression toward one another. This also echoes Usbek's statement that the principles of public law are better known in Europe than in Asia (Letter 94).

The fuller presentation is more complicated than the seemingly exuberant praise for European progress and civilization. Immediately following this exclamation, still in X.3 of *The Spirit of the Laws*, Montesquieu criticizes "our" public law for justifying the enslavement and even extermination of conquered peoples. He provides an ambiguous account of the cause of this modern harshness: "When the authors of our public right, for whom ancient histories provided the foundation, have no longer followed cases strictly, they have fallen into great error." Is it the ancient Romans who are the culprits and provide the bad example that modern public law theorists follow? Or is the issue that modern public law theorists ceased to follow these examples well? Montesquieu suggests that the Romans were responsible for the harshest right of conquest and exterminated conquered nations, while modern nations were gentler and allowed the vanquished to retain their laws. Yet the moderns are ultimately guilty of extermination, particularly in the case study of the Spanish conquest of the Americas. In fact, throughout his works, Montesquieu consistently argues that pagan Rome, for all its Tartar-like barbarism, was tolerant and left conquered nations their laws.[21] His formulation in *Considerations* makes this point clearly: "If the Spaniards had followed the [Roman] system, they wouldn't have been obliged to destroy everything to preserve everything." He continues, "It is the folly of conquerors to want to bestow on all peoples their laws and customs; that's good for nothing, as one can obey under any form of government."[22]

In X.3 of *The Spirit of the Laws*, Montesquieu briefly wears the garb of a true believer in European moral progress with respect to war and peace, only to shine a bright light on the tremendous dissonance between this smug view and reality. Part of the trifecta of modernity that was supposed to have ushered in gentleness in the law of nations was Christianity. Yet it was Christianity that hardened the hearts of the Spanish against the natives of the Americas: evangelism joined the spirit of conquest and led to the erosion of the rights of the conquered in the eyes of the conquerors. What steps Christianity had taken to soften the practice of conquest, including the ban on enslaving the conquered, did not apply to those who weren't Christian or who had different customs and habits. Both Montesquieu and his Usbek note this bit of hypocrisy (Letter 75). In his own name, Montesquieu recognizes the "special origin" of the Spanish conquest, based on the European prejudice against unfamiliar habits and bolstered by religious fervor and condescension.[23]

Montesquieu's praise of supposed advances in the modern right of nations ends up highlighting how easily so-called universal laws can be used to justify terrible practices. This darker account of modern public law—or at least its application—has an important echo in Usbek's musings. Usbek believes in the tenets of modern international law but notes with disdain how little monarchs follow these principles in practice: "This law, such as it is today, is a science that teaches princes up to what point they can violate justice without upsetting their own interests. What a design, Rhédi, to turn iniquity into a system, to give rules to that system, form its principles and draw consequences from it, all in order to harden their consciences!" (Letter 94, 151). Montesquieu and his Usbek both draw attention to the hypocrisy, poor adoption, and convenient forgetfulness of those who define rules governing conquest and then have the privilege to apply them. But Montesquieu accepts breaches of international law as a natural consequence of human nature; he views human sociability as too thin to provide the foundation for a true cosmopolitan morality.[24] Where Usbek sees a foundation for peace based on universal natural justice, Montesquieu describes a much messier scene where neither a return to simpler times nor progress rooted in enlightenment provide firm foundations for future world peace.

USBEK'S DESPOTIC STATE OF MIND

The relationship between Usbek's westward travel and his enlightenment (or lack thereof) is at the heart of *Persian Letters*, which is to say that the thorniness of the search for wisdom and knowledge separate from one's received ideas is very much on Montesquieu's mind. Usbek's most aspirational version of the genesis of his journey is that he is on a noble quest for knowledge. He speculates that he and Rica may be the first Persians to seek knowledge beyond the borders of Persia. This flirts with the troubling Orientalist premise that the "East" is static and permanently despotic, while the "West" prizes liberty and is open to change and progress. After all, for all the foibles of the

French, it is among them that sociability and communication is most developed (Letters 58, 87, and 100). Yet Montesquieu can't be said to provide fodder for Western smugness here any more than he does when he praised "progress" in the modern law of nations with tongue firmly in cheek. France, after all, was toying with despotism, and Montesquieu doesn't treat everything about their vanity and frivolousness as unproblematic. The freest individual in the work is arguably Roxane, who endures the most complete enslavement in a Persian seraglio. Indeed, if anything, the Persian protagonists are developed characters with complex and varied personalities, while the French are lampooned and stereotyped as a nation.[25] Montesquieu takes aim even (or especially) at French pretensions to their superior access to knowledge or enlightenment. Rica mercilessly dissects the knowledge industry in Paris and notes that the French are overly confident about their knowledge of countries like Persia. He describes an encounter with a French know-it-all who had consumed the travelogues of Tavernier and Chardin and therefore thought he understood Persia better than a Persian (Letter 72). Of course, now Rica is a kind of Tavernier or Chardin himself, explaining French customs and mores to the French—but perhaps without the desire to offer a definitive or essentialist account, which makes this a different sort of endeavor.

If Rica provides more insights (and experiences more profound growth) than his apparent superficiality would suggest, Usbek's abortive quest for knowledge provides the reader with the opportunity to investigate the pathologies of abstract philosophizing, devoid of self-reflection. As intimated, Usbek's motives for leaving Persia are complicated. In the very first letter, the reader's first impression of Usbek is that his sole motive for traveling is the acquisition of knowledge. He tells "his friend" Rustan that he and Rica left "the pleasures of a tranquil life in order to search laboriously for wisdom" (Letter 1, 5). In this iteration of his motives for travel, Usbek presents the acquisition of wisdom as painful rather than pleasant, thus crediting himself with a noble purpose. In letter 8, Usbek writes to Rustan again, and this time he calls attention to self-preservation as the "true motive" for his journey. In this version of the voyage origin story, Usbek feigns love of the sciences so that he can escape from court and then uses this contrived love as a pretext to gain permission to visit the West. He does say his fabricated "attachment to the sciences" turned from a charade into truth. That there are mixed motives or that he came to form an attachment to science in this way is not necessarily an indictment of his philosophic ability or his wisdom. Whether a search for wisdom or concern about his safety, Usbek ultimately thinks his motives are high-minded. He is not a coward fleeing danger, but a moral paragon who rejects a corrupt court and its sycophantic courtiers. Usbek maintains a view of himself as someone who stands for purity and is open to instruction (Letter 106). The shift in the narrative between his two letters to Rustan is enough to alert us to the possible unreliability of the most prominent narrator in *Persian Letters*, and it only becomes more notable when we begin to see that Usbek's self-presentation shifts depending on the correspondent.

Usbek maintains a facade of worldly freethinker with Mirza and Rustan, who are younger members of his friend circle and seem to look up to him (Mirza calls Usbek the "soul of our society"; Letter 10, 18; see also Letter 48, 73). But in his letters to Nessir we witness a melancholy, troubled, and ultimately stagnant and limited frame of mind. The man who professes a cosmopolitan outlook, an intrepid traveler with a yearning for enlightenment, turns out to be deeply despondent about this trip from the start. Usbek writes three letters to Nessir in which he expresses what appear to be his innermost qualms (Letters 6, 27, and 155). He confesses his "secret pain" over leaving all that is familiar behind and admits to feeling anxiety and trepidation with respect to the journey he began among the "profane" Turks (Letter 6, 10). It is clear he isn't happy in the seraglio, feeling affection for his wives only while away from them, and his fondness for scientific discovery isn't palpable either, leading us to suspect that the noble seeker story is indeed a cloak to save face with the younger members of his circle. Perhaps Usbek wants to believe what he says to his younger friends. Either way, Usbek seems to be doomed to unhappiness, both in and away from the seraglio.

In letter 27 to Nessir, Usbek writes, "My body and mind are battered; I surrender myself to reflections that become more sorrowful every day; my health, which is failing, turns me to my fatherland and renders this country more alien to me." The misgivings in letter 6 might be understandable, but letter 26 shows that Usbek doesn't progressively become more open to new knowledge or experiences. And by letter 155, Usbek is desperate to return to Persia but unable to do so. He blames Rica—whom he earlier identified as much better suited for these travels (Letters 25, 27, and 48)—for this but also clearly admits that he cannot return for the same reasons he was on the run in the first place. Usbek's self-proclaimed noble motives for travel, whether for the sake of seeking knowledge or maintaining his purity of heart, give way to real exile and mere self-preservation. Here, in his last letter to Nessir, Usbek admits that nothing about the "barbarous climate" in which he finds himself (France) interests him (Letter 155). When untangling Usbek's motives for his travels and his claims to desire knowledge and enlightenment beyond Persia, perhaps the only thing that becomes perfectly clear is his fundamental unsuitability for this sort of enterprise.

Usbek's journey of enlightenment never takes flight, no doubt because he never really leaves Persia: his obsession with the purity of his seraglio and his worries, jealousies, and wounded pride lead to the loss of what bravado he adopted toward the beginning of his exile. He finds himself hopelessly mired in his prejudices, while his disposition is marred by pride and intransigence: simply put, he is incapable of change. At the same time, he is convinced of his own philosophic insight, making universalistic metaphysical claims about natural law and justice. But the more one unpacks his claims, the more it seems to be the case that Usbek represents some of the pathologies of the knowledge industry, which Rica dedicates himself to lampooning. From the geometer who is interested in the trajectory of a bomb but not whether it was successful in a battle (Letter 128, 209) to the philosopher who "doubts everything" but "dares to deny nothing as a theologian" (Letter 66, 106), Rica looks at knowledge mongers who are too abstract or too incoherent or otherwise wanting. Through him, Montesquieu is aiming some of his sharp wit at the French *philosophes* and the salon culture that was sprouting in Europe in general and France in particular, leaving us to wonder in what ways Usbek falls short of his philosophic pretensions.

A key error of Usbek's is conflating nature and convention or mistaking the latter for the former. Letter 94 furnishes an important example of this. Usbek complains that the disembodied "state of nature" trope is overly abstract (ironic, given his own predilection for overly abstract musings), as it ignores the fundamental sociability of human beings—which, again, for him involves natural morality. In this case as in others discussed earlier, there is a surface similarity between Montesquieu and Usbek that runs the risk of burying the deeper differences between them. In *The Spirit of the Laws*, Montesquieu famously complains that the logic of the Hobbesian state of nature is too individualistic and ignores natural sociability and the spontaneity of the emergence of human society. Of course, there remain similarities between Montesquieu and the state of nature theorists from whom he distances himself, such as the inevitability of a state of war that occurs in the fullness of time in the state of nature.[26] Indeed, as outlined earlier, Montesquieu persists in attributing to international relations a fundamental state of nature. But leaving those issues to the side, Montesquieu's most potent complaint against Hobbes's conception of the state of nature is that the latter fails to imagine the psychology of human beings prior to society.[27] This is to say that he deepens the state of nature tradition and even inspires Rousseau's more radical move to consider the deep cleavages between what is by nature and what is acquired through history and society. Usbek, on the other hand, complains that the "state of nature" ignores the naturalness of the patriarchal family: "A son is born beside his father, and he remains there: here is society, and the cause of society" (Letter 94, 151). Having protested that the state of nature is overly abstract, he makes the error of importing patriarchal notions into what is universally true or right by nature. Whatever Montesquieu does or does not mean to say via his own use of the state of nature, he certainly doesn't affirm natural law underpinned by patriarchal right.

Lest we think this is an insignificant flourish rather than a core belief of Usbek's, letter 129 (also to Rhédi) provides more elaborate evidence of the ways his domestic despotism seeps into his philosophic ideas. He begins this letter by calling out most legislators for consulting "almost nothing but their own prejudices and fancies" (Letter 129, 210). The legislators who do properly consult "natural equity" have in common that "they have given fathers a great authority over their children" (211). Usbek goes on to describe in exalted tones the wisdom of paternal authority: "Of all powers, it is the one least abused; it is the most sacred of all magistracies; it is the sole one that does not depend upon conventions, and that even preceded them" (211). He speaks highly of morality as a foundation for good behavior as distinguished from law. He closes the letter by praising the French for retaining the paternal authority of Roman law, now clearly running afoul of Montesquieu's own view regarding the suitability of Roman law to France. The humor here comes from Usbek's unwittingly providing himself as an example of a "limited" man who consults only his own prejudices and fancies. Human virtue and goodness are consonant with absolute paternal power for Usbek. He notices that princes make universal public law bend to their will (Letter 94) but not that imperialism via Roman law is baked into its foundation. This parallels his inability to reflect on the ways his own despotic tendencies make their way into his universalistic principles.

Comparing Rica's very different journey to Usbek's is helpful for reinforcing the burgeoning picture of Usbek as a man whose attachment to conventions skews his view of "natural" justice. Rica is a young man, without the albatross of a seraglio around his neck, whose motives for leaving are never broached, but his suitability to the activity is commented upon by Usbek himself. He is also a young man who could choose to return to Persia but does not seem to wish to do so. Rica enjoys his travels and finds himself fundamentally changed through his encounters with the unfamiliar, particularly on the sorest of Usbek's spots: the rightful place of women in society. In letter 38, Rica considers the subjugation of women from two points of view: male utility and natural law. He weighs the French point of view against the Persian one on the matter of utility, which is to say he wonders whether men are happier when they control their wives, as the Persians believe, or when they don't, as the French contend. On this front, Rica quips that a wiser man than he might have a hard time taking a side. His tastes are already changing, as he declares, even in his willingness to entertain "extraordinary" positions (Letter 38, 62). On the normative argument, Rica quotes at some length a "gallant philosopher" who makes the point that men do not have a rightful empire over women; they use force, not right, which makes their empire a tyranny. Rather, it is women who have a natural empire of beauty over men. Rica also consults several ancient civilizations (Egypt, Babylon, Rome) and concludes that "polished" nations don't enslave women. These examples are ultimately problematic, as they all certainly subjugated women to a large degree, but they speak to Rica's willingness to compare Persian practices to those of others, seriously entertaining arguments foreign to his experience (see also letter 55). The letter concludes with a quotation from the Koran, perhaps signaling that Rica continues to treat it as an authoritative text at this moment.

Soon after, Rica announces to Usbek that his mind is "insensibly losing everything Asiatic that remains to it, and effortlessly it is conforming itself to European morals" (Letter 63, 102). He recounts that he is no longer "astonished" to see several women with several men in a house, and he finds that "this is not badly conceived" (102). He is spending time with women, rather than reading about them or speaking to gallant philosophers or consulting the Koran about them. It is only in France, he declares, that it was possible to get to know women; in Persian seraglios one does not know women. He immediately extends this statement about women to people in general: "Among us, character is completely uniform because it is forced. People are not seen such as they are, but such as they are obliged to be. In this servitude of heart and mind, one hears nothing but fear spoken, which has only one language, and not nature, which expresses itself so differently, and which appears under so many forms" (102). These declarations about human nature function as a critique of Usbek's approach to questions of right and natural law. Rica doesn't retreat into provincial, self-serving explanations or overly abstract ones. He considers utility and morality side by side and ponders historical examples, but most importantly, Rica engages directly with the customs of the French and even takes them on. Experience with embodied women seems to be the turning point for Rica in evaluating the nature of women and even nature as such. Rica teaches the reader to be suspicious of uniformity as a claim to universality. If Rica represents a way forward toward enlightenment, then one learns not by stripping away convention from nature (for this is nothing but an abstraction) but by comingling, interacting with real-life others and engaging with differences of custom and opinion.

Maybe it is hard to believe that Rica is the wiser of the two main characters of *Persian Letters*. As acknowledged earlier, his sociability may come across as unserious frivolity, and his seemingly naive commentary on manners might lack the gravitas of Usbek's ponderous philosophizing. Yet Rica is arguably the more astute of the two on key issues. When they arrive in Paris, both Rica and Usbek comment on their initial impressions of the city. Rica forms his impressions more quickly of the two because of his "vivacity of mind" (according to Usbek's description; Letter 25, 42). Rica's account seems simpleminded, as he appears to attribute much to magic, including the hold Louis XIV has on the people and the pope on him. This, however, is not the case, but works as a commentary on the naivete or even gullibility of the French, who allowed themselves to be subjected to the political and economic policies concocted by those in power. Rica grasps the financial difficulties into which the king is putting the nation and cannot find a logical way to explain how he convinces the people to go along with catastrophic policies: "If he has a war that is difficult to sustain, and he has no money, he has only to put it into their heads that a piece of paper is money, and they are immediately convinced of it" (Letter 24, 40)—or the king convinces the people that one million *écus* equals two million *écus*, and so on. It is not that Rica doesn't understand complicated financial situations; it is that the French are falling for the equivalent of parlor tricks when it comes to the crucial issue of state finances.

In contrast, when we first hear from Usbek on the situation in France, he is largely impressed by Louis XIV's power and resources (Letter 37). Admittedly, the letter focuses mostly on how much Louis's rule resembles Eastern despotism, but to the degree that we learn something about Usbek's failings at the same time, he is captivated by Louis's grandeur, if dismayed by his unwillingness to recognize and reward true merit. Usbek concludes the letter by declaring the king's resources "great" and his finances "inexhaustible" (Letter 37, 60). Usbek's slower and purportedly more considered reflections on France show him missing the mark on this important issue. Rica takes up the financial crisis of France late in the work: it is to him that Montesquieu leaves the crucial issue of John Law (Letter 138). Rica sees through French pretensions and yet is also prepared to shift his perspective based on his French experiences. Usbek, on the other hand, has predictable respect for despotic rule, such that he doesn't clearly grasp its shortfalls. While a proponent of moderate government in theory, he cannot seem to observe the difficulties of despotism in practice as they unfold before him in the French political landscape.

Usbek's failure to see the inherent weakness of the French monarchy under the Sun King recalls his praise of paternalistic versions of natural law and his approval of the persisting Roman influence on French laws and mores. Rica, by contrast, rails against the unhealthy role of Roman law in France: "Who would think that a kingdom, the most ancient and most powerful in Europe, has been governed for more than ten centuries by laws that were not made for them?" (Letter 100, 161–62). Rica provides a sophisticated account of the unsuitability of Roman law for French circumstances and marvels that the conquerors (the Franks) came to adopt the mores of the conquered. He goes on to say that while the French are ambitious when it comes to acquiring empires in beauty and cuisine, regarding "important things" they "seem to be mistrusting of themselves, up to the point of degrading themselves" (Letter 100, 161). Rica's comments on the inappropriateness of Roman law for French government point to his appreciation of the insight that not every law suits every place. There is no escape from particularity, which seems to reflect Montesquieu's own insistence that laws are necessarily plural. As Montesquieu states at the beginning of *The Spirit of the Laws*, "Laws must relate to the nature and the principle of the government that is established or that one wants to establish."[28] He starts Book I by adopting a Usbekian posture of an orderly universe with clear a priori laws, but a few short pages and chapters later he has shifted to what seems to be his deeper understanding of a necessarily fragmented human and political world—one that Rica embraces.

CONCLUSION

Usbek's desire to express or formulate universal rules that apply uniformly is itself a product of a despotic mindset. This is not to say that there isn't something simply human about this desire: he wants there to be an orderly universe with "general laws, immutable, eternal, which are observed without exception" (Letter 97, 156). We have some indication that Usbek himself wrestles with fears that standards of natural justice don't exist; his intellectual and spiritual journey is difficult, and he seems to draw no pleasure from it. Beyond his increasingly gloomier letters to Nessir, Usbek admits that he fundamentally sides with the habit of Eastern princes who drink to forget themselves than with Western thinkers like Seneca who reason about human misery (Letters 33 and 56). Leaving Usbek's psychology to the side, this chapter has focused on the ways in which he stands for larger political and theoretical trends that Montesquieu satirizes.

Most prominently, Montesquieu wants the reader to compare Usbek to Peter the Great. Nargum's commentary on the Tartars seems to stir up Usbek's counternarrative on international relations, but, as also mentioned, Nargum's first of two letters focused on Russian mores and Peter the Great. This czar is known to the reader of *The Spirit of the Laws* as the despotic reformer who could have made changes in Russia without the brutality he favored.[29] Nargum describes the czar as someone who wanted to "change everything" (Letter 51, 83). This passion for change and for carrying forth the glory of Russia beyond its borders, even as Russians were confined to Russia, went together with restlessness and agitation: at home he wandered throughout his estates "leaving marks of his natural severity everywhere," while abroad he sought to expand his domains (83–84). This can't help but remind the reader of Usbek's own ceaseless agitation. Both go about enlightenment with too great a dose of despotism, or perhaps we can say that they represent poor attempts to bring East and West together. In addition to Peter the Great, Usbek also calls to mind the great political sins of Emperor Justinian, who authored or assembled the Digest to articulate the rules of engagement in the Roman Empire. This is relevant to the issue of international law. Usbek believes that the Roman baggage offers great benefits to Europe, including the just war tradition. Montesquieu, as we have noted, is much more skeptical than Usbek about the foundations—especially the Roman foundations—of modern public law. This deep distrust of the accumulation of so-called wisdom about justice among nations is most palpable when noting that Montesquieu criticizes few rulers as mercilessly as he does Justinian. A chief issue is Justinian's intemperate passion for change, reform, and uniformity.[30] Montesquieu indicts him for contributing to the decline of the political health of Rome through his dogmatic religious intolerance. The Digest, which Grotius and his followers largely accepted, established the precedent for profoundly inhumane treatment of conquered peoples based on supposedly universal moral and religious truths.[31]

Commerce provides a better mechanism than international public law to shift the paradigm of international relations, as it recognizes a multiplicity of laws and works on a contractual model where reciprocity is a constituent component. Commerce leads to increased interactions and greater communication among nations—a model that mirrors Rica's disposition on a grand scale. Usbek's personal baggage reflects his theoretical baggage. It is significant that in *Persian Letters* it is Rica and Rhédi, the young men who are unencumbered by despotic circumstances and disposition, who leave behind the Roman patrimony of Europe and think more radically and entertain republicanism and the liberty found in the forests of Europe (Letter 100).[32] Usbek is left behind, as it were, with his despotic and universalistic frameworks. While Montesquieu sometimes seems to be more like the ponderous and serious Usbek, in the end, maybe he is closer to the playful Rica, for whom all customs and all assumptions are open for debate. In letter 143 (to Nathaniel Levi, Jewish doctor in Livorno), Rica criticizes the credulousness of Muslims and Jews and declares men "unfortunate wretches" who "vacillate ceaselessly between false hopes and ridiculous fears, and, instead of resting upon reason, they create monsters that intimidate them or phantoms that seduce them" (Letter 143, 243). Montesquieu helps puncture belief in the monsters and phantoms, bringing out the Rica in us as we entertain strange notions that become familiar and treat familiar ideas with distance such that we see their strangeness.

NOTES

1. Christian Volk, "The Law of the Nations as the Civil Law of the World: On Montesquieu's Political Cosmopolitanism," in *System, Order, and International Law: The Early History of International Legal Thought from Machiavelli to Hegel*, edited

by Stefan Kadelbach, Thomas Kleinlein, and David Roth-Isigkeit (Oxford: Oxford University Press, 2017), 240.

2. Jean Starobinski, *Blessings in Disguise; or, The Morality of Evil*, trans. Arthur Goldhammer (Cambridge, MA: Harvard University Press, 1993), 72; Judith N. Shklar, *Montesquieu* (Oxford: Oxford University Press, 1987), 25.

3. Genevieve Lloyd, "Imaging Difference: Cosmopolitanism in Montesquieu's *Persian Letters*," *Constellations* 19, no. 3 (2012): 484.

4. Montesquieu, *The Spirit of the Laws*, ed. Anne M. Cohler, Basia Carolyn Miller, and Harold Samuel Stone (Cambridge: Cambridge University Press, 1989), X.3, XX.1–2.

5. Interpreters who understand Montesquieu to stand for some universal version of international law still tend to acknowledge that he harbors realist tendencies as well. Stephen J. Rosow, "Commerce, Power and Justice: Montesquieu on International Politics," *Review of Politics* 46, no. 3 (1984): 346–66; Katya Long, "The 'Anti-Hobbes'? Montesquieu's Contribution to International Relations Theory," *In-Spire Journal of Law, Politics and Societies* 3, no. 2 (2008): 97; Haig Patapan, "Democratic International Relations: Montesquieu and the Theoretical Foundations of Democratic Peace Theory," *Australian Journal of International Affairs* 66, no. 3 (June 2012): 313–29.

6. Montesquieu, *Oeuvres Complètes de Montesquieu: Considerations Sur Les Causes De La Grandeur Des Romains Et De Leur Decadence. Réflexions Sur La Monarchie Universelle En Europe*, vol. 2, ed. Francoise Weil (Oxford: Voltaire Foundation, 2011), 360.

7. Catherine Larrère, "L'empire, Entre Fédération et République—Montesquieu," *Revue Montesquieu* 8 (2006): 116.

8. For a different interpretation of Montesquieu's take on Louis XIV's ambitions, see Michael Mosher, "Montesquieu on Conquest: Three Cartesian Heroes and Five Good Enough Empires," *Revue Montesquieu*, no. 8 (2006): 93–96.

9. Contra Long, "The 'Anti-Hobbes'? Montesquieu's Contribution to International Relations Theory."

10. Montesquieu, *Réflexions Sur La Monarchie Universelle En Europe*, 340.

11. Ibid.. See also *The Spirit of the Laws*, XIII.17.

12. Montesquieu, *Réflexions Sur La Monarchie Universelle En Europe*, 363.

13. Institute for the History of Classical Thought, "Rolando Minuti, Tartars | A Montesquieu Dictionary," accessed January 21, 2022, http://dictionnaire-montesquieu .ens-lyon.fr/en/consultation-en/.

14. Paul Rahe, "Empires Ancient and Modern," *Wilson Quarterly* 28, no. 3 (2004): 76.

15. Montesquieu, *Considerations Sur Les Causes De La Grandeur Des Romains Et De Leur Decadence,* 89.

16. Montesquieu, *Réflexions Sur La Monarchie Universelle En Europe*, 352.

17. See Belissa for a characterization of early eighteenth-century assumptions about progress in international relations, together with the assumption that Montesquieu fits neatly within it. Marc Belissa, "Montesquieu, *L'Esprit Des Lois* et Le Droit Des Gens," in *Le Temps de Montesquieu*, ed. Michel Porret and Catherine Volpilhac-Auger (Geneva: Droz, 2002), 179–80.

18. Montesquieu, *The Spirit of the Laws*, XVIII.12–17, 25.

19. Ibid., I.3.

20. On England's jealousy of trade, see ibid., XX.7, 12.

21. Cf. *The Spirit of the Laws*, X.3 and X.17.

22. Montesquieu, *Considerations Sur Les Causes De La Grandeur Des Romains Et De Leur Decadence*, 141; my translation.

23. Montesquieu, *The Spirit of the Laws*, XV.3–4.

24. Ibid., XXVI.20.

25. Roxanne L. Euben, *Journeys to the Other Shore: Muslim and Western Travelers in Search of Knowledge* (Princeton, NJ: Princeton University Press, 2006), 153.

26. Thomas L. Pangle, *Montesquieu's Philosophy of Liberalism: A Commentary on The Spirit of the Laws* (Chicago: University of Chicago Press, 1989); David Lowenthal, "Book I of Montesquieu's The Spirit of the Laws*," *American Political Science Review* 53, no. 2 (June 1959): 485–98; Stuart Warner, "Montesquieu's Prelude: An Interpretation of Book I of The Spirit of the Laws," in *Enlightening Revolutions: Essays in Honors of Ralph Lerner*, ed. Svetozar Minkov (Lexington, MD: Lexington Books, 2006), 161–89; Michael Zuckert, "Natural Law, Natural Rights, and Classical Liberalism: On Montesquieu's Critique of Hobbes," *Social Philosophy and Policy* 18, no. 1 (2001): 227–51.

27. Montesquieu, *The Spirit of the Laws*, I.2.

28. Ibid., I.3.

29. Ibid., XIX.14.

30. Montesquieu, *Considerations Sur Les Causes De La Grandeur Des Romains Et De Leur Decadence,* 253–54.

31. Ibid., 256–57. Here, Montesquieu makes clear that ancient Romans allowed "all sorts of sects" and thus strengthened their empire. Christian emperors, especially Justinian, did otherwise and destroyed whole nations while weakening the empire. Usbek isn't quite like the Christian Justinian in that he favors religious toleration (albeit with the un-Montesquieuian notion that it would provide deeper religious devotion—*The Spirit of the Laws*, XIX.27, p. 330), but he cannot help but see the world in terms of abstract ideals (Letter 85).

32. Cf. Montesquieu, *The Spirit of the Laws*, XI.6, p. 166.

BIBLIOGRAPHY

Belissa, Marc. "Montesquieu, *L'Esprit Des Lois* et Le Droit Des Gens." In *Le Temps de Montesquieu*, edited by Michel Porret and Catherine Volpilhac-Auger, 171–85. Geneva: Droz, 2002.

Euben, Roxanne L. *Journeys to the Other Shore: Muslim and Western Travelers in Search of Knowledge*. Princeton, NJ: Princeton University Press, 2006.

Institute for the History of Classical Thought. "Rolando Minuti, Tartars | A Montesquieu Dictionary." Accessed January 21, 2022. http://dictionnaire-montesquieu.ens-lyon.fr/en/consultation-en/.

Larrère, Catherine. "L'empire, Entre Fédération et République—Montesquieu." *Revue Montesquieu* 8 (2006): 111–36.

Lloyd, Genevieve. "Imaging Difference: Cosmopolitanism in Montesquieu's *Persian Letters.*" *Constellations* 19, no. 3 (2012): 480–93.

Long, Katya. "The 'Anti-Hobbes'? Montesquieu's Contribution to International Relations Theory." *In-Spire Journal of Law, Politics and Societies* 3, no. 2 (2008).

Lowenthal, David. "Book I of Montesquieu's The Spirit of the Laws*." *American Political Science Review* 53, no. 2 (June 1959): 485–98.

Montesquieu. *Oeuvres Complètes de Montesquieu: Considerations Sur Les Causes De La Grandeur Des Romains Et De Leur Decadence. Réflexions Sur La Monarchie Universelle En Europe.* Volume 2. Edited by Francoise Weil. Oxford: Voltaire Foundation, 2011.

———. *The Spirit of the Laws.* Edited by Anne M. Cohler, Basia Carolyn Miller, and Harold Samuel Stone. Cambridge: Cambridge University Press, 1989.

Mosher, Michael. "Montesquieu on Conquest: Three Cartesian Heroes and Five Good Enough Empires." *Revue Montesquieu* 8 (2006): 81–110.

Pangle, Thomas L. *Montesquieu's Philosophy of Liberalism: A Commentary on The Spirit of the Laws.* Chicago: University of Chicago Press, 1989.

Patapan, Haig. "Democratic International Relations: Montesquieu and the Theoretical Foundations of Democratic Peace Theory." *Australian Journal of International Affairs* 66, no. 3 (June 2012): 313–29.

Rahe, Paul. "Empires Ancient and Modern." *Wilson Quarterly* 28, no. 3 (2004): 68–84.

Rosow, Stephen J. "Commerce, Power and Justice: Montesquieu on International Politics." *Review of Politics* 46, no. 3 (1984): 346–66.

Shklar, Judith N. *Montesquieu.* Oxford: Oxford University Press, 1987.

Starobinski, Jean. *Blessings in Disguise; or, The Morality of Evil.* Translated by Arthur Goldhammer. Cambridge, MA: Harvard University Press, 1993.

Volk, Christian. "The Law of the Nations as the Civil Law of the World: On Montesquieu's Political Cosmopolitanism." In *System, Order, and International Law: The Early History of International Legal Thought from Machiavelli to Hegel*, edited by Stefan Kadelbach, Thomas Kleinlein, and David Roth-Isigkeit, 240–62. Oxford: Oxford University Press, 2017.

Warner, Stuart. "Montesquieu's Prelude: An Interpretation of Book I of The Spirit of the Laws." In *Enlightening Revolutions: Essays in Honors of Ralph Lerner*, edited by Svetozar Minkov, 161–89. Lexington, MD: Lexington Books, 2006.

Zuckert, Michael. "Natural Law, Natural Rights, and Classical Liberalism: On Montesquieu's Critique of Hobbes." *Social Philosophy and Policy* 18, no. 1 (2001): 227–51.

Chapter 5

Faces of Monarchy in West and East and the Limits of Traditional Jurisprudence

Montesquieu in Dialogue with Bodin in the Persian Letters

Rebecca Kingston

While both Bodin and Montesquieu are now acknowledged as defenders of limited monarchy, they offer very different ways of putting forward their vision.[1] One of the keys to understanding Montesquieu's novel approach to political analysis, especially as monarchy is concerned, begins with his literary ambitions to offer an analysis of France from the Persian perspective. The *Persian Letters* has traditionally been read as a precursor to *The Spirit of the Laws* in a call for the moderation of governments and a warning about despotic tendencies at the center. This position can sometimes suppose that Montesquieu saw the Persian regime in 1721 (at the tail end of the rule of the Safavids) in the same way as he saw it in 1748 (after a change of regime in Persia), as an exemplar of the distinct juridical category of despotism (indeed Oriental despotism, as the trope came to be known), with the rebellion in the seraglio perceived as a warning concerning the unsustainability of despotic regimes.[2] Reading the text carefully, however, in conjunction with the work of Bodin and in broader historical context of early eighteenth-century Franco-Persian relations as recently highlighted by the captivating work of Susan Mokhberi, it is evident that Montesquieu in 1721, along with the intellectual elite of France, did not regard Persia as a particularly deviant exemplar as a regime, but rather as another royal monarchy (to use the Bodinian term).[3] France and Persia were considered alike: both ruled by monarchs and characterized by attachment to mores of honor, refinement, and politeness, albeit with some distinct customs (Letter 71). Indeed, part of the literary force of the work is to demonstrate that the French and the Persians have much more in common (apart from their religion and treatment of women) than what might earlier have been supposed, despite a tendency by the French to tinge all things Persian with an element of exoticism, a tendency that Montesquieu himself mocks (Letter 28). It is a dynamic that Montesquieu would have acknowledged through the broad political and cultural discussions surrounding the official visit of the Persian ambassador to France in 1715.

I will argue in this chapter that there is a more complicated play of political models and regime types in the *Persian Letters* than has been generally supposed, and the decoupling of sovereignty and power along with a heightened sensitivity to shifts and changes in power relations makes this a unique contribution to political reflection, independent in many ways from Montesquieu's later work. To demonstrate this, I begin with examining how Montesquieu can be seen to engage with Bodin's typology, then show the ways in which those categories come to be challenged as the narrative proceeds. Through this process, Montesquieu enters into dialogue with Bodin's jurisprudence in several ways. In the first instance, Montesquieu breaks down a distinction made in Bodin's typology of regimes between legitimate seigneurial governments and despotisms. In addition, in a second moment, it becomes clear that he shifts from the purely juridical account of regimes by the recognition of a broader phenomenon of governance incorporating mores in addition to laws, leading to the acknowledgement of the centrality of certain psychosocial dynamics for political life. Third, and perhaps most significantly, in highlighting the psychosocial dynamic in political life, Montesquieu acknowledges aspects of power distinct from sovereignty that can often be more formative for politics and can shape political evolution and change, a tendency unique to this work and an emphasis that risks the undermining of regime distinctions altogether. It also provides the precondition for thinking about resistance to tyranny in terms other than juridical right. Ultimately it is less the static realities of politics, and more the realities and mechanisms of political flux and change, that are of interest to Montesquieu in this work. Overall, regarding political and regime analysis, Montesquieu in the *Persian Letters* (1721) offers a palpably distinct sensibility than what scholars generally find in *The Spirit of the Laws* (1748).

Montesquieu does not offer readers of the *Persian Letters* a precise rendering of the desirable structures of government devoted to principles of liberty, nor does he offer an account of the juridical grounds for resistance to political tyranny. However, his adoption of the satirical rhetoric of seventeenth-century moralism to matters of jurisprudence and public life opens the door to new perspectives in political reflection. I read the work as a series of reflections on differing forms of human community, questioning a traditional juridical approach to regime types by a juxtaposition and ultimate favoring of the language of social and moral psychology. Through this exploration Montesquieu offers a challenge to the notion of fixed regime types in general. The dynamics of social and moral psychology push personal, social, and political relations to constant change and evolution, and contestation. The rigid delineation of regime types as found in Bodin is surpassed by an awareness of multiple modes of the ebb and flow of power that can often have more significance than strict legal and juridical structures.

BODIN

Bodin's juridical principles as laid out in his *Six Books of the Republic* (1576) were central to a long tradition of political reflection in France.[4] With regard to an analysis of regime types, the various communities depicted in the *Persian Letters* allow Montesquieu to engage with Bodinian categories of democracy, monarchy, seigneurial government, and tyranny as well as with the more complicated mix of governance that Bodin acknowledges are possibly in conjunction with these forms of sovereignty. Still, in doing so in the idiom of fiction and through the experience of individual characters, Montesquieu adds psychological insight to traditional juridical categories. This introduces the vast category of mores and its possible impact on the exercise of sovereignty, both in enabling and constraining it. This step, in turn, as we will see, troubles the typology as conceived in purely juridical terms. The engagement with traditional categories of jurisprudence through a new perspective of social and moral psychology leads, I will suggest, to a rethinking of those categories.

Bodin is perhaps most famous for defining sovereignty in his work *Six Books of the Republic* as "the absolute and perpetual power of a commonwealth" and for positing that it is a power that cannot be divided (book 1, chapter 10).[5] Still, before elucidating the nature of sovereignty, Bodin takes pains at the outset of his work to offer a long and detailed discussion of the household to both elaborate on and improve the discussions found in both Aristotle and Xenophon. The household is considered the primary constituent unit of the republic as well as an important analogical counterpart to the political relation, with the domestic power of the male head of the household as the model and image of the exercise of sovereign power in the republic. Bodin follows Euripides in stating that the most important element in the preservation of republics is the obedience of the wife to her husband, with the only caveat that the husband should not abuse his legitimate power and should not treat his wife as a slave with recourse to battery.[6]

While the household remains subject to the same model of paternal authority, Bodin acknowledges that sovereign power at the level of the political relation of the republic can take very distinct forms. Regimes are divided into three types according to where sovereignty lies: monarchy when sovereignty is held by one, democracy when sovereignty is held by the many, and aristocracy when sovereignty is held by the few (book 2, chapter 1). In acknowledging that natural law, divine law, and the natural right to property also come into play and need to be respected in order to distinguish legitimate from illegitimate holding of power, he also acknowledges that all three forms of regime can operate according to three frameworks or "modes of operation": legitimate, despotic, or tyrannical (book 2, chapter 2).[7] This is evident most clearly in the case of monarchy. In legitimate or royal monarchy, the sovereign rules according to the provisions of natural and divine law respecting the property of their subjects; in seigneurial or despotic monarchy, certain normative constraints on sovereigns in an established realm, such as respect for the lives and properties of subjects, are no longer applicable, and the sovereign rules the realm as if it were their own household but legitimately so, due to the conquering of another state in a just war; and in tyranny, sovereignty is usurped unjustly, or an established legitimate sovereign no longer respects the normative constraints by which sovereignty should be exercised (book 2, chapter 2). In the case of usurpation of legitimate office, popular resistance can be justified for Bodin, but in the case of a legitimate sovereign becoming tyrannical, popular resistance is not justified and intervention is possible only through another legitimately appointed sovereign in a just war (book 2, chapter 5). Both royal and seigneurial monarchy can be normatively appropriate in the proper circumstances, but not, of course, tyranny, which is in its essence unlawful and illegitimate, even if resistance to it is subject to legal constraints (presumably for reasons of utility).

Bodin acknowledges that the structure of sovereignty may not always look so obvious in practice, as legitimate sovereigns can delegate responsibilities to governments of various types (again monarchical, aristocratic, or democratic), though never their ultimate symbolic, legal, and juridical power (book 1, chapter 10). By drawing on a wide array of historical evidence, Bodin demonstrates both the viability of his basic juridical categories and the diverse ways in which they have taken shape, thereby also taking great pains to correct earlier authors who may have claimed to see forms of divided sovereignty (book 2, chapter 1). So, for example, the power of the Roman Senate, while important, was still emanating from the sovereignty of the people, ensuring that Rome was a democracy, just as the powers of the *parlements* in France were emanations of royal sovereignty and not evidence of any mixed form (a view Montesquieu endorses regarding the French monarchy in his later work).

REGIME TYPES IN THE *PERSIAN LETTERS*

Against this basic Bodinian background, we see that the locus of sovereignty and the nature of its exercise appear to be a preoccupation for Montesquieu at the outset of the *Persian Letters*. We are initially presented with an array of sovereign states and modes of governance: one key example of democratic rule (the Troglodytes of letter 12), examples of republican government in Italy and Venice, four key exemplars of royal monarchy (Persia, the Troglodytes of letter 14, France, and England), one example of seigneurial monarchy (the Troglodytes of letter 11), two examples of tyranny (the Ottomans in letters 18 and 78 and the Russian Empire in letter 49), and, of course, one key example of household rule (Usbek and his seraglio). If we explore Montesquieu's discussion of each of these examples successively, and in conjunction with Bodin's discussion of these types, we can see how this work could be read as a commentary on the basic categories and analysis developed by his juridical predecessor. We see points of both continuity and contrast.

To begin, the *Persian Letters* offers little evidence of Montesquieu's later preoccupation with democratic and aristocratic forms, as they occupy a fleeting status in the work. In the three letters devoted to these forms, they appear as possible only in a very narrow geographical region (western Europe), historically rare, and sustained with enormous difficulty. In letter 125, Rhedi (writing appropriately from Venice and, as suggested in letter 29, learning about their form of government) offers reflections on republics on a historical register. Like the conjectural history presented in letters 11 to 14 in the tale of the Troglodytes, Montesquieu suggests in letter 125 that democratic government emerged historically as a reaction to abuses of single-person rule, citing the example of ancient Athens and other Greek states. Greek colonies spread the spirit of liberty to other parts of Europe and North Africa and helped to inspire the republican regimes of both Rome and Carthage. By implication, Montesquieu rejects a social contract approach found in Locke, whereby all forms of monarchical government were founded on some historical conjecture of a preexisting democracy. A more realist historical sensitivity may ally him more strongly with the work of Bodin.

The achievement of democracy appears fortuitous, sometimes partial, and even once established its capacity to sustain itself is limited. In letter 125 Montesquieu acknowledges that the uniquely European experience of democratic and aristocratic regimes could often be accompanied by practices of violent imperial oppression. As noted in letter 12, democracy is often accompanied by mores of frugality and virtue, but given the difficulties in adhering to such practices, the regime is often unsustainable in the longer term. Indeed, in letter 126 Montesquieu notes the attempts of the Romans to bring self-government to the Cappadocians in the wake of the Mithridatic wars. The Cappadocians refused, somewhat mirroring the spirit in which the Troglodytes of letter 14 rejected the burden of self-rule. In letter 87, with a focus on the place of honor in distinct regimes, Montesquieu suggests that republican motivation—that is, to excel through devoted service to the welfare of all as a good in itself—is "godlike." Overall, Montesquieu's brief references to democracies and aristocracies in the text demonstrate both a strong recognition of the ideal of liberty associated with their forms and a somewhat mystified acknowledgment that the appeal does not appear to be universal and that there have been important barriers historically to achieving them, often due to the difficulty of the social practices sustaining them. Still, it soon becomes apparent that this quality of elusiveness is not unique to republics, though not for the same reasons.

The bulk of Montesquieu's commentary about governance in the *Persian Letters* concerns various manifestations of monarchy: in Bodin's terms, royal monarchy as that in which a king rules according to dictates of natural and divine law; seigneurial monarchy, which is rule by one over a state as its own personal domain as a result of (just) war; and tyranny, in which a king rules in violation of natural and divine law.

We are offered three models of functioning royal monarchy early in the work. Still, it appears that monarchy is not only a capacious category but also an unstable one. As Usbek relates in letter 99: "Most of the governments of Europe are monarchies, or rather are so-called. For I do not know whether there has ever been a true monarchy as such; at the very least, it is difficult that they should subsist for a long time in that purity. It is a violent state, which always degenerates into despotism or a republic."[8] This suggests from the outset that the location of ultimate sovereignty in the office of a single ruler is not sufficient as a criterion of monarchical rule and leads us to think about what sorts of factors make monarchy "truly" one. It appears that for Montesquieu the functioning of monarchy involves a negotiation of responsibilities and powers between the monarch and the broader people. Still, he does not here indicate exactly what sort of factors make it unstable and pose a challenge to securing a persistent balance of power between the two.

One of the most evocative depictions of monarchy in the work is through the narrative of the last act of the virtuous Troglodytes to surrender their sovereignty to a single king. We see an echo of Montesquieu's praise of liberty in democratic governance, with the lament of its loss in the move to monarchy. Most importantly, however, we see Montesquieu's emphasis on the shift in mores that this shift in juridical governance entails. The Troglodytes will no longer have to self-regulate and follow austere and rigorous morals but will only need to follow the laws that are less rigid in their requirements, only entailing the avoidance of the most egregious behaviors.[9] This supplements the traditional juridical division between democracy and monarchy, with a focus on the impact on broader social customs and the differential nature of civil relations and internal motivations in the two types of regimes. We see already ambiguous qualities of monarchical governance. While in theory a loss of liberty, the move to monarchy also appears to be a relinquishing of a burden, and the good king does not rejoice in newly granted power but appears to mourn in the face of new political responsibility. It is a perspective that accentuates the burdens of public life and collective responsibilities. It may also help to illustrate part of an underlying tension in the nature of monarchy alluded to in letter 99 in the fact that it places much of the demands of good character and upright behavior in the hands of one with authority to govern but holds that the monarch shape others through law and through the threat of punishment rather than virtue, making a commitment to virtue and good uses of power more difficult to sustain in the long run. Yet here we are faced with a paradox. While it may seem that the move from republic to monarchy here is one that flows almost naturally from the unsustainable burden of collective republican virtue, Montesquieu also has told us that monarchies themselves are unstable and appear to naturally flow either back to republicanism or to despotism. Politics is less about stable categories and more about assessing the tendencies and shifts among them.

As Montesquieu explores the functioning of other monarchies, the tensions become apparent in other ways. The Persian regime is described in the first letter as "a flourishing kingdom."[10] While there is a tendency for Montesquieu to highlight authoritarian tendencies in what he calls "Asian" regimes, the presentation of the Persian case places it in a distinct category that cannot be assimilated to the outright despotic character of the Ottoman case. In this work, Montesquieu was not painting all non-European regimes with the same brush of "Oriental despotism" but was careful to make important distinctions among regimes of the East.

While the reader is told initially that the motive for Usbek's trip is out of his own wish to seek enlightenment, the reader is given clues in letters 5 and 8 that Usbek is somewhat in trouble with powerful individuals in the regime. Not being fearful of speaking truth to power instead of engaging in flattery, Usbek has made enemies. We are told that he initially sought to isolate himself in his home in the country to take up study, but that further concern about his position led him to decide to go into exile for a time to escape his enemies. So through the perspectives of Usbek and his friends, Montesquieu places attention to mores ahead of a strict juridical account. A power structure focused on a court servicing the rule of a single individual is associated with

competition in vying for favor, and in this context preserving one's reputation and cultivating allies is crucial. Persia here is not a corrupted France
but a fraternal twin of the French regime in which France can see herself.
Still, while sharing the status of monarchy, Montesquieu acknowledges that
the balance of power between prince and people shifts differently in each.
We are told later in letter 99 that the power of the sultans (i.e., shahs) is less
subject to the limiting power of religion and of general custom. Furthermore,
falling out of favor with the ruler in Persia can mean death. Yet such an
apparently harsh and cruel policy dealing with opponents and critics can be
a weakening and destabilizing force. Critics who face such harsh penalties
for voicing opposition may be motivated to engage in more extreme tactics
of outright insurrection and planned rebellion, an allusion to the revolt of
Mir-Weiss, the intendant of Kandahar province, against the shah, leading
to founding the Afghan state in 1719.[11] So Montesquieu presents another
paradox. Monarchical rulers who feel less inclined to limit the harshness of
penalties can ultimately make themselves more vulnerable to upheaval and
changing fortune. An attempt by the ruler to seize more control through certain strategies can have the unintended consequence of shifting power in the
opposite direction. Here the exercise of sovereignty is somewhat decoupled
from power in its effects. So it is not only that the center or concentration of
authority can appear to swing in monarchies, with sometimes the monarch
and sometimes the people having more influence in the making of policy,
but that the effects of those policies can also have the unintended effect of
swinging power the other way. Again, monarchy is not a static category but a
dynamic one, full of tensions and subject to ongoing change.

Along these same lines of shifts and paradoxes, there is also a moment
in the work when the Persian monarchy is looked on more favorably than
that of France. The parallel of the two regimes allows Montesquieu to make
not-so-veiled allusions to the ill effects of the expulsion of the Huguenots
through his invocation of a failed plan by the ministers of Shah Soliman to
expel the Armenians in Persia in letter 83, leading him to acknowledge the
often-beneficial socioeconomic effects of having different religious groups in
a state. The wisdom of the shah to block this plan for Montesquieu demonstrates the superiority of his political judgement over that of Louis XIV in an
allusion to the Revocation of the Edict of Nantes in 1685.

Usbek's arrival in Paris gives Montesquieu an opportunity to deepen the
comparison of the Persian and French monarchies and corresponding mores.
Usbek compares the position of the Persian shah to the French king (Letter
35), he notes that the courts of both share a similar preoccupation with self
and status (Letter 42), he notes differences in how noble status is achieved
(Letter 86), he remarks how greater liberty in France enhances the drive for
honor in comparison to Persia (Letter 87), he compares the force of religion

and the power of the clergy (Letters 33 and 58), and he compares the ill effects of the applications of public law in Europe (advising the prince on how much he can get away with) with the license automatically given to the shah (Letter 91). The overall effect is to come to an understanding of monarchy as a spectrum, but there is also a heightened anxiety and tension in this spectrum. The unstated anxiety is the point at which the monarchical regime begins to betray itself. At what point can it be said that the rule of one becomes corrupt? And is there a point of no return? Montesquieu does not appeal here to the dictates of natural and divine law that for Bodin serve as the regulatory standards by which a lawful and legitimate monarchy is judged. The Persian example here is a liminal one, still in the confines of a monarchy but veering perilously close to the precipice of despotism. Yet Persia also serves as a mirror in which the French can see themselves. The rather ill-defined border between the two for Montesquieu, as well as an account of the fluidity of politics that acknowledges constant evolution and inner tensions, offers little guidance here.

In one letter Montesquieu comes to depict France herself at this same liminal state and through a signaling to Bodin's categories. He notes in letter 35 that the king of France rules his family, court, and state in the same spirit. The uptake of this seemingly innocent observation, in the words of a Persian observer of the French monarchy, is that there is a tendency in the French regime toward a form of seigneurial governance, though without Bodin's legal grounds to justify it. It suggests a tendency toward a violation of the norms of royal monarchy, given a lack of respect for the natural property rights of subjects. It is an extraordinary and audacious phrase to put in the mouth of a character whose own approach to family management is revealed to be nothing short of terrorizing.

England is presented as a monarchical regime by Usbek in letter 101, but a monarchical regime underpinned by certain mores that makes the regime function in ways distinct from the rest of Europe.[12] According to Montesquieu, the English distinguish themselves by an impatient temperament that makes it difficult for monarchs to make their authority felt. The suggestion here is that the Ciceronian attributes of gratitude as the foundation of civility and commitment to mutually beneficial social ties is a particular attribute of the English, leading the people to break those ties with their monarch if they perceive an abuse of power (measured presumably by utility rather than right). Given Montesquieu's suggestion that in England the people often have more power than the king, an attribute that allows them to overthrow those kings who abuse their sovereignty, it is evident that England is an important case that permits Montesquieu to stress the instability of the monarchical regime as a type that in certain cases can flow into republicanism.

A clear example of seigneurial government appears in letter 11 in the first society of the Troglodytes. As in Bodin, Montesquieu suggests here that the first form of government known to human societies was a seigneurial one.[13] We are not told the exact circumstances of how the foreign king came to rule the first society, but clearly force was needed to try to overcome the intransigeance of the population. The "natural cruelty" of the Troglodytes and the wish to reform their dispositions led the foreign king to implement harsh measures (presumably violating certain standards of natural law), as a seigneurial monarch might "legitimately" do, according to Bodin, as a form of both punishment and correction. Yet, as we are told, this only led to more resentment, and the people took it upon themselves to rebel and execute the king along with his family. Still, the achievement of political liberty did nothing to improve their dispositions, and this experiment at republican self-rule also failed. The society was incapable of settling into any established stable institutional order.

The example is an important one. Despite its allusion to a form of seigneurial rule, as a limit case, and in context with others, it sheds light more generally on the structural tensions associated with one person rule. Here we see that regardless of Montesquieu's repeated focus on rulers and how their exercise of political power can be judged, it is also clear that a general population can be degenerate to the point of making governance, and hence a more ordered form of civil life, impossible. Yet it heightens to some degree the paradox of monarchical rule. Virtuous qualities of the population bear some relation to how moderately the government may proceed to achieve its ends. A population less inclined toward virtue can be governed only by somewhat stricter methods, such as fear of punishment, as we saw in the establishment of the second Troglodyte monarchy. Thus, monarchy by its very nature can be inclined toward harshness, not only due to the desire of the ruler to dominate but also due to concerns for the effectiveness of policy that can no longer always rely on the goodwill and better motivations of the people. The insight that the quality of collective mores sets the conditions for what is even possible in politics may suggest that utility (and not Bodinian right) may need to be a more effective standard by which to judge governance.

So the tension and instability inherent in monarchical rule highlighted in letter 99 and discussed above can be more clearly understood. The monarch needs to be considered not only in the context of juridical codes, but also in relation to the characteristics of the population at large. Monarchy itself does not rely on and thus does not encourage the civic-mindedness of the population and can be effective in motivating subjects only through other means, such as fear of punishment or hope of reward. These methods can further engender harshness and cruelty within the population, pushing the ruler to seek effectiveness in even harsher methods, leading to a spiral of political decline for both. If people come to resent such measures, they may resort to rebellion, leading to either a correction in the balance of power or regime change. *Thus, the instability and fluidity of monarchical rule is not merely a product of the overzealous motivations of a controlling monarch but is structurally embedded in its broader moral and social preconditions.* From this perspective, the *Persian Letters* can be understood as less a critique of the unique perversities of the personal rule of Louis XIV and the abandonment of the *polysynodie* initiative under the Regency and more about the structural tensions and paradoxes built into the political category of monarchy itself.[14] It also suggests that what Montesquieu sometimes presents as a spectrum—from republican to monarchical to despotic rule, depending on the relative power of the people or the single ruler—is in fact more complex. This is partly because there can be an inverse proportion between the external harshness of rule, including evident measures to assert control, and the power that it effectively demonstrates (thereby differentiating sovereign display of authority from real political power), and partly because in some limiting cases the attempt to display authoritative control can trigger a strong opposing popular reaction. The regime can tend to be experienced as successive moments of give and take, involving confrontation and struggle among competing centers of power rather than as a clear linear understanding of regime evolution.

As noted, Montesquieu does not tell us at what point a monarchy may be judged as having crossed a proverbial line into despotism, but he does offer us a couple of extreme examples of this form of rule. Along with the first society of the Troglodytes, the clearest example of violation of the rules of natural and divine law in governance is neither Persia nor France, but the Ottomans. We are told in letter 18 that Ottoman officials rule their people *as if* they were conquered. This is in contrast with Bodin's suggestion that the Ottomans did exercise seigneurial rule in a legitimate and orderly way.[15] Montesquieu suggests that the Ottomans resorted to both unlawful harshness in their methods of rule, as well as violation of basic norms of respect for private property: "The pashas, who obtain their offices only by the power of money, enter already ruined into the provinces and ravage them as conquered countries. An insolent militia is subjected only to its own caprice. Fortresses are dismantled, cities deserted, the countryside desolated, the cultivation of earth and commerce entirely abandoned."[16] The harshness of Ottoman rule is raised again in letter 78, where Usbek suggests that the severity of their punishments as dictated in law brings few of their intended effects.

To understand some of the shift between Bodin, who argues for a legitimate category of seigneurial or despotic government in the case of a conquered territory won through conflict in a just war, and Montesquieu, who appears to deny this to the Ottomans, one can invoke letter 92. There Montesquieu tells us through the words of Usbek that the right of conquest is a false right in that the use of force to subdue a society can result only in either the freedom of the society or tyrannical rule on the part of the conqueror. Thus, any idea of a "legitimate despotism" or seigneurial government as found in Bodin is erased. For Montesquieu and his contemporaries, it is objectionable that norms of natural law could be violated rightly in any circumstance. The Ottomans were using despotic methods and, given a rejection of some of the finer juridical distinctions of Bodin's analysis, Montesquieu's invocation of the spirit of despotism here carries the same connotation and negative normative force as Bodin's tyranny. Despotism in the enlightenment context, here moving beyond Bodin, came to be invoked in reference to the actual methods and practices of governance contravening reasonable limits of the use of power, regardless of the juridical context or the ways in which the ruler may have achieved power.

Another key example in Montesquieu's dialogue with Bodin in the text is his depiction of power distinct from sovereignty in the household. As has been carefully documented in the existing literature, Montesquieu offers a detailed depiction of Usbek's seraglio and of the various relations that constitute it (Usbek and his wives, Usbek and his eunuchs, the eunuchs and the wives, the wives among themselves). Each type of relation in the household has its own rules (ultimately determined by Usbek himself) and its corresponding psychosocial dynamic. This offers Montesquieu a means to depict an extreme form of power imbalance, and ways in which such power relations entail general practices of fear, suspicion, manipulation, deception, and abuse. Nonetheless, greater focus on the circulation of emotion alongside an unequal distribution of legal power gives rise to further insight into the informal dynamics of power and the ways in which the eunuchs and Usbek as master are themselves also bound by the circulation of suspicion and fear.[17] This is an effective way for Montesquieu to demonstrate how power is to be decoupled from sovereignty, but also from legal and juridical right. By making the household a site of contestation, Montesquieu is striking at the foundation of Bodin's juridical edifice.

Montesquieu's attention to the dynamics of Usbek's household, with special analysis of the psychosocial impact of Usbek's desires to control all aspects of the lives of his wives through his eunuchs, clearly sheds light on both the pathologies and the impossibility of total domination, as well as the way in which the subjected exercise a form of power on the head of the household. The resistance of Roxane at the level of the household suggests that natural right works most effectively as a motivational resource at the level of individual relations, rather than a juridical or theoretical maxim at the level of regimes. It is expressed in opposition to conventional structures of power in the family, rather than codified limits in the legal logic of sovereignty, and it comes as a cry of desire in conjunction with reason. It deepens and complicates questions of the nature and circulation of power. In Bodin and other traditional juridical analyses, the claims of power and resistance to it resided in the narrow institutional realm given that the claims of sovereignty attributed to the sovereign an "absolute and perpetual power." In the rebellion of Roxane, not only do we see a form of power decoupled from sovereignty, but it is also one where emotional appeal plays as much a role as appeal to reason, and in the realm of the household, or the building block of political community for Bodin, traditionally deemed outside the purview of natural right. Roxane's appeal was not to the basic material needs of life but to a moral one, that of liberty as independence. The broader suggestion here is that the legitimate scope of political claims reach much more widely than the foundation for sovereignty, which may be one explanation why there is constant pressure toward evolution and destabilization at the level of the regime.

One of the implications of Montesquieu's approach is that it renders the categories of regime types much more fluid. While Bodin could acknowledge that regimes shift and that it is possible to switch from one form of regime to another in juridical terms (such as Rome's transition from republican to imperial rule), the actual dynamic through which this happens remains underanalyzed in Bodin. Attention to underlying factors of motivation and social psychology in Montesquieu allows one to have a better apprehension of shifting political dynamics and the process of change and corruption that can either precede or follow institutional change. It also can better lend itself to political criticism by acknowledging the presence of tendencies rather than strict juridical shifts. Nonetheless, the shifting and fluid nature of the political realities he analyzes in this work, such as republics that are impossible to sustain, monarchies that are almost never "true" and always drifting to either republics or despotisms, and despotisms that undermine themselves with their cruelty, threatens to undermine the utility of the very types invoked. Montesquieu's rejoinder to the juridical division of regime types is to invoke it while also suggesting that it barely scratches the surface of understanding the complex dynamics through which power can circulate and shift, sometimes in unexpected ways, in public life.

Another important implication of Montesquieu's approach here is the hint in his depiction of the first society of the Troglodytes that institutional and juridical structures are an insufficient condition for broader social and political order. As the example of the first society demonstrates, if a people are naturally cruel and appear to lack any sense of civility and regard for their fellow subjects or citizens, then it may be impossible to establish any form of lasting political order, indeed, it might be difficult to think of them as a people at all. This case implies a direct criticism of Bodin, because it suggests that the existence of sovereignty, whether legitimate or illegitimate, cannot be sufficient to ensure political continuity. It also suggests that there are some basic normative considerations that must come to bear on the character and customs of the people themselves in order that they be fit for some form of governing structure. In Bodinian terms we might say that the need for minimal adherence to norms of natural law is a requirement not only for the sovereign but indeed for the population as a whole if they are to benefit from structures of governance. The question of the normative conditions surrounding the proper exercise of sovereignty and possible legitimate resistance to it dissolve in the face of a recognition that without some minimal qualities of cooperation and civility within a social order, any longer-term prospects for an established political order vanish.

CONCLUSION

Reading the *Persian Letters* as a critique of Bodin can help us to better understand the more general force of Montesquieu's message overall as well as the unique nuances of his arguments here as distinct from his later work. In the context of early eighteenth-century French-Safavid relations, the Persian regime stands as a royal counterpart to France, mainly as a point of comparison rather than contrast. While the seraglio is clearly depicted as an exotic practice, its presence in Persia does not undermine the broader understanding of the monarchical (and nondespotic) nature of the Persian regime. The quintessential exemplar of despotism of the era, the Ottomans, occupy merely a passing reference in the work.

Many read the actions of Usbek vis-à-vis his seraglio as a means for Montesquieu to comment on the despotic tendencies within his own French government, thereby offering a pointed critique of the willful policies of Louis XIV, Louis XV, and their chief ministers for being excessively overbearing and harsh. Yet, as we have seen by looking at Montesquieu's work in conversation with his predecessor Bodin, Montesquieu's concerns about monarchy and its potential instability are not unique to France or to its rulers but appear to be structurally embedded in the institutions of monarchy as such. Monarchy as a set of laws and institutions has an impact on the moral life of subjects who are no longer drawn intrinsically to seek to advance the good of all, expecting that the laws will compel behavior toward that end. Yet here the enhanced punitive authority of the law, as required by the weaker moral commitments and reduced integrity of subjects, also paradoxically lessens the power of the law, leading to a repeated spiraling and deepening of the same dynamic. At the same time, the increasing harshness of legal enforcement sparks calls for resistance and reform. Popular groups may demand an exercise of power that is responsive to their needs and concerns yet appear incapable of sustaining the type of self-government that they appear to desire, as implicit in their acts of rebellion. From this picture, there is no optimal solution or regime of moderation according to Montesquieu in the *Persian Letters*, because all regimes are depicted as inherently unstable, driven by conflicting logics, and unable to align the circulation of power with the narrower distribution of sovereignty. As an informal interlocutor, Bodin allowed Montesquieu to recognize the limits of juridical science and to reach to a broader, though complex, and ultimately darker vision of the near inevitability of political change and decline.

NOTES

1. The work of Jean Bodin (1529/30–1596) towers over the political theory tradition in France. As one of France's most erudite and reflective political theorists of the sixteenth century, his work had a lasting impact on subsequent political thinkers, and Montesquieu is no exception. A first wave of scholarship on Bodin focused on his innovations in terms of a new theory of sovereignty and the state, with a focus on the implications of this approach for a theory of legislative voluntarism and the relative independence of the monarch as a source of law; more recent interpretations have come to focus on the ways in which Bodin's theory offers some continuity with medieval jurisprudence, emphasizing his continued reliance on the normative force of divine and natural law as well as his own preference for a monarchy bounded by institutional, legal, customary, and strong normative constraints. Examples of this approach can be found with Daniel Lee, *The Right of Sovereignty* (Oxford: Oxford University Press, 2021); Daniel Lee, *Popular Sovereignty in Early Constitutional Thought* (Oxford: Oxford University Press, 2016); Daniel Lee, "'Office Is a Thing Borrowed,' Jean Bodin on Offices and Seigneurial Government." *Political Theory* 41, no. 3 (June 2013): 409–40; Mario Turchetti, "Introduction," in *Jean Bodin Six Livres de la Republique, Livre I* (Paris: Classiques Garnier, 2013).

2. Suggestion that French enlightenment thinkers took Persia for a despotic regime is found in Orest Ranum, "Personality and Politics in the Persian Letters," reprinted in *Charles-Louis de Secondat, Baron de Montesquieu*, ed. David Carrithers (London: Routledge, 2016), 3–25.

3. See the interesting and valuable analysis of Susan Mokhberi in *The Persian Mirror: French Reflections of the Safavid Empire in Early Modern France* (Oxford: Oxford University Press, 2019).

4. See for example, Nannerl Keohane, *Philosophy and the State in France* (Princeton, NJ: Princeton University Press, 1980); Benjamin Straumann, *Crisis and Constitutionalism* (New York: Oxford University Press, 2016); Howell A. Lloyd, "Sovereignty: Bodin, Hobbes, Rousseau," *Revue Internationale de philosophie* 45, no. 179 (1991): 353–79; Jean Terrel, *Les théories du pacte social: droit naturel, souveraineté et contrat de Bodin à Rousseau* (Paris: Seuil, 2001).

5. Jean Bodin, *On Sovereignty*, ed. Julian Franklin (Cambridge: Cambridge University Press, 1992), I.8, 1.

6. "Or tout ainsi qu'il n'y a rien plus grand en ce monde, comme dit Euripide ny plus nécessaire pour a conservation des Republiques que l'obeissance de la femme au mari: aussi le mari ne doit pas, sous ombre de la puissance maritale, faire une esclave de sa femme." Jean Bodin, *Six Livres de la République* (N.p., 1577), I.3, 28, https://books.google.ca/books?id=UDtGAAAAcAAJ&printsec=frontcover&dq=bodin&hl=en&ei=OqJ4Tp2aGcGWOrObgawN&sa=X&oi=book_result&ct=result&redir_esc=y#v=onepage&q&f=false.

7. See Jean Bodin, *Six Books of the Commonwealth*, ed. and trans. M. J. Tooley (Oxford: Basil Blackwell, n.d.), https://www.yorku.ca/comninel/courses/3020pdf/six_books.pdf.

8. "La plupart des Governmens d'Europe sont Monarchiques, ou plutôt sont ainsi appellez; car je ne sçais pas s'il y en a jamais eu véritablement de tels: au moins est-il impossible qu'ils ayent subsisté long-tems: c'est un Etat violent qui dégénère toujours en Despotisme, ou en République." The French edition cited here is Charles Louis de Secondat, Baron de Montesquieu, *Oeuvres complètes, vol. 1, Lettres persanes*, ed. J. Ehrard and C. Volpilhac-Auger (Oxford: Voltaire Foundation, 2004). English translations of the text are taken from Montesquieu's *Persian Letters*, ed. and trans. S. Warner (South Bend, IN: St. Augustine's Press, 2017). As Warner uses the 1758 edition as the basis for his edition (rather than the usual scholarly choice of the 1721 edition), he includes a few supplementary letters so that this quote is found in letter 102 of his English edition.

9. "Je mourrai de douleur, d'avoir vu en naissant les Troglodites libres, et de les voir aujourd'hui assujettis . . . vous aimez mieux être soumis a un Prince, et obéit a ses Loix moins rigides que vos mœurs: vous scavez que pour lors vous pourrez contenter votre ambition, acquérir des richesses, et languir dans une lâche volupté; et que pourvue que vous évitiez de tomber dans les grands crimes, vous n'aurez pas besoin de la Vertu." Montesquieu, *Oeuvres complètes, vol. 1, Lettres persanes*, 171.

10. "Un royaume florissant." Ibid., 141.

11. See n. 11 on p. 410 of ibid..

12. "Tous les peuples d'Europe ne sont pas également soumis a leurs Princes: par exemple, l'humeur impatiente des Anglais ne laisse gueres a leur Roi le tems d'apesantir son autorite: la soumission et l'obeissance sont les vertus, dont ils se piquent le moins." Ibid., 414.

13. See Etienne-Maurice Fournol, *Bodin prédécesseur de Montesquieu* (Geneve: Slatkine Reprints, 1970), 55.

14. For a reading of the *Persian Letters* as motivated by personal concerns in the context of the decisions of Orleans and Dubois to undermine the *polysynodie* reforms, see Ranum, "Personality and Politics in the *Persian Letters*."

15. Noel Malcolm, "Positive Views of Islam and of Ottoman Rule in the Sixteenth Century: The Case of Jean Bodin," in *The Renaissance and the Ottoman World*, ed. A. Contadini (London: Routledge, 2016), 206.

16. "Les Bachas qui n'obtiennent leurs emplois qu'à force d'argent, entrent ruinés dans les Provinces, et les ravagent comme des pais de Conquête. Une milice insolente n'est soumise qu'à ses caprices: les places sont démantelées; les Villes désertes; les Campagnes désolées; la culture des terres, et le Commerce entièrement abandonnés"

and "il n'y a ni titre, ni possession, qui vaille contre le caprice de ceux qui gouvernent." Montesquieu, *Oeuvres complètes, vol. 1, Lettres persanes*, letter 18, 180–81. This is also from letter 18 in the Warner English edition.

17. As the first eunuch suggests in letter 9 with regard to his relationship to the wives, "Il y a entre nous comme un flux et reflux d'empire, et de soumission" (157).

BIBLIOGRAPHY

Bodin, Jean. *On Sovereignty*. Edited by Julian Franklin. Cambridge: Cambridge University Press, 1992.

———. *Six Books of the Commonwealth*. Edited and translated by M. J. Tooley. Oxford: Basil Blackwell, n.d. https://www.yorku.ca/comninel/courses/3020pdf/six_books.pdf.

———. *Six Livres de la République*. N.p., 1577. https://books.google.ca/books?id=UDtGAAAAcAAJ&printsec=frontcover&dq=bodin&hl=en&ei=OqJ4Tp2aGcGWOrObgawN&sa=X&oi=book_result&ct=result&redir_esc=y#v=onepage&q&f=false.

Fournol, Etienne-Maurice. *Bodin prédécesseur de Montesquieu*. Geneve: Slatkine Reprints, 1970.

Keohane, Nannerl. *Philosophy and the State in France*. Princeton, NJ: Princeton University Press, 1980.

Lee, Daniel. "'Office Is a Thing Borrowed,' Jean Bodin on Offices and Seigneurial Government." *Political Theory* 41, no. 3 (2013): 409–40.

———. *Popular Sovereignty in Early Constitutional Thought*. Oxford: Oxford University Press, 2016.

———. *The Right of Sovereignty*. Oxford: Oxford University Press, 2021.

Lloyd, Howell A. "Sovereignty: Bodin, Hobbes, Rousseau." *Revue Internationale de philosophie* 45 no.179 (1991): 353–79.

Malcolm, Noel. "Positive Views of Islam and of Ottoman Rule in the Sixteenth Century: The Case of Jean Bodin." In *The Renaissance and the Ottoman World*, edited by A. Contadini. London: Routledge, 2016.

Mokhberi, Susan. *The Persian Mirror: French Reflections of the Safavid Empire in Early Modern France*. Oxford: Oxford University Press, 2019.

Montesquieu, Charles Louis de Secondat, Baron de. *Oeuvres complètes, vol. 1, Lettres persanes*. Edited by J. Ehrard and C. Volpilhac-Auger. Oxford: Voltaire Foundation, 2004.

———. *Persian Letters*. Edited and translated by S. Warner. South Bend, IN: St. Augustine's Press, 2017.

Ranum, Orest. "Personality and Politics in the *Persian Letters*." Reprinted in *Charles-Louis de Secondat, Baron de Montesquieu*, edited by David Carrithers, 3–25. London: Routledge, 2016.

Straumann, Benjamin. *Crisis and Constitutionalism*. New York: Oxford University Press, 2016.

80   *Rebecca Kingston*

Terrel, Jean. *Les théories du pacte social: droit naturel, souveraineté et contrat de Bodin à Rousseau.* Paris: Seuil, 2001.

Turchetti, Mario. "Introduction." In *Jean Bodin Six Livres de la Republique, Livre I.* Paris: Classiques Garnier, 2013.

Chapter 6

The Struggle for Recognition
and the Economy of Esteem
in and out of the Seraglio

Robert Sparling

Readers of the *Persian Letters* have often remarked on the degree to which the portrayal of the power relations between Usbek and his seraglio appears to anticipate the dynamics of Hegel's master-slave dialectic.[1] It is unsurprising that we often think of Hegel when we contemplate Usbek's tragic lack of self-knowledge, for Hegel offered the most prominent modern articulation of the self-defeating nature of mastery. This is, however, not the only mode of conceiving of the evils of mastery. We might also read Montesquieu through the lens of classical denunciations of tyranny in Plato, Aristotle, or the republican tradition. I am tempted to quote an earlier member of the Bordeaux Parlement, Étienne de la Boétie, who, two centuries before, described tyranny as unnatural, the opposite of friendship as mutual recognition: the tyrant, incapable of knowing others or being known by them, falls into the terror of mastery. La Boétie quoted the Roman emperor who looked at his wife's throat and said, "Ce beau col sera tantôt coupé, si je le commande." The tyrant "n'est jamais aimé, ni n'aime."[2] Better yet, we might reach back to someone with no connection to Bordeaux: Plato noted that "the tyrannic nature never has a taste of freedom or true friendship."[3]

But Montesquieu's argument on love, jealousy, desire, and domination is as distinct from classical arguments about the rightly ordered soul and city as it is from Hegelian dialectic. In this chapter I would like to suggest that his discussion has much more in common with the position developed by Hobbes. Most scholars recognize the importance of Montesquieu's engagement with Hobbes, but there is significant disagreement about how much his thought is a repudiation of the philosopher of Malmesbury.[4] Hobbes's view that human beings have an inherent and inextinguishable tendency to compete for esteem is at the heart of the modern debate about the nature of human sociability and the struggle for recognition. Hobbes thought the core political problem was not merely conflict derived from scarcity, but also that arising from the impossibility of a natural equilibrium between the degree to which we wish to be valued and the degree to which others value us—a problem he famously proposed to solve (or at least to mitigate) with an absolute sovereign's control of honors and values. Doubtless there is much in Hobbes of which Montesquieu disapproved: the peace afforded by Hobbes's absolute, arbitrary sovereign is something Montesquieu thought intolerable, not peace, but an ominous tranquility, "the silence of the towns that the enemy is ready to occupy."[5] The imagined seraglio, like Montesquieu's description of despotism in *The Spirit of the Laws*, is a dramatic illustration of just why a Hobbesian absolute, arbitrary power can neither bring peace nor solve the fundamental problem of recognition. But for all that Montesquieu is a critic of Hobbes, his analysis of love and reciprocity in the *Persian Letters* follows a surprisingly Hobbesian logic. In particular, this is an economic logic, a logic of value, and particularly value according to the laws of supply and demand. At its heart, this logic of values undermines the logic of essential dignity, civic friendship, and love.[6] Unlike Hobbes, Montesquieu does offer the possibility of some things being intrinsically worthy, beyond value and esteem, and of mutual recognition beyond the logic of supply and demand, but he cannot imagine social or political institutions being grounded in such absolutes.

My purpose is not primarily to add to the already rich literature on Montesquieu's reception of Hobbes; rather, it is to comment on the basic normative grounding of Montesquieu's political and social thought. If we can establish that there are certain goods beyond value—dignity, civic friendship, love—then we have an independent basis for the moral assessment of institutions and social relations that is beyond contingent conventions and subjective tastes. In examining the *Persian Letters*' account of love, we will see that while Montesquieu offered the possibility of a form of radically equal, reciprocal, and generous love, he appeared to think it could exist only on the margins of human experience. Montesquieu's defense of artificial hierarchies in monarchical regimes is apiece with his pessimism about love.

PRICE, DIGNITY, AND THE ECONOMY OF ESTEEM

Montesquieu offered a famous, oft-repeated argument that Hobbes erred in reading into natural man characteristics that only arise in collective life (SL I.2). It is when we enter into society that we begin to compete for eminence and the advantages society offers. The difficulty with this as a criticism of Hobbes is that it misreads the Hobbesian state of nature as a thought experiment meant to discover our essential nature by stripping us of our *social* trappings. But Hobbes, for all the atomism of his political thought, took for granted human sociability—after all, among the three causes of conflict is the desire for glory,[7] and his entire account of power concerns the perpetual competition not merely to dominate others but also to gain their esteem. Among all the natural sources of conflict, the competition for glory is perhaps the most intractable, since it is fundamentally comparative. Edward Andrew has observed that the natural equality with which Hobbes began gave birth to inequality as we weigh one another's value in economic terms.[8] He cites Hobbes's (in)famous claim, "The Value, or WORTH of a man, is as of all other things, his Price; that is to say, so much as would be given for the use of his Power: and therefore is not absolute; but a thing dependant on the need and judgement of another."[9] We might be tempted, with Kant, to think dignity is above such calculation. But Hobbes has no such fixed point—nothing is essentially worthy, or more fixed, than the subjective desires of evaluators. The most we can hope for is a kind of enforced consensus: "The publique worth of a man, which is the Value set on him by the Common-wealth, is that which men commonly call DIGNITY."[10] Hobbesian dignity is a product of agreement, not of nature. And given our perpetual striving and our tendency to overvalue ourselves, the sovereign must stamp the values, as on a coin: "considering what values men are naturally apt to set upon themselves; what respect they look for from others; and how little they value other men; from whence continually arise amongst them, Emulation, Quarrels, Factions, and at last Warre, to the destroying of one another, and diminution of their strength against a Common Enemy; It is necessary that there be Lawes of Honour, and a publique rate of the worth of such men as have deserved, or are able to deserve well of the Common-wealth."[11]

Montesquieu appears to share Hobbes's view (*Leviathan*, chapter 6) that most evaluative judgments are really reflections of the subjective desires of the evaluators and not essential characteristics of the things evaluated. His late *Essai sur le goût* took up an anti-Platonic line, denying that there was anything good in itself: "Les sources du beau, du bon, de l'agréable, etc.," he declared, "sont dans nous-mêmes; et en chercher les raisons, c'est chercher les causes des plaisirs de notre âme."[12] The difficulty is that tastes and desires vary. And like Hobbes, Montesquieu thought people had a basic, natural equality that was in tension with their *amour propre* and desire to be valued as they value themselves.[13] Of course, Montesquieu had a horror for the idea of values being stamped upon a society by an unanswerable sovereign (we will return to this point),[14] but like Hobbes, Montesquieu did see social life as vitiated by the perpetual struggle for distinction, and he saw stable constitutions as those in which there was a stable public rate of value. We constantly seek esteem,[15] and the beauty of the principle of honor in a monarchy was that it so structured and directed people's passions that their self-regard served to uphold the political system rather than to tear it apart. This value system ensures the existence of a stratum of people who act as an intermediary body, thus preventing the decline into populist despotism. Doubtless this celebration of countervailing powers based on a historically evolved system is a direct repudiation of Hobbes's rationalist legal positivism and his mania for unity.[16] But at the same time, regimes' principles do the task Hobbes wanted the sovereign to do: they provide a value system that orders society, mitigating the conflict that would occur in conditions of natural equality. I use the word "value" purposely, for in both Hobbes and Montesquieu we are in the realm of subjective valuing and not intrinsic worthiness. Honor mitigates conflict and turns people's self-interested ambition toward a public good. The thesis is anthropologically pessimistic in a manner reminiscent of Hobbes: human beings have a hard time with radical equality and reciprocity. This makes regimes with strong equality difficult to maintain without the most intrusive education or the most terrifying threat. There is a kind of equality of slaves under despotism, but that is held together only by fear, and it entails an ongoing condition akin to the state of war. Republican regimes in which equality exists tend to require such an extreme education as to denature people. Usbek admires the way in which republics make patriotism valuable by recompensing heroes with honors (Letter 89, 144–46), and while Montesquieu clearly celebrated this, he also thought radical republican mores a kind of mental prison (SL V.2) that is itself difficult to sustain. Republican love of country is also, Montesquieu indicated quite clearly in *The Spirit of the Laws*, dependent on a radical subjugation of women to internalized patriarchal mores almost as stifling as the external repression of the seraglio (see, eg., SL V.7, VII.8–10). Honor is a less demanding principle than virtue.

It is important to notice that those things that are valued in the system of honor are not necessarily admirable in themselves. Montesquieu can write of honor that it is, "speaking philosophically," "false" because it is clearly not the real manifestation of qualities we profess to think worthy (SL III.7). But this appears to run counter to the assertion that nothing is good in itself. There is significant debate about just what Montesquieu means by this phrase "false honor"[17]—it seems to imply that there are standards independent of appearances and opinion. Certainly, false honor is false because it is vain, a product of unflatteringly self-centered impulses.[18] But though Montesquieu writes of this passion in a manner that appears like a proto-Rousseauian satire—and though Rica can repeatedly marvel at the absurdities of this value system when he sees it in action in Paris—Montesquieu's ultimate teaching is that where it obtains, it must be preserved (SL XIX.6). These conventions are a great collection of falsities, yet they order the social universe marvelously. To see through them to the human vices beneath should not blind us to their utility; to look upon them with the naivete of the honorable is to be blind to their hidden springs. Montesquieu is at once the source of ideology critique and the great ideologist of the nobility.

He thus appears to be engaged in a contradictory pursuit, both revealing the artificial and imaginary nature of the honor system and seeking to preserve it, with all of its absurdities and hypocrisies. If the *Persian Letters* unmask social conventions, showing their underlying vanity, they also explain them and defend their utility. Would-be despots are so dangerous precisely because they truly unveil the falsity of honor.[19] By according honors based on his whims rather than on the historically evolved system of noble status, the despot devalues the prejudice of birth in favor of sycophancy.[20] There is a greater directness and even sincerity in the despot's stance, no doubt—notice, for instance, how Usbek baldly tells his wives that their virtue is merely obedience due to surveillance and threat (Letter 20, 34). His transparency and lack of hypocrisy on this score is little comfort. In contrast to despotism, monarchy requires artifice and illusion. Recall that Montesquieu's argument was not that there are *natural* aristocracies that must be respected; like Hobbes, Montesquieu began with a premise of fundamental equality. He thought that humans are driven to conflict by natural social desires for eminence and that stable regimes are those in which the avenues for eminence are fixed by custom and law.[21] We are always in some manner in an economy of eminence, but all economies have rules and dominant currencies, and the fundamental question is how those rules are established and those coins stamped. Jonathan Walsh rightly terms this a "cultural numismatics."[22]

This is why John Law is so symbolically important. The *Persian Letters* contains a mythologized John Law figure inviting people to become rich by leaving the world of crude material things and entering into "the empire of imagination" (Letter 142, 241). Interpreters have pointed out how this represents a critique of the artificial world of finance untethered from the solidity of land and commerce.[23] But we need to remember that the opinions of monarchical subjects concerning the superiority of the nobility are just as imaginary, just as based on artifice, illusion, and subjective desire. Law's despotic tendencies derived not from the fact that he manipulated the imagination, but that he was unilaterally altering values—both the values of state debt and the values involved in the status system that stabilize the social order.[24] For among Law's crimes, in Montesquieu's eyes, was the attempt to reduce independent nobility by abolishing and buying back titles with money raised by issuing company stock:[25] "He was dissolving the monarchy by his chimerical repayments and he seemed to want to buy back the constitution itself" (SL II.4). The double devaluation was despotic because the attack on venality was an attempt to destroy the intermediary power of the nobility, and hence the whole principle on which monarchy rests.[26] Again, the difficulty is not that the realm is imaginary, but rather that one set of values is being replaced by another, more arbitrary set. The realm of honor is based on artifice and vanity. Rica satirizes it well (in a letter dramatically dated 1712, so prior to the regency):

> The king of France is the most powerful prince in Europe. He does not have gold mines, as does the king of Spain, his neighbor; but he has more riches than the latter, because he extracts them from the vanity of his subjects, which is more inexhaustible than mines. He has been known to undertake or sustain great wars having no funds other than honorary titles to sell, and by this marvel of human pride, his troops paid, his fortresses armed, and his fleets equipped. (Letter 24, 39)

This is not the same thing as what is being lamented in John Law. Both traffic in something imaginary, but the vanity of the would-be nobles is inexhaustible. It is a kind of magic trick that the king plays, but it has more steadiness to it because the king's symbolic power is tied to the system of honor. It is a remarkable source of wealth incomprehensible in another regime. But if the king can raise funds in this way, he cannot without danger simply overthrow the very economy of honor on which this system is based. Because the system revolves around the monarch and his power over the imagination, it does have an inherent weakness: in the next paragraph Rica speaks of the dangers of devaluation of coin and the reckless issuing of debt, foreshadowing the crisis of Law's system that is at the heart of the book.[27] It is important that we note that these two facts, quickly linked by Rica as forms of royal subterfuge, are in fact quite distinct. The first is the heart of the regime, the love of honor—something at whose perverse artificiality Usbek marvels (Letters 89–90), and whose importance will be at the center of Montesquieu's later analysis of monarchies in *The Spirit of the Laws*. The error of Law was that he failed to understand the springs of the government, and not only did the massive reversals of fortune due to speculation overturn the order of society (Letter 132), but Law himself actively sought to eliminate the intermediary institutions that were the only brake on royal power.

In *The Spirit of the Laws* we learn, "In states that engage in economic commerce, one has fortunately established banks, which, by means of their credit, have formed new signs of value" (SL XX.10). These banks *made* new signs of value.[28] That is, a certain opinion of their substance allowed them to make values. It seems that these banks can say, "Come to the empire of imagination" (Letter 142, 241) without being subject to the same opprobrium that Montesquieu cast upon John Law. It is the form of government under which these banks were formed that made all the difference. Montesquieu goes on to say that such banks would be harmful under a monarchical government, as the excessive power of the monarch would corrupt the bank (as it certainly did in the time of Law's system). A monarchical economy must cultivate and sustain the type of desires and passions that make monarchy work. The commodities this requires are luxury goods; the desires that reign among the nobles are for approbation of their grandeur, elegance, frankness (SL IV.2). Michael Mosher has indicated how Montesquieu thought this related to the manner in which the sexes interact. Montesquieu's depiction of monarchical France as having relatively open and unconstrained relations between the sexes had much to do with the way in which he felt that the female gaze was the main lever of honor culture, reinforcing both the economic system (think of Rica's astonishment at the constant expense on style and luxury in letters 99–100 or Usbek's Mandevillian reflections on the economic benefits of vanity in letter 106) and the values system more generally.[29] Note in passing that Montesquieu's feminist credentials are not particularly strong here, for women's remarkable degree of agency and influence in monarchical regimes is due to their erotic power and their reputed reign over the world of image, glamour, and vanity.[30] There is scope, he thought, in monarchies for a higher degree of female agency and liberty than in republics (where strict mores enforce inflexible gender roles) and despotisms (where the sexual slavery of women is an integral part of the general slavery of the population), but this agency is itself highly limited to a particular role in an established economy of the passions.

In brief, Montesquieu shared with Hobbes the view that many normative terms like "good" and "beautiful" refer to subjective human evaluation, that there is a basic tension between our fundamental equality and our desire for distinction and superiority, that social life is constantly vitiated by struggles for eminence, and that these can be somewhat kept in check through a dominant "public rate of worth," which, in each regime, is defined by the regime's principle. This is intimately tied to the way in which relations between the sexes are ordered. In the next section we will see how Montesquieu's imagined seraglio serves as both a microcosm of the despotic state and an account of the sexual-social relations arising from an unfree erotic economy.

THE MARKET OF DESIRE AND
THE ABSENCE OF LOVE

Usbek is not happy, and the horrid man, for all his philosophical reflection, does not know why. He suffers from the affliction of despots: they cannot know love because they are only a source of terror. He thinks himself master, but he is thoroughly dependent. For all his mania for sincerity, Usbek lies to himself. His wives, though they flatter him endlessly, force him to confront his situation. His wife Zélis reminds him, "In the very prison in which you keep me, I am freer than you. . . . [Y]our suspicions, your jealousy, your sorrows are so many marks of your dependence" (Letter 62, 101). The women profess their love for Usbek, but it is clear that this is a mixture of flattery and Stockholm syndrome. Usbek himself is at least without illusions about his own feelings: "It is not," he writes of his wives, "that I love them. I find myself, in this respect, in a state of insensibility that leaves me without desires. In the crowded seraglio where I have lived, I anticipated love and destroyed love by itself. But from my very frigidity emerges a secret jealousy that devours me" (Letter 6, 10).[31] There is something unnatural about this sexual relation: Usbek's multiple wives have left him sexually indifferent. His only passion for his wives is an overbearing jealousy and fear of humiliation. In a sense, Usbek is in a similar condition to his eunuchs, who, deprived of sexual desire, feel nothing but a passion for domination. He cannot have his masculinity recognized because no woman will ever choose him. His wife Fatmé writes to him of her passion, "Were I permitted to choose among all of the men who live in this capital of nations—Usbek, I swear to you, I would choose only you. There can be no one in the world who deserves to be loved but you" (Letter 7, 11). If the worth of a man—or woman—is his or her price, prices are determined by buyers and relative scarcity. In the seraglio's economy of desire, Usbek's price is kept artificially high through the monopoly he holds in the market of affection. Fatmé's assertion that she would choose Usbek over all others follows her assertion that he is the only man apart from eunuchs that she has ever seen (or will ever be permitted to see). When she swears that if she had the choice of all men, she would choose *him*, the reader, much like Usbek himself, sees that this flattery only highlights her lack of choice and the worthlessness of her affirmation. There is doubtless a proto-Hegelian element to this: Usbek longs for an external confirmation of his worth, but he cannot get it from the slave precisely because it is forced. We can also see in it a product of a corrupted economy of desire.[32] His public rate of worth is as falsely inflated as stock in the Compagnie des Indes. And, like any heavily protectionist domestic economy, Usbek's seraglio, no matter the height of its walls, cannot avoid the introduction of contraband.

Usbek has only a tenuous power built on fear. The only recognition Usbek receives is from his group of male friends, and his desperate jealousy is doubtless related to his view of how he will be perceived as a man. We know Usbek is vain, for though he casts himself as a noble truth-teller indifferent to the opinions of the corrupt, he asks in his very first letter to be kept abreast of what is said about him (Letter 1). And when he thinks about the possibility of being cheated on, he laments that his friends could never help him in these very troubles—precisely because their recognition of his manliness is something he values: "Would I not a thousand times prefer an obscure impunity to a glaring correction?" (Letter 6). His gradual estrangement from Rica derives in part from the fact that Rica does not value Usbek's form of masculine domination, growing increasingly attached to a more heterosocial environment. Usbek's disgust and despair in France derives as much from the devaluation of the values he has internalized as it does from his perception of the "impurity" of their mores—he is in a disorienting economy of esteem in which the coin he carries is of less worth.

In the seraglio, the economy of desire runs according to a perverse equality. Under a despotic government, Montesquieu thought, there is a kind of equality of condition: everyone is equally a slave (SL III.8–9).[33] This only augments the struggle for recognition as courtiers jostle for the false recognition of the despot's favor. Charles Taylor points out that modern erasure of traditional hierarchies raises the stakes of competition for esteem.[34] This is what Montesquieu feared about the elimination of the principle of noble honor.[35] There is an anti-Hobbesian element to this teaching: what Hobbes thought necessary for the establishment of civic peace—unified, absolute, and arbitrary sovereignty—could itself be a source of endless conflict without intermediary institutions. Despotism, for Montesquieu, is not merely monarchy disliked, but a perpetual state of war. While a direct repudiation of Hobbes's main argument, this is in a sense an elaboration of a Hobbesian dynamic: the radical equality of condition in the state without intermediary powers leads to dangerous competition and perpetual insecurity. This is figured domestically in the seraglio, where the main currency is Usbek's desire.[36] The women compete for this scarce resource, just as the eunuchs compete for his favor. As his wife Zachi writes, glorying in the memory of a fleeting erotic victory over her rival wives, "The triumph was completely mine, and the despair that of my rivals" (Letter 3, 8). This jostling for precedence is the only thing one can expect in this perverse economy of desire.

Usbek muses on the beneficial effects of polygamy: "The plurality of wives saves us from their empire; they temper the violence of our desires" (Letter 56, 92).[37] This, too, is a question of supply and demand. The only pleasure he seems to get is from the resistance of Roxane, a resistance he wrongly attributes to the socially sanctioned cause of an extreme chastity rather than the actual, unsanctioned cause: her disgust for her husband and her desire for someone else (Letter 26).[38] That element of opposition raises her value in Usbek's eyes. The seraglio is clearly a nightmarish prison due to the radical submission and dependency of the wives and eunuchs. It is also a place of perpetually frustrated desire because there is a mismatch between erotic supply and demand.

Love can obviously not be found in such an environment. But it seems as if an economic logic obtains in almost all regimes. Where might we find love beyond the economy of esteem? The mythical tale of Ibrahim and Anaïs, which Rica recounts in letter 141, offers us an alternative universe in the next life in which a woman, murdered by her vile despot-husband for standing up to him, is transported to heaven, where she is granted an inverted, polyandrous harem in which celestial husbands indulge her every erotic wish (and many she had never thought of). There is much talk of their love, but the men are generally presented as interchangeable, and "love" is merely sensual satisfaction. It is fun for a while, but Anaïs quickly grows tired of this semibestial pleasure, and she retreats to a contemplative existence, eventually coming up with a plan to exact revenge on her murderer and give a respite to her fellow inmates of his seraglio (a story that offers mythical foreshadowing of Roxane's revenge on Usbek).[39] I have left out much detail in this tale, but I merely wish to indicate that the reciprocity of love is not really available to Anaïs in paradise. Her sex slaves are perfect in every way, but they are also lifeless. They have no independent subjectivity at all, and Anaïs grows tired even of their delightful ministrations. Even in heaven, the law of supply and demand are in force: she experiences surfeit. (Rica could have told her she would; Letter 125.) Elsewhere, Rica quotes with some approbation Europeans who criticize polygamy, lamenting "the disgust that always follows the satisfaction of the passions," observing that "a bit of coquetry is the salt that piques the appetite and prevents corruption" (Letter 38, 61). We will return to this somewhat dubious teaching; for now, let us merely notice that even heaven is no proof against the laws of erotic economy.

We have not found love in hell or heaven. Perhaps we will find it in France. Rica certainly finds much to admire in Parisian heterosocial gaiety. And doubtless Montesquieu himself thinks this is one of the better possible arrangements of sexual relations. But we are far from the ideal of reciprocity that is the opposite of the seraglio's domination. Rica describes endless stories of vain people competing for the esteem of their fellows. Paris is a great Bourdieusian battlefield.[40] And while Rica comes to find it scintillating, he does so with the ironic detachment of one who sees its absurdities and the harms that take place within the family (Letter 86). He sees endless infidelity and abuse, including an instance of a woman seduced and then left to her own devices with an illegitimate child (Letter 28). If Rica is both intrigued and concerned, Usbek is thoroughly disgusted. In his philosophical moments, he can treat notions of purity as entirely relative (Letter 17), but in sexual matters he is a fanatical purist who cannot abide the least corruption (Letter 26). Thus, he finds the indulgent French attitudes toward infidelity simply unbearable. His judgments, however, are not always merely the product of his purist patriarchal prejudice: he sees real victims of licentiousness. His greatest indignation is raised by a Don Juan he meets: "What do you have to say of a country in which such people are tolerated? . . . Where unfaithfulness, treason, rape, treachery, and injustice lead to respect? Where a man is esteemed for taking a daughter away from her father, a wife from her husband, and disturbing the sweetest and holiest of social relations?" (Letter 48, 78). The fact that this adventurer gains recognition for his perfidy is a source of quite reasonable indignation. Montesquieu thought that the constitutions in which women are freer are also the constitutions in which they have greater control over mores. But much as Montesquieu seems to have his finger on an essential psychosocial connection between misogyny and authoritarianism, the society he describes as the one in which women are the freest is decidedly patriarchal. Mary Stanley and Peter Stillman highlight the numerous ways in which Montesquieu describes French sexual mores as wanting of true reciprocity.[41] Women are still conquests, and men seek their affection as a mode of distinction. Rica opines, "The French hardly ever talk about their wives. This is because they are afraid to speak about them in front of people who know them better than they do" (Letter 55, 89). Virtuous women are only so because they are ugly, and thus undesired, he writes, and in France, "a husband who loves his wife is a man who has not enough merit to make himself loved by another woman" (Letter 55, 90). (In the *Pensées* Montesquieu wrote even less charmingly about the sexual economy: "Sans la v . . . [vérole], les honnêtes femmes seraient perdues: tout le monde prendrait des courtisanes.")[42] Women exercise a tyranny of taste. Their society "spoils mores and forms taste" (SL XIX.8). The system of honor depends on them, and much as Montesquieu appears to think this form of social relationship one of the most moderate and acceptable arrangements, it is far from a regime of reciprocity and mutual recognition.

We have yet to consider other regime possibilities such as the classical republic and the strange modern hybrid regime of the English commercial republic. On the former, we need not dwell—it entails, in its pure democratic form, an extreme, internalized social control that, while capable of producing great deeds, is a kind of psychological prison. While the mythical Troglodytes might have a brief republic of radical altruism in which marital love might flourish, Montesquieu's ultimate judgement on republican mores is less glowing. Republican love of country deprives republican citizens "of everything upon which ordinary passions rest. . . . The more austere it is, that is, the more it curtails their inclinations, the more force it gives to those that remain" (SL V.2). Of the modern commercial republic represented by England, we learn that they have a highly homosocial environment in which men are debauched and women timid (SL XIX.27). In highly commercial societies the most basic human relationships become mediated by money (SL XX.2). At one point he writes that men in England are not "esteemed" "by frivolous talents or attributes, but by real qualities, and these are only two, wealth and personal merit" (SL XIX.27). Price and worthiness are here promiscuously intermixed in Montesquieu's description. Which are we to think predominated? The young Montesquieu had certainly thought the former: "Money here," he said of England, "is sovereignly esteemed: honour and virtue, little."[43]

LOVE AT THE MARGINS

It seems we have been looking for love in all the wrong places. All we found were forms of valuing. Men and women's worth is their price, and the only question is which sexual economy does the least violence to nature. But are there relationships in the *Persian Letters* that rise beyond values to the level of love? Where might we find the radical opposite of the seraglio's torturous lack of recognition? There are two places: Roxane and her lover, and the story of Astarté and Aphéridon (Letter 67).

Roxane's heroically defiant letter closing the novel affirms that she has always been free in her pretended submission. And hers is not some sort of Stoic internal freedom—she has carried on her love affair with "the sole man who was who was holding me to life" (Letter 161, 267). She claims to have reformed Usbek's laws, replacing them with the laws of nature. Are we to see in her relationship with her lover an example of true reciprocal admiration and respect? Mary McAlpin has suggested as much.[44] This is a plausible suggestion, though little is said about him, save that he is in love. Certainly, their mutual attraction appears authentic. But in her final letter Roxane appears to value the lover for what he gives her: a secret revenge and an affirmation of her own independence. This is what she throws in Usbek's face with her final dying boast that she has always proven her freedom by cheating on him. Still, the lover surely was devoted to her—he wished to die in her gaze. There is here, then, the possibility of a truly reciprocal amorous relationship. To wax Hegelian, by risking and losing their lives, the lovers prove that they are for one another something beyond value. But this relationship, founded on the "laws of nature," is shown by Montesquieu to be thoroughly precarious. It exists as a revolutionary possibility, a delicious contraband whose enjoyment is fleeting and unsustainable.[45] Megan Gallagher has intriguingly suggested that we should read the act as mirroring Lucretia's glorious suicide that founded Roman liberty.[46] While this is an important argument, I tend to read the conclusion pessimistically: one does not imagine a great reform in Ispahan. More likely, Usbek will face a public humiliation as his countrymen shake their heads and declare him a worthless fellow paying the price for neglecting his home in foreign junkets.

Our second vision of a loving relationship beyond the economy of esteem comes from a curious story transmitted to Usbek of a Zoroastrian, Aphéridon, who marries his true love, Astarté, his sister, incest being permitted in his religion. Their tale is a complex romance in which the brother and sister must contend with sinister forces to achieve their complete, simple, and natural love. The sister is placed in the service of a sultana where she converts to Islam and is married off to a eunuch who dominates her in a manner akin to the way Usbek dominates his wives. Aphéridon convinces Astarté to run away with him, reconvert to Zoroastrianism, and live happily ever after. They undergo numerous misadventures before ultimately being united in perfect happiness. When convincing her to run away with him, he promises her a life modeled on their parents' marriage: "They lived happily, both of them, with mutual trust" (Letter 67, 111). This is a love that goes beyond price—they are ready to sell themselves into slavery for one another. We are in a realm beyond the economy of desire—and like Roxane's, this is a love described as purely natural. What is clearly shocking, however, is that their relationship is incestuous. That this should be presented as natural is an affront to the mores of Montesquieu's age and ours. Judith Shklar writes, "To make incest the condition of happiness is to say that the rules of society do nothing to make us good or happy."[47] But Shklar knows that this far from the full story—there is no preconventional natural condition to return to. Aphéridon and Astarté's religion may be "the most ancient there is in the world" (Letter 67, 112), but it is not the product of a state of nature. It is a tiny remnant of an extraordinary ancient culture. In their relationship we have a marvelous, perfectly recipro-cal affection from an already exceptional culture. What does it say that the only examples of true love are so rarified—one a desperate, quasi-suicidal pact; the other a product of a small, pariah people, where true love is a prod-uct of the near identity of the lovers? David Kettler speculates, "Perhaps it is only between brother and sister that the equality and intimate respect requisite for true love can appear."[48] Perhaps, also, it is their status as outsiders, people on the margins, that makes this possible. A domestic or political order based on such radical reciprocity beyond the economy of esteem seems a distant possibility indeed.

CONCLUSION: WHAT PRICE LOVE?

Unlike in Hegel's philosophical sketch of the master and the slave, Montesquieu's seraglio provides no grounds for *Aufhebung*. *The Phenomenology of Spirit* is a comedy—it ends in a happy state of absolute knowing and mutual recognition; the *Persian Letters*, amusing as it is, is a tragedy, ending with a catastrophic failure of reciprocity. It is a double

implosion, as both Usbek's sexual economy and John Law's political economy collapse. To dictate values despotically is a recipe for catastrophe. The
best economy of esteem is one in which there is a degree of equilibrium
between supply and demand, gratification and desire. But this is a pessimistic
claim: the struggle for esteem is a permanent and dominant characteristic of
the human condition, and for the greatest part of humanity, all relations will
be subject to some form of economy of values. Moderate regimes establish
economies of value that avoid the gravest harms; immoderate regimes multi-
ply the problems. But if one can moderate the boom-and-bust economies of
love, the fundamental logic of price continues to reign.[49]

To say that there are relations of reciprocal love that are above value, and
types of human dignity that are universal and noncomparative, is to appeal
to a realm of absolutes beyond jostling hierarchies of the economies of
esteem. Montesquieu offered the imaginative possibility of such a realm, but
he rejected it as a foundation for social institutions. His focus on the lowlier
question of what price we set on one another has some advantages—*amour
propre* and the competition for esteem are, after all, the "bread and butter"
of politics, as Christopher Brooke has it.[50] But those who seek the ground
of universal human dignity are not offering mere pie-in-the-sky moralism,
and to think comparative evaluation the only basis upon which to build is
to greatly lower our political sights. Montesquieu's moderated economies of
esteem attenuate sociosexual conflict in ways that merely alter its patriarchal
form. In its English liberal-republican mode, Montesquieu sees a charmless
segregation of the sexes and a degradingly mercenary attitude. In its French,
aristocratic mode, it involves a constant competition for a female gaze that
has been rendered vain and superficial: this comes with economic and constitutional advantages, but it also comes with all the absurdities and degra-
dations that these erotic competitions entail. More concerningly, he thought
an egalitarian republicanism would entail a strict control of the economy of
desire. We have noted the heavily circumscribed existence of women that
Montesquieu thought obtained in pure republics. The most complete psychosexual development of this idea is surely Rousseau's *Émile*, in which Sophie
upholds Émile's goodness by maintaining a constant sexual tension—*un peu
de coquetterie*, as Rica championed. If republican equality must come at the
price of half of humanity's subordination, it is a disappointing ideal indeed.
And if love must be thought of as requiring this kind of artificial manipulation of supply and demand, we must wonder if it merits the name. To say
that certain things are objectively good, objectively lovable, is to place their
importance beyond the reach of the laws of supply and demand. Perhaps the
best place to conclude is with Mary Wollstonecraft, who caviled at the type of
advice offered by Rousseau or Rica. She calls for a rational mutual affection

over "love," a term she employs to mean the sensuous gratification of desires: "Gallantry, and what is called love, may subsist without simplicity of character; but the main pillars of friendship, are respect and confidence. "[51] What Wollstonecraft is calling for is a rational admiration for the objective worth of one's friend's virtues; it is the domestic equivalent of the classical ideal of civic friendship. Montesquieu knew gallantry to be "the perpetual illusion of love" (SL XXVIII.22),[52] but he wanted French society to retain its *noble* lies. The French, after all, had "a taste for the world and above all for commerce with women" (SL XIX.6). If the reader will permit an anachronistic play on the word, we might rather wish for human relations to rise above relations of commerce.

NOTES

1. Diana Schaub, *Erotic Liberalism: Women and Revolution in Montesquieu's Persian Letters* (Lanham, MD: Rowman and Littlefield, 1995), 167; Mark Hulliung, *Montesquieu and the Old Regime* (Berkeley: University of California Press, 1996), 137; David Wooton, *Power, Pleasure, and Profit: Insatiable Appetites from Machiavelli to Madison* (Cambridge, MA: Harvard University Press, 2018), 18; Roxanne Euben, *Journeys to the Other Shore* (Princeton, NJ: Princeton University Press, 2006), 150; Jean Starobinski speculates about influence: "Hegel y songeait-il?" *Montesquieu* (Paris: Seuil, 1994), 67; Céline Spector glosses his teaching in highly Hegelian/Kojèvian language, *Montesquieu, les "Lettres persanes": De l'anthropologie à la politique* (Paris: Presses Universitaires de France, 1997), 47.

2. Étienne de la Boétie, *Discours de la servitude volontaire* (Paris: Flammarion, 1983), 168: "This beautiful throat will be cut in an instant if I command it" (my translation).

3. Plato, *Republic*, trans. Allan Bloom (New York: Basic Books, 1991), 576b.

4. Some who examine the question thoughtfully are Vickie Sullivan, *Montesquieu and the Despotic Ideas of Europe: An Interpretation of The Spirit of the Laws* (Chicago: University of Chicago Press, 2018), ch. 2; Simone Goyard-Fabre, *Montesquieu, adversaire de Hobbes* (Paris: Lettres modernes, 1980); Michael Zuckert, "Natural Law, Natural Rights, and Classical Liberalism: On Montesquieu's Critique of Hobbes," *Social Philosophy and Policy* 18, no. 1 (2001): 227–51; Spector, *Montesquieu, les "Lettres persanes,"* makes much of the connection. The bulk of readers have placed weight on Montesquieu's objections to Hobbes, but the likes of Thomas Pangle and Pierre Manent have tended to see him as closer to Hobbes in the most important matters. Pangle made this argument in his first book on Montesquieu and has returned to it in his recent *The Theological Basis of Liberal Modernity in Montesquieu's Spirit of the Laws* (Chicago: University of Chicago Press, 2010).

5. Montesquieu, *The Spirit of the Laws*, trans. Anne Cohler (Cambridge: Cambridge University Press, 1989), book V, chapter 14; hereafter cited in the text as SL

followed by book.chapter. All other in-text citations refer to *Persian Letters*, trans. Stuart Warner (South Bend, IN: St. Augustine's Press, 2017).

6. I derive this way of framing the problem from Edward Grant Andrew's *The Genealogy of Values: The Aesthetic Economy of Nietzsche and Proust* (Lanham, MD: Rowman and Littlefield, 1995).

7. Thomas Hobbes, *Leviathan* (London: Penguin, 1985), ch. 13.

8. Andrew, *The Genealogy of Values*, 36.

9. Hobbes, *Leviathan*, ch. 10, 151–52.

10. Ibid., 152.

11. Ibid., ch. 18, 235.

12. Montesquieu, "Essai sur le goût," *Œuvres complètes*, ed. Daniel Oster (Paris: Seuil, 1964), 845: "The sources of the beautiful, the good, the pleasant, etc. are in us; and to seek the reasons is to seek the causes of pleasure in our soul" (my translation). In other variants of the text, Montesquieu explicitly charges Plato with error on this score. Jean-Patrice Courois, "Les principes de l'Essai sur le goût," in *Montesquieu, oeuvre ouverte? (1748–1755)*, ed. Catherine Larrère (Bordeaux: Bibliothèque municipale, 2001), 167. Pangle, *The Theological Basis of Liberal Modernity*, 134, refers to this passage in interpreting Montesquieu's secular-liberal modernity. Usbek, in his philosophical moments, agrees: "Things in themselves are neither pure nor impure" (Letter 17, 29).

13. See the sections from *Mes Pensées* grouped under 'Amour-Propre,' esp. 1038, 1058–60. Montesquieu, *Œuvres completes*, 987–88.

14. Vickie Sullivan offers a compelling account of his anti-Hobbesianism, *Montesquieu and the Despotic Idea*, ch. 2.

15. "Les richesses, la naissance, etc., sont des médailles; l'estime publique et le mérite personnel sont de la monnaie courante." Montesquieu, *Pensées*, in *Œuvres complètes*, 1018, 986.

16. The viscount d'Orte (SL IV.2), whom Montesquieu so admired, would likely not be praised by Hobbes (though here we need to attend to the complication raised by *Leviathan*, ch. 21, in which Hobbes suggests that subjects are not bound to "execute any dangerous, or dishonourable Office.")

17. Antong Liu, "The Tragedy of Honor in Early Modern Political Thought: Hobbes, Mandeville, Montesquieu, and Rousseau," *History of European Ideas* 47, no. 8 (2021): 1243–61. Sharon Krause thinks the honor is false because "the privileges and distinctions it seeks may not be merited from the standpoint of a true or comprehensive standard of moral goodness." "Laws, Passion, and the Attractions of Right Action in Montesquieu," *Philosophy and Social Criticism* 32, no. 2 (2006): 225.

18. Scholars who read Montesquieu as critical of monarchy tend to read this passage as a critique of monarchial society more generally (See Hulliung, *Montesquieu and the Old Regime*, 30; see also the works of Paul Rahe and Thomas Pangle). Christopher Brooke has usefully surveyed some of these moves, and generally pointed the ship back in the direction of the thèse nobiliaire. "Arsehole Aristocracy (or: Montesquieu on Honour, Revisited)," *European Journal of Political Theory* 17, no. 4 (2018): 391–41.

19. Spector, in *Montesquieu, les "Lettres persanes,"* notes that the despotic turn effects a transition "de la logique de la distinction à la logique de la domination" (73). That said, the desire for distinction continues in a perverted form under despotic government. Usbek's real reason for leaving Persia is the enemies he made when he decided to attack vanity, hypocrisy and vice at court (Letter 8).

20. See Usbek's reflections on the various economies of glory (Letter 89).

21. He puts in the mouth of Usbek the important observation that speculation about nonsocial existence is vain (Letter 94, 151).

22. Jonathan Walsh, "A Cultural Numismatics: The 'Chain' of Economics in Montesquieu's *Lettres persanes*," *Australian Journal of French Studies* 46, no. 1/2 (2009): 139–54.

23. J. G. A. Pocock *The Machiavellian Moment* (Princeton, NJ: Princeton University Press, 1975), 475.

24. For an excellent discussion, see Catherine Larrère, "Montesquieu, Critique de Law. Qui Est L'ennemi Du Libéralisme?" *Cahiers D'économie Politique* 73, no. 2 (2017): 13–30.

25. William Doyle, *Venality the Sale of Offices in Eighteenth-Century France* (Oxford: Clarendon, 1996), 48.

26. In a similar way, he thought coin devaluation tended in a despotic direction, just as the necessity for exchange prevented despotism by reducing the monarch's scope for willful revaluations (XXII.14).

27. For a fine account, see Constantine Vassiliou, "'Le Système de John Law' and the Spectre of Modern Despotism in the Political Thought of Montesquieu," *Lumen* 38 (2019): 161–78.

28. The line is drawn out to good use in Clare Crowston, *Credit, Fashion, Sex: Economies of Regard in Old Regime France* (Durham, NC: Duke University Press, 2013), 35.

29. Michael Mosher, "The Judgmental Gaze of European Women: Gender, Sexuality, and the Critique of Republican Rule," *Political Theory* 22, no. 1 (1994): 25–44.

30. Montesquieu's impression of the sexualized economy of fashion and its relation to honor culture gets a powerful confirmation in Crowston's *Credit, Fashion, Sex*, which notes how the austerity of the revolutionary moment was quickly overturned in the Napoleonic order and subsequently in the restoration. One of the first things Louis XVIII did in 1814 was to ask where could be found the famous fashion merchant who had dressed Marie Antoinette, Rose Bertin (314). Legitimacy required fashion and the economy of luxury.

31. Our translator gives a note offering the original French here, signaling the awkwardness of translating it "I anticipated love." The original reads "j'ai prévenu l'amour" which has, in this instance, a sense of preventing. Margaret Mauldon's translation has "forestalled," *Persian Letters*, 8.

32. Compare Montesquieu's views on artificially high interest under despotism (SL V.15, XXII.19).

33. The depressed economy of esteem can be seen here: "People capable of much self-esteem would be in a position to cause revolutions" (SL III.9).

34. Charles Taylor, "The Politics of Recognition," in *Multiculturalism: Examining the Politics of Recognition*, ed. Amy Gutmann (Princeton, NJ: Princeton University Press, 1994), 34–35.

35. See his views on the English elimination of the lords under the commonwealth (SL II.4).

36. Notice that Usbek himself lived in such a despotic economy of esteem in the Persian court: "I had attracted the jealousy of some ministers, without having the favor of the prince" (Letter 8, 13).

37. The translation has a slight imprecision. It should read *it* [the plurality, not the wives themselves] tempers the violence of our desires: "la pluralité des femmes nous sauve de leur empire; elle tempère la violence de nos désirs."

38. Mary McAlpin notices that Roxane likely was in love with the younger lover when she was forced to become the fifth wife of the old lecher Usbek, "The Rape of Roxane and the End of the World in Montesquieu's *Lettres persanes*," *Romanic Review* 107 (2016): 63.

39. Note, in passing, that the revolution Anaïs achieves in her earthly seraglio by way of her angelic lover is not permanent—her revenge on her murderer husband is only complete when he returns to the seraglio to discover it broke and full of bastard children. We are left to infer that the oppressive mores will return once more: like Roxane's revolt, this does not truly liberate anyone; rather, it achieves a sublime revenge.

40. Spector, *Montesquieu, "les Lettres persanes,"* offers a marvelous account of this.

41. Mary Shanley and Peter Stillman, "Political and Marital Despotism: Montesquieu's Persian Letters," in *The Family in Political Thought*, ed. Jean Elshtain (Amherst: University of Massachusetts Press, 1982), 76–77.

42. Montesquieu, *Pensées*, 1273, in *Œuvres Complétes*, 999.

43. "Notes sur l'Angleterre," in *Œuvres complètes*, 332 (my translation). I have barely scraped the surface of the debate over Montesquieu's regime preference. I have tended toward a reading of him as cautiously monarchical. A judicious paper by Andrea Radasanu suggests a highly ambivalent Montesquieu who leans in favor of commercial republics: "Montesquieu on Moderation, Monarchy and Reform," *History of Political Thought* 31, no. 2(2010): 283–30.

44. McAlpin, "The Rape of Roxane," 60.

45. Mosher, "The Judgemental Gaze," 27, presents this as a utopian failure.

46. Megan Gallagher, "Fear, Liberty, and Honourable Death in Montesquieu's *Persian Letters*," *Eighteenth-Century Fiction* 28, no. 4 (2016): 623–44.

47. Judith Shklar, *Montesquieu* (Oxford: Oxford University Press, 1987), 37. But see EL XXVI.14 for a different account of incest.

48. David Kettler, "Montesquieu on Love: Notes on the Persian Letters," *American Political Science Review* 58, no. 3 (1964): 661. Schaub, *Erotic Liberalism*, 107–108, also reflects on this. She links their love to classical civic equality. I think this a powerful reading, though I tend to see the story as less optimistic for radical equality.

49. The phrase "boom-and-bust economies of love" is derived from the song "Goodbye Great Society" by singer-songwriter Paul Tyler.

50. Brooke, "Arsehole Aristocracy," 406.

51. Mary Wollstonecraft, *A Vindication of the Rights of Woman* (London: Penguin, 1992), ch. 12, 284.

52. Compare Montesquieu, *Pensées* [995], in *Œuvres complètes*, 985. Mosher points insightfully to the importance of SL XXVIII.22 in "The Judgemental Gaze," 33.

BIBLIOGRAPHY

Andrew, Edward Grant. *The Genealogy of Values: The Aesthetic Economy of Nietzsche and Proust*. Lanham, MD: Rowman and Littlefield, 1995.

Brooke, Christopher. "Arsehole Aristocracy (or: Montesquieu on Honour, Revisited)." *European Journal of Political Theory* 17, np. 4 (2018): 391–41.

Courois, Jean-Patrice. "Les principes de l'Essai sur le goût." In *Montesquieu, oeuvre ouverte? (1748–1755)*, edited by Catherine Larrère, 165–91. Bordeaux: Bibliothèque municipale, 2001.

Crowston, Clare. *Credit, Fashion, Sex: Economies of Regard in Old Regime France*. Durham, NC: Duke University Press, 2013.

de la Boétie, Étienne. *Discours de la servitude volontaire*. Paris: Flammarion, 1983.

Doyle, William. *Venality the Sale of Offices in Eighteenth-Century France*. Oxford: Clarendon, 1996.

Euben, Roxanne. *Journeys to the Other Shore*. Princeton, NJ: Princeton University Press, 2006.

Gallagher, Megan. "Fear, Liberty, and Honourable Death in Montesquieu's *Persian Letters*." *Eighteenth-Century Fiction* 28, no. 4 (2016): 623–44.

Goyard-Fabre, Simone. *Montesquieu, adversaire de Hobbes*. Paris: Lettres modernes, 1980.

Hobbes, Thomas. *Leviathan*. London: Penguin, 1985.

Hulliung, Mark. *Montesquieu and the Old Regime*. Berkeley: University of California Press, 1996.

Kettler, David. "Montesquieu on Love: Notes on the Persian Letters." *American Political Science Review* 58, no. 3(1964): 658–62.

Krause, Sharon. "Laws, Passion, and the Attractions of Right Action in Montesquieu." *Philosophy and Social Criticism* 32, no. 2 (2006): 211–30.

Larrère, Catherine. "Montesquieu, Critique de Law. Qui Est L'ennemi Du Libéralisme?" *Cahiers D'économie Politique* 73, no. 2 (2017): 13–30.

Liu, Antong. "The Tragedy of Honor in Early Modern Political Thought: Hobbes, Mandeville, Montesquieu, and Rousseau." *History of European Ideas* 47, no. 8 (2021): 1243–61.

McAlpin, Mary. "The Rape of Roxane and the End of the World in Montesquieu's *Lettres persanes*." *Romanic Review* 107 (2016): 57–76.

Montesquieu. *Persian Letters*. Translated by Margaret Mauldon. Oxford: Oxford University Press, 2008.

———. *Persian Letters*. Translated by Stuart Warner. South Bend, IN: St. Augustine's Press, 2017.

————. *The Spirit of the Laws*. Translated by Anne Cohler. Cambridge: Cambridge University Press, 1989

————. *Œuvres complètes*. Edited by Daniel Oster. Paris: Seuil, 1964.

Mosher, Michael. "The Judgmental Gaze of European Women: Gender, Sexuality, and the Critique of Republican Rule." *Political Theory* 22, no. 1 (1994): 25–44.

Pangle, Thomas. *The Theological Basis of Liberal Modernity in Montesquieu's Spirit of the Laws.* Chicago: University of Chicago Press, 2010.

Plato. *Republic*. Translated by Allan Bloom. New York: Basic Books, 1991.

Pocock, J. G. A. *The Machiavellian Moment*. Princeton, NJ: Princeton University Press, 1975.

Radasanu, Andrea. "Montesquieu on Moderation, Monarchy and Reform." *History of Political Thought* 31, no. 2 (2010): 283–308.

Schaub, Diana. *Erotic Liberalism: Women and Revolution in Montesquieu's Persian Letters*. Lanham, MD: Rowman and Littlefield, 1995.

Shanley, Mary, and Stillman, Peter. "Political and Marital Despotism: Montesquieu's 'Persian Letters.'" In *The Family in Political Thought*, edited by Jean Elshtain, 64–79. Amherst: University of Massachusetts Press, 1982.

Shklar, Judith. *Montesquieu*. Oxford: Oxford University Press, 1987.

Spector, Céline. *Montesquieu, les "Lettres persanes": De l'anthropologie à la politique*. Paris: Presses Universitaires de France, 1997.

Starobinski, Jean. *Montesquieu*. Paris: Seuil, 1994.

Sullivan, Vickie. *Montesquieu and the Despotic Ideas of Europe: An Interpretation of The Spirit of the Laws*. Chicago: University of Chicago Press, 2018.

Taylor, Charles. "The Politics of Recognition." In *Multiculturalism: Examining the Politics of Recognition*, edited by Amy Gutmann, 25–73. Princeton, NJ: Princeton University Press, 1994.

Vassiliou, Constantine. "'Le Système de John Law' and the Spectre of Modern Despotism in the Political Thought of Montesquieu." *Lumen* 38 (2019): 161–78.

Walsh, Jonathan. "A Cultural Numismatics: The 'Chain' of Economics in Montesquieu's Lettres persanes." *Australian Journal of French Studies* 46, no. 1/2 (2009): 139–54.

Wollstonecraft, Mary. *A Vindication of the Rights of Woman*. London: Penguin, 1992.

Wooton, David. *Power, Pleasure, and Profit: Insatiable Appetites from Machiavelli to Madison*. Cambridge, MA: Harvard University Press, 2018.

Zuckert, Michael. "Natural Law, Natural Rights, and Classical Liberalism: On Montesquieu's Critique of Hobbes." *Social Philosophy and Policy* 18, no. 1 (2001): 227–51.

PART III

The *Persian Letters* on Commercial Society

Chapter 7

The Plague of High Finance in Montesquieu's *Persian Letters*[1]

Emily Nacol and Constantine Christos Vassiliou

INTRODUCTION

This chapter considers how Montesquieu, in *Persian Letters*, represents and reflects on a key figure in the story of early eighteenth-century French commerce and politics: John Law. Law, a Scottish banker who served as France's controller general of finance during the early Regency period following Louis XIV's death, occupies a critical place in Montesquieu's thinking about politics. As Montesquieu writes in book II.4 of *The Spirit of the Laws*, "Mr. Law, equally ignorant of the republican and of the monarchical constitutions, was one of the *greatest promoters of despotism* that had until then been seen in Europe. Besides the changes he made, which were so abrupt, so unusual, and so unheard of, he wanted to remove the intermediate ranks and abolish the political bodies; he was dissolving the monarchy by his chimerical payments and seemed to want to buy back the constitution."[2] Law betrayed two core principles underpinning Montesquieu's vision of free, moderate government in *The Spirit of the Laws*. First, despite his success at reducing government debt, Law's "changes . . . which were so abrupt, so unusual, and so unheard of," demonstrated an insensitivity to France's general spirit. Second, his system undermined the intermediary political bodies—namely, the *parlements*—that were meant to check the sovereign's power in France. Surprisingly, however, Montesquieu offers little else throughout *The Spirit of the Laws* to justify his striking claim about Law in book II.4. This atypically personalized attack, which runs counter to the tenor of an otherwise clinical assessment of despotism throughout the book, should give readers pause. What motivated Montesquieu's brief, but profoundly negative, attention to

Law and his interventions in France's politics and economy? How should this antipathy be interpreted or explained?

Our chapter demonstrates that a close reading of *Persian Letters* further clarifies Montesquieu's dramatic contention about Law's despotism by illuminating his role as a destabilizing and corrupting actor in France during the early Regency period. We consider how specific depictions of Law in *Persian Letters* as a magician, an algebraist, a system maker, a mythic demigod, and an enlightened legislator, each point directly to the complex and delicate relationship between commerce and virtue in Montesquieu's analysis of eighteenth-century political economy. Our attention to these character depictions of Law helps us unearth a thread of argumentation that captures Montesquieu's position in the eighteenth-century commerce and virtue debates.[3] That is, he distinctly held the view that the hallmarks of eighteenth-century high finance—speculation, gambling, and luxury—were inescapable features of modern commercial life that had to be managed. Therefore, we challenge readings of Montesquieu as a radical liberal who deliberately promotes commercial innovation as a means of destroying the titled nobility[4] and Christianity[5] to accelerate Europe's modernization. Montesquieu's account of Law's system in *Persian Letters* tells a different, ominous story, demonstrating how new modes of public finance can exploit human beings' natural sense of credulity and thereby mirror existing vehicles of despotism. As such, John Law plays a key role as the epistolary novel's deuteragonist, sensitizing readers to the endogenous features of modern commerce that accommodate Europe's emergent modes of despotism.

This chapter proceeds in four sections. First, we present a brief synopsis of Law's system, featuring his work as a financial legislator. In the second section, we consider how Law's system relates to Montesquieu's assessment of modern commercial society by examining Usbek's "Tale of the Troglodytes" in *Persian Letters.* Here, we trace an argument that begins in letter 11 with Usbek's account of the mythic Troglodytes and comes full circle in letter 146, with both letters showcasing how an unmitigated spirit of avarice yields political instability, which, in our view, is the *summum malum* that unifies *Persian Letters'* interlocking narratives. In the third section, we examine Montesquieu's more episodic reflections on the character of French commercial culture, highlighting its features that created fertile ground for Law's ascent: self-interest, dishonesty, vanity, a love of gambling, and credulity. We emphasize letter 24, a hinge point in *Persian Letters* that accentuates the dangers of high finance in Montesquieu's analysis of the thorny relationship between commerce and virtue and that colors his persistent warnings about the looming specter of despotism modern European nations face. The chapter's final section begins with a close examination of letters 88–92, emphasizing the *parlements'* role as an indispensable institution of political management, one that had already proved resilient against Louis XIV's and the papacy's sustained despotic encroachments. Our analysis dovetails with a survey of Rica and Usbek's powerful illustrations of the Law debacle in letters 132 and 146, to explain how the Scottish financier became such a destabilizing force in early modern France.

LAW'S SYSTEM: AN OVERVIEW

John Law was a Scottish banker known for his mathematical genius and his penchant for gambling. By all accounts he was a charming, handsome philanderer who eventually ran afoul of British high society due to his amorous affairs with some of London's most popular debutantes.[6] He then served as France's controller general of finance shortly following Louis XIV's death and established a central bank that dealt in paper money.[7] Law is notorious, however, for instituting an innovative financial scheme to address the staggering national debt that Louis XIV accumulated during the War of Spanish Succession. In brief, Law's scheme nudged, and eventually compelled, government debt holders to exchange their securities for shares in the Mississippi Company, a government owned joint-stock company that primarily operated in the Americas. Law then disentangled the value of paper currency from the existing gold and silver standards through a series of edicts, pegging it to the Mississippi Company's fortunes instead. These policies vastly inflated the share price, producing what is famously known as "the Mississippi Bubble." The bubble burst on May 21, 1720, after Law's attempts to temper the stock frenzy precipitated an abrupt sell-off, with the shares and their tethered paper currency value becoming worthless by November 1720.

Beyond Montesquieu's bold claim concerning Law's despotism in book II.4, Law receives little sustained attention elsewhere in *The Spirit of the Laws*. Where, then, lies the evidence that he was such a worrisome figure to Montesquieu? On this question, scholars have notably emphasized the following passage in book III.3 of *The Spirit of the Laws*, which on its face reads as a neutral instantiation of the eighteenth-century commerce and virtue debates: "The political men of Greece who lived under popular government recognized no other force to sustain it than virtue. Those of today speak to us only of manufacturing, commerce, finance, wealth, and even luxury."[8] Some scholars interpret this passage as an entry point for understanding Montesquieu's protoliberalism. In Thomas Pangle's view, Montesquieu's stark opposition between the virtue of the ancients and the inward-looking commercial ethos of the moderns provides the groundwork for a radically liberal political philosophy, which precludes the possibility of classical virtue in the modern commercial world. Andrew Bibby accepts Pangle's premise but focuses his analysis on book XXIII of *The Spirit of the Laws*. There Montesquieu exhibits his expertise in banking and paper money, thus proving that he considered himself among those "who speak to us only of manufacturing, commerce, finance, wealth, and even luxury." Bibby correctly notes that Montesquieu's aversion to national banks and state enterprises distinctly pertained to Europe's existing monarchies.[9] By contrast, "in states that engage in economic commerce," such as England, " . . . one has fortunately established banks."[10] Bibby infers that Montesquieu's earlier warning about Law's despotism does not reflect a feudal, preliberal penchant for France's existing intermediary institutions; rather, it is an urgent call to emulate liberal, commercial England. In short, menacing figures such as Law will plague *European* monarchies so long as they remain wedded to their antiquated feudal institutions and practices.

Catherine Larrère, however, convincingly rejects such "monist" accounts of Montesquieu's constitutionalism, noting how they betray a primary feature of his protoliberal political philosophy: namely, his "pluralist vision of the political good."[11] She observes that Montesquieu's deliberately neutral distinction between economies of commerce (England) and economies of luxury (France) corresponds with his "external" (constitutional) pluralism, attuning readers to the "several paths commerce can take in modern times."[12] It follows, then, that Montesquieu deliberately blurs the distinction between the ancients and moderns in book III.3 to highlight the multiple intermediate possibilities for approximating virtue in the modern commercial world, with some nations better equipped than others to accommodate certain modes of high finance.

Why, then, does Law warrant special mention in Montesquieu's political writings? Does his example teach us anything apart from the antiquarian lessons that eighteenth-century monarchies are structurally too ill-equipped to face the exigencies of the modern commercial world, as Bibby supposes, or that legislators need to be mindful of their nations' institutions and practices when introducing new modes of commerce, as Larrère supposes? To answer this question, we turn to *Persian Letters*, where we find Montesquieu's most discernible, sustained commentary on Law's system and its impact on French commerce. Through our reading of this commentary, we trace how Montesquieu interprets Law's system, which fed both into and off of an alarmingly inward-looking citizenry, not merely as an economic crisis with ramifications for contemporary European monarchies but as a cultural crisis whose dangers concerned the liberal commercial world more generally.

THE MYTH OF AEOLUS: LAW'S BEWITCHING CHARM AND HIS EMPIRE OF IMAGINATION

In *Persian Letters* 132–43, we find Montesquieu—working through the voice of the Persian traveler Rica—combining "sociological analysis with bruising satire" to offer a sustained critique of Law, his strategies and ambitions, and the outcomes of his damaging financial system.[13] Nowhere is this more evident than in the "Fragment from an Ancient Greek Mythologist" that Rica transcribes into his correspondence with his comrade Usbek after finding it tucked into a letter he received from a scholar seeking Persian manuscripts. In this parable, we find Montesquieu's literary rumination on the Mississippi scheme and Law himself. It is worth reproducing here in full, for its depiction of Law's scheme, his character, and his artful persuasion of the French people.

The "Fragment" tells of a baby born to a nymph of Caledonia and Aeolus, god of the winds. The baby possessed both the gift of numeracy and an ability to tell metals apart. Aeolus also taught his son, as he grew, to bottle the wind and sell it to travelers. When the young demigod eventually surmised that wind was not a valuable commodity on his own island, he began traveling the world accompanied only by "the blind god of chance" (Letter 142, 241).[14] In his travels, Aeolus's son came upon Baetica, a land rich in gold, where he began to peddle his wares. Although Saturn, the ruler of Baetica, was not keen to receive him, he made his appeal directly to the people after Saturn departed.

The "Fragment" embedded in Letter 142 is a thinly veiled representation of how Law (the baby born to Aeolus and the nymph) left Scotland to make his way to France. Initially rebuffed by Louis XIV (Saturn), he made headway with the public as Louis faded from public life and eventually died. The public appeals Law made in his effort to peddle shares in the Mississippi Company (the wind)—fictionalized in the parable Rica transcribes in his letter—give us a clearer sense of how Montesquieu viewed both Law's system and the man himself. Consider Aeolus's son's opening appeal to the people of Baetica, as he declares, "You believe you are rich, because you possess gold and silver. Your error makes me pity you. *Believe me*: leave the country of base metals and come into *the empire of imagination*, and I promise you riches that will astonish you" (Letter 142, 241; emphasis added). This points to the core principle of Law's approach to a political economy shaped by the principles of high finance—that wealth is not a matter of holding on to "miserable metals" but is generated by financial projects that depend on speculation and investment with an eye to future profits (Letter 142, 242). Montesquieu's parable depicts Aeolus's son returning to the people of Baetica again and again, insisting each time that they place still more of their precious metals and stones directly into his hands, in exchange for future returns they can perceive only through the work of imagination. Any resistance to his plan is, he argues, simply a failure of their cognitive powers (Letter 142, 241–42). He attempts to pull the public away from their knowledge of the material world and into a realm of fantasy, and with dire consequences. At the end of the parable, Aeolus's son takes half of the wealth of Baetica before floating away on "the slightest of wings" only to return again the next day and take still more (Letter 142, 243).

That this tale represents the havoc Law wreaked in France during his time as controller general has long been clear to readers. But for our purposes, it is also notable for its critical evaluation of some of the moral and epistemological features of high finance. Here Montesquieu figures a finance-based economy as wholly dependent on imagination—that of the financial projector himself (as a "peddler of the wind" who travels only with the "blind god of chance") and that of his investors, who must trade their material wealth for so much air in the present and visualize the promise of something more tangible in the future.[15]

Although the parable of Aeolus's son in letter 142 is perhaps the most conspicuous reference to Law and his system in *Persian Letters*, it is but a small part of the text's critique of both Law and the French commercial culture that ultimately accommodated him. We next turn to Montesquieu's "Tale of the Troglodytes" (Letters 10–14), a famous allegory that also adumbrates Law's destructive impact in France, as we shall see in subsequent sections.[16] While the allegory neither mentions nor alludes to Law, we contend that it casts light on Montesquieu's deeper anxieties about the modern commercial world, ones that correspond to the variegated facets of Law's system that he presents in later letters.

TALE OF THE TROGLODYTES AND THE MORTAL POISON OF AVARICE

The Troglodyte allegory is told from the vantage point of the book's main protagonist, Usbek, who responds to a letter he received from his protégé, Mirza, asking him to expand on an earlier claim that "justice is a quality as natural to [human beings] as existence is itself" (Letter 10, 17). Usbek replies with a series of letters that detail a conjectural history of the mythical Troglodytes. He emphasizes two distinct stages of political organization mirroring the two sides of the eighteenth-century commerce and virtue debates. The first took shape in the wake of a successful coup the Troglodytes orchestrated when they overthrew a foreign king who ruled tyrannically over them. Traumatized by his rule, the newly liberated Troglodytes passed a resolution, stating that "all individuals . . . would no longer obey anyone; that each would look solely to his own interests, *without consulting those of others*" (Letter 11, 19; emphasis added). The Troglodytes' new "constitution" was grounded in an unmitigated spirit of commercial self-interest. These arrangements ultimately proved to be unstable, producing vast inequality, famine, and corruption. But it was the Troglodytes' dishonesty in daily commerce that led to their ultimate demise. Usbek recounts to Mirza that the Troglodytes faced a deadly disease outbreak and turned to a renowned doctor for his assistance. But the doctor refused them, recalling how they had swindled him the last time he helped them manage an epidemic. The Troglodytes' avarice cost them their credibility and stood as evidence of a more virulent, incurable plague, as the doctor explains in his contemptuous diagnosis: "You have a poison in your soul more mortal than the one for which you want to be cured; you do not deserve to occupy a place on earth, because you have no humanity, and the rules of equity are to you unknown" (Letter 11, 21). Nearly all the Troglodytes died as a result.

The surviving Troglodytes reorganized themselves into a republic grounded in virtue, ushering in their halcyon days. Usbek recounts how citizens developed a deep sense of the common good, evidenced by their honesty in daily commerce. Yet this more humane and equitable stage of Troglodyte history was short-lived. As the population increased, the Troglodytes' commercial activities grew more complex and demanded greater attention. Subsequently, they developed a propensity for a political life of ease and pleasure over virtue. The Troglodytes eventually appointed a king who was renowned for his magnanimity, thus relieving themselves of any burdens associated with affairs of state. The story ends with the newly chosen king lamenting the Troglodytes' decision to make themselves subjects once again, having bargained their sovereignty away to "satisfy . . . ambition, acquire riches," and enjoy a life of ease and self-indulgent pleasure (Letter 14, 27).

Montesquieu's famous allegory shaped the direction of eighteenth-century political thought on both sides of the Atlantic with its emphasis on the wealth and virtue problem advanced commercial nations faced.[17] Its message is ambiguous, however. The "republican" stage of Troglodyte history suggests that commerce and virtue are compatible under certain institutional arrangements. Yet commercial growth inevitably disturbs this equilibrium, as Montesquieu shows. Richard Sher convincingly argues that Montesquieu's ambiguity is deliberate, to highlight how moderate legislation in the modern commercial world demands a trade-off between "liberty, virtue, and commerce, and that society could not expect to have all those attributes in equal and bountiful amounts."[18] Other scholars have noted how Montesquieu developed a theoretical response to this dilemma in his later writings, arriving at different conclusions over which regime—moderate monarchy or a commercial republic—provides the best conditions for reconciling commercial gain with the public interest.[19] Michael Sonenscher captures both perspectives in *Before the Deluge: Public Debt, Inequality, and the Intellectual Origins of the French Revolution*. He traces two meaningful shifts in the evolution of Montesquieu's thought. The first shift took place in 1734, when Montesquieu unqualifiedly praised England for overcoming the wealth and virtue problem.[20] We can observe the second shift in *The Spirit of the Laws* in 1748, where Montesquieu developed a more refined theory of honor to contain the pathological features of commercial life. We do not wholly reject either of these divergent interpretations, as Montesquieu was both a distant admirer of England and a defender of civilized monarchy—a reflection of his constitutional pluralism. These interpretations overlook, however, a sophisticated theoretical response contained within *Persian Letters*, one that aims to foster a sociable, other-regarding sense of justice among an increasingly inward-looking citizenry.

In this regard, an important interchange takes place in letters 10 and 11 between Usbek and his protégé Mirza, one that anticipates Montesquieu's response to the wealth and virtue problem in *Persian Letters*. Mirza asks Usbek to elaborate on a human nature claim he presumably made in an earlier, unpublished correspondence, that "justice is a quality as natural to [human beings] as existence is itself." Usbek apparently offered this elusive response when Mirza pressed him to weigh in on a philosophical debate he was having with Rica over "whether men are happy due to the pleasures and satisfaction of the senses or to the practice of virtue." Usbek demurs from giving a rational defense of his position, stating that "there are certain truths for which it is not enough to be persuaded, but which one must also be made to feel" (Letter 11, 19). These prefatory remarks to the Troglodyte allegory cast light upon the dramatic tale's dual purpose: to educate Mirza on how to "feel" the correctness of his claims concerning justice and happiness[21] and to demonstrate that justice does not merely depend on a nation's juridical structures but on the quality of its citizens' emotional constitution. As such, we can infer from Usbek's exchange with Mirza three presuppositions that underlie good politics: (1) human beings have a natural impulse for justice, (2) the "practice of virtue" is constitutive of human beings' happiness, and (3) our theories of political justice necessarily concern the emotions. The next section provides a close reading of letters 24, 132, and 146, detailing how Law's system introduced a new plague to France that affected the emotional health of its citizens.

LAW'S SYSTEM AND THE DANGERS OF
FRENCH COMMERCIAL CULTURE

As exemplified most clearly in the parable of Aeolus's son found in Letter 142, we find a critique of an unnamed but still oft-mentioned Law running primarily through Rica and Usbek's correspondence in *Persian Letters*. Although this critical appraisal may appear disjointed, we contend that Montesquieu offers a full account of how Law damaged the fabric of French society by exploiting and enhancing a dark potential that was *already* present in its bustling commercial atmosphere. Through staging epistolary exchanges between his Persian characters, Montesquieu illustrates the vicious underside of commercial activity and prosperity in Paris in particular. While proper virtue and emotional self-government—along with robust institutions—can mitigate the dangerous aspects of commercial life, corrupt actors (in this case, Law) can still capitalize on the vice already present in many commercial settings. Here we turn to episodic reflections on commercial culture from *Persian Letters* and weave them together to reconstruct Montesquieu's account of Law, his character, and the specific weaknesses he found and exploited in French society. Among these, as we show in this section, are dishonesty, vanity, credulity, and a penchant for gambling—qualities that supported a vibrant commercial life in France (especially Paris) but also exposed the French public to manipulation by a financial schemer like Law.

In *Persian Letters*, Rica and Usbek share their observations about France's commercial dynamism and its sources, both salutary and perilous. In letter 58, for example, Rica describes Paris as an "enchanting" city in a double sense—it is full of charm, but it also mesmerizes its inhabitants and visitors in a way that arouses his skepticism (Letter 58, 94). Paris is the "mother of invention," as Rica notes that its residents' true revenue consists "in [the] spirit and ingenuity" of the people themselves (Letter 58, 94). This vibrant atmosphere framed in commercial terms is not, however, without pathologies. Rica goes on to observe that Parisians may practice their trades dishonestly— something for visitors who do not want to part with their money to bear in mind. In a pointed comment mirroring earlier commentary in letter 24, Rica notes that "an infinite number of masters of languages, arts, and sciences teach what they do not know, and this is indeed a considerable talent, for not much wit is needed to show what one knows, but infinitely more is needed to teach what one does not know" (Letter 58, 94–95). This wry observation highlights the ambiguous character of Parisian commerce: on the one hand, Rica acknowledges the ingenuity and wit it takes to teach something of which one is ignorant, but on the other hand, he foregrounds the dishonesty that underwrites some endeavors to turn a profit.[22] These impressions in letter

58 also suggest something else important: the people of Paris are credulous, willing to believe what they are told by people who seem authoritative—a recurring theme in *Persian Letters* and its representation of French society.

Letter 56 also highlights the corrupted aspects of some prominent economic activities and professions in Paris. Here Usbek observes the fate of gambling in Europe where it has become, he comments, a recognized practice that gives the gambler powerful social currency. Usbek figures gambling as a gendered practice, noting that it is most common among older women who seek to damage their husbands. He positions it as a manifestation of vanity in women, commenting that they have the capacity to ruin their husbands in all stages of their adult lives: "Clothes and carriages begin the disorder, coquetry increases it, and gambling completes it" (Letter 56, 91). But he is quick to observe that gambling has *all* of society in its grip. In a telling passage that foreshadows the critique of Law that comes late in the parable of Aeolus's son, Usbek writes, "That title [of gambler] alone takes the place of birth, property, and probity. It admits every man who holds it, without examination, into the ranks of honest men, although there is no one who does not know that one is very often deceived in so judging. *But people have agreed to be incorrigible*" (Letter 56, 91; emphasis added). What is significant here is Usbek's impression of a tacit agreement among members of a polite commercial society: that gamblers shall be let into their fold without too much questioning. Moreover, and perhaps more worryingly for Montesquieu, this letter suggests that a fascination with the professional gambler has eclipsed other long-standing norms that typically shape social interactions: rank, property holdings, and a reputation for honest dealings. Usbek notes that these are willfully ignored by people eager to associate with gamblers, and furthermore, that the desire to interact with them is so socially entrenched that it can no longer be effectively reformed. These reflections on the place of gambling in Paris make it easier to understand how a figure like Law—a notorious gambler—might have been welcomed into French society, both for his character and reputation and for his appealing financial schemes. More generally, through Usbek and Rica, Montesquieu suggests that gambling is simply one of *many* profitable endeavors that make Paris a city of activity, ingenuity, and commercial success. But it has a clear downside—one that Parisians have agreed to look away from, much like the Troglodytes who gave up on vigilance as their commercial efforts developed.

Beyond *Persian Letters*' attention to the corrupt aspects of commercial Paris—dishonesty, vanity, and excessive risk taking—the credulity of the French people is also a feature that catches the eye of Montesquieu's Persian travelers. Through their exchanges, Montesquieu raises the question of what might nurture such a guileless disposition on a large social scale. One possible answer offered by *Persian Letters* is that the French were already

socialized to it by their particular relationship to authority. Montesquieu gestures in this direction by offering intermittent commentary about the unstable
sources of authoritative knowledge in France throughout the text, beginning
with letter 24. There Rica recounts his first impressions of Paris to his friend
Ibben, turning his attention to French political and ecclesiastical powers and
considering how these authorities manipulate the minds of French subjects.
This letter deserves sustained attention, for it, too, suggests how Law could
have persuaded both French political figures and the public to follow his
advice and invest in his scheme. Tellingly, Rica's analysis of the powers of
French authorities focuses on their capacity to persuade people of the fungi-
bility of substances and the flexibility of their value and worth—key elements
of Law's financial scheme.

Rica begins with the sovereign, opening letter 24 by describing Louis XIV
as a "great magician," deeming him so for his ability to manipulate currency,
a clear reference to the various paper money schemes that the French Crown
employed to fund its wars of imperial expansion. Rica notes that if the king
"has one million *écus* in his treasury, and he needs two million of them, he
has only to persuade them that one *écu* is worth two, and they believe him"
(Letter 24, 40). Likewise, "if he has a war that is difficult to sustain, and
he has no money, he has only to put it in their heads that a piece of paper
is money, and they are immediately convinced of it" (Letter 24, 40). Rica
frames this "magical" persuasion as an act of epistemological power, commenting that Louis XIV "exerts his empire even over the minds of his subjects" by prevailing upon them to accept an approach to the value of currency
that borders on fantasy (Letter 24, 40).[23] As Rica portrays it, this takes little
exertion on Louis's part, as his subjects are ready to believe him. Of particular
interest, too, is the example Rica offers—one pertaining to the shifting value
of money in the hands of an artful king, an example that foreshadows Law's
financial manipulations in the wake of Louis's death.

In letter 24 we also find the first of several analogies between Catholicism
and the institutional culture of high finance in *Persian Letters*—namely, we
encounter the claim that high finance has provided Louis with an instrument for producing particular effects on the public mind, akin to the ways
the papacy and Catholic doctrine have affected Louis's own thinking. Rica
observes that the pope is "no less a master over the king's mind than the
king himself is over the minds of others. . . . Sometimes he makes the king
believe that three is nothing but one, that the bread that a person eats is not
bread, or that the wine one drinks is not wine, and a thousand other things
of that sort" (Letter 24, 40). That the pope exerts such control over the king
gives him even greater authority in the realm of belief, imagination, and
knowledge than Louis himself. Montesquieu also draws a parallel between

the theological claims the pope expects the king to accept and the claims about money and finance that the king expects his people to take on faith. From Rica's commentary in letter 24, we can see the influence that French political and religious authorities exert on each other and on the public, to varying effects. Rica observes sharply that both sovereign and pope are akin to magicians, who compel their subjects to imagine what they cannot see or to see things differently than the way they really are. Interestingly, when the drama of *Persian Letters* reaches its crescendo in letter 142, Montesquieu returns to Rica's correspondence once more to offer one last portrayal of a magical authority who depends on the credulity of both legislators and the public in eighteenth-century French political life: John Law. Thus, by the time Law appears most overtly in *Persian Letters* in the parable of Aeolus's son, Montesquieu has laid the groundwork to explain how Law and his system were initially so well received; that is, the French were already practiced at accepting "magical" forms of persuasion from figures with political and ecclesiastical authority, and they had also learned to tolerate some of the darker aspects of commercial prosperity (e.g., dishonesty, vanity, and an embrace of risk).

Although the parable of Aeolus's son is the most direct account Montesquieu offers of Law's effects on the French, there is another, more subtle reference to him tucked into the narrative of letters 133–36. There Rica recounts his visit to a monastery's library in Paris. While his host walks him through a section holding scientific volumes, they have a sharp disagreement about the reliability of scientific inquiry. Rica's guide evaluates works of astrology as manifestations of "occult ignorance" and deems them pitiful, but Rica asserts that these texts are in fact treated as guides to action, policy, and government in Persia. In a rejoinder meant to humble his Parisian host, Rica draws a parallel between astrology and algebra, noting that as Persia is guided by its astrologers, France is similarly led by its algebraists. He continues to press this point, asking whether all the astrologers in Persia, considered together, might have made as grievous of a miscalculation as only *one* of France's algebraists, surely here referring to Law and the disastrous effects of his purportedly rational system of finance (Letter 135, 224). By comparing Law and his intellectual and financial projects to the so-called occult ignorance of Persian astrology, Montesquieu reminds the reader yet again that Law merely drew upon and perpetuated an empire of imagination, one already put in place by king and pope.

Although Rica takes pains to show how and why the French might have found themselves in such a state of credulity, by looking carefully at their relations to specific authority figures, *Persian Letters* contains at least one admission that perhaps they were not unusual in this regard. As Rica comments in letter 143, in a longer meditation on religious belief and practices,

"Men are indeed unfortunate wretches! They vacillate ceaselessly between false hopes and ridiculous fears, and instead of resting upon reason, they create monsters that intimidate them or phantoms that seduce them" (Letter 143, 243). Here, in an epistolic reflection following immediately on the heels of the myth of Aeolus's son—a parable on how the French public was adversely affected by Law's appeals to imagination—Montesquieu allows that perhaps credulity is simply an all-too-human quality, one found in many cultures and times, including eighteenth-century commercial France. Although he offers a specific explanation for *why* France found itself in such an unfortunate position vis-à-vis Law, Montesquieu hints at the universal character of a cultural disposition to accept the fantastical.

By weaving together Montesquieu's reflections on commercial life and the production of knowledge, we argue *Persian Letters* in fact presents readers with a consistent, if scattershot, account of why eighteenth-century France might have been such a fertile environment for Law's scheme. In our reconstruction of this line of argument, we agree with Pangle that *Persian Letters* offers a critique of how religious authority and belief primed the French public to indulge in dangerous forms of imagination or fancy.[24] As we have shown, Montesquieu suggests that a certain guilelessness characterized French society, one that made it possible to accept uncritically the fantastical elements of Law's financial schemes, which they could neither see nor verify by their own senses. We submit, however, that *Persian Letters* does not go further to offer an account of how this credulity was well moderated by the commercial spirit of eighteenth-century France. In fact, Montesquieu's attention to the darker aspects of commercial activity in *Persian Letters* suggests that he thought thriving commercial societies were vulnerable *on their own moral terms* to certain kinds of projectors who capitalized on a permissive culture of dishonesty and vanity that frequently underwrote prosperity. Relatedly, he also notes the social esteem afforded to gamblers in French commercial culture, suggesting that this created a hospitable environment for Law to try his luck gambling with national finances on a hitherto untested scale. Our reading of *Persian Letters* thus submits that Montesquieu offers a complex, multicausal story of Law's success in France, one that troubles readings of him as a radical liberal who theorized how commerce might overcome or displace human frailties that render a people vulnerable to despotic rule. Instead, we contend that he was equally sensitive to the ways commerce might produce or enhance another set of dangerous foibles in individuals and the societies they comprise.

A VESTIGIAL TEMPLE OF LIBERTY TO COUNTERPOISE
THE GREATEST MONARCH ON EARTH

As we saw in Rica's letters, Paris was not free from ambition, greed, vanity, dishonesty, and false hope. Montesquieu accepted these inescapable features of modern commercial life, a reading that situates him alongside thinkers like Bernard Mandeville, whose *Fable of the Bees* famously collapses the distinction between private and public interest. To be sure, Mandevillean ideas echo throughout *Persian Letters,* insofar as Montesquieu associates vanity with public wealth.[25] As Usbek writes to Rhédi in letter 106, "[Vanity] commands and is obeyed more promptly than our monarch would be, because interest is the greatest monarch on earth," without which "this state would be one of the most miserable that has been in the world" (Letter 106, 173). At the same time, however, Montesquieu provides multiple vignettes that associate vanity with a spirit of malaise in French commercial life, inviting readers to contemplate its hazards. We saw in letter 24 how despotic rulers exploit their subjects' vanity to accommodate their imperial ambitions (Letter 24, 39). In letter 30, Rica recounts how Parisians embraced him upon his arrival for his exotic dress. He constantly felt their esteem, overhearing their praise as they filled their shops with his portraits. Yet his exhilaration was short-lived, when a melancholic Rica recognized the vapidity of their esteem once he conformed to wearing Parisian attire. He writes, "This trial made known to me what I was really worth. Free of every ornament I saw myself appreciated more correctly . . . in an instant . . . I [lost] the public's attention and esteem: for all at once I entered into a frightful nothingness" (Letter 30, 51). In letter 50 Rica recounts his stultifying conversations with Parisians who relentlessly draw attention to their merits and talents (Letter 50, 81). And in one of the book's more amusing and prophetic anecdotes, Rica overhears two friends forming a pact to praise and draw attention to each other's public utterances in a desperate effort to restore their reputations for being men of wit (Letter 54, 87). Bibby suggests that Montesquieu is deliberately ambiguous in his treatment of Parisian vanity to highlight a core obstacle preventing France from adapting to the modern commercial world—a patrician's scorn toward self-interested commerce among France's bloated noncommercial aristocratic classes.[26] According to Bibby's analysis, Montesquieu develops a sophisticated response to this challenge in *The Spirit of the Laws*, with a theory of honor, one fine-tuned to ennoble the pursuit of wealth and commercial distinctions. To be sure, vanity is a principal animating force in commercial life that Montesquieu embraces throughout his writings. But Usbek's analysis of France's honor culture in Letters 88–92, which culminates in a panegyric on the *parlements*' salutary role in French society, suggests a continual need for a noncommercial species of honor to exist alongside modes of recognition related to vanity and the pursuit of wealth.

In letters 88–90, Usbek provides a sustained account of the existing points of honor that the Bourbon Crown did not eliminate, recognizing that to do so would harm his own interests. In letter 89, Usbek asserts to Ibben that the desire for glory is an essential human need. He writes, "It is no different from that instinct that all creatures have for their own preservation. It seems that we augment our being when we can impress it upon the memory of others" (Letter 89, 145). Our desire to be remembered is a noble passion, and a key barometer for evaluating a nation's liberty: "In each state, the desire for glory grows with the liberty of the subjects, and diminishes with that liberty. Glory is never a companion of servitude" (Letter 89, 144). Usbek culminates these observations in a sober reflection on why dueling persists in France, despite the Crown's efforts to forbid this brutish feudal practice. He writes, "If one follows the laws of honor, one perishes upon the scaffold; if one follows the laws of justice, one is forever banished from the society of men. There is, then, only this cruel alternative; either to die or to be unworthy of living" (Letter 90, 146). This reflection leaves readers with a question: Are the "laws" of honor and justice in conflict with one another?

Montesquieu works through this apparent dilemma in letter 92 by juxtaposing Usbek's surprisingly prosaic announcement of Louis XIV's death with a panegyric on the *parlements*, stating how the institution, which is "hardly led to do anything more than to render justice" (Letter 92, 149), inspires a quasi-religious feeling of reverence among French citizens. The *parlements'* political power was greatly diminished by 1715, following "the destiny of human things: they yielded to time, which destroys everything; to the corruption of morals, which has weakened everything; to the supreme authority, which has laid waste to everything" (Letter 92, 149). Scholars have noted that Louis XIV's death created an opening for the *parlements* to reassert themselves in French society.[27] As Stuart Warner describes, the Parlement de Paris's officeholders forged a quid pro quo agreement with Phillipe d'Orleans, who himself was jockeying to fill the power vacuum Louis XIV left behind. In exchange for their support, the regent restored the Parlement de Paris's political right of remonstrance. But the advent of Law's system became both a boon and an impediment for the *parlements*, more generally. On the one hand, the Parlement de Paris had the opportunity to exercise its newly restored power with a series of remonstrances that aimed to thwart Law's designs.[28] More specifically, it protested the issuance of paper money and targeted Law directly with a formal request to circumscribe foreigners' powers in the administration of French finances.[29] On the other hand, if successful, Law would steer France in an opposite direction. By fully monetizing the economy, his system posed an existential threat to France's *parlements*, the one remaining intermediary political body that had the capacity to arrest France's decline, reverse the tide of destruction and corruption of morals, and check the Bourbon Crown's despotic ambitions. With Louis's death, the Duc d'Orléans "thought about again raising the temple and the idol out of the earth, he wanted the *parlements* to be regarded as the bulwark of the monarchy and the foundation of all legitimate authority" (Letter 92, 149). But France's public finances were severely impacted, having defaulted multiple times following the War of Spanish Succession, and Law, who had access to a desperate regent's ear, promised to rein in an unwieldy public debt that was enfeebling the Regency. The regent approved Law's system to restore France's international credibility, but it would come at the cost of his own citizens' creditworthiness. When Law began to make headway in French politics and finance, he disrupted an already teetering balance. Worse yet, his system would rob France of its moral foundations, as readers of *Persian Letters* witness from both Rica and Usbek's vantage points in letters 132 and 146.

Usbek's reflections in letter 146 should recall Rica's description of his experience in a Parisian café in letter 132, where he recounts how Law's system reversed the proper order of things in France. Eavesdropping, he overhears a well-to-do man complaining that he regretted having so many of his assets tied up in land, when he would rather live in Paris and have liquid assets ready to hand: "I would believe myself happier if I received a quarter of this wealth in money and portable goods" (Letter 132, 218). Returning to the same coffeehouse five or six months later, Rica hears a different story—a man sits in company, complaining that in spite of a large stash of banknotes and a good amount of silver, he is "ruined" and has nothing of consequence because he has no land. He witnesses still another man voicing hope for a social reversal of fortune under Law's system—a hope that "all the lackeys in Paris [will become] richer than their masters," should the Mississippi Company shares continue to rise in value (Letter 132, 219). Confidence in such a reversal of fortune would not have been out of place, as both travelers record in their writings home; Usbek writes of France in a 1717 letter to Ibben, "There is no country in the world where fortune is as inconstant as in this one. Every ten years a revolution takes place, which hurls the rich into extreme poverty and with rapid wings elevates the poor onto the summit of riches" (Letter 98, 158). Three years later, Rica writes to Ibben to note that he has witnessed the financial system change four times during his travels in France, and he has in fact seen Law's scheme turn the social hierarchy upside down, making the rich poor and the poor rich. He comments that Law has "turned the state like a second-hand dealer turns clothes; he appears to have placed on top what was beneath, and what was on top he reversed" (Letter 138, 228). In a further, more oblique reference to Law in letter 146, Usbek reflects on a case of ministerial corruption from his travels in the Indies, an example with obvious parallels to Law's exploits in France. There, he poses the rhetorical question: "What greater crime is there than the one a minister commits when he corrupts the morals of an entire nation, degrades the most generous souls, tarnishes the shine of high position, obscures virtue itself, and confounds the highest birth with universal scorn?" (Letter 146, 256). Law is not, in Montesquieu's representations of him in *Persian Letters*, simply an agent of chaos, a gambler, or a swindler who exemplifies the dangers of high finance and its speculative fictions. The deeper criticism levied in the text is that Law damaged the very fabric of society by reversing social norms and orders and debasing what was best about France—namely, its institutions of liberty—while elevating what was worst. His most serious crime was "the bad example he [set]" for the whole of society; this eclipsed even his "[dis-service to] his prince and [the financial ruin] of his people" (Letter 146, 255).

By stirring up the desire for riches at any moral cost and debasing the value of work, prudence, and probity, Law capitalized on and promoted the pathologies of commercial life. When combined with his poor example of civic integrity, his efforts to damage political institutions that might mitigate against the downsides of finance, and his elevation of the dishonesty and ambition that already characterized commercial life in France, Law's scheme did more than just bring financial ruin—it threatened moral and political ruin as well. Read in tandem with letter 132, it is clear that the reversal Rica and Usbek observe runs very deep, past the overturning of institutions and social orders all the way down to the morals and mores of French commercial society. It is this reversal, we argue, that made Law such a vexing figure to Montesquieu.

CONCLUSION

Law's fate as *Persian Letters'* symbolic villain is sealed when the drama comes full circle in letter 146, with Usbek detailing the system's tragic con-sequences. Other scholars have already noted the significance of the final letters' nonsequential ordering, suggesting that Montesquieu deliberately jux-taposes letter 146, the final letter that concerns Law's system, with the rapid collapse of Usbek's seraglio culminating in the suicide of his prized, virtu-ous wife, Roxane, in the remaining letters.[30] The Scottish financier's scheme aggravated commercial dishonesty in France and rendered it less manageable. The French thus came to mirror the first generation of Montesquieu's mythic Troglodytes, who, one recalls, were diagnosed with a mortal poison in their souls that made "the rules of equity . . . unknown." Not only is Law a despot with few peers, but in *Persian Letters* he becomes an avatar of political and social instability, the narrative's *summum malum*, first instantiated in the

Troglodyte allegory. In short, Law's debacle accelerated France's return to the first stage of the mythical Troglodytes' conjectural history.

It may appear bizarre that a banker represented a greater threat to liberty than the Bourbon Crown and the clergy, the two principal agents responsible for veering France toward despotism in the first place. The collapse of Usbek's seraglio forbodes the inevitable outcome of any society wholly governed by greed. It alerts readers to how commerce may accommodate despotism in the absence of robust honor-yielding institutions in place to mitigate against its pathological features. Yet in pathologizing commercial dishonesty, Montesquieu is not crafting simply a metaphor but an innovative medical analogy. When functioning optimally, a healthy human body is capable of modulating pathogens in its environment. Similarly, a healthy political body, whose institutions enliven a natural feeling of justice, can modulate and direct the so-called pathological features of commercial life—vanity, greed, ambition—to serve the public interest. Conversely, an external pathogen—in this case, Law's system—will exploit human beings' natural vulnerabilities, threatening to produce the incurable disease of self-interest and greed the Troglodyte doctor identifies in letter 11. Just as a virus proliferates itself by hijacking the body's endogenous cellular replication tools, we observe in letters 11 and 146 that once an unmodulated spirit of avarice takes hold in commercial life, it becomes self-proliferating, driven by *unchecked* but natural human passions. Yet Montesquieu's sympathetic satire of Parisian life offers an antidote to the pathologies of modern commerce that is germane to our own thinking about the morality of capitalism. Montesquieu's image of the regent "raising the temple and the idol out of the earth" should generate some optimism in the text's readers. With every generation that saw itself standing at the precipice of moral degeneration, their nations' existing institutions provided a pole of honor to keep everything on even keel. Montesquieu's panegyric on the *parlements* exhorts contemporary and future readers to unearth and build upon the existing institutions that give citizens a common pole of moral orientation to counterpoise the dysfunctional features of commercial modernity.

NOTES

1. The authors would like to thank Michael Mosher and participants in the December 2021 Conference on the 300th Anniversary of the *Persian Letters* at the University of Houston for their helpful comments on a previous draft. Parts of this chapter were originally published in Constantine Christos Vassiliou, *Moderate Liberalism and the Scottish Enlightenment: Montesquieu, Hume, Smith, and Ferguson* (Edinburgh: Edinburgh University Press, 2023).

2. Montesquieu, *The Spirit of the Laws*, ed. and trans Anne M. Cohler, Basia C. Miller, and Harold S. Stone (Cambridge: Cambridge University Press, 1989), II.4, 19, emphasis added.

3. For alternative accounts of Montesquieu's theoretical assessment of commercial society, cf. J. G. A. Pocock, *Machiavellian Moment: Florentine Political Thought and the Atlantic Republican Tradition* (Princeton, NJ: Princeton University Press, 1975); Mark Hulliung, *Montesquieu and the Old Regime* (Berkeley: University of California Press, 1976); Céline Spector, *Montesquieu: pouvoirs, richesses et sociétés* (Paris: Presses Universitaires de France, 2004).

4. Andrew S. Bibby, *Montesquieu's Political Economy* (New York: Palgrave Mac-Millan, 2016).

5. Thomas Pangle, *The Theological Basis of Liberal Modernity in Montesquieu's Spirit of the Laws* (Chicago: University of Chicago Press, 2010).

6. Janet Gleeson, *Millionaire: The Philanderer, Gambler, and Duelist Who Invented Modern Finance* (New York: Simon and Schuster, 1989).

7. For more detailed accounts of Law's system and important intellectual debates that surrounded its failure, cf. Bibby, *Montesquieu's Political Economy*, 21–26; Constantine Vassiliou, "Le système de John Law and the Spectre of Modern Despotism," *Lumen* 38 (2019): 161–78.

8. Montesquieu, *The Spirit of the Laws*, III.3, 22, emphasis added.

9. Ibid., XX.4, 340.

10. Ibid., XXIII.10, 344.

11. Catherine Larrère, "Montesquieu and Liberalism: The Question of Pluralism," in *Montesquieu and his Legacy*, ed. Rebecca Kingston (Albany: State University of New York Press, 2009), 283.

12. Ibid., 282.

13. Bibby, *Montesquieu's Political Economy*, 22.

14. All in-text citations to *Persian Letters* are from Montesquieu, *Persian Letters*, ed. Stuart Warner, trans. Stuart Warner and Stéphane Douard (South Bend, IN: St. Augustine's Press, 2017). They are cited by letter and page number.

15. Montesquieu's depiction of finance resonates with other commentaries across the Atlantic in the early 1720s, a pivotal moment in the financial revolution. In a contemporaneous literary reflection on a similar crisis unfolding in Britain—the South Sea Bubble—Jonathan Swift draws on similar imagery. He concludes a satirical poem on the South Sea scheme with a pithy account of its aftermath: "The nation then too late will find,/Computing all their cost and trouble,'/Directors' promises but wind,/ South Sea, at best, a mighty bubble." Jonathan Swift, "The South Sea Project," 1721. Like Law, the South Sea company directors bottled the wind, and invited investors into an empire of imagination that eventually collapsed in on itself.

16. Richard Sher, "From Troglodytes to Americans: Montesquieu and the Scottish Enlightenment on Liberty, Virtue, and Commerce," in *Republicanism, Liberty, and Commercial Society, 1649–1776*, ed. David Wootton (Stanford, CA: Stanford University Press, 1994), 368–402.

17. Cf. fn. 20.

18. Sher, "From Troglodytes to Americans," 402.

19. Cecil Courtney, cited in Bibby, *Montesquieu's Political Economy*, 27; Donald Desserud, "Virtue, Commerce and Moderation in 'The Tale of the Troglodytes': Montesquieu's Persian Letters," *History of Political Thought* 12, no. 4 (1991): 624.

20. Most interpreters assume that this tension was left unresolved in *Persian Letters* and draw from Montesquieu's later writings to reconstruct his theoretical response to the wealth and virtue problem. As Sonenscher notes, Montesquieu's *Considerations on the Causes of the Greatness of the Romans and Their Decline*, together with his *Notes on England* and *Reflections on Universal Monarchy*, "amounted to a . . . strong endorsement of the compatibility between wealth and virtue." Michael Sonenscher, *Before the Deluge: Public Debt, Inequality, and the Intellectual Origins of the French Revolution* (Princeton, NJ: Princeton University Press, 2009), 100.

21. For an excellent discussion, cf. Ryan Hanley's, "Distance Learning: Political Education in the *Persian Letters*," *Review of Politics* 83, no. 4 (2021): 533–54.

22. Letter 24 is full of such examples, including fraudulent "seers," women who artfully disguise their aging faces, and healers who concoct remedies against maladies both real and imagined.

23. For work on how bank paper and other financial instruments went from fantastical to ordinary in a British context, but with connections to the situation in early modern France, see Mary Poovey, *Genres of the Credit Economy: Mediating Value in Eighteenth- and Nineteenth-Century Britain* (Chicago: University of Chicago Press, 2008).

24. Pangle, *The Theological Basis of Liberal Modernity*, 4–5.

25. Lee Ward's chapter in this volume, "Female Modesty and the Spirit of Commerce in *Persian Letters*," provides an excellent discussion concerning Montesquieu's debt to Mandeville in *Persian Letters.*

26. Bibby, *Montesquieu's Political Economy*, 57.

27. Céline Spector, cited in Jonathan Walsh, "A Cultural Numismatics: The 'Chain' of Economics in Montesquieu's Lettres persanes," *Australian Journal of French Studies* 46 (2009): 147.

28. Franklin L. Ford, *Robe and Sword: The Regrouping of the French Aristocracy after Louis XIV* (Cambridge, MA: Harvard University Press, 1953), 84.

29. Antoin E. Murphy, *John Law: Economic Theorist and Policy-Maker* (London: Clarendon, 1997), 252.

30. Paul Vernière, cited in Walsh, "A Cultural Numismatics,"140.

BIBLIOGRAPHY

Bibby, Andrew S. 2016. *Montesquieu's Political Economy*. New York: Palgrave MacMillan.

Desserud, Donald. 1991. "Virtue, Commerce and Moderation in 'The Tale of the Troglodytes': Montesquieu's Persian Letters." *History of Political Thought* 12, no 4: 605–26.

Ford, Franklin L. 1953. *Robe and Sword: The Regrouping of the French Aristocracy after Louis XIV.* Cambridge, MA: Harvard University Press.

Gleeson, Janet. 1989. *Millionaire: The Philanderer, Gambler, and Duelist Who Invented Modern Finance*. New York: Simon and Schuster.

Hanley, Ryan. 2021. "Distance Learning: Political Education in the Persian Letters." *Review of Politics* 83, no. 4: 533–54.

Hulliung, Mark. 1976. *Montesquieu and the Old Regime*. Berkeley: University of California Press.

Larrèrre, Catherine. 2009. "Montesquieu and Liberalism: The Question of Pluralism." In *Montesquieu and his Legacy*, edited by Rebecca Kingston, 279–302. Albany: State University of New York Press.

Montesquieu. 1989. *The Spirit of the Laws*. Edited and translated by Anne M. Cohler, Basia C. Miller, and Harold S. Stone. Cambridge: Cambridge University Press.

———. 2017. *Persian Letters*. Edited by Stuart Warner; translated by Stuart Warner and Stéphane Douard. South Bend, IN: St. Augustine's Press.

Murphy, Antoin E. 1997. *John Law: Economic Theorist and Policy-Maker*. London: Clarendon.

Pangle, Thomas. 2010. *The Theological Basis of Liberal Modernity in Montesquieu's Spirit of the Laws*. Chicago: University of Chicago Press.

Pocock, J. G. A. 1975. *Machiavellian Moment: Florentine Thought and the Atlantic Republican Tradition*. Princeton, NJ: Princeton University Press.

Poovey, Mary. 2008. *Genres of the Credit Economy: Mediating Value in Eighteenth- and Nineteenth-Century Britain*. Chicago: University of Chicago Press.

Sher, Richard. 1994. "From Troglodytes to Americans: Montesquieu and the Scottish Enlightenment on Liberty, Virtue, and Commerce." In *Republicanism, Liberty, and Commercial Society, 1649–1776*, edited by David Wootton, 368–402. Stanford, CA: Stanford University Press.

Sonenscher, Michael. 2009. *Before the Deluge: Public Debt, Inequality, and the Intellectual Origins of the French Revolution*. Princeton, NJ: Princeton University Press.

Spector, Céline. 2004. *Montesquieu: pouvoirs, richesses et sociétés*. Paris: Presses Universitaires de France.

Swift, Jonathan. 1721. "The South Sea Project." The Literature Network. https://www.online-literature.com/swift/poems-of-swift/43/.

Vassiliou, Constantine. 2019. "Le système de John Law and the Spectre of Modern Despotism in the Political Thought of Montesquieu." *Lumen* 38: 161–78.

Walsh, Jonathan. 2009. "A Cultural Numismatics: The 'Chain' of Economics in Montesquieu's Lettres persanes." *Australian Journal of French Studies* 46: 139–54.

Chapter 8

The Political Economy of the *Persian Letters*; or, Self-Interest Wrongly Understood, in Three Lessons

Ryan Patrick Hanley

Je crois qu'il vaut mieux prendre une voie détournée et chercher

à en dégouter un peu les grands par la considération

du peu d'utilité qu'ils en retirent.[1]

"Self-interest is the greatest king in the world" (Letter 106, 288).[2] Thus claims Usbek, on the grounds that self-interest's commandments are more readily obeyed than those of any conventional king. Coming from Usbek, this is important stuff; command and control, after all, are his life. And coming in a book by Montesquieu, this is doubly important stuff; one of the pioneering political economists of the early eighteenth century, Montesquieu understood better than most the place of self-interest in moral and political and economic life.

For all these reasons, a reader who falls upon the above-quoted lesson might not unreasonably hope—even expect—to find in the text in which this lesson appears a guide to how self-interest ought to rule on its throne. But whatever else *Persian Letters* gives us, it doesn't give us this; whatever else it may be, *Persian Letters* is no normative treatise. As a result, readers seeking Montesquieu's guidance on how best to manage self-interest via moral norms and economic and financial institutions may be tempted to skip ahead to the more explicit lessons to be found in later writings such as the *Réflexions sur la monarchie universelle*, the *Pensées*, and *The Spirit of the Laws*.

Yet this, I think, would be a mistake. For while it's certainly the case that there are very few positive examples of self-interest well-managed in *Persian Letters*, the text teems with examples of mismanaged self-interest. Put differently: while *Persian Letters* is indeed conspicuously silent on the question of what ought to be done, it is a treasure house of tales and warnings of what ought not be done.[3] What follows chronicles three types of abuses of self-interest to be found in the text.

The first type of abuse might be given the heading of *excessively narrow self-interest*. Throughout *Persian Letters* we are shown examples of individuals and peoples whose self-interest restricts them to a form of a tunnel vision in which they become unable to account for any interests beyond their most immediate interests, whether the interests of others or even their own long-term interests. Among the most prominent examples on this front are the economic dysfunctions of the early Troglodytes and the economic dysfunctions that are the result of Colbert's mercantilism and Louis XIV's revocation of the Edict of Nantes. In all these cases, Montesquieu focuses on how excessively narrow self-interest impedes long-term economic growth.

A second type of abuse concerns *excessively restricted self-interest*. Institutions that aim to restrict or even obviate self-interest are prominent across *Persian Letters*, with the most prominent being Usbek's own seraglio. At first glance, the seraglio is likely to seem an unpromising place to seek out economic lessons; the primary themes of its story are less economic than political (e.g., the despotism of Usbek and his eunuchs) and moral (e.g., the relations of Usbek and his wives). Yet Montesquieu in fact depicts the seraglio and its odd commerce in ways that consistently draw on economic concepts, emphasizing that among the seraglio's failings is its perversion of self-interest in its effort to stifle it, a failing echoed in the account of the Ottoman Turks.

A third category of abuses can be gathered under the heading of *excessively enflamed self-interest*. Here Montesquieu examines the economic consequences of the interaction of rational self-interest with the passions of the imagination. By far the most prominent case of enflamed self-interest in *Persian Letters* is the frenzy unleashed by the system of John Law and the speculative risk-taking it encouraged. Yet Montesquieu's various analyses of several French social and economic institutions in place well prior to the advent of Law's ascendency reveal that this frenzy was in fact merely the apex of dispositions endemic to French society well before Law's arrival.

Taken collectively, these studies of the abuses of self-interest not only render *Persian Letters* an insightful economic text, but also reveal Montesquieu's sensitivity to the ways in which self-interest could be corrupted in a variety of distinct ways: when given too much encouragement, when given too little encouragement, and when given the wrong turn. The result is a text that repays the study of the statesman and political economist.

I

Montesquieu's economic teachings receive their first and arguably most prominent articulation in *Persian Letters* in Mirza and Usbek's famous exchange on the Troglodytes in letters 10–14. Usbek's history of the fall and rise and (potential) fall of the Troglodytes would have a long afterlife, and it remains today the first place political theorists tend to turn when they turn to *Persian Letters* for political insight.[4] But what exactly is the lesson the exchange teaches? On the face of it, it seems to be—and indeed is—a lesson about the dangers of self-interest. The obvious story of the political trajectory of the Troglodytes is that their relative flourishing as a people tracks the relative degree of self-interest to be found in the souls of their individual citizens. Yet in fact the lesson being taught here isn't simply a general warning about the dangers of self-interest, or even simply the "unlimited pursuit of self-interest,"[5] but rather a warning about the dangers of a very particular kind of self-interest.

In letter 11, Usbek begins his story. The tale of the Troglodytes begins violently: to underscore the wickedness and ferocity of the earliest Troglodytes, Usbek tells of how they not only killed their first king and "exterminated the whole royal family," but how they also went on to "massacre" the magistrates they elected in the wake of their regicide. But all of this is preparatory to Usbek's main point: the extermination of the ruling authorities gave rise not merely to a power vacuum but to a liberation of popular self-interest. Thus, after having eliminated their rulers, Usbek explains, "all the individuals agreed (*convinrent*) that they would no longer obey anyone—that each would exclusively look to their own interests without consulting those of others" (Letter 11, 146).

This moment is remarkable for several reasons. First, what Usbek is describing here is a sort of antisocial social contract, a remarkable and paradoxical collective agreement to privilege individual selfishness. Second, this liberation of individual selfishness in the wake of the death of the king will be later strikingly paralleled in the account in letter 92 of the mood in France after the death of Louis XIV (Letter 92, 247)—a discussion to which we will need to return. Third, and perhaps most importantly, the liberation of self-interest Usbek here describes is one of a very particular sort. In introducing it, he calls conspicuous attention to the fact that it is exclusive: what the

Troglodytes mean to privilege, that is, is a self-interest that looks only to the self and its needs, and indeed in the narrowest possible way. In the words of an unnamed Troglodyte: "I will think exclusively of myself; I will live happily. What does it matter to me whether others are happy? I will provide for all my needs, and as long as they're met, I won't worry that all the other Troglodytes may be miserable" (Letter 11, 146). To be self-interested in the Troglodyte manner is to be exclusively and very narrowly concerned with one's immediate and present needs at the expense of all other concerns, including both any concerns for the interests of others and any concerns for one's own long-range interests.[6]

In what follows, Montesquieu makes clear the degree to which this is a self-defeating strategy. In part it turns out to be self-defeating insofar as its exclusive focus on immediate needs blinds these narrowly self-interested Troglodytes to their future needs over the long term. Take, for example, the Troglodytes' attitude to labor: "I'll only work my field enough so that I can furnish myself with the grain that I need to feed myself: any more than that would be useless to me; I won't trouble myself for nothing." But it soon becomes clear that what seems rational to the self-interested in the short term is disastrous in the long term, and the Troglodytes' inability to think in terms of surplus, profit, and stockpiling in excess of immediate needs—as perhaps a more expansive sort of self-interest might encourage—leads almost all of them to "die of hunger" in leaner years (Letter 11, 146–47).

The commercial relations of the early Troglodytes are similarly governed by this excessively narrow understanding of self-interest. This becomes especially evident in their trading practices; later in letter 11 Usbek tells the story of a wool merchant who fleeces his evidently desperate customer only to discover that his customer is the seller of the wheat he himself needs. The result is that the price-gouging seller who arbitrarily raises the price of his wool to four times the ordinary market price finds himself forced to pay eight times the ordinary market price for his wheat (Letter 11, 147–48). This is obviously unsustainable, and it comes as no surprise at the beginning of letter 12 when Usbek says that the Troglodytes were killed off by their own wickedness and injustice (Letter 12, 148).

Usbek's history of the collapse of the Troglodytes provides a fictionalized lesson of the dangers of self-interest narrowly conceived and limited to a concern with immediate needs to the exclusion of all else. But reading on it becomes clear that this defining feature of early Troglodyte *moeurs* is also to be found in France. In *Persian Letters*, French figures are of course rarely mentioned directly by name, but one conspicuous exception is Colbert, finance minister to Louis XIV. In letter 59, Rica tells of a discussion he overheard, in which various figures mused on what things were like in the good old days, four decades earlier. The brief speech of one of the old aristocratic lords is revealing:

> My goodness! The state isn't governed anymore. Find me today a minister like Colbert. I knew him well, this Colbert: he was a friend of mine; he always made sure to pay me my pensions early. What good order the finances were in! Everyone was comfortable. But today I'm ruined. (Letter 59, 217)

Rica's old lord is cut from the same cloth as the early Troglodytes. Setting aside his tragicomic claim that "everyone" had been comfortable under Colbert (to say only the very least, Colbert's mercantilism created many losers alongside some winners), the lord shows his colors when he shifts quickly and ironically in the last two sentences from talking about the national welfare to his personal welfare, making clear in the process that it is ultimately only his personal welfare—and specifically the timely payments of his pensions—that he really cares about.[7]

This narrow-mindedness that Rica found in his old lord Montesquieu finds in French policy more generally. Take for example his very thinly veiled critique of the revocation of the Edict of Nantes in letter 85, in which Usbek recounts to Mirza the Persian shah's efforts to compel all the Armenians in the realm to convert to Islam or expatriate. Usbek explains that it was fortunate for Persia that the plan wasn't carried out, for it would have "done in Persian greatness" if the Persians had allowed themselves to be led by "blind devotion": "in proscribing all the Armenians, the upshot would be that in a single day all the businessmen and almost all the artisans of the realm would be eliminated." Usbek goes on to tell of the banishment of the Guebres from Persia, which then deprived Persia of its most industrious agricultural workers and in so doing nearly caused the nation to collapse—all the name of religious "devotion" (Letter 85, 258). Together these stories show what happens when a particular form of narrow-minded self-interest—here, religious orthodoxy—is privileged above the long-term economic interests of the nation.

II

The stories profiled above are all stories of ruin (or potential ruin) at the hands of self-interest of a certain type. Taken alone, these stories of political and economic ruin at the hands of self-interest might condition a reader to expect to find elsewhere in the text a celebration of the benefits of restricting self-interest; the lesson that too much self-interest is bad would seem to have as its concomitant the lesson that minimizing self-interest would be good. But *Persian Letters* directly contests this in its accounts of several regimes that tragically attempt to exterminate self-interest, often in the name of virtue. Indeed, far from flourishing, these are the most repressive, unnatural, and unproductive regimes described in the work.

Most prominent among these is Usbek's seraglio. The seraglio stands as one of the most important and best-studied institutions depicted in *Persian Letters*; as a number of influential studies have shown, Usbek's despotic rule over the seraglio anticipates much of the critique of despotic political rule that Montesquieu would emphasize in later works.[8] So, too, the seraglio also provides Montesquieu with an opportunity to study the dynamics of sexual and familial relations. But in addition to the political and erotic dynamics that drive it, the seraglio is also an economic institution governed by the same economic laws that govern other social institutions.[9]

In the first place, the seraglio has its origins in commerce. Usbek and his family, we are twice told, acquire their wives not through love and courtship, or even through familial agreement as marriages of convenience, but as property purchased in slave trade markets.[10] Thus, in letter 79, Montesquieu has the chief black eunuch tell Usbek how "yesterday some Armenians brought to the seraglio a young Circassian slave they wanted to sell," and how he luridly undressed and inspected her, and finding her worthy of his master, "put a golden ring on her finger" and "paid the Armenians" (Letter 79, 251). So, too, the chief eunuch soon after, writing from another seraglio (the seraglio of Ispahan rather than the seraglio of Fatmé), reports on how he "bought for your brother the governor of Mazenderan" one of the "many yellow women" just shipped in from Visapour (Letter 95, 272). Here and elsewhere, Montesquieu makes clear the degree to which the slave trade is both inhuman and economically inefficient; in the same vein Usbek later insists that the slave trade is in fact "absolutely useless," as evidenced by the fact that even as it depopulates Africa to carry slaves to America, America remains "deserted" and "doesn't profit from Africa's continual losses" (Letter 108, 307). The slave trade is thus a losing prospect all around, and it is yet on this foundation that the seraglio is built and sustained.

This is enough to suggest the flawed economic foundations of the seraglio. But these become even more evident in Montesquieu's account of how these dehumanized slaves are treated once they become Usbek's dehumanized wives. Usbek's treatment of his wives is founded on a very specific dynamic: a renunciation of freedom in the name of virtue. All his despotic control over his wives is indeed exercised with the word "virtue" on his lips (or the lips of his ministers). This trade-off between freedom and virtue invites us to consider it in both its erotic and economic dimensions. For in compelling his wives to sacrifice their private freedoms and interests in the name of "virtue," Usbek brings the ideals of classical republicanism to the seraglio, with predictable effects drawn out in detail. Specifically, the repression of natural self-interest in the name of virtue akin to self-renunciation inevitably leads not to elimination of self-interest but merely to rechanneling of it to new objects.[11]

In the seraglio we see this dynamic specifically at work in Usbek's attempts to stifle the interests of his wives in any man but himself, which only leads them to seek out other lovers in secret. The tyranny of virtue is thus tragically unsuccessful at suppressing natural desire and ultimately serves only to encourage illicit forms of sexual *commerce*. Thus the wives' reaction to the death of the chief eunuch: an event that marks both the end of the tyranny of virtue and the beginning of opportunities for "new joy" and "new satisfaction" (Letter 151, 365). This dynamic is similarly at work in the story of Usbek's eunuchs; castration eliminates neither their lusts nor their terrifying efforts to satisfy them. The futility of such efforts is well captured by Zélis in words attributed to Usbek: "One can stop being a man, but one can't stop feeling" (Letter 52, 209). And this dynamic ultimately finds its noblest expression in Roxane's defiant rejection of Usbek's "servitude" of "virtue" and her celebration of the "freedom" and "independence" that she uses to take another lover (Letter 161, 372–73).[12]

The consistent lesson across all these stories of the seraglio is that suppression of self-interest leads not to its extermination but merely its redirection. But this same lesson is to be found elsewhere in *Persian Letters*, and especially in the letters on population and growth. In this well-known sequence, Usbek and Rhédi reflect on the possible reasons for population decline over time, with Usbek particularly insistent that this decline can best be traced to "moral" rather than "physical causes" (Letter 113, 299). In his next letter, Usbek then tells Rhédi that the chief moral causes he has in mind are religious institutions that bear on the practices of marriage and reproduction.[13] Chief among his targets here are Muslim polygamy and the Christian divorce prohibition. But as interesting as Usbek's self-reflective reasons are for opposing the former of these—namely, for how it "wears out" (*épuiser*) men (Letter 114, 300)—his critique of the prohibition of divorce by the Christians especially demands attention. In letter 116, Usbek traces out the "terrible results" of this prohibition, which kills not just love but "hope." Among these results is that "a man grown sick and tired of his eternal wife soon will give himself over to prostitutes: a shameful commerce so contrary to society" (Letter 116, 304). In Western marriage, as in the seraglio, natural interests unnaturally confined lead not to withering away of such interests but to manifestations of them in ways counterproductive to the happiness of both the individual and the society.

In this way, Montesquieu's portraits of repressive sexual relationships in both the Persian east and the Christian west are tied to his conception of the difference between a healthy commerce and a "shameful commerce." Usbek further develops these lessons on the economic consequences of religious strictures on sexual self-interest in the letter that follows. Here he contrasts the "flourishing commerce" of Protestant countries with the stagnation and decline of Catholic countries that mandate priestly celibacy: in these, one finds "no longer any circulation, any commerce, any arts, any manufactures" (Letter 117, 306). And this lesson about the economic dangers of forced suppression is replicated elsewhere in Montesquieu's various accounts of other regimes that have similarly sought to repress self-interest by force. Most prominent on this front are the Ottoman Turks. For all Usbek's antipathy to the Ottomans, their imperial rule merely replicates on a grand scale his own approach to governing the seraglio. Introducing the Ottomans, Usbek describes their empire as "a sick body that sustains itself not by a gentle and moderate regimen, but by violent remedies that unceasingly wear it out [*l'épuisent*] and undermine it." And Usbek makes clear that it is their attitude to economics that is most uncompromising. Thus we learn that in Turkey, "the cultivation of the land and commerce" are "entirely abandoned"—in part because the Christians who work the land and the Jews who collect the taxes are "exposed to a thousand acts of violence," and in part because "land ownership is uncertain, with the result that the desire to improve it wanes" (Letter 19, 159). In this respect, the institutions of the Ottomans are similar to the economic institutions of their Russian enemies, who—we are told in one of the most troubling letters of the text—are similarly governed by an authority who is the "absolute master of the lives and the property of his subjects" (Letter 51, 204). The result is a people "incapable of commerce" (Letter 19, 159).

On the whole, the Eastern regimes of *Persian Letters* are depicted as hostile to self-interest. This becomes especially clear in the very way in which it characterizes Islam. Thus Usbek's key reflection on the economic consequences of Muslim *moeurs*:

> We see ourselves as travelers who must think only of another land: useful and lasting labors, cares taken to assure the fortunes of our children, projects that take longer than a short and fleeting life—such things seem to us extravagant. Tranquil in the present and without worry for the future, we take no pains to repair public buildings, or to clear uncultivated lands, or to cultivate those which are ready to be worked: we live in a state of general insensibility, and we leave it to Providence to take care of everything. (Letter 119, 308)

The lesson is clear: an indifference to the things of self-interest renders it impossible for individuals or states to flourish. Muslim *moeurs*, Usbek suggests, accomplish in the east what banishment of luxury would accomplish in the west: population decline, sapping of military strength, stifling of commerce and trade—all to the degree that "this state would be one of the most miserable ever in the world" (Letter 106, 289).[14]

III

The sins of self-interest are many, as we have seen. The early Troglodytes reveal the dangers of excessive self-interest, and the seraglio and its political analogues the dangers of attempting to excise self-interest. But where in the vast space between these two extremes does the proper middle lie? To help clarify this, Montesquieu introduces us to a third form of pernicious self-interest: the self-interest that has long defined France and its people and which tragically drew them to John Law and his system.

One of the most striking and ubiquitous themes of Usbek's and Rica's letters on the French is restlessness and impatience. Emblematic is letter 56 on the European addiction to gambling. Usbek tells us he has often watched players at a gaming table: "I have seen them in their hopes, in their fears, in their joys, and above all in their furies." And fury is the right word: obsessed with winning, devoid of reason, and caught in the grip of their passions, they seem like they "would never have time to be at peace, and that their lives would end before their despair" (Letter 56, 213). Yet this restlessness so evident in their gambling is hardly limited to their time at the table. The "disorder" (*dérangement*) so evident on their faces as they play their games of chance defines the rest of their lives as well. Rica is fascinated by the spectacle of these desperate Frenchmen running themselves ragged after wealth. In letter 87 he tells of a man who dedicated every waking moment of his life up to the day of his death to getting ahead, all of which serves only to earn him a tombstone that reads, "Here lies at rest one who never rested" (Letter 87, 262). And these sorts of figures are hardly outliers in France:

> This ardor for work, this passion of enriching oneself, passes from rank to rank, from the artisans up to the great. No one wants to be poorer than those they see immediately below them. In Paris you see men who have enough to survive until Judgement Day, who work unceasingly and runs the risk of cutting their days short in order to amass, they say, enough to live on. (Letter 106, 289).

France, and Paris in particular, is indeed a world of "continual motion," and what drives its restless and ceaseless motion is above all else the desire for wealth (Letter 24, 165). Yet alongside this restless passion for wealth, Rica and Usbek also find another and even more troubling force at work in France. This force is examined in a variety of letters, but especially in Rica's story of the deranged alchemist in letter 45. The alchemist arrives on Rica's doorstep in a crazed state, only to tell Rica that he that day discovered the secrets of Nicholas Flamel and can now transmute ordinary metals into "true gold" at will, which he believes will render him "richer than any man on earth" (Letter 45, 193).[15] For his part, Rica has nothing but contempt for this man who proposes to make something out of nothing. Yet the alchemist and his hopes are hardly outliers in France. After all, the art the alchemist claims to have discovered is the same one that the king has long practiced. Louis XIV, we are told, is himself "a great magician," for like the alchemist, he lacks gold—but unlike the alchemist, he can create some through his sleight of hand.[16] In particular, he is able to do this by selling offices, a practice that transmutes ordinary vanity into money to pay and feed and arm his soldiers. And as further evidence of his magic, we are told that "exercising his empire over the minds of his subjects, he makes them think as he wishes," and that "if he has only a million écus in his treasury and has need of two million, he need only persuade them that one écu is equal to two, and they believe him" (Letter 24, 165–66).[17]

Their restless pursuit of wealth, coupled with their willingness to subordinate their reason to their imaginations in matters of money, render the French especially susceptible to John Law's system. As Montesquieu makes clear, Law's system enjoyed the appeal it did because it appealed to both the desire of the restless to get rich quick and the propensity of those infatuated with wealth to allow their reason to be guided by their imaginations. The result of these combined desires is a particular form of self-interest, a self-interest that has been enflamed by imagination. And it is this form of self-interest that John Law—an even greater magician than Louis XIV or Rica's alchemist— was able to exploit, and in fact to such a degree that Montesquieu, with others, came to associate Law himself with despotism.[18]

Law's exploitative intentions are especially emphasized in letter 142. Here, in a fragment within a letter inside letter 142, we are given the thinly veiled story of John Law newly arrived in Bétique, a mythical land overflowing with gold and silver. In the fragment, Law's stand-in implores the inhabitants of Bétique to "leave the land of worthless metals, come to the Empire of Imagination, and I promise you riches that will astonish you." And he soon goes further: "People of Bétique, do you want to be rich? Imagine that I am very rich, and that you are also very rich; every morning put it into your head that your fortune doubled overnight; then get up, and if you have creditors, go pay them out of what you imagined, and tell them to imagine in their own right." Over time, however, the imagination of those he hopes to persuade flags, which only leads Law to "order" them to imagine again (Letter 142, 351). But the final lesson of this story comes not in this letter but in the following letter, which is on its face ostensibly dedicated to a very different topic. But here, in letter 143, Rica returns to "the virtue of amulets and the power of talismans" to remind us that all that glitters is not gold. And here Rica draws the very lesson that Montesquieu would have us draw from the spectacular failure of Law's system: "Human beings are very miserable! They float endlessly between false hopes and silly fears, and instead of trusting reason, they fabricate monsters that scare them or phantoms that seduce them"—indeed, to such a degree that they fall prey to "panic terrors" (Letter 143, 354). Panics and bubbles, driven by irrational and inflamed imaginations, are merely the economic analogues of the "ecstasies" and "raptures" and "delirium" characteristic of spiritual irrationalism (Letter 134, 333).

IV

Persian Letters can be read in a variety of ways, but at least one way it deserves to be read is as a commentary on Usbek's claim that "self-interest is the greatest king in the world." This was clearly a matter of very pressing concern for Montesquieu in the period in which he wrote *Persian Letters*. The political conditions of his world in the period covered in the text, and particularly that between the last years of Louis XIV and the early years of the Regency, he clearly found tumultuous and destabilizing.[19] The 1715 death of Louis XIV served only to liberate a wave of popular self-interest (see, e.g., Letter 92, 267), leading to cycles of inconstancy and "revolutions" in matters of riches and poverty (Letter 98, 276; see also Letter 138, 338–39). All of this seems unlikely to end well, and indeed the dominant note of letter 146, the last letter of the book in its chronological sequence, is one of tragedy. In part this reflects Usbek's experience of the collapse of his seraglio, which has just occurred. But there is also an evident economic dimension to this collapse, with Usbek lamenting he has seen "faith in contracts banished" at the very time that he has seen "suddenly born, in the hearts of all, an insatiable thirst for riches" and the emergence of a zero-sum world of economic winners and losers in which all "enrich themselves, not by honest work and noble industry, but by the ruin of Prince, State, and fellow citizens" (Letter 146, 346). With this the book comes full circle; after the collapse of Law's system, the French stand in the same precarious state as the Troglodytes at the moment of the election of their king. *Persian Letters* of course conspicuously fails to include the ending of either of these stories. So, too, it conspicuously fails to give us a normative solution to the economic problems they pose. But ultimately it is, as Paul Cheney has recently and rightly observed, "a tale of caution, not of despair."[20] As such, among the many reasons why it remains so valuable is for the reminder it offers of the urgent necessity of discovering such a solution.

NOTES

1. Montesquieu, "De la politique," in *Mélanges inédits de Montesquieu* (Bordeaux: G. Gounouilhou, 1892), 157. Albert Hirschman also cites this epigram in his influential chapter on Montesquieu's vision of commerce in *The Passions and the Interests: Political Arguments for Capitalism before Its Triumph* (Princeton, NJ: Princeton University Press, 1997), 76–77.

2. All citations to the *Persian Letters* are to the version in the *Œuvres complètes*, ed. Roger Callois (Paris: Gallimard, 1949), henceforth OC.

3. *Persian Letters* tends not to be engaged from the perspective of political economy. For important exceptions, see Céline Spector, *Montesquieu, Les Lettres persanes: De l'anthropologie à la politique* (Paris: Presses Universitaires de France, 1997), 60f.; Istvan Hont, "The Early Enlightenment Debate on Commerce and Luxury," in *The Cambridge History of Eighteenth-Century Political Thought*, ed. Mark Goldie and Robert Wokler (Cambridge: Cambridge University Press, 2006), 404–409; Jonathan Walsh, "A Cultural Numismatics: The 'Chain' of Economics in Montesquieu's *Lettres persanes*," *Australian Journal of French Studies* 46 (2009): 139–64; Florence Magnot-Ogilvy, "De l'îlot moraliste à la dissémination secrète: formes et significations de l'économique dans les *Lettres persanes*," in *Les Lettres persanes de Montesquieu*, ed. Christophe Martin (Paris: Presses de l'Université Paris-Sorbonne, 2013), 241–59; Andrew Scott Bibby, *Montesquieu's Political Economy* (London: Palgrave Macmillan, 2016), esp. 18–21; Constantine Vassiliou, "'Le Système de John Law' and the Spirit of Modern Despotism in the Political Thought of Montesquieu," *Lumen* 38 (2019): 161–78; and Paul Cheney, "Political Economy," in *The Cambridge Companion to Montesquieu*, ed. Keegan Callanan and Sharon R. Krause (Cambridge: Cambridge University Press, forthcoming).

4. I have elsewhere tried to examine the way in which these letters serve to provide a sort of political education; see Ryan Patrick Hanley, "Distance Learning: The Political Education of the *Persian Letters*," *Review of Politics* 83 (2021): 536–42.

5. Donald A. Desserud, "Virtue, Commerce, and Moderation in the 'Tale of the Troglodytes' in Montesquieu's *Persian Letters*," *History of Political Thought* 12 (1991): 608.

6. Cf. *Pensée* 1097, as quoted in Spector, *Montesquieu, Les Lettres persanes*, n. 43.

7. On Montesquieu's critique of Colbert's statism, see, e.g., Nicos E. Devletoglou, "The Economic Philosophy of Montesquieu," *Kyklos* 22 (1969): 530–41.

8. See esp. Diana J. Schaub, *Erotic Liberalism: Women and Revolution in Montesquieu's Persian Letters* (Lanham, MD: Rowman and Littlefield, 1995), 15–16 and passim.

9. Montesquieu's sensitivity to the ways in which "le sérail présente une 'économie' libidinale particulière qui tente de réguler les forces et les attributs du masculin et du féminin" has been noted by others; see Magnot-Ogilvy, "De l'îlot moraliste à la dissémination secrète," 256 and n. 32.

10. As noted in Schaub, *Erotic Liberalism*, 31.

11. In this context see especially Timothy Brennan's insightful study of the *doux commerce* thesis, which compellingly illuminates Montesquieu's association of virtue

with "inhuman repression," and shows how Montesquieu envisioned self-interest as an alternative to virtue. "Montesquieu's *Dur-commerce* Thesis," *History of European Ideas* 47 (2021): 698–712, quote at 699.

12. On the "inhumane repression" of the seraglio, see also ibid., 703–704.

13. See, e.g., Andrew Scott Bibby, "Markets and Morality in the Enlightenment: Neglected Aspects of Montesquieu's Case for Commerce," in *Are Markets Moral?*, ed. Arthur M. Melzer and Steven J. Kautz (Philadelphia: University of Pennsylvania Press, 2018), 220ff.

14. In this context see also Usbek's send-up of austerity measures in Letter 124, 1:315–16. On Montesquieu's understanding of the relationship of *moeurs* to commerce, see Bibby, "Markets and Morality in the Enlightenment," esp. 212, 224.

15. See also Rica's later comment on alchemy in Letter 135, 1:334.

16. In this context see also Usbek's pointed criticism of mining expeditions and the seemingly arbitrary values assigned to precious metals in Letter 118, 1:307. Walsh also notes the connections between the alchemist and Louis XIV and John Law; see Walsh, "A Cultural Numismatics," 142, 149–50.

17. Usbek himself at times uses a similar argument; see, e.g., his comparison of the arts of goldsmiths and other producers of luxury goods, who, like the painter, are able to transform one pistole's worth of materials into products worth 50 pistoles simply by mixing their labor (Letter 106, 1:289).

18. See esp. Thomas E. Kasier, "Money, Despotism, and Public Opinion in Early Eighteenth-Century France: John Law and the Debate on Royal Credit," *Journal of Modern History* 63 (1991): 20, 22–23; Walsh, "A Cultural Numismatics," 141–45; Paul Cheney, *Revolutionary Commerce: Globalization and the French Monarchy* (Cambridge, MA: Harvard University Press, 2010), 54; Cheney, "Political Economy"; Bibby, *Montesquieu's Political Economy*, esp. 18–21; Magnot-Ogilvy, "De l'îlot moraliste à la dissémination secrète," 248–49; and esp. Vassiliou, "'Le Système de John Law,'" passim.

19. See esp. Vassiliou, "'Le Système de John Law,'" 162–68.

20. Cheney, "Political Economy," 292.

BIBLIOGRAPHY

Bibby, Andrew Scott. "Markets and Morality in the Enlightenment: Neglected Aspects of Montesquieu's Case for Commerce." In *Are Markets Moral?*, edited by Arthur M. Melzer and Steven J. Kautz, 209–34. Philadelphia: University of Pennsylvania Press, 2018.

———. *Montesquieu's Political Economy*. London: Palgrave Macmillan, 2016.

Brennan, Timothy. "Montesquieu's *Dur-commerce* Thesis." *History of European Ideas* 47 (2021): 698–712.

Cheney, Paul. "Political Economy." In *The Cambridge Companion to Montesquieu*, edited by Keegan Callanan and Sharon R. Krause. Cambridge: Cambridge University Press, forthcoming.

————. *Revolutionary Commerce: Globalization and the French Monarchy.* Cambridge, MA: Harvard University Press, 2010.

Desserud, Donald A. "Virtue, Commerce, and Moderation in the 'Tale of the Troglodytes' in Montesquieu's *Persian Letters*." *History of Political Thought* 12 (1991): 605–26.

Devletoglou, Nicos E. "The Economic Philosophy of Montesquieu." *Kyklos* 22 (1969): 530–41.

Hanley, Ryan Patrick. "Distance Learning: The Political Education of the *Persian Letters*." *Review of Politics* 83 (2021): 536–42.

Hirschman, Albert. *The Passions and the Interests: Political Arguments for Capitalism before Its Triumph.* Princeton, NJ: Princeton University Press, 1997.

Hont, Istvan. "The Early Enlightenment Debate on Commerce and Luxury." In *The Cambridge History of Eighteenth-Century Political Thought*, edited by Mark Goldie and Robert Wokler, 379–418. Cambridge: Cambridge University Press, 2006.

Kasier, Thomas E. "Money, Despotism, and Public Opinion in Early Eighteenth-Century France: John Law and the Debate on Royal Credit." *Journal of Modern History* 63 (1991): 1–28.

Magnot-Ogilvy, Florence. "De l'îlot moraliste à la dissémination secrète: formes et significations de l'économique dans les *Lettres persanes*." In *Les Lettres persanes de Montesquieu*, edited by Christophe Martin, 241–59. Paris: Presses de l'Université Paris-Sorbonne, 2013.

Montesquieu, Charles Louis de Secondat, Baron de. *Œuvres complètes.* 2 volumes. Edited by Roger Callois. Paris: Gallimard, 1949.

————. *Mélanges inédits de Montesquieu.* Bordeaux: G. Gounouilhou, 1892.

Schaub, Diana J. *Erotic Liberalism: Women and Revolution in Montesquieu's Persian Letters.* Lanham, MD: Rowman and Littlefield, 1995.

Spector, Céline. *Montesquieu, Les Lettres persanes: De l'anthropologie à la politique.* Paris: Presses Universitaires de France, 1997.

Vassiliou, Constantine. "'Le Système de John Law' and the Spirit of Modern Despotism in the Political Thought of Montesquieu." *Lumen* 38 (2019): 161–78.

Walsh, Jonathan. "A Cultural Numismatics: The 'Chain' of Economics in Montesquieu's *Lettres persanes*." *Australian Journal of French Studies* 46 (2009): 139–64.

Chapter 9

Female Modesty and the Spirit of Commerce in Montesquieu's *Persian Letters*

Lee Ward

In a number of passages in *The Spirit of the Laws* (1748) Montesquieu acknowledged his indebtedness to Bernard Mandeville's *Fable of the Bees* (1714) for the argument that the consumption of luxury goods by the rich funds the wages of the poor.[1] In this sense, Montesquieu's political economy subscribed to Mandeville's maxim that private vices can redound to the public benefit. Here I propose to explore the less frequently observed connection between Mandeville's defense of commerce and Montesquieu's earlier work the *Persian Letters* (1721).[2] In particular, I examine the way in which Mandeville's critique of traditional arguments for female modesty is reflected in Montesquieu's observations on women in the *Persian Letters*. In his presentation of the contrast between Persian and French attitudes toward female modesty, between the confinement in the seraglio of Ispahan and the relative freedom and cultural fluidity of the Parisian salon, Montesquieu identified the importance of gender roles in shaping the political, social, and economic dimensions of modern commercial life. I conclude that, following Mandeville's lead, the early Montesquieu believed that overturning traditional conceptions of female modesty was a fundamental precondition toward the establishment of commercial society, and thus the *Persian Letters* adumbrated key themes in Montesquieu's larger project of promoting commerce in the later *Spirit of the Laws*.

My argument proceeds in the following manner. First, I will recount the main features of Mandeville's controversial argument about the public benefits of private vice. While the connection between Mandeville's praise of vice and the spirit of commerce is well known, I will highlight the less frequently remarked prominent role Mandeville assigned to the overcoming of traditional ideas of female modesty as a spur to the conspicuous consumption of luxury goods vital for the development of commercial society. I then examine Montesquieu's treatment of the theme of female modesty in the *Persian Letters*, focusing on the contrast he draws between the harshly enforced modesty of the Persian seraglio, on one hand, and the more permissive culture of gender relations in Bourbon France, on the other. The third section considers the pivotal role Montesquieu, following Mandeville, identifies with French women largely liberated from the mores of traditional female modesty, who constitute the driving social force behind the establishment of a commercial society characterized by the love of fashion, the taste for luxury, and a complex division of labor. I conclude by reflecting briefly upon the extent to which Montesquieu believed the society of women and the spirit of commerce could restrain the absolutist tendencies of the Bourbon ancien régime.

THE MANDEVILLEAN MOMENT

The genesis of the *Fable of the Bees* was the lengthy doggerel-verse style poem entitled "The Grumbling Hive: or Knaves turn'd Honest," published by Mandeville in 1705. Nearly a decade later, in 1714, he repackaged this poem in a longer study including additional essays on the origin of moral virtue and a substantive commentary on the "Grumbling Hive." The central paradox of the *Fable* is presented in the subtitle "Private Vices, Publick Benefits." The "Grumbling Hive" served as a literary illustration of the proposition that demonstrable social good can arise from the "vilest and most hateful qualities" of bees, and, of course, human beings.[3] The poem tells the tale of how a dynamic, prosperous, freedom-loving hive suffered economic and political decline due to moral regeneration. In the flourishing hive, millions of bees worked busily to satisfy their own "lust and vanity" (F 18). These bees are not paragons of austere Calvinist virtue, but rather brazen patrons of corruption: "There was not a Bee but that would, get more . . . than he should" (F 22). The sword of justice was not impartial as it checked only "the desperate and the poor" (F 23). Far from generating distrust and social breakdown, the greedy, selfish bees all pursuing their own interest strengthened the polity: "Such were the blessings of that State; Their crimes conspired to make them great" (F 24). With the advent of a moral reform movement in the hive, the newly chastened bees, now serious about virtue, precipitated a rapid decline in prosperity as luxury goods were banned, to the great detriment of trade, and a whole host of occupations tied to trade and manufacture disappeared from the economy of the hive. Eventually economic stagnation encouraged foreign attack, which was repulsed only with great loss of insect life. Reflecting on the sad fate of the moralistic hive, we realize: "Fraud, Luxury and Pride must live, while we the Benefits receive" (F 36).

The seriousness of the moral paradox at the heart of the *Fable* somewhat redeems Mandeville's palpable delight at provoking the righteous indigna-tion of the better sort of reader, for he situated his own piece of satire in the very sanctum of modern ethical realism. Echoing Machiavelli and Hobbes, Mandeville complains that "most writers are always telling men what they should be, and hardly trouble their heads with telling them what they really are" (F 39).[4] The concept Mandeville identifies to encapsulate this tendency toward hypermorality is *rigorism*.[5] In the *Fable*, rigorism primarily means rational control over selfish passions by which "Man, contrary to the impulse of Nature, should endeavor the benefit of others, or the conquest of his own Passions out of a Rational Ambition of being good" (F 48–49). The major psychological claims made by rigorists are that "there could be no virtue without Self-denial" and vice inheres in every effort "to gratify any of [one's] Appetites" (F 323, 156, 48–49). Central to Mandeville's assault on the tra-ditional ideal of virtue is, then, a reconsideration of the moral and political significance of the natural human passions and desires.

Mandeville rejects his contemporary the Third Earl of Shaftesbury's argu-ment that human beings are naturally sociable.[6] Rather, he proceeds from the Hobbesian assumption that "no Species of Animals is, without the Curb of Government, less capable of agreeing long together in Multitudes than that of Man" (F 41). How, then, does Mandeville account for the origins of the prejudice in both the classical and Christian traditions in favor of the value and naturalness of moral virtue? He provides a rather abecedarian philosophi-cal anthropology whereby "skillful Politicians" devised "the first Rudiments of Morality" in order to "render man useful to each other as well as tractable" (F 47). Indeed, for Mandeville, the major civilizational achievement of the "Lawgivers and other wisemen, that have laboured for the Establishment of Society" lies in convincing naturally passionate and selfish individuals that "it was more beneficial for every body to conquer than indulge his Appetites, and much better to mind the Publick than what seem'd his private inter-est" (F 42). The cunning of legislators and moralists produced such great effects precisely because the appeal of virtue flattered people's vanity insofar as they praised the "highest Good to which Mortals could aspire" and set forth "with unbounded Praises the wonders of our Sagacity and Vastness of Understanding" (F 43).

As is well known, Mandeville's critique of the traditional idea of moral vir-tue issued quite explicitly in service of an argument for commerce: that is, in defense of the industrious and luxuriating hive. As he concludes: "No Society can be rais'd into such a rich and mighty Kingdom, or so rais'd, subsist in their Wealth and Power for any considerable Time, without the Vices of Man" (F 229). So pervasive is the salutary effect of vice that it even animates philanthropy: "Pride and Vanity have built more Hospitals than all the Virtues together" (F 261). Perhaps what has been less discussed is Mandeville's view of the influential role of the revaluation of female shame and modesty in the emergence of commercial society.

In Mandeville's gloss commentary on the *Fable*, he singles out the idea of natural modesty among women as one of the primary legacy effects of the classical and Christian tradition of moral virtue. In particular, he targets the mistaken notion that "the difference of modesty between Men and Women" is a product of nature rather than "altogether owing to early Instruction" (F 72). In the socialization process, young girls "begin to observe how careful the women, she converses with, are of covering themselves before Men" (F 69). Little girls, unlike little boys, are habituated to develop an acute sense of shame at a very early age in order to ensure that by "Her Looks, as well as Actions" she can repel the "ever-watchful Look" of a seducer (F 70). However powerful the early education in chastity (and shame) may be, nonetheless Mandeville insists that "the Modesty of Women is the Result of Custom and Education" (F 65). The vast apparatus of traditional virtue has, then, for at least one of its major goals, the steady and dependable production of the modest, humble, and dour *hausfrau*.

Thankfully, in Mandeville's view, the education in modesty among females can be significantly undone by the proper encouragement of the very natural resources of vanity among young (as well as not-so-young) women. Indeed, the success of commercial society seems to depend upon unleashing the taste for luxury and adornments among ladies: "It is incredible what vast quantity of Trinkets as well as Apparel are purchas'd and used by Women" (F 227). Mandeville rebuts the stern moralists who traditionally laud sober women: "The variety of Work that is perform'd, and the number of hands employ'd to gratify the Fickleness and Luxury of Women is prodigious" (F 226). In a stunning reversal of the regnant theories of matronly virtue, Mandeville insists that it is "the Worst of Women and most profligate of the Sex" that contribute most through their "Consumption of Superfluities" to providing for the honest livelihood of "many peaceable Drudges" simply trying to make ends meet on the production line (F 225). Mandeville assesses that if wealthy women were to reduce their purchases of "the richest Clothes" and "other Expences [*sic*]," the loss to economic productivity would be a "Calamity to such a Nation" as commercial England (F 226).

It is perhaps fitting that the primary and vivid example Mandeville advanced to demonstrate the overarching harmony of interests that animates the laissez-faire ideal of commercial life related to women's fashion: "the silly and capricious Invention of Hoop'd and Quilt'ed Petticoats" has produced more blessings than the finest works of theology, indeed nothing "employ'd so many Hands, [and] honest industrious Hands, as the abominable improvement of Female Luxury" (F 356). In a remarkable foreshadowing of Adam Smith's theory of the division of labor, Mandeville enthuses: "What a bustle is there to be made in several Parts of the World, before a fine Scarlet or Crimson Cloth can be produced, what multiplying of Trades and Artificers much be employ'd" (F 356).[7] For Mandeville, the public benefits derived from the private vice, or at least indulgence of vanity and luxury, reflected in the crimson hooped petticoat of the debutant and manipulative young wife would provide perhaps the defining argument for the liberation of the passions in commercial society.

MODESTY FROM THE SERAGLIO TO THE SALON

Female modesty is arguably one of the central themes of the *Persian Letters*. The differing role of women in Persia and France presents perhaps the chief cultural contrast between East and West. The stark disjunction between the imagery of the cloistered harem of the Orient and the liberated women of the Occident highlights the public presence of French women. Whether at court, the salon, or the theatre, women are embedded visibly and formatively in the complex fabric of French social life. The voice of Persian women is, however, channeled through the distorted moral vision of Usbek's harem, a toxic social milieu characterized by enforced modesty and a hypereroticized conception of duty.

Persian gender relations are institutionalized in a multilayered system of slavery with both the denatured and brutalized men (eunuchs) and utterly objectified females in the seraglio all bound in service to the patriarchal Lothario (and in Usbek's case) absentee ruler. Modesty is the potent, active principle in these relations, for by Usbek's instructions the eunuchs are bondsmen of his wife-slaves until, with the "slackening of shame and modesty" among the women, they are transformed into a proxy for the master himself (Letter 2, 6). Usbek's emphasis on the centrality of preserving the sense of shame and modesty among the seraglio women penetrates into the eunuch's self-understanding as the "First Eunuch" confides to Ibbi, another of Usbek's slaves: "I have never had any words in my mouth except duty, virtue, shame, modesty (*les mots de devoir, de vertu, du pudeur, de modestie*)" (Letter 9, 16).[8] Confinement undermines Persian claims about the naturalness of female modesty inasmuch as it requires the physical and psychological mutilation of some males and the near total surveillance and repression of the social passions among the subject women.

The paradox of Persia: modesty is a public virtue masking private vice. Strictly enforced modesty encourages shamelessness and vanity. Natural modesty is replaced by brute, but spirited, physicality, as Usbek's wife Zachi recounts for him her victory in a pornographic beauty contest among the wives: "We had to strip ourselves of these ornaments that had become an inconvenience to you; we had to appear in your sight in the simplicity of nature. I considered shame as nothing; I thought only of my glory" (Letter 3, 7). Confinement not only heightens the fixation on physical attraction and sexual desire. Even in the context of Usbek's lengthy absence, vanity assumes a quasi-official role in the daily routine of the harem wives as another of Usbek's wives, Fatmé, assures him: "Think not your absence has made me neglect a beauty that you cherish" (Letter 7, 11).

The arena of frustrated sexual desire and mortifying restrictions on natural human interactions means, not surprisingly, the seraglio is in reality a den of deceit. The anxiety and emotional strain that festers throughout the decade or so of Usbek's absence in France finally, and predictably, explodes in open rebellion. Amid the chaos of the seraglio crisis, nature reasserts itself, however tragically. Usbek's favorite wife, the indomitable Roxane, reveals to him in her last moments: "Yes, I deceived you; I seduced your eunuchs; I played with your jealousy; and I know how to turn your frightful seraglio into a place of delights and pleasure" (Letter 161, 267). In her suicidal defiance of a selfish, tyrannical man, the harem wife, sexual captive par excellence, exposes the profoundly unnatural demands of a system of harshly enforced modesty that deprives women of meaningful companionship and satisfying family life with children, while the husband-despot ponders the great questions of justice in the West. Roxane taunts her tormentor: "How could you think that I was credulous enough to imagine that I existed in the world only in order to worship your every caprice?" (Letter 161, 268). The relations of men and women, and nature and convention more generally, are simplified in the savage passion and brutal repression of the seraglio.

By comparison, gender relations are at once more natural and yet also more complicated in France. Here the primary authorial gaze shifts from the mixture of sublimated hatred and obtuse moralism of the exchanges between Usbek and his wives and eunuchs, to the often playful, but typically insightful, observations of the more sympathetic Persian traveler Rica. Commentators generally conclude that Usbek's analysis is weightier intellectually than his younger companion's because the subject matter of Usbek's reflections is often explicitly philosophical and theological, whereas Rica has greater affinity for social commentary and mocking the foibles of French polite society.[9] I would suggest, however, that for purposes of understanding the connection between overturning traditional ideas of female modesty and the spirit of commerce, Rica is the most important figure in the *Persian Letters*.

Rica's observations on female modesty are introduced in one of his first letters, written soon after his arrival in Paris. In his delightfully inexpert account of a visit to the theatre, Rica confuses the audience for the actors and mistakes the finery of the wealthy women in the balcony for muffs worn "due to modesty" to hide their bare arms (Letter 28, 46). It is there Rica made the acquaintance of one of the "principal actresses," while she was undressing backstage. The content of the letter she later sent to Rica, which he transmitted to an unknown correspondent, is replete with candid revelations about the dubious status of modesty among French women of the theatrical set. Sadly, the self-described "most virtuous actress at the opera" confesses to being "the unhappiest girl in the world" after having been seduced by a "young abbé," who has left her pregnant and "now so big that I can no longer dare to appear on stage" (Letter 28, 48). The unfortunate actress, inquiring about her prospects in new pastures in Persia, offers Rica the benefit of a French woman's assessment of the significance of female propriety when she concludes "it is easier for a woman of good birth to lose her virtue than her modesty (*il est plus facile de faire perdre la vertu que la modestie*)" (Letter 28, 48).[10] Apart from the ironic reference to the role of social class in judging female moral behavior, Rica's actress friend helpfully highlights a pivotal distinction between recognizing virtue as reflecting an internal disposition of character and modesty as inhabiting an external, and socially fluid, realm of appearances.

The public-private distinction central to the Persian conception of enforced modesty effectively dissolves in France, where culturally permissive attitudes toward marital infidelity sever even the most basic connection between female modesty and chastity, or at least between the external appearance of modesty as a signifier of sorts of sexual restraint. As Rica relates: "The French hardly ever talk about their wives. This is because they are afraid to speak about them in front of people who know them better than they do" (Letter 55, 89). The societal agreement not to allow infidelity to destroy the family is, in Rica's view, a "tacit convention" among the French "that brings happiness to both sexes" (Letter 55, 90). Rica hastens to add, rather impishly, that his French guides assure him that there are indeed some virtuous French women, but "they were all so ugly one would have to be a saint in order not to hate virtue" (Letter 55, 90).

The convention that enforces permissive attitudes toward infidelity in France is in its own way a soft form of tyranny against the hapless cuckold who weakly seeks recourse in "the necessity of law" in order to "make up for the charms he lacks" (Letter 55, 90). Such a character is castigated as a "disturber of the public peace" (Letter 55, 90). There is, of course, a certain rough natural justice underlying French permissiveness: namely, the individual man or woman's capacity and effort to generate love, affection, and sexual desire.

As Rica relates, the marriage vow in France includes an implicit caveat that each partner promises "to be loveable always," and if this promise is broken, "they no longer believe themselves to be bound by theirs" (Letter 55, 90–91). The private is made public in France because an underlying philosophy of erotic naturalism pervades public attitudes and social institutions, if not necessarily the formal laws and religious strictures of the church.

Perhaps the defining image representing the collapse of the public ideal of modesty in Rica's account of Regency France is contained in the hilarious scene at the courthouse in letter 86. Here Rica expresses to an unnamed correspondent his impression that scarcely any vestiges of traditional patriarchy are left in France, where the civil law always sides against the "jealous husband, the sullen father, and the disagreeable master" (Letter 86, 140). The French Palace of Justice is a veritable eighteenth-century *Jerry Springer Show* wherein on any given day "a modest girl comes to confess the torments of her virginity too long guarded," a "shameless woman comes to make known the outrages she has committed against her husband," while yet another woman "with similar modesty" announces publicly her disappointment in "bearing the title of wife without enjoying it" (Letter 86, 141). The legal process is a reflection of public opinion, for in these tribunals "they follow the voice of the majority," even though Rica insists experience proves "it would be better to heed the voice of the minority" (Letter 86, 141–42). It is in the public space in France that one glimpses into "the secrets of the families," exposed to the light of day amid the scattered debris of "agitated fathers, abused girls, unfaithful lovers, and sullen husbands" (Letter 86, 141).

The more serious political implications of the spectacle in the courthouse relate to Montesquieu's pessimistic judgment on the state of legal and political institutions in France at the time. It is Usbek who most directly verbalizes Montesquieu's concern for the future of moderate government when he observes: "The *parlements* resemble those ruins that we tread underfoot . . . their authority will continue to languish unless some unforeseen situation comes to be and gives back strength and life to it" (Letter 92, 149). The debauched judicial process of Rica's telling is perhaps the predictable outcome of the long-term centralization of political power in Bourbon France that has sapped much of the vitality out of the intermediary institutions that once anchored the nation's moderate monarchy.[11] In lieu of a strong institutional foundation for constitutional balance, the permissive cultural attitudes toward modesty that, as Mandeville proposed, support commercial mores would assume great significance for Montesquieu's vision of political liberty.

The position of women in French public and social life provoked Rica's most important reflections on the nature of gender relations. Among his very early impressions of Paris was his astonishment at the leading role French women played in their opposition against Pope Clement XI's papal bull, which forbade them to read the Bible (Letter 24, 41). French women, "indignant over this insult to their sex," launched a "revolt, which divided the entire Court, the entire Kingdom, and every family" (Letter 24, 41). The matrons of the salon and belles of the theatre in France have a degree of political and social valence that their cloistered sisters in Persia could scarcely imagine. The newly arrived Rica finds the whole debate about women's status in the Christian faith perplexing because, to his mind, the Catholic "mufti" was merely confirming the general principles of Islamic Holy Law, according to which women are inferior to men and "will not enter into paradise" (Letter 24, 41).

Later Rica will admit to harboring doubts about his inherited religious prejudices about the inferiority of women. He confides to his Turkish friend Ibben that in Europe "there is a great question among men to know whether it is more advantageous to deprive women of liberty or to allow then to keep it" (Letter 38, 60). Characteristically for Rica, the question of the intrinsic rightness of female emancipation rather quickly devolves into a comparison of the degree of sexual satisfaction offered to men relative to the immodesty of their wives. The deciding factor in this debate seems to be a man's aptitude for uneasiness: that is, whether "the Asiatics" are correct to confine their women in order "to calm their uneasiness (*inquiétude*)" or whether European men with their coquettish wives are "right not to have any uneasiness at all" (Letter 38, 61).[12] The issue of natural equality or inferiority of the sexes is explored most directly not by Rica but by a "gallant philosopher," who argues that by the standard of natural law, the "empire" that men hold over women "is a veritable tyranny" deriving from the simple fact that women "are gentler than we are, and, consequently, more humane and reasonable" (Letter 38, 61). That is to say, in most places women allow men to rule them despite the "natural empire" they have over men, "that of beauty, which is irresistible" (Letter 38, 61).

The gallant philosopher clearly made an impression on Rica.[13] The Persian voyager admits to one Muslim correspondent, "although it shocks our morals," history does indicate that "among the most polished peoples, women have always had authority over their husbands" (Letter 38, 62). As a point of comparison, the natural power of beauty can in some sense hold its own historically against brute physical force. But Rica confesses some guilt about adopting the Occidental taste for paradox instead of simply embracing the Prophet's injunction that husbands "have the advantage of one degree" over their wives (Letter 38, 62). Is France one of those "most polished nations" in which women rule husbands? As we have seen, the relaxed attitude to sexual promiscuity seems to apply evenly in France. But where women do exercise a kind of rule in France is in the informal network of noble women who serve as mistresses to powerful men in the government. These women, Rica informs us, "form a kind of republic" that shapes the political agenda of the nation (Letter 107, 175). But unlike the handful of women related by blood or marriage to the Persian king, the "republic" of politically connected noble women in France constitutes simply an elite expression of the more basic condition of the country, "where women in general govern, and not only take in all of the authority wholesale, but even parcel it out among themselves retail" (Letter 107, 175).

Perhaps the greatest power women exercise in French society is, however, not political per se, but on the level of fashioning mores. When Rica admits that he finds himself "effortlessly" conforming to European morality, his primary evidence is that he is "no longer so astonished to see five or six women in a house with five or six men, and I find that this is not badly conceived" (Letter 63, 102). Frequent exposure to women in social settings leads Rica to the realization that "I know women only since I am here" (Letter 63, 102). The mores of Persian life are derived from fear, not nature, and as such they produce a uniformity of character that is false precisely because it is forced. The naturalness of social relations in France does not mean that gender roles are free of dissimulation and superficiality. Indeed, Rica mocks French women's susceptibility to the "bantering wit" of the gallant whose charms "naturally made for the boudoir" have succeeded in forming the French national character as a whole (Letters 63, 102; 82, 135).

Nonetheless, despite French women's predisposition toward frippery, there is a certain pragmatic wisdom in their attitudes toward male power. For instance, one beautiful lady at court, "worthy of being looked upon by our monarch," inquired broadly of Rica about various aspects of Persian morality, especially "the way of life of Persian women" (Letter 141, 232). She found the idea of one man shared by multiple wives in a suffocating confinement utterly repugnant: "She could not see the happiness of one without envy, or the condition of the others without pity (*Elle ne put voir sans envie le bonheur de l'un et sans pitié la condition des autres*)" (Letter 141, 232).[14] There is a degree of moral seriousness in her reasoning, given that in the contrast between her envy for the satisfied sexual desires of the one and the pathetic servitude of the others, this French noblewoman felt a certain disgust at the spiritualized libertinism animating Persian polygamy.[15] This challenge to Persian mores by a beautiful Western woman elicits Rica's creative talents (and no doubt his sexual desire) as he composed for her entertainment an elaborate story, a "travestied" version of a Persian tale that amounts to a mystical fable of female empowerment and revenge fantasy for the seraglio wives seeking ultimate justice against their cruel oppressor. There is little reason to doubt this French noblewoman would appreciate Rica's efforts and likely delight in the imaginary triumph of her Persian sisters.

The contrast between Rica's and Usbek's perceptions of French women in comparative context is arguably Montesquieu's version of Mandeville's project to reevaluate a commercial society's attitude toward female modesty. While Rica is perhaps somewhat naive about the degree to which French women expose their true thoughts to him, he compares remarkably well to the self-satisfied and morally obtuse Usbek. When Usbek lauds his slave-wife Roxane for her spirited resistance against his repeated attempted rapes, he described it as a "battle between love and virtue" (Letter 26, 43). But Usbek's attempt to contrast the "virtue" of the desperate denizens of the seraglio, on one hand, and the women of France, "where neither shame nor virtue is known," on the other, backfires spectacularly as he reveals his incapacity to acknowledge genuine moral agency in women (Letter 26, 43). If the relative freedom of French women from the strictures of Persian-style modesty does not lead to "horrible excess" of debauchery, it is not so much that "nature revolts" against women's freedom (Letter 26, 45). Rather, as Rica gradually seems to recognize, overturning harsh ideals of female modesty and gender segregation illuminated greater possibilities for equality between men and women than the stifling pseudonaturalism of traditional patriarchy and religious orthodoxy could likely ever countenance. Moreover, as we shall see, this new orientation toward female modesty would be a vital element in Montesquieu's conception of commercial society.

WOMEN AND THE SPIRIT OF COMMERCE

It is my contention that there is a strong possibility that Mandeville's *Fable of the Bees* inspired, or at least informed, Montesquieu's account in the *Persian Letters* of the role women play in encouraging the spirit of commerce. At the very least, Montesquieu in this early work traversed well-marked Mandevillean terrain by highlighting the importance of female vanity and women's desire for luxury as a major spur for economic prosperity. What Montesquieu added to Mandeville's basic insight by way of the cultural contrast between Parisian society and the Persian seraglio is, of course, his keen awareness of the significance of French women's public presence. That is to say, Montesquieu's Persian observers sensitize his readers to the profound social and economic transformation in France rendered possible by the reevaluation of traditional ideas of female modesty.

Rica's impressions of French society provide the reader with a sense of how much the intensity of Western life struck the Persian travelers. Rica relates that in France and Italy, he was astonished at the densely populated metropolitan areas inhabited by individuals in continual motion. For Rica, the "great confusion" he experienced in Paris was merely the physical manifestation of the cultural predilections of a people programmed to register fast changing attitudes and tastes (Letter 24, 39). The economic dimension of this cultural vitality was profoundly materialistic, but it bore little evidence of the thrift and work ethic of Calvinist Europe. Rather, in France Rica intuitively recognized that vanity was the primary spur for French industry and prosperity. In contrast to the thrifty *Homo economicus* exemplified by the entrepreneurial Benjamin Franklin,[16] Montesquieu reveals that the promotion of acquisitive habits in France was very much a state affair as the vast apparatus of the Bourbon monarchy sought to finance its continued existence by way of selling tithes and sinecures. Rica assessed this source of revenue was even richer than territorial possessions because the French king extracted his wealth from the "vanity of his subjects, which is more inexhaustible than mines" (Letter 24, 39). The patronage system of the French monarchy was, then, itself a dimension of the national economy as the selling of honors illuminated the psychological basis of commercial society: namely, the social passion of vanity that proved more plentiful and dependable than all the gold in the mythical Eldorado.

Rica's initial perception of the trickle-down model of French economics upon his arrival in France gradually became more refined over the course of his time in the West. This was especially true with respect to his growing appreciation of the role of French women as the arbiters of taste and consumers of luxury items par excellence.[17] The vital precondition for women playing this role in economic development was not only a repudiation of the harsh gender segregation present in Persia. The secret to prosperity in France was nothing less than the total integration of men and women in a shared public and quasi-public space that constituted the ideal venue for education in the personal traits and social habits suited to commercial life. It is women in France who are the agents of seemingly perpetual change: "The caprices of fashion among the French [are] astonishing" (Letter 99, 16). The great fluidity of sartorial and ornamental taste comes, of course, at a cost, especially to French men. As Rica relates, "It would not be believed just how much it costs a husband to keep his wife in fashion" (Letter 99, 160). The expectations placed on French men, whether by the demands of love or reputation, achieve the same result: namely, dramatic release of the acquisitive passions of the male providers of fashionable wives and mistresses. The rapid movements of fashion mirror the constantly changing social milieu of urban France, as the "woman who leaves Paris to spend six months in the country returns as antiquated as if she had been forgotten for thirty years" (Letter 99, 160). A child sees a portrait of his or her à la mode mother and assumes that "it is some American woman who is represented there," so drastically do fashions change in a short period of time (Letter 99, 160).

In France, Rica discovers "daughters are made differently from their mothers" inasmuch as even the most basic assumptions about female anatomy are subject to alteration: "In the past, women had waists and teeth; today they are out of the question" (Letter 99, 160). The styles of women's coiffure and chapeau fluctuate so radically that French architects routinely have to "raise, lower, and widen their doors according as women's attire demanded that change" (Letter 99, 160). But Rica warns one of his unnamed correspondents not to dismiss French fashion as mere frivolity. For women at least, fashion is a deadly serious affair. To the French, fashion in clothes and hair styles represents "the rule by which they judge everything that other nations do" (Letter 100, 160). But the importance of this *en vogue* theory of international relations pales by comparison with the impact the vagaries of fashion have on the lives of individual men and women. Rica confides to an unnamed (almost certainly male) correspondent: "The role of a pretty woman is much graver than is thought" (Letter 110, 178). A chic French woman at her toilette resembles the general of an army, strategically placing a beauty spot here and some makeup there in a manner "she hopes or predicts success will come" (Letter 110, 178). The desire to please that Montesquieu presents as natural to the psychology of women extends beyond crafting attractive physical appearance to include even the communicative arts. Rica applauds a certain transparency in French manners: "Everything speaks; everything is seen; everything is heard; the heart is as visible as the face" (Letter 63, 102). However, the dialogic character of French social conventions that encourages a pleasing idiom of badinage suggests that the skills of the gallant only reciprocate the esthetic toils of the society lady laboring grimly at her maquillage.

Women's participation in French social life is also intergenerational. Once again, it is Rica who perceives the significant role women of all ages—not just marriageable young women—play in the milieu of fashionable society. In a letter to Usbek, Rica relates his experience at one "social gathering" where he "rather enjoyed" himself (Letter 52, 84). Rica mischievously engaged in conversation with four females ranging in age from twenty to eighty, each of whom either critiqued the absurd vanity of the elder women or implausibly claimed to be twenty years younger than they were. It is the censorious women themselves who mock their fellow socialites for "wearing flame-colored ribbons" and spending "more than an hour dressing up" (Letter 52, 84). French women of all ages contribute with spirit and verve to the conspicuous spending that fuels the national economy. There is clearly something morally dubious about the deceit exercised by society ladies, but Rica resists condemning these women who are fundamentally in denial about aging and mortality: "They make every effort to deceive themselves and to escape the most distressing of thoughts" (Letter 52, 85). Indeed, Rica reflects forbearingly: "Perhaps it is good fortune . . . that we find consolation in the weakness of others" (Letter 52, 85). With this rather generous observation Rica both anticipated and departed from Jean-Jacques Rousseau. Whereas Rousseau famously criticized vanity or *amour propre* as the spur to anxiety and psychologically unhealthy comparisons with others,[18] Montesquieu, speaking through Rica, highlights the economic benefits of the traumatic rituals of comparison on the catwalks of Parisian haute couture. One women's desire to shine with a crimson ribbon is a greater impetus to industry than all the moral exhortations imaginable.

One of the most distinctive features of Bernard Mandeville's argument for private vices and public benefits is his appreciation for the specialization of skills and division of labor. Montesquieu, once again following Mandeville, situates women at the heart of the economic harmony of interests. However, it is the pensive Usbek, rather than the more gregarious Rica, who sketched out this Mandevillean vision most powerfully in an exchange of letters with a Persian named Rhedi, who is a resident of Venice. Rhedi's attitude toward the West is conflicted. On one hand, he condemns the famed commercial republic of Venice as a "profane city" that is an "abomination to our sacred prophet" (Letter 31, 52). However, on the other hand, Rhedi is obviously attracted to the fast pace of life in a "city where every day my mind takes shape," and in which he is "educating [himself] in the secrets of commerce" (Letter 31, 52). In a further letter to Usbek written several years later, Rhedi reveals the deep disillusionment with the West that was the ultimate product of his cultural exchange. In particular, he expresses a once again rather proto-Rousseauian distrust of the progress in the arts and sciences: "I do not know if the utility that is drawn from them compensates men for the ill use that people make of them every day" (Letter 105, 169). Out of all the advances made in Western society, Rhedi focuses on the invention of money—the lifeblood of commerce—as especially problematic. The adoption of gold and silver currency "has been very pernicious" in the countries in which they were discovered: "Entire nations have been destroyed; and men who have escaped death have been reduced to servitude so severe that the account of it makes Muslims shudder" (Letter 105, 170). For Rhedi, disillusionment with Western commercialism leads to a reenchantment with the "amiable simplicity" of the ideal Islamic life reminiscent of the prophet, which produced the "tranquility that reigned in the hearts of our first fathers" (Letter 105, 170). Religious fundamentalism appears to Rhedi as the natural reaction to the bewildering pace of change in European commercial society.

In response to his friend, Usbek homes in on commerce as perhaps the distinctive factor in the creation of Western Enlightenment morality. Usbek defends progress in the arts and sciences, especially with respect to technology and military affairs, against the accusations of the disappointed Rhedi. Usbek rebuffs Rhedi's quasi-civic republican assertions about progress in the arts and sciences producing effeminate citizens. Usbek admits the driving force behind French prosperity does, indeed, have a distinctly feminine form. But the cultured tastes of the denizens of the fashionable metropolis reveals that "where pleasures are the most refined . . . it is perhaps the place where people live the hardest lives (*une vie plus dure*)" (Letter 106, 172).[19] The hardness of French life is a function of industry and work ethic, not scarcity. The pleasures of some are built upon the labors of others. In fine Mandevillean form, Usbek cites women's fashion as the prime fillip to industry: "A woman gets it into her head that she should appear at a gathering in a particular dress, and they no longer have the leisure to drink and eat. She commands and is obeyed more promptly than our monarch would be, because interest is the greatest monarch on earth" (Letter 106, 172). The desire for luxury, like the love of gain, is pervasive and "runs through every rank, from artisans to nobles" (Letter 106, 172). The spirit of competition, and implicitly social mobility, injects demonstrable dynamism into French society that cannot help but impress the reflective Usbek.

Perhaps the most unmistakable gesture to the influence of Mandeville's teaching in the entire *Persian Letters* is Usbek's thought experiment by which he challenges Rhedi to think through the consequences that would follow if "a kingdom only upheld those arts absolutely necessary to the cultivation of the earth, which are actually very numerous, and that the arts that only serve voluptuous pleasures or fantasies be banished from it" (Letter 106, 173).[20] How does Usbek assess the quality of life in his version of Mandeville's reformed hive? In keeping with the famed Dutch doctor, Usbek judges that the state in which all the arts devoted to serving "voluptuous pleasures or fantasies" are banished "would be one of the most miserable that has been in the world" (Letter 106, 173). The entire society would soon become enfeebled as "the income of individuals and, consequently, that of the Prince, would cease almost completely" (Letter 106, 173). The negative effects of sumptuary laws would include stifling "that circulation of riches and increase of income that arises from the dependence that the arts have upon one another" (Letter 106, 173).

The poverty natural to a condition of enforced individual autarky clearly illuminates the social benefits of cooperative—but self-interested—commercial enterprise and transactions. Usbek also frames his treatment of commerce and luxury in terms of population growth, one of his fixations in the exchange with Rhedi. If luxury goods were banished from the state, the number of inhabitants would "diminish proportionately" such that only 5 percent of the population could survive solely by cultivating the land (Letter 106, 173). To illustrate his preference for trade over agriculture, Usbek claims "with a pistole's worth of colors, a painter will produce a canvas that will yield him fifty," whereas the owner of land produces "only a twentieth part of its value"

(Letter 106, 173). The upshot of Usbek's paean to commerce is his conclusion that the political strength of a nation depends on unleashing the acquisitive passions and superfluous desires of its people: "For a prince to be powerful, his subjects have to live delightfully; he has to work to procure for them every kind of superfluity as attentively as he does to procure the necessities of life" (Letter 106, 173). Given Usbek's own admission about the role women play in French public and social life establishing the psychosexual foundations of commercial mores, it is difficult to see how the master of the Persian seraglio could not appreciate the political and economic consequences of his own tyranny back home.

CONCLUSION

I have tried to trace the theme of commerce, well established in Montesquieu's masterpiece *The Spirit of the Laws*, back to his earlier *Persian Letters*. I also hope to have illuminated the distinctive echoes in the *Persian Letters* of Bernard Mandeville's general teaching on private vices and public benefits, as well as his more specific preoccupation with revealing the connection between commerce and the overturning of traditional ideas of female modesty represented, albeit in extreme form, in the Persian seraglio. In this way, Montesquieu's famous treatment of the role of women in the formation of national character in book XIX of *The Spirit of the Laws* was, in my view, adumbrated in the satirical observations of the fictional Persian travelogue decades earlier. Needless to say, for Montesquieu, the liberating effects of the commercial spirit, viewed both in terms of female modesty and acquisitive passions, clearly represents a potential counterforce against the absolutist tendencies looming over the closing half century of the ancien régime (see Letters 92 and 140). There is also considerable truth in the argument that even if Montesquieu's account of the public role of women in French society is not necessarily protofeminist, it is at minimum subversive of traditional patriarchy.[21] At the very least, in the diverse array of perceptions, observations, and judgments related by Rica and Usbek, Montesquieu presented the reader with an index of possible outcomes for France ranging from the bloody and suicidal revolt of the harem prisoners to the more benign vision of a stable and prosperous national government restrained by the consumer demand for luxury and entertainments among its vain and industrious subjects.

NOTES

1. See Charles-Louis de Secondat, Baron de Montesquieu, *The Spirit of the Laws*, eds. Anne M. Cohler, Basia C. Miller, and Harold Stone (Cambridge: Cambridge University Press, 1989), VII.1 and XIX.5, 8, and 11, for the connection to Mandeville. For Montesquieu's expression of his agreement with Mandeville in his *Pensées*, see Montesquieu, *My Thoughts*, ed. and trans. Henry C. Clark (Indianapolis, IN: Liberty Fund, 2012), 448, #1553, and Catherine Larrère, "Montesquieu on Economics and Commerce," in *Montesquieu's Science of Politics: Essays on the Spirit of the Laws*, ed. David W. Carrithers, Michael A. Mosher, and Paul A. Rahe (Lanham, MD: Rowman and Littlefield, 2001), 372, n. 28. While to my knowledge there is no evidence that Montesquieu read the *Fable of the Bees* prior to 1721, other scholars have also seen a connection between the *Persian Letters* and Mandeville. See for instance, E. J. Hundert, "Sexual Politics and the Allegory of Identity in Montesquieu's Persian Letters," *Eighteenth-Century: Theory and Interpretation* 31, no. 2 (1990): 112, and Tjitske Akkerman, *Women's Vices, Public Benefits: Women and Commerce in the French Enlightenment* (The Hague: Het Spinhuis, 1992), 17. For a good treatment of Mandeville's role in the eighteenth-century debate about commerce and luxury, see Istvan Hont, "The Early Enlightenment Debate on Commerce and Luxury," in *The Cambridge History of Eighteenth-Century Political Thought*, ed. Mark Goldie and Robert Wokler (Cambridge: Cambridge University Press, 2006), 387–95.

2. For treatments of Montesquieu's political economy in the *Persian Letters*, see Andrew Scott Bibby, *Montesquieu's Political Economy* (New York: Palgrave Mac-Millan, 2016), 18–19; Paul Cheney, *Revolutionary Commerce: Globalization and the French Monarchy* (Cambridge, MA: Harvard University Press, 2010), 54; and Henry C. Clark, *Compass of Society: Commerce and Absolutism in Old-Regime France* (Lanham, MD: Rowman and Littlefield, 2007), 84–89.

3. Bernard Mandeville, *The Fable of the Bees or Privates Vices, Publick Benefits*, ed. Frederick Kaye (Indianapolis, IN: Liberty Fund, 1988), vol. 1, 4. Hereafter in notes and text simply F and page.

4. Compare with Niccolò Machiavelli, *The Prince*, trans. Harvey Mansfield (Chicago: University of Chicago Press, 1985), 61, and Thomas Hobbes, *Leviathan* (Indianapolis, IN: Hackett, 1994), sec. 4, 5.

5. The intellectual provenance of the term lies in seventeenth-century French thinkers such as Saint-Evremond and Pierre Bayle, whose critique of austere Christian arguments against luxury greatly influenced Mandeville; see Thomas A. Horne, *The Social Thought of Bernard Mandeville* (New York: Columbia University Press, 1978), 56.

6. See Anthony, Third Earl Shaftesbury, *Characteristicks of Men, Manners, Opinions, Times* (Indianapolis, IN: Liberty Fund, 2001), vol. 2, 18, 47, 100, 123–26.

7. Cf. Adam Smith, *An Inquiry into the Nature and Causes of the Wealth of Nations*, ed. R. H. Campbell and A. S. Skinner (Indianapolis: Liberty Fund, 1981), vol. 1, 13.

8. For the original French, see Charles-Louis de Secondat, Baron de Montesquieu, *Lettres Persanes/Persian Letters* (Bilingual Text) (London: JiaHu Books, 2013), 50.

9. See for example, Akkerman, *Women's Vices, Public Virtues*, 46, and Judith Shklar, *Montesquieu* (Oxford: Oxford University Press 1987), 34. However, Diana J. Schaub, *Erotic Liberalism: Women and Revolution in Montesquieu's Persian Letters* (Lanham, MD: Rowman and Littlefield, 1995), 111, discerns a certain "seriousness" in Rica's observations.

10. For the French original, see Montesquieu, *Lettres Persanes/Persian Letters*, 106.

11. See Montesquieu, *Spirit of the Laws*, VIII.6, 116–17, and Lucas A. Swaine, "The Secret Chain: Justice, and Self-Interest in Montesquieu's Persian Letters," *History of Political Thought* 22, no. 1 (spring 2001): 101.

12. "Uneasiness" is my translation for *l'inquiétude.*

13. Thus, I disagree with Kra's assertion that Montesquieu signals through Rica his objection to the "polemical exaggeration" of the gallant philosopher. Pauline Kra, "Montesquieu and Women," In *French Women and the Age of Enlightenment*, ed. Samia I. Spencer (Bloomington: Indiana University Press, 1984), 276.

14. For the original French, see Montesquieu, *Lettres Persanes/Persian Letters,* 418.

15. For a more critical view of this French woman's response to polygamy, see Mary McAlpin, "Between Men for All Eternity: Feminocentrism in Montesquieu's *Lettres persanes*," *Eighteenth-Century Life* 24 (winter 2000): 53.

16. See Benjamin Franklin, *The Autobiography of Benjamin Franklin* (Mineola, NY: Dover, 1996), 63–70.

17. See Schaub, *Erotic Liberalism*, 121.

18. See Jean-Jacques Rousseau, *The Second Discourse on the Origins of Inequality*, trans. Roger D. Masters and Judith R. Masters (New York: St. Martin's, 1964), 149.

19. For the original French, see Montesquieu, *Lettres Persanes/Persian Letters*, 318.

20. The editors of a recent translation of the *Persian Letters* also recognize the unmistakable resemblance to Mandeville in Letter 106; see Charles-Louis de Secondat, Baron de Montesquieu, *Persian Letters*, trans. Stuart D. Warner and Stéphane Douard (South Bend, IN: St. Augustine's Press, 2017), 173, n. 202.

21. E.g., Mary Lyndon Shanley and Peter G. Stillman, "Political and Marital Despotism: Montesquieu's Persian Letters," in *The Family in Political Thought*, ed. Jean Bethke Elshtain (Amherst: University of Massachusetts Press, 1982), 67, and Michael Mosher, "The Judgmental Gaze of European Women: Gender, Sexuality, and the Critique of Republican Rule," *Political Theory* 22, no.1 (1984): 33.

BIBLIOGRAPHY

Akkerman, Tjitske. *Women's Vices, Public Benefits: Women and Commerce in the French Enlightenment*. The Hague: Het Spinhuis, 1992.

Bibby, Andrew Scott. *Montesquieu's Political Economy*. New York: Palgrave MacMillan, 2016.

Cheney, Paul. *Revolutionary Commerce: Globalization and the French Monarchy.* Cambridge, MA: Harvard University Press, 2010.

Clark, Henry C. *Compass of Society: Commerce and Absolutism in Old-Regime France.* Lanham, MD: Rowman and Littlefield, 2007.

Franklin, Benjamin. *The Autobiography of Benjamin Franklin.* Mineola, NY: Dover, 1996.

Hobbes, Thomas. *Leviathan.* Indianapolis, IN: Hackett, 1994.

Hont, Istvan. "The Early Enlightenment Debate on Commerce and Luxury." In *The Cambridge History of Eighteenth-Century Political Thought*, edited by Mark Goldie and Robert Wokler, 370–418. Cambridge: Cambridge University Press, 2006.

Horne, Thomas A. *The Social Thought of Bernard Mandeville.* New York: Columbia University Press, 1978.

Hundert, E. J. "Sexual Politics and the Allegory of Identity in Montesquieu's *Persian Letters.*" *Eighteenth-Century: Theory and Interpretation* 31, no. 2 (1990): 101–15.

Kra, Pauline. "Montesquieu and Women." In *French Women and the Age of Enlightenment*, edited by Samia I. Spencer, 272–85. Bloomington: Indiana University Press, 1984.

Larrère, Catherine. "Montesquieu on Economics and Commerce." In *Montesquieu's Science of Politics: Essays on the Spirit of the Laws*, edited by David W. Carrithers, Michael A. Mosher, and Paul A. Rahe, 335–73. Lanham, MD: Rowman and Littlefield, 2001.

Machiavelli, Niccolò. *The Prince.* Translated by Harvey Mansfield. Chicago: University of Chicago Press, 1985.

Mandeville, Bernard. *The Fable of the Bees or Privates Vices, Publick Benefits.* Edited by Frederick Kaye. Indianapolis, IN: Liberty Fund, 1988.

McAlpin, Mary. "Between Men for All Eternity: Feminocentrism in Montesquieu's *Lettres persanes.*" *Eighteenth-Century Life* 24 (winter 2000): 45–61.

Montesquieu, Charles-Louis de Secondat, Baron de. *Persian Letters.* Translated by Stuart D. Warner and Stéphane Douard. South Bend, IN: St. Augustine's Press, 2017.

———. *Lettres Persanes/Persian Letters* (Bilingual Text). London: JiaHu Books, 2013.

———. *My Thoughts.* Edited and translated by Henry C. Clark. Indianapolis, IN: Liberty Fund, 2012.

———. *The Spirit of the Laws.* Edited by Anne M. Cohler, Basia C. Miller, and Harold Stone. Cambridge: Cambridge University Press, 1989.

Mosher, Michael. "The Judgmental Gaze of European Women: Gender, Sexuality, and the Critique of Republican Rule." *Political Theory* 22, no.1 (1984): 25–44.

Rousseau, Jean-Jacques. *The Second Discourse on the Origins of Inequality.* Translated by Roger D. Masters and Judith R. Masters. New York: St. Martin's, 1964.

Schaub, Diana J. *Erotic Liberalism: Women and Revolution in Montesquieu's Persian Letters.* Lanham, MD: Rowman and Littlefield, 1995.

Shaftesbury, Anthony, Third Earl. *Characteristicks of Men, Manners, Opinions, Times*. 3 volumes. Indianapolis, IN: Liberty Fund, 2001.

Shanley, Mary Lyndon, and Peter G. Stillman. "Political and Marital Despotism: Montesquieu's Persian Letters." In *The Family in Political Thought*, edited by Jean Bethke Elshtain, 66–79. Amherst: University of Massachusetts Press, 1982.

Shklar, Judith. *Montesquieu*. Oxford: Oxford University Press, 1987.

Smith, Adam. *An Inquiry into the Nature and Causes of the Wealth of Nations*. 2 volumes. Edited by R. H. Campbell and A. S. Skinner. Indianapolis, IN: Liberty Fund, 1981.

Swaine, Lucas A. "The Secret Chain: Justice, and Self-Interest in Montesquieu's *Persian Letters*." *History of Political Thought* 22, no. 1 (spring 2001): 84–105.

Chapter 10

Rica in Paris

Sociability and Cosmopolitanism in the Persian Letters[1]

Megan Gallagher

It is good to know that the cosmopolitan has a history as an idea; it is better understood when we examine it as lived experience.

—Margaret C. Jacob[2]

INTRODUCTION

Montesquieu's *Persian Letters* is a tapestry composed of many threads, some of which, such as despotism, foreignness, and religion, have gained the most attention from readers and commentators. This chapter grabs hold of a thread that has garnered less attention and, without claiming its centrality to understanding the text, makes the case for its presence and purpose. While Usbek is often considered by scholars to be the novel's central character, the one around whom most of the major events revolve, the transformation of his companion Rica is remarked upon but not often analyzed. Focusing on Rica's contributions to the *Letters*, I argue that the novel offers a vision of cosmopolitanism built on the practices of sociability—specifically, by Rica and not Usbek. In addition to reportage—and satire—of Parisian trends, Montesquieu outlines Rica's journey from a young and impressionable traveler to a sensitive cosmopolitan, learned in the forms of modern sociability that dominate the ancien régime's elite society. Yet to become cosmopolitan, in this case, is not identical with "becoming Parisian." Rica does not simply adopt Parisian, French, or, even more broadly, Western values uncritically. Rather his observations gain a critical edge, refined both by his exposure to Parisian norms and the cultivation of his capacity for judgment that his outsider's perspective affords him.

"Cosmopolitanism" is an embattled term with a complex history, so what does it mean, and what is at stake, in calling Rica a cosmopolitan? For Margaret Jacob, "as early as the 1640s in English, the cosmopolitan came to mean someone who identified beyond the nation. At the same moment in French, the cosmopolite offhandedly appears as a 'habitué of all the world.'"[3] In labeling him thusly, I mean to imply that Rica adopts a posture of epistemic humility with respect to his knowledge and understanding of the world(s) in which he travels. He learns through the experience of moving between different cultures that an attitude of mastery and domination prevents intercultural understanding and collapses differences that should be, if not celebrated, then at least probed and understood. No less an authority on Montesquieu than Melvin Richter has argued that "Montesquieu understood himself to be a cosmopolitan and humanitarian, who held a pluralist view of human differences and cultural diversity"[4]. This aligns with what Pauline Kleingeld has labeled "cultural cosmopolitanism": "the view that humanity expresses itself in a rich variety of cultural forms, that we should recognize different cultures in their particularity, and that attempts to achieve cultural uniformity lead to cultural impoverishment."[5] Indeed, while Usbek's world *seems* to expand, only to collapse in on itself with the news of his wives' rebellion, Rica's horizons continue to expand, implicitly beyond the novel's end.

In the following section, I argue in favor of reading the *Letters* as an account of Rica's, rather than Usbek's, transformation. I demonstrate that while Usbek is the ultimate consumer of scientific, religious, and even political knowledge, Rica is a consumer of social knowledge. While often positioned as a lesser form of inquiry, if we accept that the *Letters* participates in a cosmopolitan inquiry, then Rica's discoveries about Parisian culture ought to be weighted as heavily as Usbek's inquiries into science and religion. While Usbek's inquiries reflect on and, yes, affect his sense of self, Rica's inquiries change how he relates to others and ultimately render him adaptable to his new environment, contrary to Usbek, who remains personally inflexible and endures an existential crisis in consequence. In the chapter's third section, I return to Kleingeld's "cultural cosmopolitanism" and argue in favor of interpreting Rica as a cosmopolitan who offers a model of being in the world that would benefit French and Persians alike. I detail three qualities—curiosity, reciprocity, and humility—that contribute to the development of Rica's cosmopolitanism, and contrast them to Usbek's attitude. In a brief fourth section, I suggest that cosmopolitanism bubbles under the surface of the *Letters* most especially through Rica's engagement with commerce. In a fifth section, I consider a possible objection to Rica's characterization as cosmopolitan: his detached and ironic style of writing, which draws into question the seriousness with which we should regard his transformation. I conclude by suggesting that further interpretations of the *Persian Letters* would benefit from exploring the relationship between sensibility and sociability in the character of Rica.

READING FOR RICA

For most interpreters of the *Persian Letters*, Usbek is not only the central character; he is the novel's supreme cosmopolitan figure. Jean Starobinski, for example, regards Usbek as a mirror of Montesquieu himself and observes that "Rica merely complements Usbek, who plays the leading role"[6] For another critic, Rica is "the livelier but less complicated Persian, [who] reports French political and social absurdities and comes to see the world with a cynical, if superficial, aplomb."[7] Thus the novel's cosmopolitan leanings, if they exist, ought to be revealed via Usbek's letters to his far-flung correspondents, who do indeed constitute a diverse and worldly bunch of interlocutors. But Usbek himself pushes back on this interpretation of Rica as the lesser intellectual of the two, remarking in the very first letter that "Rica and I are perhaps the first among Persians who left their country out of a longing for knowledge, and who renounced the pleasures of a tranquil life in order to search laboriously for wisdom."[8] He thus presents himself and Rica as traveling similar paths toward enlightenment. Though their paths diverge (indeed, the two spend most of the novel apart from one another), we should at least maintain that they are starting from similar places of curiosity and commitment to inquiry.[9]

Lisa Lowe is one of the few commentators who recognizes that Rica is "a complex figure," "a central voice and authority who presents French customs, attitudes, and society, as well as an invented foreigner."[10] Rica flourishes (and, as I argue in the next section, his cosmopolitanism flourishes) in large part due to his induction into the ways of sociability during his travels. According to Céline Spector, Montesquieu "distinguishes between two models for the formation of civil society through a convergence of interests. The first, identified with England, is a 'paradigm of commerce.' The second, identified with France, is a 'paradigm of manners.'"[11] It is principally the latter that Rica encounters during his stay in Paris, where he is educated into the ways of French sociability through his encounters with the nameless Frenchmen who people his anecdotes.[12] Sociability can be defined as the social practices grounded in the belief in man's natural goodness, which is best refined and expressed via certain norms of *politesse* in the informal domains of society, such as the salon, as opposed to the state. "It was common to affirm in the Enlightenment that France was the model of sociability to the rest of the world. The aristocratic ideal of a polite individual was transposed with the help of natural law into the Enlightenment ideal of a polite nation."[13] For example, in a well-known passage, Rica himself observes that "it is said that man is a sociable animal. On this basis, it appears to me that a Frenchman is more of a man than any other. He is man *par excellence*, for he seems to be made solely for society" (Letter 87, 142). Already when we meet him, Rica has an uncommonly strong ability to identify with others; there are hints that Rica is predisposed to a heightened sensibility, as when he writes, "I confess to you, Usbek, that I have never seen anyone shed tears without being moved" (Letter 126, 206).

Nonetheless, in spite of his sensibility, Rica's development into sociability is not without challenges. Roxanne Euben remarks that "Rica's letters often undermine not only the view of travel as a linear progression from parochialism to universal truth but also the very opposition on which such a view of knowledge is built."[14] The way this undermining occurs is not exactly flattering to Rica. For instance, he occasionally demonstrates binary thinking, even when his experiences to that point would ideally guard against it, as when he describes his habit of thought, which is, he says, "insensibly losing everything Asiatic that remains to it, and effortlessly it is conforming itself to European morals" (Letter 63, 102). What is especially interesting is that exposure to "European morals" has so rapidly led to an evaluation of them as superior to his own "Asiatic" inheritance. In the same letter, he expands on what he finds stultifying about Persian culture compared to French culture:

> Among us, character is completely uniform because it is forced. People are not seen such as they are, but such as they are obliged to be. In this servitude of heart and mind, one hears nothing but fear spoke . . . and not nature. . . . Dissimulation, that art among us so practiced and so necessary, is here unknown. Everything speaks; everything is seen; everything is heard; the heart is as visible as the face. (Letter 63, 102)

If the first thing that strikes one about the passage is its clean-cut juxtaposition of the Persian and French way of doing things, the second must be the substance of that juxtaposition and Rica's sense that French society has a wider remit for behavior, grounded in nature rather than in fear. (We know from the much later *The Spirit of the Laws* that fear, the spring of despotism, immobilizes.)[15] Whereas Rica's fellow Persians must dissimulate to appear *the same*, the French go to great lengths to differentiate themselves from one another, whether through wit (Letter 54, 87), fashion (Letter 99, 160), or the cultivation of "scientific" knowledge (Letter 45, 68). The recurring emphasis on banter, or chatter, in the *Letters* highlights the degree to which the French strive to demonstrate their uniqueness and learning with pride and, more importantly, through discourse and discussion.

Compare Usbek's attitude toward society. We know he considers himself "a man of intelligence,"[16] and such a man, he tells us, "is usually rather difficult in society. He likes very few people, and he is bored with the great number of people he refers to as 'bad company.' His contempt is eventually impossible to disguise, and then they all turn into his enemies."[17] This is plausibly what happened at the court of Isfahan that led to his departure. In any case, it describes his preference for conducting his inquiries into science, nature, and faith on a one-on-one level that sees him engage directly, and singularly, with a series of knowledgeable interlocutors. Whereas Rica absorbs, Usbek masters. And ultimately, whereas Rica will transform, Usbek will break.

RICA THE COSMOPOLITAN

Insofar as cosmopolitanism is discussed in secondary literature on the *Letters*, it is not received with much enthusiasm. For instance, in one of the few explicit discussions of cosmopolitanism in the novel, Mary Helen McMurran concludes that "writers [in the eighteenth century] could not reinvest in a freightless classical source and yet did not attach new, specific content to the terms. Then, alleviated of philosophical distinctiveness, but broadly distributed among a range of discourses, the cosmopolitan was nothing, or a nobody.[18]" In this telling, cosmopolitanism is little more than a warmed-over notion of rootlessness. In a more positive light, as Montesquieu's translator Raymond MacKenzie describes cosmopolitanism, it "suggests that nation-states are not inevitable, and that geography is not destiny."[19] Pauline Kleingeld argues that "eighteenth-century cultural cosmopolitans are neither relativists nor ethnocentrists. They want to have it both ways: they wish to preserve open-minded engagement with other cultures in a way that takes their particularity seriously, and yet they reject relativism. They do this by grounding the standard for evaluation in a common humanity that underlies all cultural forms."[20]

This sense of what Kleingeld calls "cultural cosmopolitanism" aligns more neatly with what we see happening in the *Letters*, where both Usbek and Rica both struggle with the seemingly contradictory desires to hold on to their "Persianness" while opening themselves to Parisian, or even worldly, influences. The charge of relativism might seem to stick, as on first glance when Rica remarks to his associate Ibben that "it is indeed the same earth that carries us both, but the men of the country where I am living, and those of the country where you are, are different men indeed" (Letter 24, 42). Yet on second reading, what first appears as relativism—"two very different sorts of men"—instead takes on the appearance of a healthy pluralism—"the same earth supports both peoples." In other words, Rica's emphasis is on the capacity of very different sorts of people to live together, not the relativistic desire to rank one above the other. This pluralism is different from the universalism with which cosmopolitanism is sometimes associated. See, for example, Starobinski's claim that

> confronted with the relativity of the absolutes that people have revered in different times and different places, the reader becomes aware of the need to rise to the level of the universal and experiences the awakening of a cosmopolitan concern for the happiness and prosperity of all peoples. The groundwork has been laid for the triumph of the universal concepts of Reason, Justice, and Nature, in whose name local fanaticism and regional prejudice can be condemned.[21]

On the contrary, Rica does not seem particularly interested in banishing "regional prejudice" so much as he is interested in exploring it, distinguishing it from his own upbringing, and, on more than one occasion, marveling at it: he is an enthusiastic traveler. Rica's cosmopolitanism is thus something of a happy medium between relativism and universalism, without the egoism that both of those positions essentially require.

In the chapter's introduction, I remarked that cosmopolitanism entails a form of epistemic humility. One characteristic of epistemic humility, as I am using the concept here, is curiosity. Unlike what I will argue are the other two qualities of epistemic humility (reciprocity and humility itself), curiosity is shared by Usbek and Rica alike. It is what brought them out of Isfahan and, as discussed in the previous section, should be equally attributed to both characters. Curiosity matters because it is a motivational force—it explains Usbek's many letters to his different interlocutors (and is conspicuously absent, replaced by suspicion, in letters to the eunuchs and his wives), as well as Rica's eager exploration of Paris. To be curious is also to admit that there is knowledge one does not possess, and rather than being ashamed or proud of the fact, one chooses instead to pursue knowledge for its own sake. Again contrary to Starobinski, to be curious is to defer "the triumph of the universal concepts of Reason, Justice, and Nature" in favor of the unfamiliar and the strange. This of course may have negative outcomes—recall Rica's observation that "there is no one who does not leave this city more cautious than when he entered it; by dint of parting with one's wealth to others, one learns to conserve it. This is the sole advantage for strangers in this enchanting city" (Letter 58, 95)—but these are presented as manageable costs of a cosmopolitan approach. (Indeed, I suggest below that commerce and cosmo-politanism are in fact intimately linked.)

Another quality of cosmopolitanism's epistemic humility is reciprocity, or a willingness to engage with others on their own terms. For instance, Rica remarks of Parisians that "when I say to you that they despise everything for-eign, I speak only of trifles, for on the important things . . . they wholeheart-edly admit that other peoples are wiser than they are, provided that it is agreed that they are better dressed" (Letter 100, 161). Enclosed in a larger joke about the vanity of the French is an important revelation about Rica's reception, which is often lost in comparison to the more famously quoted lines, "Ah! Ah! Monsieur is Persian? That is a very extraordinary thing! How can anyone be Persian?" (Letter 30, 51). Even that anecdote opens with Rica's observa-tion that "the inhabitants of Paris are curious to the point of extravagance."

Admittedly, Rica complains that "so many honors cannot fail to be a bur-den" and chooses to dress a Westerner as a sort of "experiment," after which he attracts far less attention: "Free of all my foreign ornament, I found that people took me more nearly for what I am really worth" (Letter 30, 51). However, his regret appears to be presented in an overly dramatic fashion, such as when he claims that he "would have been justified in complaining about [his] tailor . . . for he had made me lose in a moment all that public attention and esteem" (ibid.). And for our purposes, the important thing is less the fickle nature of Parisians' curiosity, but the willingness of Rica to engage it with good humor and an interest in learning what he can about the culture in which he is immersed. If anything, the exchange illuminates Rica's own cosmopolitan frustration with the limits of those he encounters, because while "cosmopolitanism converts novelties back into the persons who cre-ated or sustained them and strangers back into the familiars they would be in their own societies," the Frenchmen he encounters as often as not fail to make that move from stranger to familiar.[22] Theirs is a failure of cosmopolitan imagination.

A third crucial quality of cosmopolitanism's epistemic humility is, unsur-prisingly, humility itself. Rica demonstrates two kinds of humility—existential and interpersonal. Regarding the first, Rica famously observes the compara-tive "pettiness" of most humans in face of their relative insignificance:

> My dear Usbek, when I see men who crawl upon an atom, that is to say, the earth, which is nothing but a speck in the universe, directly proposing them-selves as models of providence, I do not know how to reconcile so much extravagance with so much pettiness. (Letter 59, 97)

Rica demonstrates what, in Montesquieu's hands, feels like an incredibly modern insight into the limits of humanity's authority over, and place within, the cosmos. But Rica's humility also extends to his fellow humans, petty or not. In at least one instance, when he was engaged in playing a dupe to several vain women (and acting in a rather petty fashion himself), it leads to the reconsideration of his behavior: "'Ah, good God!' I said to myself. 'Shall we only ever be sensible of the ridiculousness of others?'" (Letter 52, 84). This form of self-examination and recalibration—indeed, this kind of learning—is characteristic of Rica.

Together, these three qualities of curiosity, reciprocity, and humility contribute to the novel's much-lauded perspectivalism. By perspectivalism, I mean the novel's ability to reflect, and refract, the worldviews of multiple characters without necessarily ordering them in terms of correctness or authority. It is central to the pluralist vision of cosmopolitanism. That's not to say Montesquieu does not indicate a preference for certain beliefs: compare Rica's attitude to that of Usbek, who approaches a cosmopolitan stance in his dealings with, for example, religious difference. It is correct that "for Usbek the pursuit of knowledge implies mobility, openness to the outside world, and above all refusal to submit solely to the authority of his native 'culture.'"[23] Yet by his own standard, Usbek fails miserably to embrace a similarly cosmopolitan position, most obviously with respect to the treatment of his wives in Isfahan. For Montesquieu, this failure to reconcile his conflicting beliefs and practices mirrors the larger failures of despotic government, but it also gestures to the limits on the supposedly learned Usbek's cosmopolitan leanings.

COSMOPOLITAN COMMERCE

It is a curiosity that while much critical ink has been spilled over the precise nature of Usbek's political leanings and what they represent for Montesquieu, there has been little to no discussion of what type of political system Rica might represent. Returning to Kleingeld's typology of cosmopolitanisms, I have suggested that Rica's attitude and disposition toward others is thoroughly cosmopolitan, even if it remains detached from any particular type of government. His views certainly do not fit into the typology later established by Montesquieu in *The Spirit of the Laws*. But a cosmopolitan outlook is in harmony with another key piece of Montesquieu's thought, and that is the ability of commerce to facilitate smooth international relations and thus the possibility for a cosmopolitan world order. While above I focused on the "paradigm of manners," here I turn to Spector's "paradigm of commerce."

As is well known, Montesquieu appreciates the capacity of commerce to successfully counter conquest as the chief means of operating in the international realm. What is referred to as *doux commerce* ensures that in pursuing their own interests, men—and states—do as a little harm to one another's interests as is possible. With states united in the pursuit of profit and thus less interested in the art of war, the political consequences of the increasing power of commerce would seem to be cosmopolitan, or what Kleingeld classifies as "market cosmopolitanism." This is characterized by "the view that the economic market should become a single global sphere of free trade, and that this will promote world-wide peace while enhancing individual freedom and reducing the role of states."[24] This is consonant with, in the words of Stephen Rosow, Montesquieu's "historical view of the development of capitalist commerce in Europe [which] implied a cosmopolitan appreciation of rules for cooperation and the limitation of force in international politics."[25]

Where is commerce in the *Letters*? Nearly everywhere! Many of the interactions that Rica commits to paper are either transactional or, more often, his observations on the consequences of engaging in commerce. Though Rica does not demonstrate particular interest in international politics, he does engage with cosmopolitanism's domestic effects. For example, he writes to Usbek, "What would be the use for me to give an exact description of their dress and attire? A new fashion would come along to destroy all my work . . . and even before you had received my letter, everything would have changed" (Letter 99, 160). Thus, layered underneath the social commentary about the fickleness of French fashions is a more serious comment on the importance of commerce to social niceties—indeed, about the ability of markets to influence and be influenced by social mores.

According to Kleingeld, market cosmopolitanism implies endless mobility, as people move to where there is work, and thus "cultural differences would be lost insofar as they depend on a habitat or economic system that would now become obsolete; and insofar as they are portable, they would lose their original moorings and be mixed in a global potpourri of cultural forms."[26] This strikes me as an accurate rendering of what Rica undergoes as he learns to wear his newly acquired French-ness outwardly and to conceal the "Asiatic" quality of his mind. Contrary to Usbek, whose Janus-faced attempt to hold onto two different selves is ultimately ruined by the collapse of the seraglio and who hardens into a total despot by the last of his letters, Rica engages in multiple kinds of commerce—literal, intellectual, and social. Yet rather than lose himself in the process, Rica learns and grows. He becomes cosmopolitan. And, not coincidentally, he is far more content with his lot than Usbek is by the novel's end.

RICA'S IRONIC DETACHMENT

The following objection may be made to this reading of the *Persian Letters*: my emphasis on Rica's earnestness and growth is overstated. In fact, much of Rica's commentary is characterized by an ironic detachment that finds humor but not necessarily deeper meaning in the stories he recounts. On this view, his cosmopolitanism should be interpreted primarily as satirical critique, precisely distanced at the points where I suggest he is most engaged. Surely—for example—referring to the pope as a magician (Letter 24, 40) is tongue-in-cheek on Rica's part, an example of his "cynical, if superficial, aplomb."[27]

However, this interpretation does not seem quite correct to me. It is true that Rica often serves as Montesquieu's vehicle for making ironic remarks, but Rica *himself* is rarely detached, nor is he especially ironic, even when the results of his observation feel that way for the reader. Stuart Warner, for instance, argues that "many of the examples that Rica presents are unintentionally humorous, and while Rica sometimes fails to understand what he observes . . . these examples cut to the satiric quick of some significant political or religious matters."[28] In other words, Montesquieu communicates satirical commentary via Rica, but Rica himself is—*often*—speaking in earnest.

This is not to say that Rica is not sometimes facetious or playful. For example, think of his oft-quoted remark about not having seen anyone walk in Paris, as "no people in the world make better use of their machines than the French; they run; they fly" from house to house, which "are so tall you would swear that only astrologers live in them" (Letter 24, 39). To claim he means this literally would be to show little regard for Rica's intelligence. But as Rica himself reminds Ibben, and the reader, "Do not expect me currently to be able to comment to you about European morals and customs. I myself have only the slightest idea of them, and I have scarcely had enough time to be astonished, but nothing more" (Letter 24, 39). These observations, after all, come relatively early in his time in Paris; the awe in his authorial voice is tempered in later letters by a wryness. But this is distinct from the ironic detachment that Montesquieu orchestrates as part of his own authorial voice, via the interplay between the impressions of Rica and Usbek.

This interpretation is more compatible with the notion that, over the course of the novel, Rica becomes increasingly well-educated and cosmopolitan. If we think back to the three qualities I argued above are fundamental to cosmopolitanism—curiosity, reciprocity, and humility—there is no reason to think Rica possessed these qualities in great quantity before leaving Isfahan, even if he was predisposed by his sensitivity to cultivate them. Instead, it is as he is exposed to the ways of Paris and his various associates and interlocutors that he develops both his cosmopolitanism and an impish sense of humor.

CONCLUSION

The legacy of cosmopolitanism is not without issue. In the words of Ian Coller, "ideas about cosmopolitanism coming out of Enlightenment Europe intersected with cosmopolitan practices at the boundaries of Europe and the Muslim world, drawing new lines and boundaries of identity and difference, and that in turn these reconstructions of identity practice cleared the ground for new—and exclusively *European*—philosophical articulations of cosmopolitanism."[29] Thus, what had the potential to be a generative and polyvocal political position also eventually hardened into an identity bound to, if not totally static, then increasingly rigid notions of self and other, navigated along the line of the nation-state. We see some of this in Usbek, who sinks into apolitical despotic excess just as control of his seraglio escapes him.

In Rica, however, we see the twin effects of sensibility and sociability, which combine to produce a cosmopolitan subject invested in exploring the new culture in which he finds himself—and, to give him slightly more credit—which he has actively sought out for that very purpose. If there is some suggestion of a predisposition towards cosmopolitanism—a heightened sensibility—it is all the more the case that Rica's cosmopolitanism emerges from his encounters and engagements with French men and women who, albeit unwittingly, instruct him in the ways of cultural pluralism, tolerance, and the common humanity of all. His cosmopolitanism does not come with a particular political agenda—he is not proposing an international federation, after all. Instead, it depends on the fuzzier and thus more easily dismissed realm of culture. Rica has long been written off as the sillier and less consequential of the *Persian Letters'* two central characters, but in his embrace of cosmopolitan commerce, we find a vision that aligns more closely with Montesquieu's than we might have imagined.

NOTES

1. Thank you to Jeffrey Church for his thoughtful feedback on an earlier draft of this paper presented at the Persian Letters Conference. Thank you to Constantine Vassiliou and Jeffrey Church for the invitation to participate.

2. Margaret C. Jacob, "The Cosmopolitan as a Lived Category," *Daedalus* 137, no. 3 (2008): 25.

3. Margaret C. Jacob, *Strangers Nowhere in the World: The Rise of Cosmopolitanism in Early Modern Europe* (Philadelphia: University of Pennsylvania Press, 2006), 13.

4. Melvin Richter, "Montesquieu's Comparative Analysis of Europe and Asia: Intended and Unintended Consequences," in *Charles-Louis de Secondat, Baron de Montesquieu*, ed. David Carrithers (London: Routledge, 2016), 350.

5. Though Kleingeld's focus is Germany, her typology is useful beyond that specific country. Pauline Kleingeld, "Six Varieties of Cosmopolitanism in Late Eighteenth-Century Germany," *Journal of the History of Ideas* 60, no 3 (1999): 515.

6. Jean Starobinski, *Blessings in Disguise; or, The Morality of Evil*, trans. Arthur Goldhammer (Cambridge, MA: Harvard University Press, 1993), 68.

7. Charles A. Knight, "The Images of Nations in Eighteenth-Century Satire." *Eighteenth-Century Studies* 22, no. 4 (1989): 503.

8. Charles-Louis de Secondat, Baron de Montesquieu, *The Persian Letters*, trans. Stuart D. Warner and Stéphane Douard (South Bend, IN: St. Augustine's Press, 2017), letter 1, 5. Further citations will be made in text.

9. Indeed, given that we later learn Usbek's more pressing reasons for leaving Isfahan (Letter 8, 13–14), Rica may seem more like the one truly seeking out knowledge.

10. Lisa Lowe, *Critical Terrains: French and British Orientalisms* (Ithaca, NY: Cornell University Press, 1991), 231.

11. Cited in Antoine Lilti, *The World of the Salons: Sociability and Worldliness in Eighteenth-Century Paris* (Oxford: Oxford University Press, 2020.), 276, n. 170.

12. Rica's Parisian education is by and large free from the influence of women, though women are nonetheless the subject of several letters. Letter 52 (84–85) is an exception, where a visit to a salon appears to be the occasion.

13. Daniel Gordon, *Citizens without Sovereignty: Equality and Sociability in French Thought, 1670–1789* (Princeton, NJ: Princeton University Press, 1994), 75.

14. Roxanne L. Euben, *Journeys to the Other Shore: Muslim and Western Travelers in Search of Knowledge* (Princeton, NJ: Princeton University Press, 2008), 148

15. See also Megan Gallagher, "Fear, Liberty, and Honourable Death in Montesquieu's Persian Letters," *Eighteenth-Century Fiction* 28, no. 4 (2016): 623–44.

16. I prefer this translation of "un homme d'esprit" to Warner and Douard's "witty man" as it more clearly distinguishes between Usbek's self-understanding and the depiction of "wits" in letter 54. See Charles-Louis de Secondat, Baron de Montesquieu, *Lettres persanes*, ed. Laurent Versini (Paris: GF Flammarion, 1995), 590, and *The Persian Letters*, trans. Raymond N. MacKenzie (Indianapolis, IN: Hackett Publishing, 2014), 227.

17. Montesquieu, *The Persian Letters*, Warner and Douard's edition, letter 145, 227.

18. Mary Helen McMurran, "The New Cosmopolitanism and the Eighteenth Century," *Eighteenth-Century Studies* 47, no. 1 (2013): 32.

19. Montesquieu, *The Persian Letters*, MacKenzie's edition, appendix, 282.

20. Kleingeld, "Six Varieties of Cosmopolitanism in Late Eighteenth-Century Germany," 515.

21. Starobinski, *Blessings in Disguise*, 70–71.

22. Srinivas Aravamudan, "Response: Exoticism beyond Cosmopolitanism?" *Eighteenth-Century Fiction* 25, no. 1 (2012): 230.

23. Starobinski, *Blessings in Disguise*, 69.

24. Kleingeld, "Six Varieties of Cosmopolitanism," 518.

25. Stephen J. Rosow, "Commerce, Power and Justice: Montesquieu on International Politics," *Review of Politics* 46, no. 3 (1984): 365.

26. Kleingeld, "Six Varieties of Cosmopolitanism," 520.

27. Knight, "The Images of Nations," 503.

28. Montesquieu, *The Persian Letters*, Warner and Douard's edition, 13.

29. Ian Coller, "East of Enlightenment: Regulating Cosmopolitanism between Istanbul and Paris in the Eighteenth Century," *Journal of World History* 21, no. 3 (2010): 448.

BIBLIOGRAPHY

Aravamudan, Srinivas. "Response: Exoticism beyond Cosmopolitanism?" *Eighteenth-Century Fiction* 25, no. 1 (2012): 227–42.

Coller, Ian. "East of Enlightenment: Regulating Cosmopolitanism between Istanbul and Paris in the Eighteenth Century." *Journal of World History* 21, no. 3 (2010): 447–70.

Euben, Roxanne L. *Journeys to the Other Shore: Muslim and Western Travelers in Search of Knowledge*. Princeton, NJ: Princeton University Press, 2008.

Gallagher, Megan. "Fear, Liberty, and Honourable Death in Montesquieu's *Persian Letters*." *Eighteenth-Century Fiction* 28, no. 4 (2016): 623–44.

Gordon, Daniel. *Citizens without Sovereignty: Equality and Sociability in French Thought, 1670–1789*. Princeton, NJ: Princeton University Press, 1994.

Jacob, Margaret C. "The Cosmopolitan as a Lived Category." *Daedalus* 137, no. 3 (2008): 18–25.

———. *Strangers Nowhere in the World: The Rise of Cosmopolitanism in Early Modern Europe*. Philadelphia: University of Pennsylvania Press, 2006.

Kleingeld, Pauline. "Six Varieties of Cosmopolitanism in Late Eighteenth-Century Germany." *Journal of the History of Ideas* 60, no. 3 (1999): 505–24.

Knight, Charles A. "The Images of Nations in Eighteenth-Century Satire." *Eighteenth-Century Studies* 22, no. 4 (1989): 489–511.

Lilti, Antoine. *The World of the Salons: Sociability and Worldliness in Eighteenth-Century Paris*. Oxford: Oxford University Press, 2020.

Lowe, Lisa. *Critical Terrains: French and British Orientalisms*. Ithaca, NY: Cornell University Press, 1991.

McMurran, Mary Helen. "The New Cosmopolitanism and the Eighteenth Century." *Eighteenth-Century Studies* 47, no. 1 (2013): 19–38.

Montesquieu, Charles-Louis Secondat, Baron de. *Lettres persanes*. Edited by Laurent Versini. Paris: GF Flammarion, 1995.

———. *My Thoughts*. Edited and translated by Henry C. Clark. Indianapolis, IN: Liberty Fund, 2012.

———. *The Persian Letters*. Translated by Raymond N. MacKenzie. Indianapolis, IN: Hackett, 2014.

———. *The Persian Letters*. Translated by Stuart D. Warner and Stéphane Douard. South Bend, IN: St. Augustine's Press, 2017.

Richter, Melvin. "Montesquieu's Comparative Analysis of Europe and Asia: Intended and Unintended Consequences." In *Charles-Louis de Secondat, Baron de Montesquieu*, edited by David Carrithers, 347–66. London: Routledge, 2016.

Rosow, Stephen J. "Commerce, Power and Justice: Montesquieu on International Politics." *Review of Politics* 46, no. 3 (1984): 346–66.

Spector, Céline. *Montesquieu. Pouvoirs, richesse et société*. Paris: Presses Universitaires de France, 2004.

Starobinski, Jean. *Blessings in Disguise; or, The Morality of Evil*. Translated by Arthur Goldhammer. Cambridge, MA: Harvard University Press, 1993.

PART IV

The *Persian Letters* as a Critique of Modernity

Chapter 11

Who Is the Hero of the
Persian Letters?

Jeffrey Church

The animating question of this chapter is a deceptively simple one: who is the protagonist of the novel the *Persian Letters*? This question turns out not to be easy to answer, as a brief survey of the scholarship on Montesquieu's work shows. In general, much of the older scholarship assumes that Usbek is the hero of the novel, as he appears at several points in the work to serve as a mouthpiece for Montesquieu's political and philosophical views. By contrast, Rica was regarded as an amusing sidekick, a diversion, comic relief, but not central to the aim and drama of the work.[1]

Conversely, recent scholarship—including several of the essays in this volume—has reversed the conclusion of the older scholarship. According to this new view, Usbek is no hero of the novel but rather, in his tyrannical arguments and action, an expression of the despotism that Montesquieu abhors.[2] He is, then, the villain of the novel. On this view, the novel critiques Usbek as a representative of the blindness to eros or the despotic tendencies in Enlightenment philosophy. Instead, scholars now regard Rica as the unsung hero of the *Persian Letters*, who champions the liberation of women and exhibits a cosmopolitan toleration in his letters, reflecting Montesquieu's considered views.[3]

On my view, both of these interpretations are one-sided in regarding only one of the main characters as the hero of the novel. My argument in this chapter is that Usbek and Rica are both the imperfect protagonists of the *Persian Letters*. In the first section below, I will argue that Usbek indeed espouses Enlightenment views on politics and religion, and so he represents one of Montesquieu's heroes in the novel. At the same time, I will argue that Montesquieu critiques Usbek as a despotic character, which prevents him from being the sole protagonist of the novel. In the second section, I claim that Rica reflects modern views on society or manners, so he must also be regarded as a hero. At the same time, I bring out Rica's limitations, as Montesquieu portrays him as a character who abstracts from political engagement and does not act in the novel.

Why does Montesquieu include two imperfect protagonists in his novel, rather than, say, one protagonist (or three, etc.)? The reading I develop in this paper is that Usbek and Rica represent for Montesquieu two irreconcilable tendencies of modernity. Usbek stands in for the modern Enlightenment rationalism that, due to its laudable emphasis on depersonalizing politics, faces difficulties in guiding individuals in their personal lives. Rica, by contrast, represents the tendency of modernity toward critique and skepticism that, for all its worldliness, nevertheless veers into ironic detachment. Ultimately, it seems that Montesquieu included two protagonists in this novel to suggest that these two tendencies, toward action and toward reflection, can never be fully reconciled but rather must be kept in some friendly tension lest modern societies veer into despotic or ironic detachment.

USBEK

Usbek's Moderate Rationalism

In several ways, the older scholarly assessment of Usbek is correct. Usbek displays several virtues of a Montesquieuian hero. First, Usbek is a *philosopher*. In the very first letter of the work, Usbek portrays his motivation for undertaking the journey as philosophical: "Rica and I are perhaps the first among Persians who left their country out of a longing for knowledge, and who renounced the pleasures of a tranquil life in order to search laboriously for wisdom" (Letter 1, 5). Like Montesquieu himself, Usbek recognizes that philosophical investigations conducted in one regime will not yield the truth about human nature. Different regimes produce different human characters, so a proper philosophical investigation of human nature would involve comparing different regimes, as Montesquieu himself does. To understand human beings, Usbek sees, one must travel to a radically different country in order to distinguish what is universal from what is merely particular and conventional.

Second, a result of Usbek's philosophical outlook on the world is that he is *skeptical of religious or traditional authority*. In letters 16–17, Usbek expresses his "doubts" about his religious faith to a "divine mullah," launching into a critique of the arbitrary positive dogmas surrounding food in Islam (Letter 16–17, 28–29). The response Montesquieu composes for the mullah indicates Montesquieu's own reservations about religious dogma. The mullah recounts a fantastical and absurd story about animals spontaneously emerging from excrement on Noah's ark (Letter 18, 31–32). Later, Usbek expresses exasperation with the hypocritical casuistry of some religious practice (Letter 57, 93–94), and raises concerns about core dogmas of the Judeo-Christian tradition, particularly related to chastity and the marriage prohibition on the part of Christian priests as inhibiting population growth and modern prosperity (Letter 116, 188–89). Instead, Usbek elsewhere calls for a more rationalistic approach to religion, one whose core beliefs are grounded on reason—a form of natural theology (Letters 69, 116–19; 83, 135–37, 97, 156–58)—as well as an emphasis on religious toleration. Usbek's critique of Shah Soliman's persecution of the Armenians is an unmistakable allusion to the unwise and unjust Revocation of the Edict of Nantes. As Usbek points out, religious toleration can be quite useful, as a "multiplicity of religions" in one regime can animate our "zeal" for obeying the law much more reliably than one religion can (Letter 85, 138–39).

Third, Usbek speaks truth to power and is *critical of despotism* in Persia. In letter 8, in which he elaborates on his motivation for his journey, he professes that in the despotic "court" of Persia, he "dared to be virtuous there" and "spoke a language there until then unknown" and "confronted flattery." This "sincerity" made him "enemies" in the form of the "jealousy of some ministers, without having the favor of the prince." As such, Usbek resolved to flee despotism for the freedom of the West, feigning a "great attachment to the sciences" but then eventually forming this "attachment" after all (Letter 8, 13). Like Montesquieu himself, Usbek's critical stance toward Persian despotism leads him to critique the despotism he finds in the West. In letter 37, for example, Usbek draws parallels between Persian despotism and the absolute monarchy of Louis XIV, noting that Louis's despotic power arouses his fear of the military officers who keep him in power (Letter 37, 60).

Finally, fourth, his criticism of despotic government brings him to a *defense of moderate government*, much like Montesquieu himself. In letter 80, Usbek writes that the "government" that "most conforms with reason" is the one that "proceeds to its end with the least difficulty": that is, the one that is most in line with human nature: a "gentle government" (Letter 80, 131). A moderate government does not cultivate slavish souls, nor does it arouse a furious backlash. Rather, it accords space for and facilitates human ambitions and desire for honor, fueling a dynamic modern society (Letter 89, 144–46). "Foreigners" are constantly attracted to modern government because of the "liberty and the opulence" found there, and industriousness follows, as all individuals seek riches (Letter 122, 200). Usbek, like Montesquieu, longs for the return of the *parlements* to reestablish moderate government in France. These *parlements* are the "bulwark of the monarchy and the foundation of all legitimate authority," that aristocratic institution that could function to check and balance the monarch and thereby uphold "public liberty" (Letter 92, 149).[4]

Taking these four traits together, we can conclude that Usbek represents a tendency of modern Enlightenment political rationalism. This tendency seeks to enlighten modern peoples to embrace reason and reject benighted religious superstition. It also aims to reform political regimes such that they cease to be governed by the arbitrary will of men but instead are governed by the rule of reason. Montesquieu himself is a well-known example of this type of moderate Enlightenment rationalism, so the older scholarship is quite correct to see in Usbek a reflection of Montesquieu's own views and hence an admiration that readers ought to have for this character.

Usbek's Tyrannical Rationalism

However, recent critics also correctly identify some major problems with Usbek's activity and his character. First, for all his criticism of despotism, he himself exhibits *despotic control* over his seraglio. In the second letter, following Usbek's philosophical self-aggrandizement in letter 1, Montesquieu has Usbek write to his chief eunuch reminding him of the absolute "mastery" he wields over the seraglio and the mastery that Usbek still has over the eunuch. Usbek asks him to "remember the nothingness out of which I took you" (Letter 2, 6). The framing drama of the *Persian Letters* consists in the unraveling of Usbek's despotic government. Following Usbek's futile efforts to confer "unlimited power" and to engender "fear and terror" (Letter 148, 257), his chief eunuch is killed, his wives are caught with lovers, and Roxane commits suicide in protest of his rule. If the novel is itself a critique of despotic government in all forms, then the novel must be indeed also engaged in criticizing Usbek himself.

Second, Usbek exhibits a striking *lack of self-knowledge* about the contradiction between his principles and his practice. Montesquieu has him make arguments whose wisdom he ignores in his own seraglio. For example, Usbek identifies a "contradiction" in the "human mind" that the more the "law" seeks to restrict "licentious debauchery," the more human beings rebel against the law and engage in it (Letter 33, 54). His own severe restriction on sexual behavior in the seraglio—and the resulting "licentious debauchery" that occurs—suggests that Usbek is unable to internalize his own views. In letter 146, Usbek castigates ministers who set a "bad example" (Letter 146, 255). Montesquieu underscores the irony of this comment by dating the letter after the destruction of the seraglio and Roxane's suicide, suggesting that Usbek still does not understand his own responsibility for these dramatic events. Despite his philosophical ambitions, Usbek fails to heed the fundamental injunction of the Delphic oracle: know thyself. In this way as well, Montesquieu portrays the limits of Usbek's philosophical credentials.

Third, Usbek's tyrannical drive to hold on to power makes him *unhappy and unfeeling*. Of course, as I have already suggested, Usbek's despotism is unjust. As Jaron exclaims to the first eunuch, "Great god! How many things are needed to make only one man happy!" (Letter 22, 37). Many individuals must be enslaved in order to serve the happiness of one. However, Montesquieu also points out that the precarious situation of the despot undermines this end of the happiness of one. Because human beings tend to resist and rebel against severe authority, as Usbek himself points out, that authority is always in jeopardy. Usbek thereby harbors a "secret jealousy that devours" him, a jealousy of all potential threats to his absolute rule (Letter 6, 10). Indeed, Usbek confesses in this same letter that too much satisfaction of his desires—too many wives, too much love—has led him to a "state of insensibility." He has "destroyed love by love itself" (ibid.). As Zelis points out to Usbek, his "suspicions" and "jealousy" are "so many marks of your dependence" and thus a source of his unhappiness and enslavement (Letter 62, 101). Usbek's Enlightenment philosophy and virtue are supposed to promise happiness, but ultimately Usbek finds himself the unhappy object of scorn and rebellion.

What are we to make of Montesquieu's critique of Usbek? Why does Montesquieu put these flaws into a representative of the kind of moderate Enlightenment that Montesquieu himself extols? Other scholars have suggested that Montesquieu indicates limits to Enlightenment's capacity to "cure our souls."[5] Others have argued that Usbek's form of Enlightenment rationalism contains in principle the aspiration to despotism that he exhibits in practice. In this volume, Peter Lund argues that Usbek's rationalism aims at political and social control and so reflects his own despotic personality.[6] Diana Schaub has argued that Usbek's philosophy is a form of Hobbesian rationalism, which is blind to the complexities of human eros. On Schaub's view, Montesquieu's critique of Usbek points toward an "erotic liberalism" that takes into account a more complete picture of the human being.[7]

I agree with these scholars that Montesquieu uses Usbek to display the dark side of modern rationalism. However, I disagree with their interpretation that Usbek represents a diminished, limited, or cramped vision of Enlightenment liberalism. If it were the case that Usbek represents an imperfect version of modern rationalism, Montesquieu would not portray Usbek's views and virtues as so close to his own. Any critique of Usbek's commitments, in other words, will at once be a critique of Montesquieu's commitments as well.

As such, on my view, Montesquieu's critique of Usbek is a critique of modern Enlightenment political rationalism as such. In other words, the problem facing modern rationalism is inherent to and inextricable from its benefits.[8]

The virtue of modern rationalism, as Montesquieu suggests it through the character of Usbek, is its depersonalization of politics. Usbek defends a vision of politics that replaces the rule of a personal ruler with the rule of law, that displaces the historical dogmas and idiosyncrasies of positive religion with an abstract natural theology, and that minimizes the role of personal virtue for the maintenance of a healthy political regime. A moderate government is one that pays less attention to individual desires and ambitions—or rather gives them freer rein—than a despotic government. However, this depersonaliza-tion of politics ironically leads modern political rationalism to abstract from the personal vices of the political rationalist himself. The perspective of the political rationalist is on the welfare of society as a whole. Individuals' wel-fare is only intelligible, on this view, as a function of the welfare of the group. As such, the rationalist perspective makes it difficult to have knowledge of particulars, of this or that individual, or especially myself as an individual. It can thereby blind one to the infractions of the individual when one is so caught up in what is general and universal, as Usbek is. It also renders it dif-ficult to find one's own happiness as distinct from the happiness of the group.

Consider a few examples from Usbek's letters. In letter 76, Usbek gives a rationalist account of the worth of human life, one that adopts the perspective sub specie aeternitatis. He argues that laws against suicide are unjust. They are motivated by "pride" in the worth of our individual lives as an "impor-tant object" in the universe. By contrast, the rational understanding of worth would not begin from my own perspective, but from the perspective of the whole. From that perspective, "all men together, a hundred million heads like ours, are only a tenuous and minute atom," and so if we kill ourselves, all that happens is that we change our form from a human to "an ear of corn, a worm, a piece of turf" (Letter 76, 126). From a rational perspective, individual life does not matter that much.

For a more political-economic example, consider Usbek's defense of modernity against Rhedi in letter 106. There, he defends the arts on the basis that it generates great industry. However, at the same time, Usbek indicates that this industry is unceasing, that "in order for a man to live delightfully, a hundred others must labor without letting up." All individuals are engaged in a competition to outdo the others, for "nobody likes to be poorer than the person whom he sees immediately beneath him" (Letter 106, 172). Here, Usbek adopts the rationalistic perspective that looks to the greatest benefit to the greatest number, extolling the means that will produce the greatest pros-perity. However, this very perspective takes no heed of the lack of individual satisfaction that is taken in the competitive struggle for status.

Modern political rationalism has the laudable aim to transcend the partial and personal perspectives of tradition and adopt a "view from nowhere," a universal perspective on human nature as such that can serve as a general standard for political criticism. Yet this Enlightenment universalism necessarily abstracts from and pays no heed to individuality and individual differences, to the arbitrary and the traditional. It remains in danger of being like Peter the Great, who, "restless and ceaselessly agitated," sought to "change everything," to reform and rationalize away the "ignorance of his subjects" and "make the arts flourish." Ultimately, Peter "wanders throughout his vast estates, leaving the marks of his natural severity everywhere" (Letter 51, 83). Unlike ancient rationalism, modern political rationalism does not equip individuals with the capacity for self-knowledge that can bring its universalism down to earth.

RICA

Rica's Cosmopolitan Criticism

In recent scholarly work, Rica has made a meteoric rise in stature. Far from the sidekick or sideshow of the *Persian Letters*, Rica is regarded by several scholars as the hero of the work.[9] I agree with these scholars in part, but in my view, they miss the imperfections in Rica's character, which I will draw out as well below. Rica's virtues and vices are important to bring out because I will argue that he represents a second tendency in modern rationalism, an ironic skepticism, that is irreconcilable with the political rationalism I argued was implicit in Usbek's character.

Rica's first positive characteristic is that he advocates for the *emancipation of women*. Montesquieu takes great care to characterize the seraglio women in a complex and insightful way, to give them deep personalities in a striking contrast to the "Orientalist" novels of the time, which would portray the women of "the East" in superficially erotic terms. He gives Roxane the final words of the novel, even though hers is not the final letter chronologically. In doing so, Montesquieu demonstrates great sympathy for the plight of women in such an unequal condition. He gives voice to this sympathy in the character of Rica, who provides the most masterful critique of Usbek's despotism in his story of Ibrahim and Anaïs. That letter contains a reversal of the seraglio relationship, with one female master and many male slaves, but then concludes with an egalitarian relationship between the men and women, in which the new Ibrahim "dismissed all of the eunuchs, making his home accessible to everyone. He did not even want his wives to be allowed to veil themselves." The result is great happiness and fecundity—"thirty-six children" (Letter 142, 238). In addition, Rica expresses admiration for the freedom that women enjoy in the West and defends it against his Islamic practices (Letter 38, 60–62).

Second, Rica also demonstrates the achievement of a *cosmopolitan perspective*. In contrast to Usbek, Montesquieu portrays Rica as undergoing a personal transformation. Usbek remained a despotic personality throughout the novel. By contrast, Rica gradually loses "everything Asiatic that remains to it" in the course of his travels (Letter 63, 102). He demonstrates a keen interest in the social customs of the West and comments on them at length. As such, he exhibits curiosity about the world's diverse ways of being human. What he admires so much about Paris is that "nature" speaks in its manifold individuality, as it "expresses itself so differently, and which appears under so many forms." By contrast, in Persia, "character is completely uniform because it is forced" (Letter 63, 102). There is no room for the diversity of humanity to manifest itself as it does in the West.[10]

Third, at the same time, Rica reveals a capacity for *universal criticism*. Just as he shows a curiosity about the manifoldness of humanity, he also enjoys finding problems with the customs, often in a quite amusing way. For example, the freedom accorded in Parisian society leads individuals to engage in a competitive struggle for status to appease their vanity. This struggle gives rise to hypocrisy and egoism. Rica identifies one such talkative socialite who, in response to a criticism about the vanity of society, exclaims that he "never speaks about all" his many accomplishments and riches and boasts about his "modesty" (Letter 50, 81). More broadly, this drive for social vanity, Rica observes, leads individuals to die of "weariness" (Letter 87, 143). Throughout his letters, Rica finds hypocrisy, vanity, and vice penetrating all sectors of society, and he brings these features to light for criticism.

In sum, then, Montesquieu includes Rica as a modern philosophical tendency of a different type than Usbek. Like Usbek, he challenges traditional modes and orders and adopts a universal perspective on human conventions. Unlike Usbek, however, he is interested in what distinguishes human beings from one another rather than what we share in common. Usbek seeks the universal principles of human nature. Rica examines the individual idiosyncrasies embedded in the customs of each regime. Usbek tends to focus on politics and religion with universal, encompassing principles. Rica tends to focus on social customs that are diverse and personalistic. Usbek is serious and brooding, befitting his cold rationalist perspective. Rica is cheerful and funny, finding the humor in human things, which involves identifying what is contradictory in our personalities. Humor is found in the conflict between the general roles that we adopt and the divergent, inner, individual disposition we take toward these roles. Consider the humor Rica finds in two men who play the general role of witty men in Parisian society, yet individually, behind closed doors, they practice at and plagiarize their humor (Letter 54, 87–89). Conventional appearance prescribes men and women to adopt particular roles, but hidden from view is an individual who diverges from these roles and uses them for his own advantage. Rica's humor involves bringing this hidden individual idiosyncrasy to light and juxtaposing it next to the social expectation.

Rica's Detached Impotence

Recent scholars are correct to have identified Rica as a hero of the *Persian Letters* but have gone too far in overlooking the imperfections Montesquieu gives to Rica's character. In general terms, Montesquieu portrays Rica as an individual without any agency, any action undertaken in the world, but a mere detached observer of the world.

First, Rica *abstracts from politics* and reveals himself to be *politically impotent*. As is often noted, Usbek demonstrates a deep interest in politics, whereas Rica does not, preferring instead to comment on social customs. His primary interest resides in the mores surrounding women, while also taking up matters concerning, for example, vanity or wit or feigned intelligence (Letter 66, 106–107). Rica does, of course, touch on political and religious matters. Yet when he does so, it is always more critical than constructive. For example, in letter 24, he refers to Louis XIV as a "great magician" in his financial shenanigans, while the pope is a "magician" for making "the king believe that three is nothing but one" (Letter 24, 40). He points out the hypocrisy of Christian priests and critiques the Inquisition (Letter 29, 48–50), and details at length the absurd financial schemes of John Law (Letters 132, 217–20; 142, 239–43). In these letters, Rica critiques politics but offers no vision of a positive order, as Usbek does.

The problem, of course, with Rica's abstraction from politics is that he leaves himself thereby unable to act for the benefit of individuals when it really matters. The most important political opportunity Montesquieu gives to Rica is in letter 141, in which Rica writes a letter critical of seraglio despotism directly to Usbek. Montesquieu dates this letter in the midst of the downfall of Usbek's seraglio, indicating that it could play a pivotal role in its fate. The letter comes after Usbek's third grant of authority to his eunuchs (Letter 153) and his letter rebuking his wives (Letter 154) and bemoaning his fate (Letter 155), but before his wives' response (Letters 156–58) and of course Roxane's suicide (Letter 161). In other words, Rica's letter comes at a pivotal time in the drama—or it perhaps comes too late, after Usbek's desperate interventions. If it comes at the right time, Montesquieu shows Rica to be an ineffective counselor. His advice in this letter—become an egalitarian Ibrahim!—is not heeded by Usbek. But if Rica's letter comes too late, it shows Rica to be inattentive and detached from his friend's plight. In other words, Rica's abstraction from politics reveals him to be either politically impotent or imprudent.

Second, Rica's criticism and humor veers into *ironic detachment* from the world around him. Often his humor involves some innocent fun, as when he tells each woman of three different ages what they want to hear to satisfy their vanity (Letter 52, 84–85). But where does he belong in the world? Rica confesses he feels in "continual motion" upon arrival in France, without a stable place to be (Letter 24, 58). He found that he was mobbed by Parisian socialites who were curious about his exotic dress. Rica thereby "quit my Persian dress" and instead dressed like a European. When he did so, it revealed, he says, "what I was really worth . . . for all at once I entered into a frightful nothingness," with no Parisian even giving him a second glance. But once they learned he was Persian, then the "buzz" around him resumed (Letter 30, 51). Rica feels alienated from Paris when recognized as a foreigner but feels even more alienated from belonging when he is recognized as a Parisian.

Furthermore, Rica's irony can leave him detached from the very real injustices and suffering of individuals in society. In one of his most discussed letters, letter 28, Rica ironically describes the Parisian audience as the actors and actresses putting on a play, feigning social roles and the like. It is all great fun and quite funny the way Rica describes the theatricality of modern social manners. However, he concludes by reproducing a letter from an actress who confesses that a "young abbé . . . ravished [her] innocence" and left her penniless and with child. The actress pleads with a stranger she only met the day before to travel with him to Persia to make a new "fortune" as a "dancer" (Letter 28, 48). Though commentators have discussed the first half of the letter, no one has pointed out the striking contrast between the lighthearted playacting of the first half and the suffering of a poor young woman in the second half of the letter who "grows older" and "loses some of [her] charms" and her "salary . . . seems to diminish every day" (Letter 28, 48). Yet Rica describes them both in the same detached, ironic tone. Indeed, we only have Rica's recapitulation of the actress' letter, which has a desperate and fantastical plea to make a new fortune in a country she has never visited. In the face of this very real suffering, in other words, Rica laughs. The idiosyncrasies of individuality are more interesting to him than the political project of reforming society to end these injustices.

What is Montesquieu trying to convey in according these flaws to Rica? On my view, Rica represents for Montesquieu a second tendency of modernity that, like Usbek's political rationalism, contains both benefits and flaws. Rica embodies the skeptical tendency of modernity, born like Enlightenment political rationalism out of a critique of all given, dogmatic authorities in nature and in tradition. This tendency, again like the Enlightenment tradition, seeks to liberate individuals from the trappings of all these customs and allow them to live as they please. Unlike Enlightenment rationalism, however, the skeptical tradition extends its skepticism to reason's deliverances as well. Reason purports to discover universal norms implicit in all human life. For the skeptic, reason's claims are no different from any other universalizing claim of tradition or religion that claims to have discovered a single truth about human life. For the skeptic, philosophers have disagreed and will continue to disagree about which claims are in fact true, and no philosophy or religion has been able to develop an infallible argument in its favor. As such, as a skeptic, Rica engages in very little philosophy of human nature. Instead, in line with this skeptical tendency, Rica surveys the multiplicity of particular ways of being human on view in Paris. The skeptic thereby gains satisfaction in surveying the many ways of being human, while standing above each of them with the cosmopolitan ability to mix and match these different ways into a hybrid construct, much as Rica does when he reverses a Persian seraglio with Western egalitarian gender norms (Letter 141, 232–38).

However, the problem with this skeptical tendency of modernity, Montesquieu is suggesting through Rica, is that it tends to estrange individuals from a sense of belonging in any particular place. The radical critique of all customs and the hovering above them as a cosmopolitan bricoleur means that one can call no particular convention home. As such, it engenders a form of ironic detachment from one's fellows who indeed belong to a tradition or convention. Rather than conceiving of oneself as part of a common or universal project, the ironist critically reflects on the presuppositions underlying all such projects and so cannot ever become part of one. The ironist sees only individuality and recognizes the legitimacy of nothing common or universal, which renders all form of community suspect. Of course, Rica does not embody this ironic detachment in an extreme way. Nevertheless, Montesquieu indicates through Rica that the otherwise laudable modern tendency toward skepticism and cosmopolitanism contains a danger. His suggestion here, I think, is much the same as his take on what Usbek represents: a positive development of modernity that nonetheless contains some dangers that we should be conscious of as modernity develops.

The parallel between Usbek and Rica raises this final question, why does Montesquieu create a second imperfect protagonist? Why not one protagonist who embodies both tendencies, for example? My reading is that Montesquieu places these two tendencies in two divergent characters to indicate their ultimate irreconcilability. One might compare, as other scholars have done on other topics, Montesquieu and Hegel on this matter.[11] Hegel, for example, identifies similar problems with the universalism of modernity and with its tendency to ironic self-critique.[12] However, Hegel argues that ultimately such tendencies can be reconciled in a differentiated modern state that recognizes the value of both universal rational autonomy and individual distinctness or difference. In a contemporary context, following Hegel as well, Charles Taylor has defended the reconcilability of universal Enlightenment reason with the difference-sensitivity of multiculturalism with a nuanced account of recognition.[13]

Montesquieu, by contrast, is not as sanguine as these thinkers. It is hard to conceive of a possible character who might synthesize Usbek and Rica. Any such characterization would verge on incoherence. Montesquieu shows through these highly distinct characters that modernity itself contains highly distinct tendencies, and that any attempt to synthesize them would result in losing the distinctness of one or both, the tendency toward universalism or the tendency toward individual difference. The wisest approach to the problems of modernity, Montesquieu suggests through his characters, is to find the kinship between the two tendencies. Usbek and Rica, after all, are friends. Why are they friends, given their great differences? They share a pursuit of wisdom and a distaste for arbitrary authority. By emphasizing this commonality, Montesquieu suggests, the two tendencies can be bound together in friendship. This friendship could arrest the worst effects of each tendency. Each keeps the other one grounded: Rica reminding Usbek of the individuality of the women who are oppressed under his despotic system, and Usbek reminding Rica of his particular homeland and heritage. Each would thereby recognize a shared pursuit of wisdom that might ultimately, in the case of Usbek, incline him to self-knowledge, and, in the case of Rica, push him to genuine human connection.

NOTES

1. See, for example, Jean Starobinski, *Blessings in Disguise; or, The Morality of Evil* (Cambridge, MA: Harvard University Press, 1993), 67–68.

2. "There is an unbridgeable chasm in Usbek's life separating speech and deed." Stuart Warner, "Montesquieu's Literary Art: An Introduction to the Persian Letters," in *Persian Letters*, trans. Stuart Warner and Stéphane Douard (South Bend, IN: St. Augustine's Press, 2017), xxxviii. See, in this volume, Vickie B. Sullivan, "Hiding in Plain Sight: Montesquieu as a Friendly Influence in the *Persian Letters*," and Peter Lund, "The Unknown Chains of Enlightenment: The Irony of Philosophy or an Ironic Philosopher."

3. See, in this volume, Stuart Warner, "The Book of Relations: Reflections from Montesquieu's *Persian Letters*"; Megan Gallagher, "Rica in Paris: Sociability and Cosmopolitanism in the Persian Letters"; Andrea Radasanu, "Pitfalls of Abstract Ideals: Usbek on the Law of Nations," understands the book to be a criticism of Usbek's approach to natural law and a defense of Rica.

4. See Rylan Hanley, "Distance Learning: Political Education in the Persian Letters," *Review of Politics* 93, no. 4 (2021), on Usbek's method of educating his interlocutors on his views.

5. Sullivan, "Hiding in Plain Sight," 18.

6. Lund, "Unknown Chains."

7. Dianna J. Schaub, *Erotic Liberalism: Women and Revolution in Montesquieu's Persian Letters* (Lanham, MD: Rowman and Littlefield, 1995), ch. 2.

8. In this critique of modern political rationalism, Montesquieu's view anticipates that of Oakeshott's; see Michael Oakeshott, "Rationalism in Politics," in *Rationalism in Politics and Other Essays* (Indianapolis, IN: Liberty Fund, 1991). For Oakeshott, modern rationalism transforms all knowledge into an algorithmic process accessible to everyone, which overlooks the personal "know-how" implicit in individual human practices.

9. See note 3 above.

10. See Gallagher, "Rica in Paris," for a helpful elaboration on the different types of cosmopolitanism Rica embodies.

11. See, for example, Michael Mosher, "The Particulars of a Universal Politics: Hegel's Adaption of Montesquieu's Typology," *American Political Science Review* 78, no. 1 (1994): 179–88.

12. See, for example, Georg Wilhelm Friedrich Hegel, *Elements of the Philosophy of Right*, ed. Allen W. Wood (Cambridge: Cambridge University Press, 1991), sec. 138–140.

13. See Charles Taylor, "The Politics of Recognition," in *Campus Wars: Multiculturalism and Politics of Difference*, ed. John Arthur, 25–73 (Boulder, CO: Westview Press, 1995).

BIBLIOGRAPHY

Hanley, Ryan. "Distance Learning: Political Education in the Persian Letters." *Review of Politics* 93, no. 4 (2021): 533–54.

Hegel, Georg Wilhelm Friedrich. *Elements of the Philosophy of Right*. Edited by Allen W. Wood. Cambridge: Cambridge University Press, 1991.

Mosher, Michael. "The Particulars of a Universal Politics: Hegel's Adaption of Montesquieu's Typology." *American Political Science Review* 78, no. 1 (1994): 179–88.

Oakeshott, Michael. "Rationalism in Politics." In *Rationalism in Politics and Other Essays*, 5–42. Indianapolis, IN: Liberty Fund, 1991.

Schaub, Diana J. *Erotic Liberalism: Women and Revolution in Montesquieu's Persian Letters*. Lanham, MD: Rowman and Littlefield, 1995.

Starobinski, Jean, *Blessings in Disguise; or, The Morality of Evil*. Cambridge, MA: Harvard University Press, 1993.

Taylor, Charles. "The Politics of Recognition." In *Campus Wars: Multiculturalism and Politics of Difference*, edited by John Arthur, 25–74. Boulder, CO: Westview Press, 1995.

Warner, Stuart. "Montesquieu's Literary Art: An Introduction to the Persian Letters." In *Persian Letters*. Translated by Stuart Warner and Stéphane Douard (South Bend, IN: St. Augustine's Press, 2017).

Chapter 12

Hiding in Plain Sight

Montesquieu as a Friendly Influence in the Persian Letters

Vickie B. Sullivan

Many readers of the *Persian Letters* have seen something of Montesquieu in his fictional character Usbek, "who in many ways resembles his author."[1] Indeed, at times Montesquieu's Persian character utters ideas and opinions that Montesquieu himself will repeat in his own name in his later political works, *Considerations of the Greatness of the Romans and Their Decline* and the magisterial product of his mature years, *The Spirit of the Laws*. This similarity of views was so apparent to those who knew Montesquieu best, not only to his intimate friends but also to his son, that they jokingly referred to the French author as Usbek.[2]

As understandable as this is, given the likeness of views on some issues such as population, criminal punishment, commercial activity, and the desirability of religious toleration, there is something so deeply inapt about the equation that even to entertain it seems to border on the absurd because in many respects the character embodies what Montesquieu regards as the greatest of societal evils—a despot.[3] A Persian aristocrat who is the victim of the machinations of a court under a despotic ruler, Usbek is himself a despot in his domestic life as he maintains a seraglio, keeping his several wives cloistered from the world at large so as to secure their "virtue." Usbek commands eunuchs—slaves denied the prospect of their own family—to guard his female treasure by enforcing his wives' virtue. In his larger household, Usbek maintains other slaves, those who serve his wives and eunuchs as servants, and concubines, whom his agents purchase on the international slave market to adorn his seraglio and to help satisfy his carnal desires. All the members of his extended seraglio subordinate their wills to Usbek's. Stuart Warner comments that "Montesquieu directs us to recognize the degraded world of the seraglio as representative of tyranny, and Usbek as the principal exemplar of the tyrant."[4] Not only in *The Spirit of the Laws* but also in the *Persian Letters*, Montesquieu aims his acerbic insight against despotism, the subjection of women, and the inhumanity of slavery, for example. What association could there be between Montesquieu—whose very purpose as a writer is to combat despotism as the scourge of humanity—and his character, this murderous despot who occasionally expresses some enlightened opinions as he acclimates himself to the Paris of the early eighteenth century?

One possible explanation is that Montesquieu's *Persian Letters* shows his character Usbek absorbing not just any Enlightenment philosophy, but his own specifically. The preface, in fact, features the fictional translator and editor of the letters, who hosted these Persian visitors to France and came to know them well, announcing his vehement desire to remain anonymous. The letters themselves do not explicitly refer to any such friend and host, thus presenting readers with an apparent lacuna in the fictional story the work presents. There is a way to read the work that fills this lacuna, however. The assembler of the letters, to maintain his desired anonymity, has made sure that his engagement with his Persian friends is cloaked. He does admit to taking several other liberties with his friends' letters. This assembler is very much akin to Montesquieu. Thus, Montesquieu seems to hide in plain sight, exerting a friendly influence in the fiction of the work. That influence is great enough for Usbek to mouth some enlightened views, but certainly not great enough for Usbek to see himself for what he is—a despot—and to renounce his rule. In failing these tests, he is ultimately responsible for the deaths that ensue with the collapse of his seraglio.

THE PREFACE AND THE FICTIONAL ASSEMBLER OF THE LETTERS

Montesquieu published the titillating and politically provocative epistolary novel anonymously in Geneva. Montesquieu's caution in hiding his own identity is mimicked by the character he creates who provides in the work's preface the fictious explanation as to how these letters came to be published as a book.[5] He offers the current collection of letters, he explains, "to try out the public's taste"; if he finds that it is well received he will publish others from among the "great many others" that remain in his "portfolio." He has selected which letters to bring forward and which to suppress—at least for the time being. He then emphasizes his intense desire to maintain his anonymity, using the prospect of the public's desire for more such letters as leverage:

"But [the possibility of a sequel] is on the condition that I shall remain unknown—for if my name comes to be known, from that moment on I shall be silent," he threatens (Preface, 3).

The fictitious assembler of the collection then proceeds to offer an explanation of his intense caution surrounding his association with the work: "If it were known who I am, it would be said, 'His book clashes with his character. He should use his time for something better. This is unworthy of a serious man.'" The fictional author of these words, of course, sounds very much like Montesquieu, who had by this point in his life established his gravitas by having served as the Président à Mortier in the Parlement of Bordeaux and been welcomed as a member of the Academy of Bordeaux. Such an apparent turn to levity would provoke "[c]ritics" who, the assembler notes, "are never lacking in these kinds of reflections, because they can make them without trying to think much" (Preface, 3). Thus, this anonymous author of the preface together with Montesquieu as this character's author, encourage the reader to think much rather than little, so as to avoid being lumped in with this group of thoughtless critics.

The assembler of the letters proceeds to explain that the two Persians "who are writing here were lodged with me; we spent our lives together." Thus, he claims that he became the intimate friend of Usbek and Rica such that these three characters spent their fictional "lives together" in France (Preface, 3). Obviously, this claim provides a prima facie explanation as to how these letters came to exist as a collection, but without more reflection, this explanation cannot be said to be adequate. The letters, for instance, make explicit reference neither to such a Frenchman who spent his life with Usbek and Rica nor to the occasion of their first encounter nor to the venues of their subsequent meetings. In confronting this apparent lacuna in the story, a reader could reject the claim of the preface's author out of hand as being an ill-conceived and ill-integrated attempt on Montesquieu's part to provide a fictional explanation for the origin of these letters. There is, however, an alternative way to read the work so as to substantiate this claim: the fictional assembler of the letters who announces his desire to hide his identity has, in fact, redacted identifying information from the letters.

Such a disingenuous act would be entirely in keeping with the types of interventions the assembler reveals he has taken with the letters as he elaborates on his relationship to the Persians. Claiming that "people transplanted from so far away could no longer have any secrets," he explains that Usbek and Rica "looked upon me as a man from another world" and therefore "hid nothing from me." In this manner, the author suggests that their forthrightness induced the Persians to share their correspondence freely with their French host. This quality of the Persians would explain, of course, how the Frenchmen came into the possession of the letters that he would make public.

His subsequent comments undermine this claim to the Persians' utter transparency, however. Immediately after claiming that the Persians hid nothing from him, he explains that they did endeavor, in fact, to hide things from him, which he proceeded to uncover: "I even fell upon several others that they were careful not to confide to me, so mortifying were these letters to Persian vanity and jealousy" (Preface, 3).[6] Because he explicitly contradicts his immediate prior claim of the utter transparency of his Persian friends, the reader is thus warned not to take his assertions at face value. The preface of the work establishes that the assembler of the letters dissembles.

In addition, it must be noted that the assembler does not specify whether none, some, or all such embarrassing letters are included in the ones he now publishes. Given that the *Persian Letters* reveals that the wife whom Usbek had judged most virtuous had long been conducting an illicit affair and that the resistance she offered to her husband's sexual advances derived not from virtuous modesty but rather from revulsion, such that Usbek's ultimate success in consummating their marriage constituted rape,[7] the reader might well conclude that he includes at least some such embarrassing letters in the current publication.

Immediately after this manifest contradiction, the preface's author offers another such transparently false claim when he declares that he acts "only as a translator." Now, we know that this is not strictly true, as he has already acknowledged that he has selected which letters to publish. Nevertheless, he again makes a statement in order to revise it so significantly as to make the first articulation into a falsehood. Far from merely translating the letters, he here explains that he deemed it necessary to adapt their Persian letters "to our morals." What that means precisely and how such adaptations changed the originals he does not say. He proceeds to note that he also saw fit to delete what he deemed extraneous: "I have spared the reader from the Asiatic language as much as I could, and have saved him from an infinite number of sublime expressions" (Preface, 3). His purported solicitude for the reader guided his interventions with the text: "But that is not all I have done for [the reader]," as he notes that he has also "cut out the lengthy compliments that the Orientals use no less lavishly than we do." Perhaps, as he suggests, nothing of value was lost in these extractions, but then he points to even greater intervention on his part: "I have passed over an infinite number of trivialities that have so much difficulty withstanding the light of day, and that must always die between friends" (Preface, 4). The first part of the sentence suggests that he merely excised comments on the quotidian, but the subsequent description of the excised matter as reflections that "must always die between friends" suggests discussions of far greater import. Contrary to his overt claims, then, he is no mere translator, but rather an editor with a most interventionist bent. We have known this fact from the very beginning of the preface, however, where he explains to his readers, as we have seen above, that he has for the moment suppressed some letters so as to have leverage in maintaining his anonymity. The *Persian Letters* have been curated by this Frenchmen who, like Montesquieu himself, is just well-known enough as a man of gravity to wish to remain aloof from the matter of the letters that he publishes.

The assembler shares another characteristic with Montesquieu. Both may be accused of deception with regard to the texts for which they are responsible. We have already noted above that the assembler's descriptions of his actions contradict his statements regarding them. Montesquieu himself admits to being less than candid with his readers in this epistolary novel. The posthumous 1758 edition of *Persian Letters* contained "Some Reflections on *Persian Letters*," in which Montesquieu describes how the form of the novel "allows" "the author" to combine "philosophy, politics, and morality" in "a secret, and, in some fashion, unknown chain" ("Some Reflections," 269). He thus confesses to keeping secrets from his readers. He later seeks to claim his innocence with respect to any such subterfuge: "Certainly the nature and design of *Persian Letters* are so apparent that they will deceive only those who want to deceive themselves" ("Some Reflections," 271). This claim hardly offers absolution, however, because the nature and design of the work are hardly "so apparent," as he himself has confessed above. In this manner, in avowing his innocence, he actually confesses to his deceptive techniques.

USBEK'S OBSCURED HAVEN AND HIS UNNAMED FRIEND

Asterisks appear in the work to mask the identity of the recipient or recipients of letters as well as the location or locations outside of Paris from which correspondence originates or to which it is sent. These asterisks appear in Montesquieu's manuscript, so they are intentional on his part and are not the product of any defect of his manuscript. For the purposes of this chapter's examination of Usbek's relation to Montesquieu, only the asterisks that obscure locations will be examined here.[8] Because they are a part of the story Montesquieu creates, one must reflect on what purpose they serve within that fiction of the novel. One intriguing possibility has already presented itself. Perhaps these asterisks, which obscure a location outside of Paris, serve to cloak the identity of the fictional assembler of the letters. It is the assembler, after all, who claims to have spent a great deal of time with these Persians and, in fact, to have hosted them during their stay in France. He also has expressed a keen desire for anonymity. The host who offers Usbek a haven from Paris could very well be the fictional assembler who exerts a friendly influence, schooling Usbek in enlightened thought—that is, in the thought of Montesquieu.

The location of this unnamed friend first becomes an issue in letter 45 when Rica, who is in Paris, writes to Usbek at a location that is redacted. The Persian friends are now separated—far enough apart that they need to write, as Rica wrote to his French friend, but not so far apart that Usbek does not return periodically to the bustle of the Parisian streets.[9] Thus, the country house that Usbek finds so charming appears to be just outside of Paris. Indeed, at one point, Rica notes that he sends a letter to Usbek even though he knows he will see his correspondent "at the end of the week" (Letter 141, 247). Thus, it appears not to be a fictionalized version of Montesquieu's chateau in Bordeaux, because travel to and from this rather distant province would be longer and more arduous than what is depicted in the novel.

Rica prefers Paris as his abode, while Usbek clearly prefers the quiet of the country.[10] In letter 63, writing to Usbek from Paris, Rica complains of his friend's penchant for quiet: "I believe that you want to spend your life in the country. I lost you at first for two or three days, and now it is fifteen and I have not seen you." Rica acknowledges the appeal of Usbek's undisclosed situation, writing to his friend that "you are in a charming house; that you find a society that is agreeable to you; that there you reason completely at your leisure." Rica concludes of Usbek's attachment to this country home: "Nothing more is needed to make you forget the entire universe" (Letter 63, 101–102).

Although the assembler of the letters does not permit this French host and companion of the Persians to speak directly by means of a letter or letters authored by him, he does speak indirectly, because his Persian friends make reference to individual Europeans whose opinions they hold in high regard. Frequently, the European whom they respect both reveals interests and holds views that are widely associated with Montesquieu. For example, Usbek writes to Ibben that "a man of good sense [*un homme de bon sens*] said to me the other day, 'People are in many respects freer in France than in Persia; thus they love glory more'" (Letter 89, 144).[11] The remainder of the letter consists of Usbek's continuing quotation of this man's remarks. Every detail of the quotation could come from Montesquieu, who is, as this very work shows, intensely interested in the contrast between Eastern and Western mores and political forms. Moreover, in treating the topic of glory in this letter, Usbek quotes this man as discussing antiquity—Athens, Lacedaemonia, and Rome—and the features of Persian despotism that beat down the spirit of those with responsibility in the despotic regime. The words of this man, which Usbek transcribes and transmits to his Turkish friend, are very much akin to those of Montesquieu, the philosopher.

Another such instance occurs when again writing to Ibben, Usbek recounts "what a rather sensible European [*un Européen assez sensé*] said to [him] the other day" (Letter 103, 166).[12] Again, this letter consists of a long quotation that could be a part of a treatise written by Montesquieu. The quoted passage reflects on the history of Europe and the differences between France and Persia that suggest why despotism is so deeply entrenched in Asia. Thus, Usbek again transmits ideas to Ibben that are entirely in harmony with Montesquieu's political thought.

Rica, too, writes to Ibben of a European who has challenged his thinking, and yet again the remarks are strikingly similar to views that Montesquieu expresses. Having grown up in a society in which women do not appear in polite society but are rather enclosed in the households of their fathers or husbands, Rica uses his sojourn in Paris to learn of women, of whom he says he knew nothing until he came to Paris. In writing to his Turkish friend, he pursues the question "of knowing if natural law subjugates women to men." Rica then refers to a conversation he had recently had with a noteworthy European: "a very *galant* philosopher [*un philosophe trés galant*] said to me the other day" that "the empire that we hold over [women] is a veritable tyranny." Rica elaborates that this philosopher explained that this lamentable condition of women has resulted from the fact that they are "more humane and reasonable" than men. Moreover, these very "advantages" "should have given them superiority over us, have made them lose it, because [males] are not reasonable" (Letter 38, 61).[13] On the basis of humanity and reasonableness, this philosopher of Rica's acquaintance responds to his question regarding the natural subservience of women to men by maintaining the natural subservience of men to women.

In this way, Rica reveals the intriguing detail of his life that he is in conversation with a European philosopher regarding the nature of females and their proper role in society. It is, of course, tempting to speculate on the identity of Rica's interlocutor. The editor and translator of the Penguin edition suggests that Rica is probably making reference to Fontenelle, "whom Montesquieu very probably knew before 1721."[14] By contrast, Stuart Warner suggests that "Montesquieu comes to mind as a possibility."[15] There is much to corroborate Warner's suggestion. First, the work itself shows that Montesquieu is intensely interested in women and their oppression. Indeed, one commentator writes that "the considerable attention Montesquieu devotes to sexual equality in the *Persian Letters* makes this work an important philosophical source for the women's liberation movement."[16]

This interest on Montesquieu's part continues in his later *Spirit of the Laws*. For example, in a chapter entitled "On Administration by Women," he concludes that women can make very fine rulers of states and of empires. He observes that in the "Indies government by women turns out very well" and then notes that "if one adds to this the examples of Muscovy and of England, one will see that they succeed equally well in moderate and in despotic government," apparently pointing to the rule of Elizabeth of Russia and Elizabeth I of England. He also declares in this chapter that "their very weakness" in terms of physical strength "gives them more gentleness and moderation, which, rather than the harsh and ferocious virtues, can make for a good government."[17] Montesquieu, like the philosopher of Rica's acquaintance, believes that feminine gentleness makes women admirable rulers.

Another possible identifying element is Rica's application of the term "very *galant*" to his philosophical acquaintance. If Rica means by *galant* a philosopher who pays special attention to women and has an especial appreciation of their charms, it is certainly the case that Montesquieu displays just such sentiments elsewhere in *The Spirit of the Laws*. When treating the spirit, mores, and manners of various nations in book XIX, Montesquieu emphasizes the critical role that women play in French society in chapters 5 and 6. Montesquieu speaks of France quite coyly in these passages in book XIX, never identifying the nation by name. He does, however, use the plural first person as subjects and objects in the second of these two chapters, thus indicating that he speaks of himself and his French compatriots.

Montesquieu begins this consideration in chapter 5 by reflecting: "If there were in the world a nation which had a sociable humor, an openness of heart; a joy in life, a taste, and ease in communicating its thoughts; which was lively, pleasant, playful, sometime imprudent, often indiscreet," then "one should avoid disturbing its manner by laws, in order not to disturb its virtues." He then asks rhetorically, "If the character is generally good, what difference do a few faults make?" He further resists any effort at reform of this people's character when he observes that "one could restrain its women, make laws to correct their mores and limit their luxury, but who knows whether one would not lose a certain taste that would be the source of the nation's wealth and a politeness that attracts foreigners to it?" He concludes the chapter with the admonition that this nation should be left to "do frivolous things seriously and serious things gaily."[18] Montesquieu thus offers a keen appreciation of the politeness and softening effects that women bring to a society very much like France.

In the chapter that follows, Montesquieu corroborates the sentiments of the prior one as he brings forward an unnamed "gentleman" to express his views. The chapter begins with this character's admonition: "May we be left as we are, said a gentleman of a nation closely resembling the one of which we have just given an idea." Montesquieu is, of course, the gentleman who here speaks, and the nation to which he refers in the first person is his own. This gentleman notes that "nature" "has given us a vivacity capable of offending and one apt to make us inconsiderate; this same vivacity is corrected by the politeness it brings us, by inspiring us with a taste for the world and above all for commerce with women." The French social life is distinctive; many who do not partake of its pleasures may very well regard it as requiring reform, but the gentleman in this chapter, like Montesquieu in his own name in the prior one, rejects that call: "Our discretions joined to our harmlessness make unsuitable such laws as would curb our sociable nature."[19] Just as Montesquieu cloaks his views of the importance of women behind an unnamed "gentleman" in *The Spirit of the Laws*, so he seems to hide similar views behind the "very *galant* philosopher" of Rica's letter.

If Montesquieu intended this philosopher to be a fictionalized version of himself, as Warner and I both suggest, then he has been quite open indeed with Rica about his views of the proper place of women in society. If the fictional Montesquieu was so forthcoming with Rica, one might ask whether he was similarly forthcoming with Usbek, the ruler of a seraglio and hence one who wields this most awesome, unjust, and unnatural power over the female sex. If this philosopher did broach the topic of women's unjust subjugation to men with Usbek, those reflections do not seem to have permeated his consciousness, as they do not come out in his letters.

In the two instances we have examined, Usbek and Rica report to Ibben the reflections of a particular European—one who sounds very much like Montesquieu. But there are several other very prominent instances in which Usbek appears to convey elements of Montesquieu's thought without attributing the views to a European of his acquaintance. Instead, Usbek offers these views in his own name. What is significant about this is that Montesquieu shows this Persian character so imbibing his thought with respect to issues that do not touch on Usbek's rule of his wives and slaves that he seems to embody Montesquieu himself. No greater example of Usbek thus becoming a veritable mouthpiece for Montesquieu exists than the ten letters he writes on the issue of the depopulation of the world. This series of eleven letters, counting Rhedi's letter that initiates the topic, constitutes by far the most sustained focus on a single topic in the novel.[20] Rhedi reflects to Usbek that the modern world is vastly devoid of population compared to ancient times. He continues that this depopulation is "the most terrible catastrophe that has ever happened in the world"—one that "has been scarcely perceived, because it has happened insensibly over the course of a great number of centuries" (Letter 112, 182). Rhedi's remarks set Usbek off on this extended dissertation on the causes of the world's depopulation. That Montesquieu shares these very concerns of Usbek, one need look no further than book XXII of *The Spirit of the Laws*, entitled "On the Laws in Their Relation to the Number of Inhabitants," where Montesquieu will offer a similar analysis in his own name. Among the topics Montesquieu there considers is how the Christian devotion to "perfection" at first "permitted celibacy soon imposed the necessity of that celibacy."[21] With more individuals committed to a life devoted to God rather than to family, fewer marriages occurred and thus fewer children were born.

It might be said, however, that Usbek, in a private letter to a Turkish friend, is much more critical of this aspect of Christianity than is Montesquieu in his own treatise. Usbek condemns the Christian virtue of chastity. "I am speaking about the priests and dervishes of both sexes who take vows to eternal continence." He continues that chastity "is, among Christians, the virtue *par excellence*," noting that he does "not understand [it], not knowing how that which is a virtue results in nothing." He continues that the monasteries and nunneries of Christian lands that commit their denizens to chastity are "like so many pits [*gouffres*] in which future generations are to be buried" (Letter 117, 191).[22] Usbek speaks here, but how can a reader doubt that the Persian character received this vituperation of clerical life from a philosophical Frenchman? This result suggests that the fictionalized Montesquieu was more forthcoming in a private conversation than he would actually be in his great work of political philosophy, which he would publish anonymously but which would ultimately bear his name. Nevertheless, as author of the *Persian Letters*, Montesquieu shows the friendly influence of an unnamed Frenchman of "*bon sens*" who befriended these Persians. It is from this friendship that Usbek learns such arguments and comes to embrace them.

USBEK'S OTHER ENLIGHTENED FRIEND

If a fictionalized Montesquieu is the character who befriends Rica and Usbek in France, he is not the first friend they make from a foreign nation during their travels. Ibben, a Sunni Muslim who resides in Turkey is another such acquaintance who becomes an intimate friend of both Persian travelers. Ibben is at first a favorite correspondent of Usbek and an intimate confidant. Ibben responds to these confidences by attempting to educate Usbek regarding his status as a despotic ruler of a seraglio. Usbek responds to Ibben's efforts at enlightenment by increasing silence, to which Ibben pleads for Usbek's renewed commitment to their friendship. Nevertheless, Usbek appears to be uneducable by the hand of Ibben. Ibben's influence on Usbek prefigures and mirrors that of the fictionalized Montesquieu on Usbek.

Ibben makes his first appearance when Usbek writes to him upon reaching the shores of Europe on April 12, 1712. Usbek explains that after a voyage of forty days, the travelers arrived in Europe at the port of Livorno on the Italian peninsula. Although he and his Turkish friend belong to different sects of Islam, Usbek appeals to their common faith on this occasion: "It is a great spectacle for a Mohammedan to see a Christian city for the first time" (Letter 23, 38). He then explains that he and Rica will depart for Marseilles the next day, with the intention of settling in Paris.

Upon having been in Paris for a month, Rica, true to his character as a keen observer with an acerbic wit, writes to Ibben to offer his reflections both on the king of France, who functions, in his estimation, as a "great magician," and on the pope, who functions as an even "stronger" "magician," as well as on various French religious and political controversies of the time (Letter 24, 40). Usbek writes a much briefer letter to Ibben on the same day, offering expressions of gratitude for the hospitality the Turk had extended to Rica and him in Smyrna. Usbek also offers Ibben warm friendship, telling his Turkish friend that he is "the subject of our most tender conversations" (Letter 25, 42).

Two years later, however, Ibben sees fit to complain of the neglect Usbek has shown him. He begins by noting that "three ships have arrived here without having brought me any news from you." He then asks if Usbek is ill or whether it pleases him "to worry me." Ibben then comments, "If you do not love me in a country where you are tied to nothing what will it be like in the middle of Persia and the bosom of your family?" (Letter 67, 107). This comment reveals that Ibben and Usbek did not know each other before the Persians passed through Turkey on their way to Europe. Because Ibben does not know how Usbek will treat him when he is home, they had not somehow met prior to Usbek's trip to Europe.

Ibben then says perhaps he is "mistaken." What he apparently means by this is that he might be wrong to presume that Usbek has not established new and deep ties in France: "You are amiable enough to find friends everywhere. The heart is a citizen of all countries. How can a well-made soul prevent itself from making commitments?" (Letter 67, 107). Thus, Ibben implies that he is being neglected now, when Usbek is in France, just as he would be when Usbek returned to Persia, where he would be distracted by the friends and family of his native land. Perhaps this is a wry acknowledgement of Usbek's growing commitment to his French friend, who offers views very much in keeping with Montesquieu's views and which Usbek recounts in his letters to Ibben. Indeed, by this time, Usbek has written several letters to Ibben that recount the views of one or more Europeans that are akin to those Montesquieu offers in his treatises.

We have noted two such letters above, but there are several others. The first such letter in which Usbek conveys to Ibben the views of such a Frenchman is letter 34, which Usbek begins by examining Persian culture as something akin to an outsider, noting that the "gravity of the Asiatics comes from how little interchange [*commerce*] there is among them." Persians do not have true friendship, as they seek company within their extended families, but each family is "isolated" one from another. He then refers to "a man from this country" with whom he "was conversing about these things." The remainder of the letter is a quotation in which Usbek transmits to Ibben the thoughts of this Frenchman: "What shocks me most about your [Persian] morals is that you are obliged to live with slaves whose hearts and minds are always affected by the baseness of their condition." The Frenchman then advises the Persian to "get rid of your prejudices." A slave, he observes, who guards a man's wives "consents to being tyrannized by the strongest, so long as he can afflict the weakest" (Letter 34, 55–56).[23] It is quite plausible that the conversation that Usbek here recounts could have been had with a particularly blunt Montesquieu. After all, in the preface to *The Spirit of the Laws* he says that he would be "the happiest of mortals if [he] could make it so that men could cure themselves of their prejudices."[24]

Perhaps fortified by his knowledge that Usbek is receiving such advice that challenges the justness of his position as the pinnacle of a despotic order that keeps slaves to guard the virtue of his wives, Ibben undertakes himself to influence the manner in which Usbek thinks of his position. In letter 67, after complaining of Usbek's silence and reflecting on what is surely his ability to make friends in his new circumstances, Ibben speaks of his own capacity for friendship with good people from disparate cultures. He then encloses the letter that just such a man had written to him, with the ostensible purpose of fostering a new friendship between the author and Usbek. It depicts the efforts of a Guebre and adherent of Zoroastrianism, the pagan religion that preceded Islam in Persia, to steal a woman—his sister—from a seraglio. The brother and sister marry and thus consummate the love that has blossomed since their childhoods. It is, as Diana Schaub points out, the only letter that depicts a happy and loving marriage—and one, at that, in which the wife makes critical decisions for the couple and the husband shares in the domestic labor of the wife with alacrity.[25] Usbek never acknowledges this letter with its radical message.

Like the Frenchman of "*bons sens*," Ibben befriends Usbek while he travels, assesses the Persian's predicament as a domestic despot, and attempts to counsel him, showing him his true position within his society and his seraglio. On this matter, Usbek shows himself to be uneducable. He orders the sternest possible measures when he discovers the rebellions of his wives. In attempting to maintain his status and his reputation, Usbek loses both. In the collapse of his seraglio, however, others lose more. Roxane dies by her own hand as her lover dies at the hands of the vengeful eunuchs.

For all the enlightened views that Usbek espouses—views that he may very well have imbibed at the fictional Montesquieu's dinner table as well as in his salon and gardens—Usbek fails to see his own position as despot. How fortunate Usbek was to have Montesquieu as his friend, from whom he could learn about European politics and religion, about the ravages of Asiatic despotism, and about the needs of human nature. Despite these lessons, Usbek could not overcome his own despotic character. "Usbek's philosophical reflections remain completely detached from his actions as regards his life in Persia,"

Warner remarks.[26] Thus, someone very much like Montesquieu fails to "make it so that" Usbek was "able to cure [him]self of [his] prejudices."[27] A successful cure would surely have been the fictional Montesquieu's greatest wish for his Persian guest. Montesquieu's hiding in plain sight in the *Persian Letters* depicts his own failure with respect to his Persian friend. Perhaps the lesson of Montesquieu's friendly influence on Usbek is that the Enlightenment could not cure all our souls of all their ills.

CONCLUSION

Montesquieu has constructed the novel so that he is an essential but unnamed character in it. He hides, as it were, in plain sight. The author of the preface claims to be only a "translator" of these letters, but he is much more, as he himself concedes. He baldly states in the preface that he managed to uncover letters that Persian "vanity and jealousy" had been "very careful not to confide to me." Then he admits that he has excised what must amount to significant portions of the letters, as he admits to leaving out "an infinite number of sublime expressions," "the lengthy compliments that Orientals use no less lavishly than we do," and "an infinite number of trivialities" (Preface, 3–4). He thus implies, without explicitly confessing, that he is no mere translator but rather a most interventionist editor. Having so depicted the degree of intervention in the fictional text, it should come as no surprise to the reader that he obscures his identity from the novel, as well as any explanation as to how the Persians came to meet this quite extraordinary Frenchman.

The fiction of the *Persian Letters* shows Usbek gaining from the greatest mind of the Enlightenment an enlightened education. The Persian learns to speak as does Montesquieu to such an extent that the two, the real author and his character, become interchangeable in the mind of Montesquieu's friends and family.

But ultimately, Usbek and Montesquieu diverge in a most decisive way, as Usbek shows himself to be intractable on the matter of his personal tyranny. In his role as author, Montesquieu shows the futility of the friendly influence that Rica, Ibben, and even a fictionalized version of himself attempt to exert over the Persian despot of a seraglio. Montesquieu declares in the preface to *The Spirit of the Laws* that "it is not a matter of indifference that the people be enlightened." Enlightenment is an important factor, but it cannot be a panacea—even to Montesquieu. The ultimate lesson of Montesquieu's friendly influence on Usbek is that despotism is often intractable from the human soul, even when that soul is tutored by the most insightful and enlightened of teachers.

NOTES

1. Eric Nelson refers to Usbek as "Montesquieu's *porte-parole*"; Eric Nelson, *The Greek Tradition in Republican Thought* (Cambridge: Cambridge University Press, 2004), 155. Earlier versions of this argument were presented at Boston College, "Montesquieu's *Persian Letters* at 300," November 11–12, 2021. as well as at the University of Houston, "*Persian Letters*," December 10–11, 2021. I gratefully acknowledge the insightful comments and suggestions of Pauline Kra, Ourida Mostefai, Diana Schaub, and Stuart Warner. Any errors that remain are my own.

2. Judith N. Shklar, *Montesquieu* (Oxford: Oxford University Press, 1987), 25.

3. Craiutu comments that for Montesquieu, despotism was an "absolute evil"; Aurelian Craiutu, *Virtue for Courageous Minds: Moderation in French Political Thought, 1748–1830* (Princeton, NJ: Princeton University Press, 2012), 64.

4. Stuart Warner, "Montesquieu's Literary Art: An Introduction to *Persian Letters*," in *Persian Letters*, trans. Stuart D. Warner and Stéphane Douard (South Bend, IN: St. Augustine's Press, 2017), xi.

5. Starobinski notes that "most fiction writers" "pretended to be nothing more than editors" in the period when *Persian Letters* was written; Jean Starobinski, "Exile, Satire, Tyranny: Montesquieu's Persian Letters," in *Blessings in Disguise; or, The Morality of Evil*, trans. Arthur Goldhammer (Cambridge, MA: Harvard University Press), 60.

6. See Warner, "Montesquieu's Literary Art," vii–viii. Warner refers to this admission of the translator as "an act of dissimulation."

7. Diana J. Schaub, *Erotic Liberalism: Women and Revolution in Montesquieu's Persian Letters* (Lanham, MD: Rowman and Littlefield, 1995), 46–47.

8. Many more letters contain asterisks that obscure the name of the recipient. Rica writes almost twenty such letters. At least some of the recipients seem to be Persian. See letters 73 and 122; see also letter 135, in which Rica refers to "our Persia," and letter 130, 212, in which he refers to "our august Sultan." For a thoughtful treatment of the mystery of these asterisks in the text, see Aurélia Gaillard, "Les Lettres persanes ou la logique du secret," in *"Les Lettres persanes" de Montesquieu*, ed. C. Martin (Paris: Presses universitaires de Paris-Sorbonne; Oxford: Voltaire Foundation, 2013), 297–302.

9. For example, letter 56 (10 of the moon of Zilhagé 1714) is Usbek's missive to Ibben from Paris. But two months later, Usbek is back at the country house, as letter 59 (14 of the moon of Saphar 1714) shows.

10. The sole letter that Rica writes from a location obscured by the asterisks is letter 74.

11. Charles-Louis de Secondat, Baron de Montesquieu, *Œuvres complètes*, ed. Roger Caillois (Paris: Gallimard, 1949), 1: 264.

12. Ibid., 283.

13. Ibid., 186.

14. Betts, in Charles-Louis de Secondat, Baron de Montesquieu, *Persian Letters*, trans. C. J. Betts (London: Penguin, 1993), 309 n.1.

15. Warner continues that Montesquieu would be a viable possibility because he "was in Paris until, 1713, so he would have been there, so to speak, for Rica to meet" (Letter 38, 61 n.73). I concur entirely with Warner's suggestion here. We differ, however, on the degree to which the fictionalized Montesquieu appears in such a cloaked manner in the work, whether or not the real Montesquieu happened to be in Paris at any given time.

16. Sanford Kessler, "Religion and Liberalism in *Persian Letters*," *Polity* 15, no. 3 (1983): 390–91. See also Michael Mosher, "The Judgmental Gaze of European Women: Gender, Sexuality, and the Critique of Republican Rule," *Political Theory* 22, no.1 (1994): 28.

17. Charles-Louis de Secondat, Baron de Montesquieu, *The Spirit of the Laws*, trans. Anne M. Cohler, Basia C. Miller, and Harold S. Stone (Cambridge: Cambridge University Press), VII.17, 111.

18. Ibid., XIX.5, 310.

19. Ibid., XIX.6, 311.

20. The next longest series of the letters is the one Rica writes to *** regarding the "great library in a monastery" (Letter 133, 220), which consists of five letters. By contrast, the series on the Troglodytes is comprised of four letters, including Mirza's letter that provides the occasion for Usbek's extended response.

21. Montesquieu, *The Spirit of the Laws*, XXIII.21, 448–49.

22. Montesquieu, *Œuvres complètes*, 1: 305.

23. Ibid., 1: 180. The original published version attributed the letter to Rica; see letter 34, 55 n.65. It is certainly the case that the Frenchman would be speaking extremely bluntly to a man who maintains a seraglio, a fact that would appear to suggest that Rica would be a better choice as the letter's author. Nevertheless, the Frenchman's admonition to a Persian to rid himself of his prejudices and do away with the tyranny of a seraglio is much more relevant to Usbek's situation than to Rica's. In either case, though, the letter shows a Persian visitor developing close ties to a Frenchman whose views encapsulate some of Montesquieu's.

24. Montesquieu, *The Spirit of the Laws*, preface, xliii.

25. Schaub, *Erotic Liberalism*, 107. See also Warner's helpful comments on this letter; Warner, "Montesquieu's Literary Arts," xxxiii–xxxviii.

26. Warner, "Montesquieu's Literary Arts," xxxviii.

27. Montesquieu, *The Spirit of the Laws*, preface, xliii.

BIBLIOGRAPHY

Craiutu, Aurelian. *A Virtue for Courageous Minds: Moderation in French Political Thought, 1748–1830.* Princeton, NJ: Princeton University Press, 2012.

Gaillard, Aurélia. "Les *Lettres persanes* ou la logique du secret." In *"Les Lettres persanes" de Montesquieu*, edited by C. Martin. Paris: Presses universitaires de Paris-Sorbonne; Oxford: Voltaire Foundation, 2013.

Kessler, Sanford. "Religion and Liberalism in *Persian Letters*." *Polity* 15, no. 3 (1983): 380–96.

Montesquieu, Charles-Louis de Secondat, Baron de. *Lettres persanes.* Volume 1 of *Œuvres complètes de Montesquieu,* edited by Jean Ehrard and Catherine Volpilhac-Auger. Oxford: Voltaire Foundation, 2004.

———. *Œuvres complètes.* 2 volumes. Edited by Roger Caillois. Paris: Gallimard, 1949–51.

———. *Persian Letters.* Translated by C. J. Betts. London: Penguin, 1993.

———. *Persian Letters.* Translated by Stuart D. Warner and Stéphane Douard. South Bend, IN: St. Augustine's Press, 2017.

———. *The Spirit of the Laws.* Translated by Anne M. Cohler, Basia C. Miller, and Harold S. Stone. Cambridge: Cambridge University Press, 1989.

Mosher, Michael. "The Judgmental Gaze of European Women: Gender, Sexuality, and the Critique of Republican Rule." *Political Theory* 22, no.1 (1994): 25–44.

Nelson, Eric. *The Greek Tradition in Republican Thought.* Cambridge: Cambridge University Press, 2004.

Schaub, Diana J. *Erotic Liberalism: Women and Revolution in Montesquieu's Persian Letters.* Lanham, MD: Rowman and Littlefield, 1995.

Shklar, Judith N. *Montesquieu.* Oxford: Oxford University Press, 1987.

Starobinski, Jean. "Exile, Satire, Tyranny: Montesquieu's *Persian Letters.*" In *Blessings in Disguise; or, The Morality of Evil.* Translated by Arthur Goldhammer. Cambridge, MA: Harvard University Press, 1993.

Warner, Stuart. "Montesquieu's Literary Art: An Introduction to *Persian Letters.*" In *Persian Letters,* translated by Stuart D. Warner and Stéphane Douard. South Bend, IN: St. Augustine's Press, 2017.

Chapter 13

What Did Usbek—and the Reader—Know, and When Did He Know It?

John T. Scott

Montesquieu's *Persian Letters* is comprised of 161 letters, each carefully dated using a curious hybrid of Arabic or Muslim lunar months and Gregorian or Christian solar years. Along with the date, each letter also includes the locations of the sender and recipient (except when the recipient or destination is unnamed).[1] The combination of Arabic months and Gregorian years reflects the two main plot lines of the "kind of novel" Montesquieu has written: namely, the travel of Usbek and Rica to the West and Usbek's seraglio back in the East. East and West themselves reflect one another, often uneasily, like the hybrid calendar itself. Most readers probably ignore the dating of the letters, unfamiliar with Arabic lunar months. Yet even glancing at the more familiar Gregorian solar years would reveal an anomaly: the letters as presented by Montesquieu are not in the order in which they are dated. To take one important example, letter 146 is compositionally the last one dated in the entire collection, specifically 11 Rhamazan 1720 (November 11, 1720), but the very next epistle, letter 147, was penned more than three years earlier, in 1717. What is the reader to make of the differences between the order of presentation of the letters and their compositional sequence?

Not only readers, but scholars have generally paid little heed to the anomalous relationship between presentation and composition. To be fair, interpreters already have their hands full trying to understand the relationship between the two main plotlines of the work. They also face the challenges posed by the epistolary form Montesquieu gives the work, with the polyphonous voices of various correspondents and unclear relationships among the letters, which in general do not appear at first glance to have any particular order. The form of the work puts an unusually large interpretive burden on the reader. As Dena Goodman writes, "The epistolary form of the *Lettres persanes* makes this transfer of textual dynamism possible by requiring the reader to make connections between the letters as discrete textual units."[2] Although she does not attend to the relationship between the presentational and compositional ordering of the letters, what Goodman says about Montesquieu's assignment of interpretive labor to the reader would apply to this feature of the text as well.

Those scholars who do note the anomalous relationship often limit themselves to suggesting that Montesquieu places the concluding seraglio letters, letters 147–61, out of compositional sequence at the end of the novel in order to provide a dramatic dénouement.[3] This explanation is hardly satisfying, however, for it ironically takes Montesquieu at his word when he poses in the preface as the mere editor of the letters, as opposed to the author who is master of dating the letters as he chooses. More satisfying is the argument that this same rearrangement serves to give the novel two endings: the breakdown of the seraglio culminating in Roxane's suicide in the last letter in order of presentation, letter 161, and the breakdown of absolutist monarchy, principally in relation to French finances under the minister John Law and the exile of the Parlement of Paris, culminating in letter 146, the last letter in compositional sequence.[4] These two endings therefore relate the two main plotlines through a parallel and nearly simultaneous collapse of order in East and West, of the despotism of the seraglio and the absolutism of the French monarchy.

A further layer of complication in comparing the presentational and compositional orderings of the letters is introduced when we consider the order in which the letters were read. Montesquieu makes it possible to calculate the timing of the receipt of letters, if only roughly, by providing the locations of sender and receiver. He makes this possible by including exchanges between a sender and recipient where the second letter in the exchange is a reply to the first. For example, letter 8 of August 20, 1711, from Usbek to Rustan, written from Erzerum and sent to Ispahan, is a reply to Rustan's letter of May 28, 1711, from and to the same destinations, meaning it took about two and a half months for the letter to travel that distance. Most importantly for most of the letters in the work, the exchanges between Paris and Persia—that is, to and from Usbek to his wives or eunuchs, or to other correspondents back home— take about five months in each direction. (The fact that Usbek states in letter 155 that the letters take up to six months is not definitive, since the phrase "six months" seems to mean "a long time," and is used in this way elsewhere in *Persian Letters*, e.g., in letters 52, 59, 75, 78, 99, etc.) Consulting the dates of the letters enables readers to ascertain what Usbek knew and when he knew it, and consequently to assess what this says about Usbek's character and to understand how Montesquieu manipulates the reader's own responses through the relationship between the presentational and compositional orderings of the letters.

My aim in this chapter is to present an analysis of the relationship between the presentational and compositional orderings of the letters in Montesquieu's epistolary novel with an eye both to how they affect the action of the plot in relation to its main protagonist, Usbek, and to what effect they have on the experience of the reader of the work. As for Usbek, this analysis will help to highlight the division in his personality as a self-proclaimed seeker of wisdom through travel to the West, on the one hand, and as the tyrannical master of the seraglio he has left behind in the East, on the other. Far from being the "hero" of *Persian Letters* or a kind of alter ego for Montesquieu himself, this division reveals a tragic lack of self-understanding in Usbek.[5] As for the reader, I argue that the discrepancies between the presentational and compositional orderings of the letters obscures Usbek's self-deception to some degree, thereby putting the reader in the position to discover Usbek's character where Usbek himself does not.

My interpretation of Usbek's character is similar to the readings of *Persian Letters* by other scholars, but my emphasis on the relationship between the presentational and compositional orderings of the letters is largely novel and further underscores the reading of Usbek as self-deceived. My analysis builds on the work of several scholars who have given more sustained attention to the relationship between the presentational and compositional orderings of the letters, especially the fine studies by Theodore Braun, Diana Schaub, and Stuart Warner. My interpretation is especially indebted to Warner, who writes, "How exactly one should understand the divide that exists within Usbek himself, a divide that appears to be pivotal to the understanding of the whole of *Persian Letters*? More specifically, why does Montesquieu craft a character who is both philosophical and tyrannical? This divide . . . is apparent at the beginning of the book, is sometimes hidden from view later on, in no small measure because of the discrepancy between the orders of presentation and composition."[6] My hope is that focusing on this relationship more systematically will lend additional help in navigating Montesquieu's first great labyrinthine work.

SOME PRELIMINARY REFLECTIONS ON *PERSIAN LETTERS*

In the postscript, which first appeared in the posthumously published 1758 edition of *Persian Letters*, Montesquieu offers his own reading of the work he first published more than three decades earlier. His reading has naturally influenced interpreters, but consideration of the relationship between the presentational and compositional orderings of the letters contained in the work introduces some complication into the author's reading of the text.

Writing of the success of the "kind of novel" (*espèce de roman*) he published, Montesquieu explains,

> The novel's beginning, development, and end can be seen; its various characters are placed in a chain that binds them together. As they lengthen their stay in Europe, the morals of that part of the world take on in their heads a less marvelous and bizarre air, and they are more or less struck by these bizarre and marvelous matters in accord with the differences of their characters. On the other hand, disorder in the Asian seraglio grows proportionately with the length of Usbek's absence, that is to say, as fury increases and love diminishes. ("Some Reflections," 269)[7]

He goes on to explain that the epistolary form of the work enabled him to be able to join philosophical, political, and moral reflections into his novel. Then he asserts that "a secret and, in some fashion unknown chain" binds the whole work together: a famous remark that has intrigued and frustrated many a Theseus who has tried to navigate the maze. Finally, after some apologetics concerning the parts of the work some found too bold, Montesquieu concludes his "Reflections" by instructing the reader: "He is entreated to pay attention to the fact that all the charm consists in the eternal contrast between things as they really are and the singular, naïve, or bizarre way in which they are perceived. Certainly the nature and design of *Persian Letters* are so apparent that they will deceive only those who want to deceive themselves" ("Some Reflections," 269–71). Despite my usual proclivities, I will not attempt to identify the "secret and unknown" that allegedly ties together the whole.[8] Let me instead consider the initial and concluding remarks Montesquieu makes about his work.

At first glance, Montesquieu's description of the novel seems entirely fitting. He identifies the two main plotlines of his novel and the inversely proportionate relationship between them: as the West becomes gradually more familiar to the Persian travelers, the East becomes more distant and disorderly. But what about his initial claim: "The novel's beginning, development, and end can be seen" ("*On en voit le commencement, le progrès, la fin*")? If we consult the dating of the letters and compare this chronology to the order in which Montesquieu presents them, not one, but two beginnings of the work are seen: namely, letters 1 and 2 in presentational order form one beginning, while letters 3 and 4, which precede their predecessors in compositional order, constitute another beginning. Likewise, not one, but two endings are seen. As already remarked, letter 146 is the compositional end of the work, whereas letter 161 is the presentational conclusion. The reader sees the two beginnings and endings only if the dating of the letters is consulted. So the beginning and end of the novel are in fact not so easily seen as Montesquieu claims.[9]

The complexities Introduced by comparing the presentational and compositional orderings of the letters affect how we read Montesquieu's concluding remarks about the "charm" of the novel and its "nature and design." First, what the "nature" and "design" of the work may be is less certain and more enigmatic than Montesquieu claims. The "nature" of the work seems to refer to what he earlier said about it being a "kind of novel" with an epistolary form that enables him to interject philosophical, political, and moral reflections without interrupting the narrative, a proceeding he also says there "would shock the design and nature" of a more traditional novel form ("Some Reflections," 269). Returning to his concluding remarks, what he means by the "design" (*dessein*) of the work seems to refer to the "plan" of the work in the sense of how it is designed or constructed, although the term can also mean "aim" or "intention."[10] In any case, the twofold presentational and compositional orderings of the letters makes the "nature" and especially "design" of the work more complicated than at first sight.

Second, his statement that the "charm" of the work "consists in the eternal contrast between things as they really are and the singular, naïve, or bizarre way in which they are perceived" seems to refer primarily or initially to the charm the reader finds in the often unintentionally perceptive incomprehension with which the Persian travelers see and relate what they witness. Two delightful examples are letter 24, with Rica reporting on the king of France and the pope as wonderous "magicians," and letter 28, also from Rica, describing the theater, where the spectators are more actors than the thespians themselves.

Third, in this light, then, the "nature and design" of the work "will deceive only those who want to deceive themselves" insofar as Montesquieu's readers fail to recognize themselves in the funhouse mirror provided by the Persians. As the morals of the West become more familiar to the travelers across the work, they should become less familiar, more exotic in the eyes of the reader. Yet what about the characters themselves, and especially Usbek? Is he self-deceived? As he becomes more accustomed to the mores of the West, does the master of the seraglio gain any understanding of his home back in the East? The relationship between the presentational and compositional orderings of the letters will, I argue, underscore Usbek's self-deception. If the reader of *Persian Letters* should not deceive themselves, Usbek is a self-deceived reader of the letters *he* receives from Persia.

TWO PERSIANS GO ON A DOUBLE DATE

I turn now to an analysis of the relationship between the presentational and compositional orderings of the letters in *Persian Letters*. As mentioned earlier, the two most conspicuous resequencings of the letters occur at the beginning and end of the work, giving it two beginnings and two endings. However, there are other instances of stretches of the text in the "development" of the novel where Montesquieu also manipulates this ordering. Let me examine the most important instances of resequencing in the beginning, middle, and end of *Persian Letters*.

In the Beginnings

The divide between the presentational and compositional orderings of the letters in *Persian Letters* is evident from the very outset of the novel. Let us begin with the presentational ordering. Letters 1 and 2 are both from Usbek from Tauris, with letter 1 (April 15, 1711) to his friend Rustan, back in Ispahan. In this letter the reader is introduced to Usbek and his claim that he has left his country "out of a longing for knowledge" and to "search laboriously for wisdom" (Letter 1, 5). Letter 2 (April 18) is to the first black eunuch, also back in Ispahan, commanding him to be a faithful guardian of the seraglio: "You command them, and you obey them; . . . you serve them as the slave of their slaves. But by means of a reversal of authority, whenever you fear the slackening of the laws of shame and modesty, you command as master like myself" (Letter 2, 6). The question of whether being master and slave simultaneously is possible is not raised or addressed by Usbek, but we might wonder about what sort of motives actuate both the eunuchs and the wives in his absence. Finally, Usbek gives permission to the eunuch to take the wives to the countryside if they so wish. The first two letters therefore exhibit two very different faces of Usbek's position and personality. The first is a letter between friends and equals, and it effectively launches the Western plotline of the novel. The second is from a master to a slave who is himself simultaneously master and slave, and inaugurates the Eastern plotline.

Ah, but the plot is already in motion if we turn to the compositional ordering, unbeknownst to Usbek and to the reader who does not consult the dates. Letter 3 is to Usbek from one of his wives, Zachi, and is dated March 21, 1711, from the seraglio in Fatmé, that is, from the countryside. It is therefore the first letter in compositional order. Letter 4 is to Usbek from another wife, Zéphis, dated March 29, also from Fatmé. The letter from Zachi comes a day after Usbek's departure, and reports that the wives have ordered the chief eunuch to take them to the countryside. The wives' order to the eunuch therefore predates Usbek's letter giving permission to the eunuch to take them to the countryside. Although Zachi alleges that she cannot bear to remain in Ispahan without her beloved Usbek, in a later letter (Letter 47) she associates the countryside with freedom, perhaps here freedom from Usbek's authority.[11] Letter 3 is also among the most titillating of the collection, with Zachi recalling a contest among the wives for Usbek's attentions, complete with lewd poses by the naked contestants, culminating in Zachi's victory and her voyeuristic desire that the other wives could have witnessed the prize. As we shall see, Zachi's erotic energies will not be confined to her husband. In any case, a mere day after Usbek's departure, then, the wives assume authority.[12]

The letter from Zéphis, in turn, complains about one of the black eunuchs who has forced her to give up her slave girl, Zélide. "Neither my seclusion nor my virtue can shelter me from his extravagant suspicions," she complains (Letter 4, 9). Although the letter does not reveal what the eunuch may be suspicious about, we later learn from letter 20, from Usbek to Zachi, that he is aware that she has taken familiarities with the slave girl: in other words, that the young Zélide has been providing sexual favors for his wife. Since Usbek is in Erzeman, in the Ottoman Empire, he will not receive these letters until about three months later, so around the end of June, or shortly before the series of letters he writes about the Troglodytes (Letters 11–14). These letters are written in answer to letter 10, from his friend Mirza back in Ispahan, asking to seek his wisdom concerning the question of whether happiness is due to pleasure or virtue. In short, immediately after Usbek's departure, his growing distance from the East is accompanied by a decline in his authority and the seraglio is already descending into disorder. As Warner writes, "The discrepancy between the orders of presentation and composition and what follows from it thus signals at least an erosion if not an inversion of authority beginning to seep into Usbek's seraglio immediately upon his departure."[13] We may also wish to question Usbek's wisdom.

There is another sort of second beginning to the novel revealed by the contrast between the presentational and compositional orderings: namely, whereas in letter 1 Usbek claims to Rustan that his voyage is for the sake of wisdom, in letter 8 to the same he reveals that he has left Persia because his outspokenness at court has earned him dangerous enemies. He has left Persia for his own protection under the pretense that he wishes to educate himself in the sciences of the West. Of course, the two reasons he gives are not mutually exclusive, although at minimum his claim that he travels to seek wisdom is rendered suspect.[14] The letter is dated August 20, 1711, from Erzerum, meaning that Usbek is now safely out of Persia. The dating of letter 8 means that it is actually number 17 in compositional order, penned just after the Troglodyte series. In fact, letter 8 is written the same day that as letter 17, which is a second letter to Muhammed Ali (the first one being letter 16, nine days earlier) revealing that among a profane people he is entertaining doubts that need resolving. "I feel my reason is straying," he writes, asking, "lead it back to the right path" (Letter 17, 29). (In reply, in letter 18 the imam relates a scatological story of the birth of the pig from excrement on Noah's ark, with the added bonus of the creation of a cat from a lion sneezing.) Is Usbek's letter to the imam seeking wisdom another subterfuge? At any rate, it also might make us question Usbek's wisdom.

Finally, at about the same time he writes both to Rustan about his real motivation for leaving Persia and to Muhammed Ali allegedly seeking wisdom, one of Usbek's eunuchs has written to inform him of the bad behavior of one of his wives. The letter from the eunuch is not included in the collection, but letter 20 from Usbek to Zachi is dated from Smyrna on January 12, 1711, allowing us to interpolate the date of the missing letter given a travel time of about four months, so late August. Usbek has learned that his wife has been found alone with Nadir, a white eunuch. Since letter 9 by the first eunuch to another eunuch traveling with Usbek reveals that his castration removes the ability to satisfy erotic desire without ceasing to feel it, we have reason to suspect that Zachi's dalliance with the eunuch was not entirely innocent.[15] Certainly, the love she professes for Usbek in letter 3 from late March has quickly waned. At any rate, in letter 20 Usbek preaches duty, virtue, and honor to his wife, saying, "You should thank me for the discomfort which I make you live, since it is only due to that that you still deserve to live" (Letter 20, 35). He also writes of the love he feels for his new wife, Roxane, about whom more later.

The letters surrounding letter 20 from Usbek to Zachi throw further light on Usbek's situation. As for the preceding letter, letter 19 (November 2, 1711), it has Usbek writing to his friend Rustan from Smyrna, so at the juncture of East and West, stating, "I have seen with astonishment the weakness of Ottoman empire" (Letter 19, 32). He writes this at the same time as his own seraglio is growing increasingly weak, a development of which he will be made aware a couple of months later, and just before he departs for Europe.[16] The two letters following letter 20 further underscore the situation facing Usbek, all the more so because they are dated on the same day. Letter 21 from Usbek to the first white eunuch is chilling: "And what are you but vile instruments, which I can break at my fancy; which exist only so long as you know how to obey; which exist in the world only in order to live under my laws or to die as soon as I order it" (Letter 21, 36). Usbek's authority in relation to at least the eunuchs is despotic. The need for such despotic measures and Usbek's relation to his wives is nicely captured in letter 22 to the first eunuch from Jaron, the eunuch who is traveling with Usbek: "As Usbek proceeds further and further from the seraglio, the more he turns his head toward his sacred women. He signs, he sheds tears; his sorrow becomes bitter; his suspicions are becoming stronger. He wants to increase the number of their guardians" (Letter 22, 37). We know from letter 6 that Jaron is not quite correct about the reasons for Usbek's sorrows, for there he admits to a friend, "It is not, Nessir, that I love them. I find myself, in this respect, in a state of insensibility that leaves me without desires. In the crowded seraglio where I have lived, I anticipated love and destroyed love by love itself" (Letter 6, 10). Once again, there is growing disorder in the seraglio in the East as Usbek travels to the West.

In the Middle: The Development of the Design

The Persian travelers arrive in Europe, landing at Livorno, as reported in letter 23, dated April 12, 1712, after almost exactly a year since departing Ispahan. "The women enjoy great liberty here," Usbek relates (Letter 23, 38), with the obvious implied contrast to their lack of liberty in the seraglio. A month later they finally reach Paris, as reported by Rica in letter 24, dated June 4. The two plotlines of East and West that constitute the principal "development" (*progrès*) of the novel according to Montesquieu are now firmly established.

The first two letters from Paris written by Usbek belong to each of these plotlines. Letter 25 (June 11, 1712) is written to Ibben and relates that he should expect a long letter from Rica about what they have observed so far in Paris. This is in fact letter 24, which Ibben may in fact have already received, apparently unbeknownst to Usbek. The other, more important thing of which Usbek will turn out to be ignorant is contained in letter 26 (September 7) and written to his favorite wife, Roxane. He begins, "How fortunate you are, Roxane, to be in the gentle country of Persia, and not in these poisoned climates, where neither shame nor virtue is known. How fortunate you are! You live in my seraglio as in the abode of innocence, beyond the outrages of all human beings; you joyfully find yourself in that fortunate condition of being powerless to fail. No man has ever soiled you with his lascivious gaze." The self-deception he displays is staggering, in the letter itself and given what remains to come of the story. As for the letter, Usbek recounts what can only be termed the rape he committed on his reluctant new wife. The story renders ironic what he has said about her "fortunate" situation of "innocence" and free from anyone's "lascivious gaze": "I cannot imagine that you have any object other than that of pleasing me. . . . I cannot, Roxane, doubt your love" (Letter 26, 43–44). Usbek displays a tragic lack of imagination and overabundance of confidence.

During the development of the novel there are several inversions of the presentational and compositional orderings of the letters that shed further light on Usbek's role and character. I examine two sequences of letters.

The first set of letters are letters 37–43, which include several seraglio letters. The compositional ordering of these letters is: 37, 40, 41, 42, 38, 39,

43. The first of these letters, letter 37 from Usbek to Ibben (March 7, 1713), frames the following letters. Usbek writes of the aging king of France: "It is said that he possesses a very high degree of talent for making himself obeyed," and that he governs his family, court, and state "in the same spirit." The monarch has also been heard to say that he admires the "Oriental politics" of the Persian sultan above all the governments in the world (Letter 37, 59). Note that the French monarch "is said" to possess this talent for making himself obeyed, but other details in the letter undermine this appearance. At any rate, if Montesquieu establishes a parallel between West and East through the comparison between the French king and the Persian sultan, a further parallel is suggested between the French monarch and Usbek himself. The doubts we might have about Usbek's power to make himself obeyed color the following sequence of letters.

The "mis-sequenced" letters in this series are letters 41 and 42, which in compositional order are numbers 38 and 39. The presentational ordering places these letters together with letter 43, forming a trio of letters concerning the seraglio. Letters 41 and 42 are both dated March 7, 1713—that is, the same day as Usbek to wrote to Ibben about the French king, therefore further underscoring the parallel of the king to Usbek. Letter 41 is from the first black eunuch to Usbek and concerns his plan to replace a deceased black eunuch with a fresh recruit who is resisting the necessary procedure. Letter 42 is from the would-be castrato, Pharan, begging his master not to let them unman him. Finally, letter 43 is from Usbek to Pharan, forbidding the operation and instead ordering that a new eunuch be purchased. Why Usbek spares him is unclear. At any rate, although the presentational sequence of these letters suggests Usbek's immediate reply and therefore mercifulness, the compositional dating may suggest otherwise. Namely, letter 43 is dated September 25, six and a half months after letters 41 and 42, meaning that, with about five months of travel time for these letters to reach Usbek, he may have waited a month or more before replying with his orders. In any case, due to distance and Usbek's delay, the poor gardener had waited an entire year to learn of his fate.[17] Meanwhile, in a letter written on September 20, just days before his reply to Pharan, Usbek writes to Ibben, "One should weep for men at their births and not at their deaths" (Letter 40, 64). Usbek's self-pity makes for an ironic contrast to Pharan's predicament.

The second series of letters to be examined are letters 63–71. The compositional ordering of these letters is: 64, 63, 67, 68. 66. 69, 70, 65, 71, and they are written over a period of seven months. As in the previous sequence of letters I just examined, the first letter in presentational order frames the following ones. In letter 63 (May 10, 1714) Rica writes to Usbek to complain of his absence in the countryside. In addition to a potential parallel between Usbek and the French monarch, who rules from Versailles rather than Paris (see

Letter 37), Usbek's absence in the countryside highlights his absence from the seraglio. In addition, Rica writes that he has only come to know women in Europe, for in Persia, "among us, character is completely uniform because it is forced" (Letter 63, 102). The relevance of Rica's remarks for Usbek is strengthened by the preceding letter, letter 62, in which Zélis writes to Usbek of erotic desires known only to women, without specifying what they may be. She warns him, despite his authority over them, "do not imagine that your situation is happier than mine. I have tasted here a thousand pleasures unknown to you. . . . I have lived, and you have only languished. . . . In the very prison in which you keep me, I am freer than you" (Letter 62, 101). The apparently interchangeable wives, highlighted by several having similar names, turn out to have their own thoughts and desires. As the following letters will testify, Usbek's rule and understanding grows ever weaker with his distance.

The next letter in presentational order from the chief of the black eunuchs to Usbek confirms this conjecture. This letter, letter 64, precedes letter 63 by a day in terms of composition. "The seraglio is in a horrible disorder and confusion; war reigns among your wives; your eunuchs are divided," he reports to his master. He dares to place the blame squarely on Usbek: "Shall I reveal to you, magnificent lord, the cause of all these disorders? It lies completely in your heart and the tender regard that you have for your wives" (Letter 64, 103). Is the eunuch correct? Usbek does earlier tell the wayward Zachi in letter 20 that he wishes to rule through love rather than fear. However, as we have seen, as early as letter 6 he admits that what afflicts him is the memory of his wives, but not for the reasons one might think: "It is not, Nessir, that I love them." Returning to letter 64, the eunuch urges despotic measures, and perhaps he is right for the wrong reason: rather than counterbalancing Usbek's supposed tenderness for his wives, these measures are the only replacements for the missing erotic motives for his wives' obedience. Although the switch in presentational and compositional orderings between letters 63 and 64 is slight, it intimates that the disorder in the seraglio stems from Usbek's absence.

The next letter in presentational sequence, letter 65, finds Usbek writing to his wives, having learned from the black eunuch about the disorder and divisions in the seraglio. He acknowledges his absence and speaks to them having entrusted the eunuch with their virtue and his honor. Urging them to change their conduct, he concludes, "For I would like to make you forget that I am your master, so that I remember only that I am your husband" (Letter 65, 106). In short: he ignores the eunuch's advice. Placing this letter immediately after letter 64 from the black eunuch makes Usbek's letter to his wives seem closer in time than it is, for letter 65 is dated October 5, 1714, or soon after he would have received letter 64 from the eunuch, given the five months needed for the letter to reach him in Paris. In turn, his letter to his wives would not reach them until March 1715, meaning that the disorder in the seraglio has ten months to develop in Usbek's absence, including his absence in epistolary terms.

A further resequencing of the letters underscores Usbek's despotic rule over his wives by way of a contrast to one of the only stories in *Persian Letters* about true romantic love. The story is told in letter 67 from Ibben to Usbek, dated August 17, 1714, so a letter written shortly before Usbek learns about the disorder in the seraglio from the black eunuch and then writes to his wives. The story involves true love between a brother and sister, a love authorized and even encouraged by their religion, Zoroastrianism, but forbidden by the Islamic law under which they live. The implied contrast to their incestuous love is the sort of love allowed under Islamic law, that is, the polygamous and despotic marriage represented by Usbek himself. If the story of Aphéridon and Astarté is meant by Ibben as a kind of fable to teach Usbek, the four or five months his letter would take to travel from Smyrna to Paris means that it arrived too late to serve that purpose. Yet it might serve the purpose for the reader, and especially the reader who consults the dating of the letters.

The final two letters in the sequence under examination are letters 70 and 71, which in compositional ordering are numbers 65 and 71. The first is from Zélis to Usbek, dated July 9, 1714, so two months after the black eunuch writes to Usbek about the disordered seraglio but about three months before Usbek would have received that letter. She relates to Usbek a story about a newly married man who rejects his wife after accusing her of not being a virgin. "If my daughter received a like treatment," she writes, "I believe that I would die of grief from it" (Letter 70, 119). The next letter is Usbek's reply (December 5, 1714), in which he tells his wife that although the law allowing the groom to return the bride is harsh, especially since proofs of hymen are not reliable, it was nonetheless the law. He then praises his wife for the care she has taken in the education of their daughter, which he sees as preparing her for being guarded by eunuchs in her own future husband's seraglio. It does not occur to Usbek that Zélis's letter to him criticizing the marital customs exhibited by the unfortunate story of a matrimony gone wrong should lead him to question the laws of the seraglio.

In sum, the two sequences of letters from the middle or development of the plot in *Persian Letters* that I have examined all reveal Usbek's waning authority over his seraglio as he grows more distant, both physically and otherwise, and they also cast doubt on his understanding of his role and his self-understanding.

At the Endings

As I mentioned at the outset, the fact that Montesquieu manipulates the ordering of the letters toward the end of *Persian Letters* by placing letters written compositionally earlier in order to build to a dramatic conclusion is the most common observation by scholars concerning the relationship between the presentational and compositional orderings. Similarly, the fact that resequencing the letters in this manner gives *Persian Letters* two different endings, one for the Western plotline and another for the Eastern, has been noted. As such, I will perhaps have little new to say about this particular example. Yet I believe that backing up a few steps in terms of the development of the novel may shed further light on how the double ending of the novel functions, both in terms of understanding Usbek's character and understanding and in terms of the reading experience.

The principal case of "mis-sequencing" of the concluding series of seraglio letters involves three letters placed out of order with respect to both the presentational and the compositional orders: namely, letters 147, 148, and 149, which are numbers 105, 110, and 113 compositionally. These are the letters with which the concluding series of seraglio letters begin, but they were written considerably earlier than the rest. If these letters had been put in their "proper" place, then the Eastern seraglio letters would have been interspersed among the Western letters more like the general pattern of the novel as a whole, alternating between the Western and Eastern plotlines.[18] More substantively, if they had been put in something more like their compositional order, then Usbek—and the reader—would have been aware earlier of the growing turmoil in the seraglio.[19] However, my attention to the relationship between the presentational and compositional orderings of the letters underscores the fact that the disorder of the seraglio has been long in the making, indeed from the outset of the novel. Certainly, Montesquieu's grouping the seraglio letters as a single sequence despite their chronology creates a spectacular denouement, but it cannot come as much of a surprise to the reader who has consulted the dates of the letters throughout the novel.

Let us examine the portion of the work where the "mis-sequenced" seraglio letters "ought" to have been placed to see if doing so sheds light on Montesquieu's proceeding.

The first thing to note is that doing so not only makes the concluding seraglio letters of the Eastern plotline seem to be a single sequence but also makes the Western plotline also seem to be a single sequence, concluding in the other "end" of the work in terms of composition. The last seraglio letter in presentational order before the concluding sequence is letter 96 from the first eunuch to Usbek, dated February 8, 1716. The eunuch reports purchasing a slave as a wife for Usbek's brother. The eunuch also exhibits a sadistic streak, imagining how introducing a new wife into the seraglio will lead to jealousies and conflicts among the wives, with their inner turmoil hidden beneath the exterior tranquility of the seraglio due to the eunuch's authority. Perhaps we are meant to recall Zachi's account in letter 2 of the exhibitionist contest among Usbek's wives for his favor and Usbek's account in letter 26 of the rape of Roxane. The eunuch concludes, "But all this, magnificent lord, all this is nothing without the master's presence. What can we do with this vain phantom of an authority that can never be entirely communicated?" (Letter 96, 155). So he writes, urging Usbek to return. Moving the remaining seraglio letters to the end of the novel accentuates Usbek's continued absence.

As with other cases we have examined, the letters preceding the first "mis-sequenced" seraglio letter—namely, letter 147 in presentational order and number 105 in compositional order—frames that letter and, indeed, all of the remaining seraglio letters. Letter 104 is the last of a set of three letters from Usbek to Ibben, all written in June 1717, which contain his reflections on political authority. Letter 102 concerns European monarchies and their tendency to degenerate into despotisms or republics, letter 103 relates what a "sensible European" said to him about the error of Asian princes hiding themselves, and then letter 104 speaks of the submissiveness of European peoples to their princes and the dangers of trying to rule them by too much force. Of course, all these reflections might be applied to Usbek himself in relation to his seraglio, although also of course he does not do so. The letter that should follow these three letters is from the great eunuch to Usbek (September 1, 1717), and commences, "Things have come to a state that can no longer been maintained. Your wives have imagined that your departure allowed them common impunity. Horrible things are taking place here" (Letter 147, 257). Usbek's reply in letter 148 (February 11, 1718) grants the eunuch "unlimited power over the entire seraglio" and commands him: "Let fear and terror walk with you" (Letter 148, 257–58). Usbek does not apply the reflections he has made on political authority to his own rule.

A similar deficit in Usbek's self-knowledge can be seen by putting letter 149 back in compositional sequence as number 113. This letter is from Narsit to Usbek (July 5, 1718), informing him of the great eunuch's death and the fact that he dared not open the letter Usbek sent to the deceased, namely, letter 148, meaning that Narsit has not exercised the authority Usbek has granted over the seraglio. I will return to these letters. Usbek would have received Narsit's letter at the same time he writes a series of letters concerning the supposed depopulation of the earth and related issues. These contain his reflections on how both the Christian and Mohammedan religions contribute to this depopulation, including the drawbacks of polygamy (Letter 114), the damaging effects of the sort of slavery practiced in modern times for commerce (Letter 115), the benefits of permitting divorce such as the Romans did (Letter 116), the bad effects on population of having eunuchs in the East and celibate priests in the West (Letter 117), a series culminating in letter 122 recommending mild government. Usbek's reflections exhibit the growing insight he has gained by distance from the East, the alleged reason for his travels proffered in letter 1. When the "mis-sequenced" seraglio letter is inserted in this context, however, it once again seems that Usbek has learned nothing from these reflections in relationship to himself. As Warner remarks, "Wondrously, Usbek appears completely oblivious of any division in himself. Indeed, he shows no semblance of understanding that his own philosophical reflections are anathema to the world of Persia and the seraglio to which he clings even from afar."[20]

At about this point in *Persian Letters* the Western and Eastern plotlines unfold approximately simultaneously in terms of chronology, but they are separately sequenced in terms of presentation. Once again, the last letter in the Eastern plotline is letter 96 from the first eunuch to Usbek (February 8, 1716). Letters 97–146 are confined to the Western plotline, with two minor exceptions that do not involve the seraglio (the two exceptions being letter 97 from Usbek to Hussein, an ascetic dervish, and letter 123 from Usbek to Méhémet Ali). Letters 97–146 cover the period from February 1716 to November 11, 1720, with letter 146 being the last letter in the novel in compositional ordering. After the sequence of letters on depopulation and other matters concluding with letter 122, discussed above, the remaining letters in the Western plotline include gradually fewer letters from Usbek, underscoring his growing absence.[21] Beginning with letter 147, the Eastern plotline takes over, covering almost the same time period as the Western plotline, beginning with letter 147, written on September 1, 1717, and ending with the last letter, letter 161, dated May 8, 1720. As noted above, the way Montesquieu sequences the letters in terms of presentation gives his work two endings, one for each of the two main plotlines.

The Western plotline culminates with the collapse of absolutist monarchy in France with John Law's fiscal policies and the exile of the Parlement of Paris, creating a parallel between the failures of absolutism in the West and the unraveling of Usbek's despotic seraglio in the East. This parallel has been remarked by previous scholars. What I wish to note is how the last three letters by Usbek in the Western series foreshadow the concluding seraglio sequence which follows. In letter 144 (October 22, 1720) Usbek writes Rica about two learned men he has encountered who display their vanity and lack of wisdom, and he praises his correspondent for his modesty and wisdom.[22] Letter 145, from Usbek to an unidentified recipient (October 26, 1720) is also on the theme of wisdom, in this case including a letter within the letter about a ridiculous scholar hounded by his neighbors for having dissected a dog, which leads to reflections by Usbek on those who profess "an arrogant ignorance."

The question of Usbek seeking and having wisdom is of course present from the beginning, with him claiming in the very first letter to be traveling to the West to seek knowledge. Letters 144 and 145 therefore solicit us to ask what wisdom Usbek has in fact gained. Finally, as for letter 146, Usbek writes to Rhédi about ministers to princes, alluding to the disastrous ministry of John Law in France. By reordering the letters Montesquieu, so to speak, buries the lead concerning his critique of French absolutism.[23] Further, Usbek's remarks about bad ministers should make the reader recall that Usbek was himself a kind of minister, for in letter 8 he admits that he has left Persia because he has made enemies in the court by speaking too freely. Usbek states there, "I even formed a great design: I dared to be virtuous there" (Letter 8, 13). This is his self-understanding, but perhaps he is self-deceived. If so, then Usbek himself was a failed minister as well. Whether as minister or master, Usbek will now be revealed to have failed to rule his seraglio.

Finally, we come to the concluding seraglio sequence commencing with letter 147. As mentioned, this letter is from the great eunuch to Usbek telling him of the uncontrollable disorder of the seraglio, to which Usbek replies in letter 148 granting him full authority. Unfortunately, letter 149 from Narsit to Usbek informs him of the great eunuch's death and relates that the eunuch he has not dared open Usbek's letter to his predecessor. Finally, Narsit tells him that has been informed that a young man has been seen in the seraglio. Usbek replies in letter 150, dated December 25, 1718, and so therefore soon after receiving Narsit's missive, admonishing him for not opening the letter and investing him with the authority he attempted to convey to his predecessor: "The least delay may lead me to despair, and you tranquilly rest under a vain pretext!" Letter 151 is to Usbek from another eunuch, Solim (May 6, 1719), telling him that he has learned that a letter sent by Usbek, apparently letter 150, has gone astray. He further tells him, "Your wives no longer restrain themselves" since the great eunuch's death, apart from the faithful Roxane. His wives are in the countryside, and apparently two men have been smuggled into the seraglio there. We will soon learn that Solim is tragically wrong about Roxane. Another letter from Solim to Usbek dated the same day, letter 152, reports that his letter has been lost, and he urges Usbek to write him promptly.

What I wish to point out is that the news of the unopened letter and of the letter gone astray have the effect on the reader of making the quickening collapse of the seraglio much more sudden and unexpected than it would seem, if the dates of the letters are consulted:[24] namely, the seraglio has been falling apart for at least two or three years, if not from the time of Usbek's departure seven or eight years earlier.

The final letters show Usbek's increasingly frantic and futile attempt to regain control over the seraglio from afar. His reply to Solim in letter 153 and his letter to his wives in letter 154, both dated October 4, 1719, arrive too late. The next letter is also written the same day, with Usbek confiding to his friend Nessir in Ispahan that he is despondent: "I sometimes wait six whole months for news from the seraglio; I count every instant that passes; my impatience makes each one longer; when what has been long awaited is about to arrive, a revolution suddenly takes place in my heart, and my hand trembles in opening a fatal letter" (Letter 155, 262). He can no longer live in "this dreadful exile" and longs to return home. The letter reveals a kind of disintegration of Usbek's identity as master of his wives.[25] One might sympathize more with him if he hadn't been in absentia for more than eight years, with long periods of epistolary silence. A batch of letters from his wives are written on March 2, 1720, apparently in answer to letter 154, in which Usbek tells them that the eunuchs will no longer merely guard them but will punish them. In letters 156, 157, and 158, Roxane, Zachi, and Zélis complain of the eunuch's harsh treatment. In letters 159 and 160, both dated May 8, 1720, it is Solim's turn to complain, revealing Roxane's infidelity and saying that he will punish the wives.

We arrive at the second ending. Roxane writes the final letter in the presentational order of *Persian Letters*, also dated May 8, defiantly telling Usbek while dying at her own hand: "I might have lived in servitude, but I have always been free. I have reformed your laws by those of nature, and my spirit has always remained independent. . . . You were astonished not to find in me the ecstasies of love. If you had known me well, you would have found in me all the violence of hatred." She has found love with another: "We were both happy: you believed me deceived, and I was deceiving you" (Letter 161, 268). Usbek has been deceived, but more than anything he was self-deceived.[26]

NOTES

1. For the details of how Montesquieu constructed this complex system, see Robert Shackleton, "The Moslem Chronology of the *Lettres persanes*," *French Studies* 8 (1954): 17–27. See also Stuart D. Warner, "Editor's Note on the Calendar in *Persian Letters*," in *Persian Letters*, ed. Stuart. D Warner, trans. Stuart D. Warner and Stéphane Douard (South Bend, IN: St. Augustine's Press, 2017), lxi–lxiii.

2. Dena Goodman, *Criticism in Action: Enlightenment Experiments in Political Writing* (Ithaca, NY: Cornell University Press, 1989), 21.

3. See R. L. Frautschi, "The Would-Be Invisible Chain in *Les Lettres persanes*," *French Review* 40 (1967): 604–12; Robert F. O'Reilly, "The Structure and Meaning of the *Lettres persanes*," *Studies on Voltaire and the Eighteenth Century* 67 (1969):

108; Nick Roddick, "The Structure of the *Lettres persanes*," *French Studies* 28 (1974): 396–407.

4. See Diana J. Schaub, *Erotic Liberalism: Women and Revolution in Montesquieu's Persian Letters* (Lanham, MD: Rowman and Littlefield, 1995); Stuart D. Warner, "Montesquieu's Literary Art: An Introduction to *Persian Letters*," in *Persian Letters*, ed. Stuart D. Warner, trans. Stuart D. Warner and Stéphane Douard (South Bend, IN: St. Augustine's Press, 2017). See also Theodore E. D. Braun, "Montesquieu, *Lettres persanes*, and Chaos," in *Disrupted Patterns: On Chaos and Order in the Enlightenment*, ed. Theodore E. D. Braun and John A. McCarthy (Amsterdam: Rodopi, 2000), 79–90.

5. As for similar interpretations of Usbek's character, see Roxanne L. Euben, *Journeys to the Other Shore: Muslim and Western Travelers in Search of Knowledge* (Princeton, NJ: Princeton University Press, 2006), 144–56; E. J. Hundert, "Sexual Politics and the Allegory of Identity in Montesquieu's *Persian Letters*," *Eighteenth Century* 31 (1990), 101–15; G. J. Mallinson, "Usbek, Language and Power: Images of Authority in Montesquieu's *Lettres persanes*," *French Forum* 18 (1993), 23–36; O'Reilly, "The Structure and Meaning of the *Lettres persanes*"; Schaub, *Erotic Liberalism*; Warner, "Montesquieu's Literary Art." Jean Starobinski argues that Usbek is Montesquieu's alter ego; *Blessings in Disguise; or, The Morality of Evil*, trans. Arthur Goldhammer (Cambridge, MA: Harvard University Press, 1993), ch. 3.

6. Warner, Montesquieu's Literary Art," xiv–xv.

7. All quotations and references from *Persian Letters* are to Montesquieu, *Persian Letters*, ed. Stuart D. Warner, trans. Stuart D. Warner and Stéphane Douard (South Bend, IN: St. Augustine's Press, 2017). Quotations from the original French are from *Oeuvres completes*, vol. 1, ed. Roger Caillois (Paris: Gallimard, Bibliothèque de la Pléiade, 1949.

8. For a review of attempts to unravel the chain in the 1970s and 1980s, see Theodore E. D. Braun, "'La Chaîne secrète': A Decade of Interpretations," *French Studies* 42 (1988): 278–91.

9. See Warner, "Editor's Note on the Calendar in *Persian Letters*," ix–x.

10. See Frautschi, "The Would-Be Invisible Chain," 606.

11. See Warner, "Montesquieu's Literary Art," xliv–xlv.

12. Warner, "Editor's Note on the Calendar in *Persian Letters*," x–xi. See also Schaub, *Erotic Liberalism*, 44–45.

13. The story continues in letter 47, in which Zachi writes to Usbek: "I have great news to tell you. I have reconciled with Zéphis; the seraglio, which was divided between us, has reunited." One possibility is that they have decided to share Zélide's favors. Later, in letter 53, Zélis writes Usbek to tell him of the passion of the white eunuch for her slave Zélide and her disgust at such a union, although we might also conjecture that she would not oppose the marriage because it would leave her slave girl free to continue their relationship.

14. See Warner, "Editor's Note on the Calendar in *Persian Letters*," xiv.

15. Likewise, in letter 53, speaking of the passion of the white eunuch for her slave girl, Zélis tells Usbek, "I have heard you say a thousand times that eunuchs feel a

certain voluptuousness toward women that is unknown to us; that nature compensates them for their loss" (86).

16. As also noted by Mallinson, "Usbek, Language and Power," 26.

17. See Braun, "Montesquieu, *Lettres persanes*, and Chaos," 81.

18. As noted by Roddick, "The Structure of the *Lettres persanes*," who argues that Montesquieu places these letters out of sequence for largely stylistic reasons.

19. See Schaub, *Erotic Liberalism*, 91, 133.

20. Warner, "Editor's Note on the Calendar in *Persian Letters*," xv.

21. See Schaub, *Erotic Liberalism*, 88.

22. Letter 144 is problematic because although it is said to be by Usbek to Rica, the letter writer addresses Usbek, praising him for his modesty and wisdom. Nonetheless, not only would my point here still stand if we were to attribute the letter to Rica, but it would in fact be strengthened if we consider whether Usbek is in fact wise.

23. See Schaub, *Erotic Liberalism*, 86.

24. See ibid., 85.

25. See Euben, *Journeys to the Other Shore*, 151.

26. Mallinson notes the linguistic echo between Roxanne's statement in letter 161, "This language, without doubt, appears new to you," and Usbek's claim in letter 8 about his conduct in the Persian court, "I spoke a language there until then unknown" ("Usbek, Language and Power," 32).

BIBLIOGRAPHY

Braun, Theodore E. D. "'La Chaîne secrète': A Decade of Interpretations." *French Studies* 42 (1988): 278–91.

———. "Montesquieu, *Lettres persanes*, and Chaos." In *Disrupted Patterns: On Chaos and Order in the Enlightenment*, edited by Theodore E. D. Braun and John A. McCarthy, 79–90. Amsterdam: Rodopi, 2000.

Euben, Roxanne L. *Journeys to the Other Shore: Muslim and Western Travelers in Search of Knowledge*. Princeton, NJ: Princeton University Press, 2006.

Frautschi, R. L. "The Would-Be Invisible Chain in *Les Lettres persanes*." *French Review* 40, no. 5 (1967): 604–12.

Goodman, Dena. *Criticism in Action: Enlightenment Experiments in Political Writing*. Ithaca, NY: Cornell University Press, 1989.

Hundert, E. J. "Sexual Politics and the Allegory of Identity in Montesquieu's *Persian Letters*." *Eighteenth Century* 31 (1990): 101–15.

Mallinson, G. J. "Usbek, Language and Power: Images of Authority in Montesquieu's *Lettres persanes*." *French Forum* 18 (1993): 23–36.

Montesquieu. *Oeuvres completes*. Volume 1. Edited by Roger Caillois. Paris: Gallimard, Bibliothèque de la Pléiade, 1949.

———. *Persian Letters*. Edited by Stuart D. Warner. Translated by Stuart D. Warner and Stéphane Douard. South Bend, IN: St. Augustine's Press, 2017.

O'Reilly, Robert F. "The Structure and Meaning of the *Lettres persanes*." *Studies on Voltaire and the Eighteenth Century* 67 (1969): 91–132.

Roddick, Nick. "The Structure of the *Lettres persanes.*" *French Studies* 28 (1974): 396–407.

Schaub, Diana J. *Erotic Liberalism: Women and Revolution in Montesquieu's Persian Letters.* Lanham, MD: Rowman and Littlefield, 1995.

Shackleton, Robert. "The Moslem Chronology of the *Lettres persanes.*" *French Studies* 8, no. 1 (1954): 17–27.

Starobinski, Jean. *Blessings in Disguise; or, The Morality of Evil.* Translated by Arthur Goldhammer. Cambridge, MA: Harvard University Press, 1993).

Warner, Stuart D. "Montesquieu's Literary Art: An Introduction to *Persian Letters.*" In *Persian Letters*, edited by Stuart D. Warner. Translated by Stuart D. Warner and Stéphane Douard. South Bend, IN: St. Augustine's Press, 2017.

———. "Editor's Note on the Calendar in *Persian Letters.*" In *Persian Letters*, edited by Stuart D. Warner. Translated by Stuart D. Warner and Stéphane Douard. South Bend, IN: St. Augustine's Press, 2017.

Chapter 14

The Book of Relations

Reflections from Montesquieu's **Persian Letters**

Stuart D. Warner

A man walks alone in a park and beside him a woman walks, also alone.
How does one know? It is as though a line exists between them, like
a line on a playing field. And yet in a photograph they might appear a
married couple, weary of each other and of the many winters they have
endured together.

—Louise Glück, "The Couple in the Park," *Faithful and Virtuous Night*

The way of *Fortune*, is like the *Milken Way* in the sky; which is a meeting or knot, of a number of small stars; not seen asunder, but giving
light together.

—Francis Bacon, "Of Fortune," *Essays or Counsels, Civil and Moral*

Persian Letters is an elegantly enticing book. But no matter how often one
revisits its terrain, new perplexities and, perchance, new discoveries await. It
is a cornucopia of wonders.

It is tempting, especially upon first encounter, to read most of its letters as
self-contained, each conveying a meaning distinct from the others; however,
no single letter can be understood, fully or even for the most part, on its own.
By repeatedly traveling back and forth along the literary topography of the
book, one is able to discover singular ways in which myriad letters, both
distant from and in close proximity to each other in presentation, transfigure

and impress themselves upon the meaning of others, but in a manner through which the initial meaning is not lost. Far from being a work simple to navigate, *Persian Letters* is staggeringly dense, and thus it is difficult know where one has been and where one is headed.

In Montesquieu's *orbis litterarum*, relations are the coin of the realm. This is true in the most obvious way. As a work of epistolary fiction, *Persian Letters* consists of letter writers and letter recipients, and this implies certain reciprocal relationships. In this respect, it is no different from other works of that genre that preceded it, for example, *The Turkish Spy*. Nevertheless, unlike all other such works of fiction, Montesquieu's contains an order of composition—the fictional date each letter is written—and an order of presentation, which are discordant with each other—thus there are two beginnings and two endings to it: letters 3 and 146 are the first and last letters composed, and letters 1 and 161 are the first and last letters presented. What conceals this divergence from immediate view is that the letters are dated using unfamiliar Arabic (Muslim) names of lunar months and familiar Gregorian (Western) solar years. Imagine reading the book upon its initial publication and encountering "*the 18th of the moon of Saphar, 1711*," the date of letter 2, written by Usbek, or "*the 21st of the moon of Maharram, 1711*," the date of letter 3, written by Zachi—how would one understand this? Would one realize that the latter letter was not later, and it was written not only prior to letter 2 but also to letter 1—that is, that it is the first letter in the order of composition? Would one have been able to calculate that Usbek would have received Zachi's letter prior to writing to the first black eunuch, and that the decision of the wives to go to the country was made independent of any judgment by Usbek, a decision Usbek was merely seconding, lest the chief black eunuch believe a fissure had formed between his wives' actions and his guiding authority?

It is only by always having the dates of the letters firmly in mind that one can notice that letters 6 and 8 provide one of two remarkable framing devices for the Troglodyte letters. Letter 6, from Usbek to Nessir, is ninth in the order of composition, and it immediately precedes Usbek's response to Mirza in letter 11, which is tenth in the order of composition—and it does so because the old man in letter 14, who bemoans the demise of the interest in virtue among the then still domestically organized Troglodytes and the corresponding rise in interest for law and public life, provides something of a mirror image of Usbek, devoured by sorrow, concerned that the virtue of faithfulness within the seraglio has lost (or soon will lose) its hold on his wives in his absence—all of which takes us back to the second letter's *now* problematic coupling of law and virtue: that is, what is of a piece in letter 2 is rent asunder in letter 14. Letter 8, on the other side, is seventeenth in the order of composition, and it is written by Usbek to Rustan ten days after he has sent the final Troglodyte letter to Mirza (and on the very same day that he sends his second letter to Méhémet Ali, who, like the Troglodytes, is cast underground). So rather than thinking of Letter 8, which points to "the true motive" for Usbek's journey, as being related only tangentially to that famous series of letters, it appears we would be better served by considering the possibility that it is informed by them, and cannot be understood except through a lens of understanding that they must provide.

The hybrid calendar that governs *Persian Letters* is complicated enough, but offstage, so to speak, another calendar is at play: the Persian solar calendar, instituted in 1079. Under the aegis of that calendar, we can determine that Usbek and Rica departed for Paris on the very last day of 1710, the twentieth day of its first month (*Farvardin*), and the wives departed for the country the very next day, on *Nowruz* ("new day"), the vernal equinox, the first day of 1711, the most festive day in Persia. In the country they stay at the seraglio of Fatmé, the name of Usbek's oldest wife, a place to which they repair throughout the course of the book, a place where men hide in walls, and where Roxane, Usbek's youngest wife, will rendezvous with her lover. The seraglio at Ispahan is left behind. Of the eleven letters Usbek's five wives write to him, four are written from that country seraglio (as is a letter from Narsit, a black eunuch, to Usbek). It is the place the wives go in the hope "to be freer" (Letter 47).[1] Almost synchronically, Usbek will, with the possible exception of his first year in France, spend most of his time outside of Paris, at a country estate, just as prior to deciding to leave Persia, he withdrew to a home of his own—perhaps the seraglio of Fatmé—in the country outside of Ispahan. To the contrary, Rica will, except for a few brief visits to Usbek, remain in Paris. However, while cut off from Paris, Usbek is not cut off from Persia, as the twenty-nine letters he sends and the twenty-five letters he receives from home attest. Rica, though, *appears* to be entirely cut off from Persia—as *Persian Letters* contains not a single letter sent or received by Rica from Persia—but his relationship to his homeland is more entangled, postally and otherwise, than it seems.

Persian Letters is replete with interpolated letters—letters with other letters, speeches, or stories embedded within them, which the respective letter writer attributes—sometimes intentionally falsely, as is the case with letters 67 and 141—to someone other than himself. Letter 28 is the first instance that takes the form of a letter within a letter. Rica, who does not write before arriving in Paris—but who will write the first letter from there—regales us with an account of visiting theatrical performances—comedic and operatic. Given his description of the various scenes, one might conclude that he naively misjudges what he witnesses, confusing actors and actresses with spectators. However, given that he is in fact recounting tales of seduction, it is fair game to say that the spectators, some in "loges" (Letter 28) are, in fact, acting out certain scenes, perhaps scenes they have planned, even written out in advance, and rehearsed with some care. Of course, on the basis of Rica's accounting, it is far from clear whether the spectators know that they are playing a role, or whether what might have been a mask has come to be the face itself.

Toward the end of this letter, which is the first in the work sent to an anonymous recipient—the first of eighteen that person will receive from him—Rica remarks that one of his friends brought him to a "loge," where one of the principal actresses was undressing. They got along so well that she sent him a letter requesting his aid in finding a position as a dancer in Persia—a highly valued position there—which he is including with his own. After claiming at the outset of her letter that she has always been "the most virtuous actress at the opera," she informs Rica that "as I was getting dressed for my role as a priestess of Diana, a young *abbé* came and found me there, and, without any respect for my white habit, my veil, and my bandeau, he ravished my innocence." The abbé succeeded in this quest, she proclaims, because he had promised to marry her—but, alas, he proved to be "unfaithful" (Letter 28): what a surprise! But was he really an abbé, or simply playing the role of one, perhaps dressed appropriately from a previous performance of that part? Her claim is that her innocence was ravished, but was it *her* innocence or the innocence of a virgin priestess of the virgin Diana? It rather appears that Rica's operatic actress is a simulacrum of herself, but to such an extent that her image and her being are virtually indistinguishable—to Rica, to Rica's correspondent, and maybe even to herself.

To get to letter 28, we must first traverse letter 26, written by Usbek to his youngest wife, Roxane, who, we can discover, uniquely shares with our letter-writing European actress the fashion of wearing a bandeau—which in and of itself serves as a semantic marker directing us to read these two letters in relation to each other—and whose virginal innocence was also ravished (or should we here say "ravaged"), by her husband, something brought into graphic relief with his disturbing, matter-of-fact characterization of her "dying virginity" (Letter 26). This morbid expression of loss, which does not dwell in the realm of images, portends Roxane poisoning herself, as well as Usbek's eunuchs from the seraglio at Ispahan, in the last letter in the order of presentation.[2] She has been led to take her own life because her lover, who she presumably was able to meet in the countryside and not in Ispahan, was brutally killed by one of Usbek's black eunuchs: life no longer holds any value for her. In her final sentence she announces to Usbek, "I am dying" (Letter 161), words that echo the same formulation of the chief black eunuch while on his deathbed.[3] But just before that, as Roxane can taste her end, she reveals to Usbek that "the pen falls from my hand" (ibid.). This formulation, which scarcely seems worthy of anyone's attention, is copied word for word from a French manual for writing letters for specific occasions: in this case, "the pen falls from my hand" is advised for a letter in which a wife will inform others of the death of her husband.[4] Of course, we have an instance here of ironic reversal, but at the same time, the death of Usbek's eunuchs and one of his wives sounds a death knell of any chance Usbek ever had of returning to Persia: indeed, as letter 141 foreshadows and letter 155, although written earlier, reinforces, there is no going home for Usbek. As Usbek intimates in the final line of the last letter in the order of composition, which he would have written after first having received Roxane's letter of denouement, John Law's France and Usbek's life have been reduced to a "frightful nothingness" (Letter 146), an expression that bears a close resemblance to Usbek's characterization of his chief black eunuch's circumstance prior to acquiring him from his service within another seraglio (Letter 2).[5]

The thematic element of female virginity in letters 26 and 28 reoccurs in letter 70 with Zélis's account to Usbek of the impending marriage of his friend Soliman's daughter. This will be the third in a sequence of letters about daughters. In letter 51, embedded in a letter about Peter the Great, a Muscovite daughter writes to her mother bemoaning that her husband does not beat her sufficiently, the marks from which would truly signal his love for her. Following that, in letter 62, Zélis writes to Usbek that "with your daughter having reached her seventh year, I believed that it was time to have her enter into the interior apartments of the seraglio, and not wait until she was ten to entrust her to the black eunuch." Now, in letter 70, Soliman's daughter arrives at her prospective husband's home on horseback, which immediately results in a request from the husband-to-be for an increase in the stipulated dowry. Soliman offers a "small present" to be added to it, which proves to be a sufficient inducement. Immediately following the wedding, Soliman's daughter is violently taken to bed, where after an hour the young man "furiously arose" and slashes her face, because "she was not a virgin," at which point "he sent her back to her father" (Letter 70). Yet, how indeed could she be a virgin: the young man had had *his* way with her for the previous hour! The image of a virgin remaining a virgin had somehow become an expectation reality had to satisfy, as if a woman could be, like a houri, resurrected continually as a virgin: Persian women have to be pure, which appears to mean that they cannot be women. Reality could not live up to the image and had to be punished for its impotence, or perhaps the young man was at work playing a confidence game, or both.

It is on this occasion, for the only time in *Persian Letters*, that Usbek answers a letter from one of his wives, and he does so immediately upon receiving it.[6] His concern is not directed toward Soliman's daughter, however: "I pity Soliman, especially as his distress is without remedy" (Letter 71); yet he notes that science has shown that there is no sure test of a woman's virginity. But in the second half of his letter he responds to Zélis's earlier missive about their daughter, and in so doing reinforces the importance of purity: "I learn with pleasure about the care that you are taking with the education of your daughter. God grant that her husband finds her to be as beautiful and pure as Fatima" (ibid.). This is not the only time Usbek broaches the matter, though. Towards the end of letter 48, Usbek castigates a young French philanderer who had been intimate with women (others' daughters and wives) to whom he was not married, thereby making him, by Usbek's lights, culpable of rape and treason. This incites Usbek to wax poetic:

> Happy are the children of Hali, who protect their families from disgrace and seduction! The light of the day is not purer than the fire that burns in the hearts of our women; our daughters never think without trembling of the day that must deprive them of the virtue that renders them akin to angels and incorporeal powers. Native and cherished land upon which the sun casts its first glances, you are not soiled by the horrible crimes that compel this luminary to hide himself as soon as he appears in the darkened West. (Letter 48)

Thus, the consummation of a marriage renders women less than pure.

Virgins, young women and eunuchs alike, do not fare particularly well in *Persian Letters*; however, the *image of women* who are virgins finds at least one saving grace in the work, as we can see from the starting point of letter 1, which commences with the virgin Fatima—conflated, though, with another Fatima—giving birth to twelve children, all accomplished while remaining pure. However, perhaps we should also harken back to Usbek's very early gnomic declaration to Nessir that in the seraglio in which he lived, he "anticipated love and destroyed love by love itself" (Letter 6). Perhaps this allusive apothegm stands illuminated by the matter at hand, for the consummation of love seems to require undermining the purity that Usbek most admires.

It is worth reminding ourselves at this juncture that the structure of the thematic constellations of letters that we find in *Persian Letters* varies. There are the often-noted series of letters, for example, the Troglodyte letters (Letters 11–14) and the library letters (Letters 133–37); there are letters such as 70 and 71, where one letter is a direct response to another; there are those that are quite distant from each other yet intimately connected (of which more shortly); however, there are also those that follow each other, which appear thematically to differ but do not. An instance of this relational device occurs in letters 35 and 36, both written by Usbek—the first to his cousin, Gemchid (in Persia), and the second to Rhédi (in Venice). In the former letter, Usbek writes with wonder at some length about a host of similarities between Islam and Christianity, which is a bit surprising given the disgust Usbek expressed to Nessir shortly after entering the profane Turkey, land of the Sunnis (see Letter 6); in the latter, Usbek is taken aback by the inflamed passions he finds in the petty disputations taking place in a café concerning "a quarrel of the ancients and moderns"—whether Homer is superior to modern poets. The issues in these two letters appear quite different until, guided by the seemingly off-topic last paragraph of letter 36, one realizes that the dispute about poetry serves as a surrogate for religious sectarian zealotry, which is internal to both Christianity and Islam and hence identical in both. In presenting Christianity and Islam as similar, Usbek is revealing that what might be offered as critique of one would be able to function thereby as a proxy for the other. Ironically, the dualities that appear in letters 35 and 36 are strangely mimicked in Usbek himself, for in the latter letter, for the only time in the seventy-eight letters he writes, he divides himself so as to speak to himself.

Let us here move on to a not obviously connected sequence of missives—letters 81–86, which will lead us to something fundamental about Rica and Usbek.

Nargum, Persian envoy to Muscovy, writes two letters to Usbek, the first of which is letter 51 and the second of which is letter 81, of which more shortly. In letter 51, Nargum includes a letter from a daughter to her mother, complaining because her husband does not beat her enough: a good beating every now and again, as we pointed to earlier, would testify to his love for her. Of some importance is that we do not learn how Nargum came into the letter's possession. Setting that aside, though, Nargum's own letter draws attention to Peter the Great. Peter does not allow his citizens to leave Muscovy, and they are left thinking that there are no customs other than their own. However, Peter seeks to further the place of the arts and sciences in his country, and to advance the reputation of Muscovy in Europe and Asia. Yet, "restless and ceaselessly agitated, he wanders throughout his vast estates, leaving the marks of his natural severity everywhere" (Letter 51). This description of Peter maps onto the description of Usbek and the seraglio that Zachi—who intimated she reveled in Usbek leaving the marks of his love upon her—and Fatmé—who vows that she has seen no other man—provide in letters 3 and 7, as well as mapping onto Usbek's claim in letter 8 about going to the king, indicating to him "the longing that I had to educate myself in the sciences of the West" (Letter 8).[7] It further maps onto Zachi's description of Usbek's wandering in "barbarous climates," and her *assertion* about wandering "from apartment to apartment" (Letter 3) following Usbek's departure.

Letter 81 is of a piece with Nargum's first letter, for in it he presents a sketch of the history of the Tartars, of Genghis Khan in particular. These people are "the true dominators of the universe." To be sure, Usbek's name alone ties him to this people. Despite apparently knowing a great deal about them, Nargum, at the end of the letter, bemoans their lack of historians and asks how many of their glorious achievements, their conquests of others, have been lost in the mists of time, for absent the creation of a historical record, silence reigns.

Whatever further taste we might have for silence might be satisfied by letter 82, for there Rica writes to Ibben about a taciturn people, the Carthusians, who cut off their tongues as part of their religious commitment; thus, they too are silent and cannot be heard. He further suggests that "it would be very desirable for all other dervishes to cut off in the same manner everything that their profession renders useless to them" (Letter 82), no doubt alluding to the eunuchs of Persia and elsewhere.

Usbek presents his most sustained discussion of justice in letter 83, and it bears a striking resemblance to his first overtly philosophical argument on the compatibility of God's omniscience and free will in letter 69: both are turgid and strained, appearing sophistic, and it is less than obvious what their arguments are. Consider the opening line of letter 83: what exactly does it mean to say that "*La justice est un rapport de convenance*"? The line mines a remark from Leibniz's *Theodicy* (1710), but there Leibniz is discussing punitive justice and the agreement or congruence is between wrongdoing and punishment. Is that what Usbek's letter about? Surely his letter aims at minimizing God's role, although not completely, but how exactly does he do that without grounding justice upon convention, something he vows to avoid at all costs? Three times in the letter he nods in the direction of that perhaps there is no God at all—"If there is a God"; "even if there were no God"; "and who, if he existed"—nevertheless, the argument for justice being "eternal" and that "we ought always to love justice" is premised on the idea of a God:

> So, even if there were no God, we ought always to love justice, that is to say, *to endeavor to resemble that being of whom we have such a beautiful idea*, and who, if he existed, would necessarily be just. Free though we might be from the yoke of religion, we ought not to be free from the yoke of equity. Here is, Rhédi, what makes me think that justice is eternal and does not depend on human conventions; and were it so dependent, it would be so terrible a truth that it would be necessary to hide it from ourselves. (Letter 83; emphasis added)

But why should we resemble the being of whom we have a beautiful idea, irrespective of whether he exists or not? What seems to make the idea beautiful for Usbek is that God cannot commit injustice, because only a being who has interests and can pursue them come what may can be unjust. However, to be without interests is not to be human—neither man nor woman: how can that be the basis of justice, something that presumably positions human beings to adjudicate divergent interests? The determining factor for Usbek is a beautiful idea, not a beautiful being: the idea or image replaces the reality. Thus, Usbek seemingly allows for the possibility that justice is indeed reducible to human convention; nevertheless, that would be such an ugly truth, it would have to be papered over and hidden from sight. Is Usbek's letter—which begins with a rhetorical question to Rhédi, "You would never have imagined that I could have become more of a metaphysician than I already was" (Letter 69)—not an exhibition of sophistry?

However, we should step back a bit because of a remark Usbek makes earlier in letter 83. He notes there that "it is true that men do not always see these relations; when they see them, they often even turn away from them; and their own interest is always what they see the best. Justice raises its voice, but it has trouble making itself heard amidst the tumult of the passions." The contrast between seeing and hearing is curious, but we should focus our attention on the latter, in part because unlike the prior two letters, here justice is not silent: it must make its voice heard—and we think what he means by that is that caught in the swell of the thumotic impulses that lead to injustice, the voice of justice has to be persuasive for a variety of reasons, even if it dissimulates.

Another reason to focus on the voice of justice is that it is the driving force in Rica's treatment of justice in letter 86, written to the same unnamed correspondent to whom letter 28 was sent. Here, the abstract, strained, and distant qualities of Usbek's characterization of justice are absent: Rica's presentation is particularized and populated entirely with examples of women. But just as Usbek's letter on justice was preceded by Nargum's letter on the violent, warlike Tartars, Rica's is preceded by a letter dealing with war, which he writes to the same anonymous individual about *Les Invalides*, a hospital for old or wounded army veterans, "victims of their fatherland" (Letter 84). Rica concludes letter 84 by a clarion call for a temple in which "the names of those who die for their fatherland were preserved," for without that, their names would soon be forgotten—just like the achievements of the Tartars— and, indeed, have been.

Rica begins letter 86 with what will come into focus as an image of Usbek and the seraglio: "It seems that families here govern themselves entirely alone. The husband has only a shade of authority over his wife, the father over his children, and the master over his slaves. Justice is concerned with all of their differences, and you may be sure that it is always against the jealous husband, the sullen father, and the disagreeable master." This is a far cry from the punitive justice of letter 83; here we seem to find something akin to distributive justice. In any case, Rica announces that he went to a place where justice is rendered; it is a "sacred place where all the secrets of the family are revealed and the most hidden actions are exposed to the light of day." Before arriving there, one must pass by tradeswomen who beckon in a "beguiling voice"—prostitutes, ribbon makers, or perhaps both. But in that "tribunal" of justice, women come to make things known, to make their voice heard— they speak of what presumably are the injustices of men, which absent their voices will remain invisible: fathers, husbands, daughters, unfaithful lovers, and abusers. In one of Rica's examples, a woman with "similar modesty" to a shameless woman seeks to be turned over and examined, her husband perhaps not having consummated the marriage properly, if at all, and that "a judgment restore to her all the rights of virginity" and thereby restore her to purity and make her whole again. Justice here is inextricably connected to a pleading voice; justice here is a claim against men. Yet at the end of this letter we read, "In this tribunal, the voice of the majority is followed, but it is said that it is recognized by experience that it would be better to heed the voice of the minority; and that is natural enough, for there are very few just minds, and everyone agrees that there are an infinite number of false ones" (Letter 86).

Now, whatever this process is, there is something profoundly false and disingenuous about it, and thus about justice, for while the majority is heeded, everyone agrees that there is a superior path to be had. But what exactly is the tribunal of justice that Rica describes? It appears twisted and contorted around two institutions: a court of law and the confessional; the contractual and the sacramental. From whom, after all, are the women seeking relief from the men in their lives—judges, who are men, or priests, who also are men? Whatever the case may be, the women's complaints eerily echo life in Usbek's seraglio.

By looking at Usbek's letter on justice and then Rica's, we have stumbled upon a striking disparity between them, one that exhibits itself throughout the weft and warp of *Persian Letters*. On the simplest level we can say, along with many others, that Usbek leans toward the more abstract—hence his letters on the nature of God's omniscience, justice, religious toleration, criminal punishment, severe and moderate governments—while Rica dwells in the land of convention—hence his letters on the theatre, fashion, and books. But how does that difference express itself, and what accounts for it? Perhaps it manifests itself most in a divide we canvassed earlier: other than the first year that the two of them are in Paris, Usbek will spend almost the entirety of his time while in France outside of the city; Rica, however, is out and about in Paris, always finding new things to do and meeting new and different people.[8] Usbek is fundamentally secluded, whereas Rica is attentive to the divergent nuances of Parisian social life. Indeed, the description Usbek gives of himself in the opening paragraph of letter 48 seems to fit Rica better than it does himself.[9] We must recognize that unlike Usbek, Rica is a master of images, a master of credit, and a master of belief, all of which culminate in a distinctive form of irony and humor.[10] This allows him to be insightful in the most oblique and impressionistic ways about the relation of convention and nature, dual themes he pursues especially through his reflections about women. Perhaps it is because of such mastery that Rica is able to transform himself and to flourish in Paris, whereas Usbek proves incapable of doing either. Usbek wants to return to Persia, but, he writes to Nessir, Rica does not: "I have pressed Rica a thousand times, but he opposes all of my resolutions. He keeps me here by a thousand pretexts. It seems he has forgotten his fatherland, or rather, it seems that he has forgotten me, so unfeeling is he to my displeasures" (Letter 155).

Yes, it appears Rica wants to stay, but why did he leave Persia to go to Paris in the first place? In letter 1, Usbek writes to Rustan and declares that "Rica and I are perhaps the first among Persians who left their country out of a longing for knowledge," a claim he will qualify in letter 8, yet only with respect to himself—Rica goes unmentioned in the latter letter. So why did Rica leave for Paris? Is it as Usbek describes it in letter 1, or might that only be a part of Rica's reasons for departing Persia?

A clue to the resolution of these questions is to be found in letter 127, a strange letter on any reading. The opening of it takes us into the history of Sweden, in particular to the reign of Charles XII. In 1716, Sweden found itself with several enemies, not the least of which was Russia and therefore Peter the Great. It was in that year that Charles met the German Georg Heinrich von Görtz, who thought, with prudent decisions, that Sweden could pursue a path of peace. Charles was so impressed by him that he appointed him chief minister of his government, on the basis of which he came to be known as the "Grand Vizier" of Sweden. But Sweden continued to find herself at war on several fronts, and funds were needed, so Görtz hatched a twofold plan: to mint emergency coins, *Nottaler*, and to print paper money.[11] Görtz, being German, was not a favorite son of the nobles in Sweden, and when Charles was felled by a bullet in late 1718, it was easy to trump up charges against Görtz, find him guilty, and have him beheaded—particularly since Sweden's financial system began to suffer greater and greater strain after its monarch's death.[12]

Immediately following his remarks about Görtz and Sweden, Rica turns to himself:

> You know that, in the sacred banquets in which the Lord of Lords descends from the most sublime throne in the world to communicate with his slaves, I formed a severe law for myself to control an intractable tongue. I have never been seen to utter a single word that could be bitter to the lowliest[13] of his subjects. When it was necessary for me to cease being sober, I did not cease being an honorable man; and *in that trial of our faithfulness*, I have risked my life, but never my virtue. (Letter 127; emphasis added)

We cannot be certain what Rica said when he could not be silent, but whatever it was, it put his life in danger. This no doubt points to a reason for leaving, to say nothing of never returning. And in this respect, his reason seems akin to the reason Usbek offered in letter 8. However, what is remarkable is where his actions took place—at an all-important banquet for the king. This suggests that however young he was, Rica was a significant figure in Ispahan, something that is borne out in several letters. Consider, for example, the various individuals who turn to Rica for help: the operatic actress in letter 28, the alchemist in letter 45, the Capuchin in letter 49, and the woman at court in letter 141. But we should also observe how in letter 30, Rica reports that he is the object of everyone's attention: "I found portraits of myself everywhere. I saw myself multiplied in every shop, on every mantel, so much did they fear not having seen me enough."[14]

In letter 126, Rica writes to Usbek to tell him that despite expecting him back in Paris the following day, he is forwarding his letters to him. The mention of this to Usbek becomes the occasion for Rica to speak of his own letters that have arrived, including at least one that informs him that "the ambassador of the Grand Mogul has received orders to leave the kingdom" (Letter 126). Of course, we do not have these letters, but it seems clear that he is receiving correspondence informing him of political news that might be of interest to him or might have some bearing on his own circumstances. Moreover, as the first two letters that Rica writes show, he knows a good deal about French political life—not details that could have been easily gleaned in a month's time in Paris, but details about which a politically well-placed individual might already have been privy.[15]

If we are correct about Rica's status in Persia, this might provide some guidance in making sense of one peculiarity in eighteen of the forty-six letters that Rica writes—namely, why it is that the letter recipient in those letters is anonymous, the person's name and location signified by the notation * * *, which appears in the letter headings and also in the body of letter 109, where Rica is directly addressing the recipient of the letter. All of these letters save one deal with specific scenes of Parisian life; they embody the kinds of things about which a foreigner might write home.[16] These letters in which the addressee is unknown appear destined for Persia, and most likely Ispahan, or at least this is what we think can be inferred. If this is a veridical inference, the question is why they are anonymous, and we think the answer has to do with protecting the person to whom they are being sent. Be that as it may, if the letters are being written by Rica to someone in Persia, this means that he is maintaining some form of hidden relationship to Persia—that is the crucial point.

What is also hidden from view is Rica's relationship to the ending of *Persian Letters*. Within the order of presentation, the collapse of Usbek's seraglio and Usbek's having to deal with it dominates the final scene. However, within the order of composition, it is Rica who brings the curtain down, writing twelve of the final twenty-one letters, including letter 141, which stands the whole of *Persian Letters* on its head,[17] and is thus a rewriting of it from his perspective and what he has learned; letter 142, one of the two detailed letters he writes about John Law, and thus about corruption; and letter 143, which vitiates the notion of purity upon which the Persian view of women rests. We can say that the deepest understanding of *Persian Letters* turns on how to understand the relationship between Usbek and Rica, what each represents, and how each brings *Persian Letters* to a conclusion.[18]

NOTES

1. All translations from *Persian Letters* are by the author and drawn from his edition: Montesquieu, *Persian Letters*, ed. Stuart D. Warner, trans. Stuart D. Warner and Stéphane Douard (South Bend, IN: St. Augustine's Press, 2017); henceforth PL. Quotations from this work are cited parenthetically by letter number.

2. Earlier in PL 26, Usbek takes comfort that Roxane is not in the "poisoned climates" of France and Europe.

3. Cf. PL 151.

4. Jean Puget de la Serre, *La secrétaire à la mode* (Amsterdam, 1646), 112.

5. Cf. PL 30, where Rica remarks upon taking off his Persian clothes and putting on European ones: "Free of every foreign ornament . . . I entered into a frightful nothingness."

6. This allows us, along with PL 64 and 65, to establish a timeline for how long a letter takes to get from Ispahan to Paris and vice versa.

7. Cf. PL 1.

8. Cf. PL 45, 48, and 141.

9. Cf. the first and fifth paragraphs of PL 48, and the second paragraph of PL 155.

10. PL 141 testifies to Rica's irony, and PL 143—which is, along with letters 133–37, an imitation of Rabelais—testifies to his humor.

11. The episode involving Görtz should be read in parallel to PL 132, 142, and 146, which deal with John Law.

12. Cf. R. Nisbet Bain, *Charles XII and the Collapse of the Swedish Empire—1682–1719* (New York: G.P. Putnam's Sons, 1895), 277–301.

13. Cf. PL 127, par. 3: "For, after all, if it is an evil action to blacken the lowliest of his subjects in the mind of the prince."

14. Cf. PL 91 about the visit of the Persian ambassador, Mohammed Reza Beg. Concerning the ambassador's ill-fated visit to France, which sheds some light on letter 30, see Susan Mokhberi, *The Persian Mirror: Reflections of the Safavid Empire in Early Modern France* (New York: Oxford University Press, 2019).

15. Cf. PL 24.

16. Usbek writes four letters to an anonymous addressee, perhaps the same individual to whom Rica writes.

17. And in part offering an imitation of Shahrazad's role in *One Thousand and One Nights*, via the character of Zuléma.

18. This paper grows out of a presentation at a conference commemorating the 300th anniversary of the first publication of *Lettres persanes*, which took place at the University of Houston in December 2021. I am ever so thankful to Constantine Vassiliou and Jeff Church, the organizers of that meeting, for their generous hospitality and patience. For conversations over many years about *Persian Letters*, I owe more than I can say to Stéphane Douard, John Gibbons, Ryan Hanley, Marina Marren, Tom Merrill, Svetozar Minkov, Andrea Radasanu, John Scott, Vicki Sullivan, Kathlynn Thomason, and especially Ralph Lerner.

BIBLIOGRAPHY

Bain, R. Nisbet. *Charles XII and the Collapse of the Swedish Empire—1682–1719*. New York: G. P. Putnam's Sons, 1895.

Mokhberi, Susan. *The Persian Mirror: Reflections of the Safavid Empire in Early Modern France*. New York: Oxford University Press, 2019.

Montesquieu. *Persian Letters*. Edited by Stuart D. Warner. Translated by Stuart D. Warner and Stéphane Douard. South Bend, IN: St. Augustine's Press, 2017.

Serre, Jean Puget de la. *La secrétaire à la mode*. Amsterdam, 1646.

Chapter 15

The Unknown Chains
of Enlightenment

The Irony of Philosophy or an Ironic Philosopher[1]

Peter Lund

SOME REFLECTIONS ON "SOME REFLECTIONS"

"You are never as divine as when you lead to wisdom and truth through pleasure."[2]

Montesquieu's reflections can be contrasted subtly with Usbek's, the character that often sounds like Montesquieu. In fact, it would seem that "Some Reflections" might even be Montesquieu's response to Usbek's reflections in letter 33, in which Usbek discusses the problem of our attachment to the material world. Montesquieu and Usbek may agree that our bodies can be conducted to pleasure or pain through chemistry. They might even agree that fundamentally, human beings seek pleasure and avoid pain. Montesquieu sees this as a feature, not a bug. Usbek, on the other hand, has a tragic view and vain hope is above it all: "It is much better to rise above these reflections and to treat man as a sentient being rather than to treat him as a reasonable one. The soul united with the body is thereby ceaselessly tyrannized" (Letter 33, 54).[3] Thus, the body and the soul are at war with each other. What is life without a body? In Usbek's mind, humans are pleasure-seeking machines. For Usbek, the body is the cause of our sentiments, and it is for this reason he disapproves of drinking. It drags our soul down through its effect on the body. Alcohol suppresses reason and allows us to "rebel against all precept"

239

(Letter 33, 55). Thus, drinking or not, there is for Usbek a human's desire for a "secret pleasure," to shuck the burdens of our knowledge. On the flip side, stimulating drinks uplift us and allow those who imbibe them to be able to "charm away" the memories of our troubles. Whatever we imbibe, we as human beings are destined to the enormous weight of our reason or drink the draft of Lethe. Thus, to Usbek, it is no wonder that the most thoughtful Europeans turn to Stoicism as a kind of acceptance of the burdens of this world and tug-of-war that is human nature.[4] He, however, hopes he can remove himself from the material world, that is, he is an exception to nature. While imbibing the stimulants, he may draw a brief respite from the curse of his knowledge and for a fleeting moment recover life.

What sort of book is the *Persian Letters*? Like one explaining a joke, the explanation is less comical than the joke itself. The *Persian Letters* does not read like a different hand than *The Spirit of the Laws*. In fact, if one reads the 1758 edition, which includes letters featuring the character Jaron and most notably "Some Reflections," the hand that wrote *The Spirit of the Laws* becomes most clear. Perhaps this author is a bit less witty or more direct in his late sixties than when the first edition was published. "Some Reflections" more explicitly points to secrets and silence the reader might have missed. Moreover, these same reflections express his pleasure in finding a narrative and his surprise to discover an interesting and humorous story in the work for which the demanding public who do not see his more penetrating wisdom clamor for a sequel. "Some Reflections" seems more a eulogy than an epilogue. It is less chiding of the popular reading than the preface and in this way less comic and more clinical. Nevertheless, it highlights the importance of the body of his work and not just the spirit. In "Some Reflections," Montesquieu takes up the theme of the "nature of the work" by exploring the "body of the work." He uses philosophic nomenclature to discuss what might appear a literary contention. The epistolary novel is free to expose a secret or unknown chain that an ordinary novel cannot. It is on reflections of a body, a particular type of novel, that nature is revealed. By reflecting on the body, Montesquieu says a reader can see more deeply than if the reader abstracts from the body of the work.

In "Some Reflections," Montesquieu clarifies his philosophic methodology. Montesquieu's philosophy, on the other hand, embraces partial perceptions so that one can apperceive a whole. This absurdity is practiced out of love, as a lover sees the best in his beloved. The charm of love is that it gives divinity to the instantiate, the very imperfections of the beloved become beauty marks. This aspect of love is essential for philosophy. For Montesquieu, the philosopher ties "our truths" and "our dogmas" together as a whole. He "makes this *justification* out of love for those great truths" and refrains from striking at our "most tender places" ("Some Reflections," 271, emphasis added). That is, for Montesquieu, the task of philosophy is not to liberate us from "our dogmas" or tear down "our truths." On the contrary, love is not a delusion but it heightens awareness and makes us "pay attention." In love, the particulars become meaningful. This should be seen in contrast to how Usbek sees love. Usbek sees love as rose-colored glasses and our sentimentalities, compromises.

In this way, Montesquieu might resemble Socrates as he depicts himself in Plato's "Apology of Socrates," who, either out of a peculiar piety or public service, exposes the public dogmas as dogmatic. In a singular moment of public speaking, he presents the philosopher to the "Athenians" as an anti-dogmatist. The appeal of such an image is found in its radical freedom. Such a philosopher is no longer chained by the shadows of his time and place. This image of philosophy is one that dies on the cross of reason, giving up the most dear convictions and conventions to dispel ignorance. One might wonder with no dogmas if Athens or any community can hang together. The public image of Socratic philosophy must excuse the practice of philosophy by its good motives, his piety or public service.

There is a thread of Montesquieu's scholarship portraying him as a force against tyranny. This invites many scholars of this perplexing work to explore how the bits of the work add up to a warning of political means that may lead to tyranny or advice to lead a society away from tyranny.[5] On its face, this seems a noble endeavor, turning one's perverse interest in the thoughts of an eighteenth-century thinker to the advantage of the current political era. The problem of tyranny is not in its means for the means of a tyrant and a benevolent monarch or government might be necessary for the health of the people.[6] If such means are necessary then they are not just legitimate but just because where is the justice in watching the city burn when the law is silent or even proscribes the solution.[7] It is good policy to be vigilant against such means because it is difficult to distinguish between tyranny and necessary tools that appear like tyranny.[8] Montesquieu distinguishes himself from Usbek and thus from enlightenment not by image of good and serious intentions but by the reality of good and serious intentions.

Montesquieu distinguishes himself from the public image of philosophy by contrasting the popular reading with a more philosophical reader. In both the preface and "Some Reflections," Montesquieu presents his philosophic method. A good philosopher is like a good reader. He pays attention to the contrasts between the unreliable and very particular perspectives present in a work and *can* see the forest *because* of the trees. Montesquieu expresses his certainty that the work speaks for itself, and only Usbek and his analogous reader will be deceived: "Certainly, the nature and design of the Persian Letters are so apparent that they will only deceive those who want to deceive themselves" ("Some Reflections," 271). It is through Usbek's ambition that

Montesquieu explores how the rationalist became enslaved to his task of enlightenment. Powerless, he expresses his tyranny over everything else. Usbek, certain the material world is an immense, chaotic, and constant flux of matter in motion, tragically longs to mean something in that world.

WHAT IS PHILOSOPHIC FREEDOM?

"The author allows himself the advantage of being able to join philosophy, politics, and morality into a novel, and of binding the whole together by a secret chain, and in some fashion unknown." —Montesquieu, "Some Reflections," 269

Satirical writing requires subtle readers. These subtle readers not only are aware of Montesquieu's design; Montesquieu wants them to be aware of the popular reading. In the preface, he focuses on the critics. The critics are just as demanding and tyrannical as the popular reading in "Some Reflections." The popular reader demands the conventional. This is contrasted with the nature of the work and apperceptions of "the way things really are." The good reader must be subtle enough to understand convention and uncover nature that is not revealed easily. This is a tall order. In "Some Reflections," he elaborates on this demand both for a sequel and, more damning, that Usbek and Rica exhibit a parochial or "singular" understanding of the world. Montesquieu refuses to be cowed by the clamoring of the crowd. He is lucky that the booksellers take the haranguing for him. This tyrannical readership imagines that these backward barbarians ought to go through a conversion and to be enlightened by the universal and "evolved" society in the West. One should recognize the parallel between Usbek's universalism and the demands of this audience. By demonstrating an audience burdened with such an expectation and an alternative audience which he portrays as more clear-eyed, he entreats his reader to not accept blithely the supposed divorce between Usbek's philosophic commitments and his despotic nature.

The satirization of Usbek does not portray him as a fool or naive. On the contrary, he is respected among his friends in Persia as "the soul of their society," the mullah expects that he understands religious law, and he enjoys respect from the Persians in the West. Moreover, his philosophy would be well received by French readers; as Stuart Warner in his interpretive essay remarks, his philosophical leanings are "anathema" to his origins in Persia.[9] This, Warner notes in order to highlight Usbek's duality: "Wondrously, Usbek appears completely oblivious of any division with himself."[10] This divide Warner sees in Usbek manifests itself in the apparent difference between Usbek's philosophic side, which resembles Western philosophy, and his tyrannical or despotic side, which is most clearly exhibited in his rule of the

seraglio, and thus tied to Persia (compare Letters 2 and 97). This oblivious-
ness is wondrous if his philosophy is truly distinct from his despotic soul.
Perhaps wonder, not certitude, is the beginning of philosophy. No one can
read the *Persian Letters* without seeing the contrast between Usbek's rule
of the seraglio and his seemingly enlightened philosophy.[11] This contrast is
clearest if one thinks of Persia and her ways as inherently despotic. There
is a contrast between the secular enlightened world and "the backward" and
"religiously closed" world of Asia. The placing of the chronologically third
and fourth letters as the first and second leads to an ambiguity. The readers
may see Usbek as unique among Barbarians and that the Persian world is not
bereft of rational men. Alternatively, the reader may conclude that Usbek is
not wholly a creature of the East. The French readers, as Montesquieu points
out, are also demanding that their fictional foreigners not be revealed as
enlightened from the start (see "Some Reflections," especially 270). Neither
conclusion sits well with these audiences. This unsettling claim is intended
to shift readers to reconsider their demands that Persians be singular or that
the West be wholly free. With this reordering, Montesquieu both proves the
mettle of the readers and invites them to see the limits of Usbek.

Thus, the order of the letters is a source of intrigue. Free of the narratological chain, he shuffles the letters to serve the arguments rather than the narrative. The first two letters tempt one to see Usbek's division as the source of
his unhappiness. They are reordered in front of the third and fourth, showing
Usbek's character as philosophic and despotic. This is to tempt the reader to
believe that Usbek is merely "saving face"; that is, in the first letter he presents an image of himself, while the second letter reveals the "true" Usbek.
The heart of this contention is the conceit that philosophy is complete and
self-sufficient. In short, under this view Usbek's despotism is incompatible
with his philosophy. This would incline one to think that the complex of mastery and slavishness depicted in the second letter is a contradiction with the
philosophic life presented in letter 1. Letter 1 not only presents a philosophic
life that has a complexity of freedom and unfreedom but reveals that Usbek's
philosophic life involves an insufficiency. Thus, only in a certain way is the
letter a mask: it attempts to paint what is done for selfish reasons as noble.
Usbek wants Rustan to see his departure as an act of freedom and a mark of
his philosophic independence, but neither Rustan nor a reader who is paying
attention will think that he is free. It might appear that his "longing for knowledge" is genuine, but in its resemblance to the "plausible pretext" of letter 8,
a careful reader will reexamine what he presumed about his resemblance to
the philosopher, a lover of wisdom.

Although letter 1 can be seen as establishing Usbek's philosophical constitution, at the heart of his departure is his dissatisfaction. Perhaps his friends
share this dissatisfaction, and it is certain that the "refined" and "enlightened"

believe it of a person who lives under the "Oriental light." Montesquieu, through Usbek, relies on an image of a philosopher who has come to know the shadows to be shadows on the walls of a cave. While Montesquieu's enlightened reader might feel this dissatisfaction and would find it plausible one be dissatisfied with the narrow world of Islam, it is precisely this dissatisfaction that distinguishes Usbek from Socrates. The first letter is a temptation that is more risible than laudable to the careful reader. Montesquieu uses the conceits of the enlightened reader to believe Usbek a noble iconoclast unhappy to be ruled by superstition, but to the careful reader, he is revealed as just as much a puppet of the strings of his desires and the chains of his opinions of his own self-importance.

Usbek is unable to be at home in his own city because any city is too small. He has big dreams. It is his desire that drives him out. This longing is so great, it tears him from the "tranquil life" to the "laborious" search for "wisdom" (Letter 1, 5). There is implied freedom that Usbek and his friends seem to share. In the tenth letter, Mirza expresses this more directly. When he speaks to the mullah he does not "speak to them as a true believer but as a man, a citizen, and a father" (Letter 10, 18). The letter begins with a mystery of Usbek's religion. Warner notes that this is a conflation of two Fatimas. This conflation turns Fatima into a mystery more familiar to his readers: a virgin birth. This mystery should be profoundly perplexing. Mysteries of faith serve for some as sources of doubt, while for others, mysteries have the opposite effect, affirming their faith in a power higher than themselves. We get no direct comment from Usbek about how he understands Fatima in this letter. This mystery is left unexplored for a discussion of how Usbek and his friends did not "believe that [Persia's] borders were those of 'our' [i.e., Usbek's and his friends'] knowledge." Usbek implies that others are bound by beliefs of the East. He and his friends, on the other hand, are liberated enough to seek enlightenment, not from "Oriental light alone." The silence regarding the mystery indicates he is not dissatisfied with the East because of its particular positions so much as its partiality. "Oriental light" is incomplete. Usbek seeks knowledge without borders.

Usbek, unsatisfied with his "Oriental light," does not "expect a great many to approve" of his journey; unstated is his expectation that Rustan will approve. This expectation may be falsely placed. Do they share this same longing and lack of belief? He is both chained to a life of labor by his longing for wisdom and free of chains of his "culture" and his "religion." This letter reveals a tension in Usbek's philosophical life, that of freedom and unfreedom. Usbek is evidently leaving the domain of Islam to a place that would treat the mystery of Fatima as a delusion, and also within the borders of Islam, by his group of friends not satisfied with Islam's borders of knowledge.[12] Thus, he treats the philosophic life as one seeking truth beyond the borders of his community, just as if it is a peculiar dissatisfaction only true for his small society. This might lead one truly concerned with truth above satisfaction to ask, "Is my freedom experienced in the philosophic life only true within the borders of my little community of friends?"

What does this dissatisfaction mean? This image of philosophical longing portrays it as both a blessing and a curse. While "the philosopher" shares with his philosophical friends a liberty from the small and singular horizon, he is never truly at home in the world he must live. This means that this type of philosopher, perhaps all philosophers, must cherish his friends, but his love of wisdom supersedes his love of his friends. Usbek ends the letter with what might seem the same tenderness and earnestness of purpose that Aristotle has for Plato in the *Nicomachean Ethics*.[13] Implying that he must travel to satisfy his search for the truth, he writes, "be assured that in whatever part of the world I am, you have a faithful friend" (Letter 1, 5).[14] One might be touched by such tender words between friends who share a passion for wisdom. Yet Usbek cannot help but point out his "selfless sacrifice." What a martyr for philosophy! Montesquieu's audience perceives this either as courageous or as a comically self-congratulatory and self-effacing claim. Usbek portrays himself as a sort of explorer: "Rica and I are perhaps the first among Persians who left their country" for this noble purpose. Usbek would have Rustan believe he does things selflessly, in fact at his own expense. The service he does for the Persians is more serious than their friendship. However, Montesquieu's reader understands him; in letter 5, despite Usbek's "reasons" and in contrast to Rustan's "inclinations," Rustan is unable to pardon Usbek. We can see that Usbek is heartless and that Rustan is unconvinced of his nobility.

However, Montesquieu evaluates Usbek's departure, in Usbek's two accounts one cannot help but see a resemblance between letter 1's "longing for knowledge" and "the plausible pretext, [he] indicated to [the prince that he had a] longing . . . to educate himself in the sciences of the West" in letter 8 (Letter 8, 13). Warner paradoxically sees letter 8 as a more honest presentation of Usbek's "true motive" and an incomplete explanation that requires letter 1 to inform his reasons for leaving. Warner offers an alternative interpretation of letter 1 that a reader could suppose: it perhaps maintains the pretext that is dangerous to dispel while he remains in Persia. On the other hand, it could be that the story of Usbek is more complicated than the practical impulse or theoretical impulse alone can explain.[15] While Warner may favor one, both hold a strong line between the theoretical needs and practical needs. It is on this strong line that Warner can describe what letter 8 calls "the prudence of his enemies" as "political persecution." Thus, Warner is able to pretend his "longing for knowledge" is what catches the ire of his enemies. The transition from the love of wisdom to wisdom places one at odds with the authority of the city. Such a theoretical impulse is antidogmatism. By pitting the impulse of letter 1 at odds with the impulse depicted in letter 8, Warner is able to say his philosophy is his true drive and he would practice it at his own peril for it is at odds with his self-preservation: "Usbek's own circumstances thus turn out to enact a tension within an intricate web of philosophy, political persecution, and self-preservation." This, he believes, is a tension both Montesquieu and Usbek share.[16] If letter 8 shows this tension, then he also shares this with Socrates. It seems that to Warner all philosophers would share this tension.[17] Thus, the irony of this hard and fast line between theoretical and practical impulses is that letter 8, rather than revealing that Usbek in fact leaves for self-preservation alone, reveals to Warner that he leaves for *both* his philosophy and his self-preservation. This would seem to push against how Usbek presents it himself. He takes care to say it is his "prudence" that is his "true motive," while if there is any truth to letter 1, it is done without his intention. The "longing for knowledge" is a pretext he thought would appeal to Rustan and resembles the pretext he tells the king. It is his *virtue* that ensures the jealousy of the flatterers. Usbek's philosophy is his *right opinion* rather than *knowledge of ignorance*. Thus, letters 1 and 8 tie the theoretical to the practical, in general, but in the particular case of Usbek his version of the theoretical, his "*design*," is incompatible with the practical, his *life*.

The practical reason or practical impulse should keep you out of trouble. In the philosopher, it should be contrasted with high-mindedness. In the manner of Donald Rumsfeld, "You go to war with the army you *have*, not the army you want." Practical impulse reconciles one's wishes and wants with reality. It is on account of his "*feeble virtue*" that Usbek ran right into this trouble; it is Usbek's high-minded virtue that ensured the enmity of the flatterers. It seems that rather than being perceived as the enemy of the city, he is a friend of the tyrant. The whole letter is an inversion of the Socratic life: he "appeared in court at a young age," "dared to be virtuous," which was all part of his "great design," and "astonished worshippers and the idol." This is the very opposite of Socrates. He appeared in court at an old age. He was finally allowed to do so by the silence of the daemon, the mysterious voice that forbids, which is by no means his design. Usbek stands as a poor imitation of the Athenian who refused Crito's offer of escape. Socrates constantly professed his ignorance of virtue, a far cry from Usbek's false humility, claiming possession of only a "feeble virtue" but implying the opposite relative to the sycophants of the court. To some, Usbek's virtue might resemble Socratic nobility. One must, however, consider the difference between the Delphic activity in the Apology. Socrates presents his service to the city as the gadfly of Athens finding ignorance. He did so because he was perplexed by Chairophon's report that he was the wisest. Usbek, on the other hand, "knowing vice," set about "unmasking vice." It seems where Socrates is humble, Usbek is proud, and where Socrates is ignorant, Usbek boasts wisdom.

Usbek's vanity bleeds through as his words express humility. Usbek would seem to be ambivalent about the purpose of this letter. On one hand, Rustan is to understand that it was not his choice; that is, he was driven out. On the other hand, Usbek would be the first to tell this tale of his exile as if he cleverly got the best of the flatterers and the powerful despot. On account of his bravery, the corrupt target him. The "lion," however, is swallowed by the fox; he creates a "plausible pretext." He is all fox in his "plausible pretext." One may expect Usbek to say to his friend, "We must ignore our hearts and listen to reason," for his life is at stake. It would not occur to Usbek to concern himself with his own heart, much less his friends' hearts. Rather, he admonishes his friend for listening to his enemies' reason over his own.

Driven out by his enemies, he perfected a ruse to leave. He feigns an interest in the sciences of the West. Thus, if Usbek is a satire of the enlightened philosopher, enlightenment's love of wisdom or longing for knowledge may also be a clever ruse to disguise a deep certainty. The despot was not his enemy; a despot has flatterers and those who confound flattery, not enemies. Usbek insists his trip is on account of having the ear of the despot. His curiosity would serve the prudence of the despot. Warner contends that his philosophy is the antipode to despotism. Rightly, Warner sees letter 8 as a confirmation of Usbek's philosophic nature, or rather, of Usbek's philosophic life, but that philosophic life is despotic. Usbek seems to portray himself as the Persian gadfly goading the court to virtue. The examined life has costs. Socratic knowledge of ignorance means one doubts even the dearest convictions of those at home in the city. For these personal psychic costs, philosophic zeteticism provides a kind of pleasure in the form of self-knowledge, or at the very least a clearer sense of what is at stake in knowing one's own self. Such knowledge is dangerous for the political order that relies on those conceits being held by those who call the city their home. Montesquieu expects his enlightened reader would see letter 1 as a demonstration of Usbek's philosophic freedom and letter 8 as a demonstration of his conflict with the city. One reader might contrast his philosophical life portrayed in the first letter with his despotism, his slavishness, and his unhappiness portrayed in letters 2, 3, and 4 in their minds. This is their prejudice for the West and taste for enlightenment. Montesquieu uses this to "test the taste" of his reader. To the careful reader, this duality forces a revaluation of their enthusiasm for Usbek. It is not his longing for knowledge but his dissatisfaction with the narrow horizon of the Orient that drives philosophic life. Moreover, it is not practical wisdom and courage that is his "true motive" for leaving, but high-minded designs and cowardice that led him to flight. The philosophical freedom of letter 1 might appear to be confirmed in letter 8 if it was his doubt that led him to grief, but it was his *certitude* that incurred the jealousy of his enemies.

The different accounts of Usbek's reasons for departure from Persia ought to force the enlightened reader to revisit his earlier assumption that letter 1 portrayed philosophic longing for knowledge. This "longing for knowledge" becomes itself what Usbek would suppose is a "plausible pretext" to satisfy Rustan. If Rustan is not satisfied, should we be? Thus, his reader is asked to turn back on himself and wonder if his philosophic commitments are not at the same time expressions of dissatisfaction and vain desires for a great design.

Upon examination, both letter 1 and letter 8 portray Usbek as the inversion of the philosopher. Montesquieu uses Usbek to satirize not only a version of philosophic life but also the enlightened reader who may be tempted to view him unironically. The irony of Usbek is that he is not himself ironic in his claims about the philosophic life. The joke is, as it were, on him and on Montesquieu's reader, since Montesquieu is portraying in him an irony of enlightenment, that is, its dissatisfaction and its unfreedom. While the "enlightened" reader would cheer the microphone drop of the righteous Usbek as he leaves Persia, those who pay attention see a "philosopher" who wishes to turn the world to his own ends and has found himself forced to turn away from his own happiness. He got away with his life, and his "great design" was abandoned. Even in this letter, intended to excuse and explain his departure, he is saddened by the possibility that he may be forgotten. Even his friends must bend their minds in accordance with his will. Despite his despotic will—more despotic than the despot—the champions of freedom will be cheered by the victory of the idealist over the flatterers. One might ask, "Who was driven out?" Usbek, in the telling, acts as if he has deprived the flatterers of the prize. Who is the victor, the ones chasing or the one being chased?

FAR TOO GOOD FOR THIS WORLD

"[Women] possess a natural empire over us—that of beauty which is irresistible. [T]he empire of beauty is universal." —Montesquieu, Letter 38, 61–62

What does Usbek think of the wisdom of the West? Usbek addresses this question most directly in letter 97. Speaking to the dervish of Jaron, "You will believe [a free tongue] is the fruit of independent life one lives in this country. No, thanks be to heaven, the mind has not corrupted the heart" (Letter 97, 158). He lives among philosophers who devote themselves to petty research. This might lead one to think that Usbek, whatever his disposition before coming, upon his arrival rejects them as mistaking the small for the large. To Usbek, these scientists are as good as the Koran. All they are lacking is "bold figures and mysterious allegories." This is a double-edged claim. On one hand, Western science is petty; on the other hand, so is the Koran. What distinguishes the Koran from other writings is its "force and liveliness of expression" (157). This claim is what leads him to try to reassure the dervish of his faith. His doubt of his Koran is in reality a sign of his commitment to the "summit of Oriental wisdom" that was achieved by marveling at the miracles. The West, led by the "tracings of *human* reason" have "resolved the chaos" with "simple mechanics" (156; emphasis added). This conclusion leads to political laws that "change" to suit the purpose of those who make them or are governed by them and a physics of "immutable and eternal [laws] without exception." The mutability of the political laws only serves to underline the immutability of the laws that govern the beings that political laws are meant to serve. That is, he accepts neither the Koran nor Western science, with its permissive political laws and sweeping deterministic physics. Human reason simply cannot fathom the mysterious and immense universe. On one hand, the West is destined to adopt an insufficient doctrine on account of its incomplete experience. On the other hand, in letter 106 to Rehdi, Usbek embraces the capitalism of Locke, proclaiming self-interest the ruling principle on earth (Letter 106, 172). Usbek may be a child of the East, but he is a subject of Western philosophy. Usbek believes in the material world and disdains it. Usbek's tyranny is exhibited in both the seraglio and his philosophy and driven by his desire to matter in this ephemeral and vast world.

Usbek's metaphysics is tied to his household management. Letter 3 portrays the tie between sensibility (rational) and sensibility (feeling), or rather how in Usbek these two senses of the word are untethered and lead to both his and his wives' unhappiness. If the women were to have happiness in the seraglio, it would be through enchantment and ornament, but Usbek wants reality, not fantasy; reason, not passion. Stemming from his fundamental truth, the world is matter in motion. The power he wields to make sensible— that is, rational—the woman and slaves of the house is his effort to make meaningful the chaotic seraglio. The tyranny of the seraglio is reflected in his metaphysics, and his metaphysics is the ground of his tragic worldview. Usbek implies that he is a sensible philosopher; there is a duality here in the word sensible (worthwhile) and sensible (those who rely on their senses). All sensible philosophers conjecture about God. Godlike ideas are not perceived by the senses, but they can be known by induction, a mode of knowing Usbek finds senseless.

"Ah my dear Usbek, if only you knew how to be happy!" (Letter 3, 8).[18] This line follows the description of the contest of virtue in the seraglio. In the seraglio, Usbek wishes to see the world as it is and refuses to let his eros drive reason from his mind. This, as Zachi indicates, has its costs on his happiness and demands a despotic rule of his household. The words she uses indicates what Montesquieu wishes for his reader to understand about

Usbek's disposition toward eros. According to Zachi, at first it was by art that they tried to win his affections, but Usbek would have no "ornament" or "finery" to tease his imagination. He would rather judge as a naturalist and see with "his eyes" "the simplicity of nature." Described from Zachi's perspective this was no "shame," but "glory." How is this a glory? She still thinks that even in their nakedness she has charm over him, but he is immune to their charms. He seems to be incapable of being entranced by their illusions. He is surveying "from enchantment to enchantment," but he commands still further. He not only dominates their bodies but also their words and thoughts. She "confesses" she became "insensibly the mistress of [his] heart" (7–8). While she may be the mistress of his heart, one might ask, "What heart does he have?" Although he is not blind, he "considers the benefits of being loved *nothing* . . . love breathes in the seraglio, and your insensibility takes you from it." The shared description of Zachi and Usbek as "insensible" only serves to highlight his disconnect from the human feeling one might expect from the erotic and intimate interactions described in this letter. These words portray Usbek's position in the seraglio still more poignantly: his sensibility and insensibility is a description of his philosophy and detached disposition.

To Montesquieu's reader, Usbek's rule of Zachi's seraglio would be both enticing with its pageantry and disgusting with its despotism. What would the reader make of this conflict? Nevertheless, Usbek's rule of the seraglio is rooted in his dualistic philosophy. In letter 69, unprompted, Usbek shares with Rhédi his metaphysics, which has absorbed him lately.[19] This insight about metaphysics is set up in letter 17, establishing his concern that it is spurious to generate universal or general principles in a world of matter in motion. Rather, he is concerned with how the material world can be composed of anything wholly impure or pure. Our senses are averse or attracted to things, but things are only their material and are neither good nor bad in themselves. This conviction about the material has not changed despite the best efforts of the mullah to convince Usbek that pigs spring abiogenetically from excrement.

The material world, in Usbek's mind, remains composite and nonmiraculous in letter 69. Playing on the double entendre of "sensible," this mundane conclusion does not prohibit him from maintaining that "most sensible philosophers" reflect on the nature of God. Whatever other sensible philosophers think about the material world, such conclusions as Usbek has made about it would place him among those philosophers who trust their senses. Yet he is going to conjecture about a being, a perfect being, who necessarily cannot be perceived by the senses (Letter 69, 116–17). Any conjecture about such a being would have to be bereft of contradiction. This means he cannot be known in the same way all other knowledge has come to be known: induction.

If he were truly a *sensible* philosopher, he would accept the limits of the sensible world. Despite all appearances, Usbek insists there is an insensible world. How can particular sensations lead to knowledge? For Usbek, induction of these sorts of ideas is not possible because it incorporates contradiction. Induction would be good enough for a painter but is not for a "sensible philosopher." Usbek insists that the ideal can never come from the particulars. Zeuxis, the painter, hopes to compile a goddess from the parts of beautiful women. Usbek's complaint imagines Zeuxis is like the blind men who encounter only part of an elephant and cannot put it together. This is to assume that Zeuxis is unaffected by the empire of beauty on one's mind. While Zeuxis is impressed with the woman's nose or any part in particular, it is, as Zero Mostel in the movie *The Producers* might say, "the whole package" that makes her beautiful. Usbek seems to forget beauty's grip on us.[20] This is also an inversion of a Socratic example.[21] In the *Republic*, Socrates attempts to explain to his interlocutors how philosophy works. He uses the experience all sensible human beings have when in love: "When we say a man loves something, if it is rightly said of him, he mustn't show a love for one part of it and not for another but must cherish all of it?"[22] Socrates goes on to explain that while anyone in love might pick a part of their beloved and remark his "hooked nose" is kingly, but it is nevertheless the "bloom of a youth" that one loves. Setting aside the Greek pederasty—a thing not easy to set aside—we should point out the details of this practice. First and foremost, is how love skews one's preferences, turning imperfections into marks of perfection. Secondly, loving the boy is what makes one pay attention to his sensible qualities. Thus, to Socrates, philosophy is first and foremost a sort of love not bereft of eroticism, but they go together hand in glove. The Socratic example emphasizes how love takes the particulars of one's beloved and elevates them. To say something is beautiful is to take the sensible particular and express how it is a universal. It seems that Usbek is either immune to beauty's charm or willfully denying it.

Whatever Socrates thinks philosophy is, Usbek insists that despite the divine being unavailable to our senses, God's perfection means he, unlike human beings, cannot have limits on his knowledge. Usbek's insistence that there is an omniscient divinity turns on his concern for human freedom, and specifically his own. Moreover, his own freedom hinges on there being a truth behind the divine that even God chooses to know or not know. The troubling thing for Usbek about this deduction is that with foreknowledge, human freedom would be as "a billiard ball is free to move when it is struck by another one" (Letter 69, 118). Usbek's argument for human freedom begins with Usbek's desire. It is his "desire" not to limit God, implying it might be easier if he could limit God's knowledge, as other philosophers have done. Thus, to comport to Usbek's will, God becomes despotic. Even a benevolent despot is despotic. God "makes creatures act at his own fancy, [and] he knows everything that he wants to know" (118) Thus, as any good despot would, he delegates. He allows his creatures to do "the acting or not acting," leaving him "the capacity to be worthy or unworthy." God, in order to comport to Usbek's will, is now *mixed*.

To ask a very Captain Kirk–like question, "What is God capable of being worthy or unworthy of?" While God has not the same limits that humans have, that is, our senses, he is limited by "the number of pure possibilities." The verb he uses to describe God learning his limits is "draws," as if he picks out of his quiver the proper arrow, expressing a freedom but implying a necessity that governs his actions. This imperious metaphor is further ham-mered home by the analogy that Usbek uses with some hesitancy because he worries it is too mundane to fully express his thought. The decrees of God are done, as ambassadors obey their monarch, but ambassadors of all his ministers are outside his territory and answer to necessity. Thus, Usbek conceived of himself as a creature of another world under the command of an alien king. Usbek asks Rhédi, "Why so much philosophy?" Recognizing the precepts of the divine and the knowing of his composite nature, he feels the weight of the expectation that he live as God commands, according to a self-determinate will. If God is a learner who can be worthy or unworthy, why cannot Usbek? Usbek knows this is a fantasy: "We do not feel our pettiness, and in spite of ourselves we want to be counted in the universe, and to act and to be an important object in it" (Letter 76, 126). There is a tragic irony in this statement, for while Usbek expresses his deepest desire, his reason forbids its realization, so Usbek of all people feels his pettiness and his lack of freedom.

Perhaps if Usbek had not left Persia or the seraglio, he would not be so disposed to consider his ambitions as so vain. He begins his discussion of suicide in letter 76 with a criticism of the "laws of Europe." He is critical of Europe not because her laws make him miserable but because they "deprive him of a remedy" to the "grief," "misery," and "contempt" he will inevitably experience. These laws are unjust because they lack his consent. European laws lack his consent because he played no part in their creation, and laws from any prince, because he has "no advantage" from his subjugation to that prince.[23] Usbek takes great pains to explain he has no allegiance to the tem-poral powers either in the West or the East, less on account of the latter more than the former. He sees no advantage in being forbidden from taking his own life. More important than his lack of obligation to this world is his lack of obligation to the eternal world. "We imagine that the annihilation of a being as perfect as we are would degrade all of nature and we do not conceive of the fact that one man more or less in the world—what am I saying?—that all men together, a hundred million heads like ours, are only a tenuous and minute atom in [God's] immense knowledge" (Letter 76, 126). This intimation of his insignificance is the mourning of his own will. Usbek wants to be free of this world's limits, but in the limitless, materially he will become corn and spiritually he is as an atom is to the whole of the universe. In short, while Usbek hates the limits of this life, he is overwhelmed by the meaninglessness of the next. Even a belief in his soul is a wish to be more than matter in motion. It is for this reason Usbek does not know how to be happy; he is insensitive to the means by which any of us are happy.

Usbek's enlightenment is an unyielding desire for an unskewed truth. This dogged rationalism rebels against the imperium of beauty and thus brings about an epistemological problem that is also his eudaimonistic problem. Zeuxis, in supposing he could find suitable subjects for his work of art, must have found them beautiful or understood what it meant that others did. Usbek cannot seem to make the sensible world matter enough for beauty to hold sway not only over our senses, but our minds and souls. Those we find beautiful in their particularity are a universal. To admit they are beautiful is to admit the empire they have (compare Letter 69, 117 to Letter 38, 61–62). For Usbek to admit the beauty, a universal, it would accede that he is under their spell. He is not seeing things as he would suppose they really are. In his insistence on sensibility (rationality), he is insensible (unfeeling) about the meaning of a beautiful person. To Usbek, induction cannot apprehend a whole and leads only to delusion; the whole is God's knowledge. He wishes in letter 76 to impress upon Ibben that if one apprehends the sheer immensity of the totality of things, one will inevitably be overwhelmed by one's own meaninglessness. Thus, his epistemological problem drives him to his tragic perspective.

SILENT REALITY AND EXPRESSED APPEARANCE

"I am going, then, to live under your laws and share your cares. Great God! How many things are needed to make only one man happy!"[24] — Montesquieu, Letter 22, 37

Perhaps this is the fate of all philosophers, to live in the world but never truly find happiness there. While Usbek clearly is a satire of enlightenment and its pretentions of being a scientific Socratic philosophy, he also serves as a warped reflection of Montesquieu. The satirical use of Usbek reveals enlightenment's epistemological problem as a eudaimonic problem. It seems that the freedom yearned for by the enlightenment is only one face of a coin whose other side is the tragic determinism and meaninglessness of matter in motion. The irony of Usbek's philosophy is that it brooks no delusion. Even if we are not as convicted of this truth as Usbek, we cannot run from its possibility. The truth, no matter how terrible, is something with which we must contend. Montesquieu's satire is an attempt to contend with this very fact by forcing the reader to look at Usbek as a reflection of Montesquieu's own philosophy. It is a feature of this reflection that scholars can mistake Usbek for Montesquieu, treating his words for Montesquieu's voice. However the additions in the 1758 edition may change his voice, this irony is made more apparent. A reader who is concerned with the work understands its features as partial elements of a whole. An epistolary novel is inherently preceded by a conversation. Presented in letters, it can only be presented in parts. Just as the old bit of wisdom claims about chains and their weakest link, the coherence of the work relies on its parts. In fact, the wholeness of a chain is determined by the qualities of its links. The irony of Montesquieu's philosophy is that our freedom is felt by ties we have to "our truths." Thus, there are three chains pointed at in "Some Reflections": a narratological chain that can "be seen" and is "unexpected"; a more mysterious chain that is "secret" and "in some fashion, unknown"; and the third chain, an unspoken chain, which remains only indicated and not named. This final chain binds the philosopher to the whole of which he is a part. Philosophic freedom depends on his commitment to that whole. Montesquieu utilizes key contrasts to lead the reader to explore this ambiguity or duality in his letters. The critique of Usbek's freedom serves as a reflection of Montesquieu's own philosophic freedom.

Just as letters reveal partial perspectives that the reader must link together, so do the untitled preface and "Some Reflections." On first blush, the preface is a comic critique of prefaces of this style, placing Montesquieu in contrast with his rather serious character, Usbek. Montesquieu is more coy and playful, standing on the pretense of fiction, than in "Some Reflections," where he explicitly portrays the letters as fiction. In the preface, he teases his reader with suggestive pairings.[25] Usbek had his dualism: the world of being and the world of becoming. Montesquieu, on the other hand, with these pairings shows that dualities are contrasts that if recognized indicate something is behind the contrasts. These dualities all share a contrast between what is expected by a conventional reader and what he expects a good reader to notice.[26]

This is not the ancient contrast between nature and convention. For the ancients, the notion of nature is a question. Is anything that is not artificial rational? In short, is reality rational? Montesquieu seems to hide these questions for a prior question: Can we know reality? Since reality always reveals itself in apparent, expressed, and particular ways, the reality is hidden. Montesquieu supposes that if it is revealed, it will do so like the woman he knows who walks well, but in public always limps. Reality will appear dysfunctional, funny, and "with an unnatural gait." The comedy of human life is that reality, if it reveals itself, certainly is not revealed completely, but in its partial or particular manifestations. The deep truth to which Montesquieu is pointing is one that Usbek will never see. Usbek is dubious of the world of his senses. He is repulsed by the tyranny of his particularity, his partiality, and his material life. This can be contrasted with what Montesquieu only hints at: that the material world with its "hooked-noses" is a partial truth. He can care for it because it is perhaps the only world.[27]

Perhaps Montesquieu only intended to hint in 1720 at this deeper truth that later in life he could treat explicitly. He is comfortable showing how serious Usbek is about shaping the world or shuffling off this mortal coil. Montesquieu makes plain his concerns about Usbek and the possibility of a more humane enlightenment.[28] This is marked by the addition of two letters and "Some Reflections." Montesquieu's hand becomes apparent with these changes, whereas it was far more hidden before.

Both letters concerning Jaron, the additions to the Persian letters, demonstrate an inversion of freedom. Letter 15 from the first eunuch confesses that despite his servitude, he "still has a heart." One cannot read the letter and not notice paternal pride and discussion of slavery as honors. Love is not jealous, and although he explicitly claims to not intend to tell his pleasure at Jaron's promotion, this is a sign enough that he is happy about his friend's success. Although his slavery left him childless, he enjoys the joy of a father. That is, a slave can have the happiness of a free man with love. In letter 22, Jaron begins with a description of Usbek, like the caricature of a teenager: "He sighs; he sheds tears; his sorrow becomes bitter." While this is not unexpected, it is an aspect of Usbek that has been hidden from us. While Zachi portrays him as unfeeling, Jaron shows a man who is all hysteria. He is sent this way and that for fear of the status of his wives. This is the immediate sequel to the letters concerning Zachi's indiscretion with the white eunuch. He is not torn up by erotic desire but by fear that the seraglio will not be as he wills. Far from mastering himself, he is destroyed by their indiscretion. He is a slave to this even though he appears to "master" slaves and the seraglio. Jaron, too, is the inversion of freedom. His "will is [Usbek's] property." Although his pleasure would be in the West, he must go back. Jaron, unlike Usbek, will be visibly happy, but inside discontent: "My exterior will be tranquil, and my spirit unquiet." This is how Jaron will "live under the laws" of the first eunuch and the seraglio and "share his cares." It seems that Jaron is an alternative to Usbek's comical imperious will. While Jaron appears tranquil living "under another's gaze," this is just a another. Jaron, like the philosopher depicted in the first letter, longs for the West and is not content with the boundaries of Persia. He is forced to live by another's laws even though he has heard of his overseer's affection. Jaron's unhappiness is being compelled by another's will that is not his own but is most disappointed in being under Usbek's will, which has been revealed to him to be all emotion.

Montesquieu, in these letters, raises the possibility that there are two destinies for an "enlightenment" philosopher such as Usbek. Jaron's slavery appears only when we know what is hidden. Usbek's slavery is revealed to us in his every sigh, lashing out, and exposition of philosophy. Both are tragic and live at the expense of their freedom and happiness. Montesquieu, through the character of Jaron, reveals the curse of Usbek's philosophy. He is always dissatisfied with how the world will not conform to his will, even when it wishes him well.

It seems there are two types of drama in the *Persian Letters*. The first is among the characters and the second, among the ideas. The letters concerning Jaron and "Some Reflections" tie the epistemological claim with the question of freedom. The first eunuch is free despite his destiny being under Usbek's control. This we can attribute primarily to his love. His attachment gives his lack of liberty meaning and liberates his soul to be attached to the world. Yet Jaron and Usbek, who have tied their happiness to the ability to go and possess what they want, are forever captured by the determinants of the world around them. Thus, love, which allows one to justify one's own truths as great truths, also liberates one's soul.

The changes to the *Persian Letters* are subtle but more tightly connect the theme of happiness to Usbek's philosophy. What is the alternative? We cannot return to our narrower world as Usbek really cannot return to his Persia. In "Some Reflections," Montesquieu wishes to explicitly contrast himself and his philosophy with Usbek's to those unwilling to "pay attention." The experience of the good reader is contrasted with the more popular reader. Montesquieu's philosopher is a good reader. He contrasts a reader who pays attention with one who is demanding, that is, tyrannical. The European audience, perhaps even the philosophic audience, expects that these foreigners find enlightenment among the Europeans. The Persians should marvel at the great and grand European world. To some degree they did, but the interest in "these features [is] always bound to the sentiment of surprise and astonishment" ("Some Reflections," 270). This wonder might be the beginning of wisdom. Montesquieu points out this expectation that the Persians are small, "singular," and incapable of recognizing that the universal is singular as well. The Persians in reflecting on the European world may discover that even the "enlightened" world is singular and "find *our* dogmas singular" (ibid.). Through the eyes of the Persians, we might see how the enlightened world hangs together. Just as a good reader is not dissatisfied when expectations are dashed but perceives the design or the nature of the work, so does a good philosopher look at the laws, opinions, and "truths" that manifest in the world to see how they hang together.

The philosopher is not content with observing the shape of his horizon. Usbek is not alone in claiming that boundaries of our knowledge are not simply "our truths." This dissatisfaction led Usbek to "enlightenment," but Montesquieu thought that by the light of his own truths, he could see the "eternal contrasts." To borrow from the preface of his great work *The Spirit of The Laws*, "Many of the truths will make themselves *felt* here only when one sees the chain connecting them with the others. The more one reflects on the details the more one will *feel* the certainty of the principles."[29] These stand as an introduction of a set of conditions for the work on Montesquieu's happiness. These conditions are hopes for one reading Montesquieu's *Spirit of the Laws* that he has "new reasons for loving his duties, his prince, his homeland and his laws," and that by such examination he may come to know himself. It may be thought that such reflections are beyond the scope of a narratological claim about Usbek's characterization. This, however, would not recognize the radicality of the claim Montesquieu is making in his prefatory remarks. If the recognition of the singularity of even "our truths," which claim to be universal, obtain in the great regimes of the East and the West, they would be recognized by reflection on the chain that binds them as a whole in our minds. This would easily be considered knowledge, but Montesquieu takes care to show that this chain is "felt." Usbek would have the world hang together on reason. He acquiesces to the fact that most humans are sentimental rather than rational, but his freedom hangs on a desire to be released from the fettering and distorting effects of passion. Out of this desire, Usbek insists the world comport to his superior and despotic reason. The difference between Usbek and Montesquieu, in short, may be characterized by the difference between desire and love.

NOTES

1. I would like to thank Professor Jeffrey Church for his calm and clear-eyed advice. I am very grateful for our discussions concerning the *Persian Letters* and political philosophy. They have reminded me again and again of my deep commitment to political philosophy. It must be said that this chapter would not have happened without the encouragement and friendship I have found with Dr. Constantine Vassiliou. Moreover, Professor Stuart Warner and the other contributors to this volume have shaped my ideas about this work.

2. The proem is an invocation of the muses placed at the beginning of the book on commerce. Charles Montesquieu, *The Spirit of the Laws*, trans. Anne M Cohler, Basia C. Miller, and Harold S. Stone (Cambridge: Cambridge University Press, 1989), 377.

3. A discussion of how cost is as much a barrier to alcohol as religious proscriptions. Usbek prefers the economic incentives over the religious proscriptions because religious proscriptions work contrary to their purpose: rather than deterring proscribed behavior, proscribing behavior invites it all the more. It is not that humans are insensitive to moral principles; on the contrary, "the human mind is a contradiction."

Usbek sees the very same instrumental reason that is such an aid to achieving desires as the thing that recognizes the limits to our will and rebels. By our guilt we know ourselves to be prisoners of our own desires.

4. It seems here Usbek is pointing out for Montesquieu a parallel problem that both Usbek and the enlightened reader suffer. This makes the appeal of whatever "beverage" Usbek praises at the end of the letter equivalent to Seneca and stoicism, reducing the soul still further as an emergent quality of the body.

5. See Jonathan Walsh, "A Cultural Numismatics: The 'Chain' of Economics in Montesquieu's Lettres Persanes," *Australian Journal of French Studies* 46, no. 1–2 (January 2009): 139–54; also see Leo Strauss, "On Tyranny" in Leo Strauss and Alexandre Kojève, *On Tyranny: Including the Strauss-Kojève Correspondence*, ed. Michael S. Roth and Victor Gourevitch (Chicago: University of Chicago Press, 2013), 103–105. He ties by way of analogy the efforts of John Law to the image of alchemy and the dissolution of Usbek's seraglio: "This is unworthy of a serious man" (preface, 3). In the untitled preface, Montesquieu expresses his concern that if he were to attach his name to the *Persian Letters*, his audience find his work silly and would reevaluate him for his lack of seriousness. There is an irony in the concern. The attachment of his name can only motivate readers to look more deeply into the work or find him more ridiculous. Contemporary scholarship must feel the duty this concern places on the reader. Much ink has been spilled to illustrate the seriousness of the *Persian Letters*. This volume includes many pieces that are an examination of how the *Persian Letters* speaks on the whole and in part to bigger issues than the narrative of Usbek's and Rica's journey west. Many scholars are struck by the "Secret Chain" indicated in "Some Reflections." Jonathan Walsh, in his "A Cultural Numismatics: The 'Chain' of Economics in Montesquieu's Lettres Persanes," begins with a survey of this scholarship. Out of his concern that his readers take him seriously, Walsh portrays the events in Usbek's household as a satire of the events in France and appeals to authorities, great and small, ignoring the way each of the authorities might "join philosophy, politics, and morality" as Montesquieu did ("Some Reflections," 269). He then turns to the advantages for a community to have an economy driven virtuously (i.e., for the right reasons, at the right time, in the right way): that is to say, the benefits of good commerce and the disadvantages of bad commerce. This is not unfair to the *Persian Letters*, but it ignores the reasons these elements of human life are connected. He favors revealing the places that reflect the more directly expressed claims in *The Spirit of the Laws*. He ultimately seems to want to rename the *Persian Letters* the *l'espirit* of currency, as a kind of epilogue to *The Spirit of the Laws*. This narrows the scope of the wisdom of the *Persian Letters* to how economics leads to or avoids tyranny at the expense of anything not confirmed in *The Spirit of the Laws*. Walsh is intrigued by the Secret Chain so long as it is of opaque political consequences primarily through economics. This is to ignore that the Secret Chain for Montesquieu is a literary claim, remarking the epistolary novel affords him an advantage that an ordinary novel cannot. He may place in "conversations," so to speak, arguments that in a narrative would never come into contact. Walsh, on the other hand, demonstrates a chain of despotism. He claims Montesquieu gives the image of seraglio in order to

hammer home the snowball of the effect of vicious economics, and in contrast to how virtuous economics lead to liberalism.

6. See Locke, *Second Treatise on Government,* chapter 13, section 158.

7. See Strauss, "Restatement," in *On Tyranny*, 180–81.

8. Leo Strauss ends his *On Tyranny* with a discussion of piety and law. On the authority of Aristotle, tyrants would be well advised to utilize a theocracy to rule, but to Strauss, this seems a sort of paradox for two reasons. From the point of view of the philosopher, he contends that tyranny is a rule without law and piety is being lawful or just to the gods. Secondly, a pious regime rules by praise and blame, i.e., virtue, and the tyrant, or the tyrant defined in this way, would rule by compulsion. It is this need for compulsion that scholars find so antithetical to enlightenment and suppose that is the heart of Montesquieu's criticism of Usbek and the Persians. Strauss begins his discussion of the paradox with a declaration of the tyrant's hubris to seek honors only owed to the gods. The examination is particularly of an "enlightened tyrant." Such a tyrant shares with the philosopher a desire to understand nature for albeit different reasons. Strauss suggests in Xenophon's dialogue that both Simonides (the philosopher) and Hiero (the tyrant) ignore the question of "What is a god?" because "what they mean by 'the gods' is chance rather than 'nature' or the origin of the natural order" (104–105). The implied preference for order rather than divine will, or what is meant by "divine will," means that at least this tyrant wishes to improve on "God's order" or nature's chaos. Thus, the act of the "enlightened" tyrant is to improve the seemingly chaotic work. It is not lost on this reader the irony of Walsh in his last paragraph translating *l'esprit* as nature.

9. Stuart D. Warner, "Montesquieu's Literary Art," in *Persian Letters*, trans. Stuart D. Warner and Douard Stéphane (South Bend, IN: St. Augustine's Press, 2017).

10. Ibid., xv.

11. Compare PL 2–3 and 17, his thought that the senses are the sole source of knowledge, PL 97. His preference for scientific knowledge over mystical knowledge. Mohammed Ali's response to Usbek's questions concerning the need for revelation show how philosophy is pitted against religious proscription: "Your vain philosophy is that lightning flash that announces the storm and darkness; You are in the midst of the tempest and you wander about at the mercy of the wind" (Letter 18, 31).

12. The discussion of enlightenment cannot be made without considering its disposition toward revelation. Usbek's silence here fits his assumption of his small society of friends but also allows the reader to project his disposition on Usbek. He is not silent elsewhere, and where Usbek, a Persian, would not make such a conflation of the important women in Islam, a French author might, and thus a French reader may read without pause. Since this conflation makes Fatima appear more like the virgin birth that the audience is familiar with and as *enlightened readers* are suspicious of miracles, they would assume Usbek, too, is suspicious. This assumption would make Usbek's resemblance to an enlightened philosopher all the more agreeable.

13. Aristotle, *Nicomachean Ethics* (1096 11–18).

14. There is an ambiguity in this assurance. It is to reassure Rustan that circumstance may tear them apart but they remain friends. Alternatively, is the fact that Usbek is leaving Persia reason that Rustan may doubt their friendship?

15. Warner, "Montesquieu's Literary Art," xiv–xv.

16. Ibid., xiv.

17. Ibid.

18. Zachi's letter is presented third but is the first letter chronologically. The letter is devoted to describing the lost happiness of both the seraglio and Usbek. In many ways, the theme of the *Persian Letters* is happiness. The Troglodytes seek it, Usbek is constantly searching for it, and religion and law are often evaluated in terms of happiness (c.f. PL 18 and 38 especially). The first two letters are devoted to the limits of happiness. The description of the rule in this letter and subsequent letters reveal what is mechanically a despotism. Contrary to expectation, Zachi portrays the condition of the women as a practical political virtue of a sort. The devotion to Usbek's pleasure and the description of naked wives presenting themselves are at least evidence to Zachi of Usbek's happiness. While this would seem quite alien to the French experience of women, the contemporary mind cannot help but think this would appeal to French readers as an E. L. James novel appeals to our contemporaries. It does not seem a stretch to think that this letter was at least slightly appealing. The tension between what seraglio is and how it is perceived is hidden, at least for a certain type of reader, by the degree that image stokes the imagination. Zachi's rhetoric seems to intentionally work on a paradox that Rica discusses in letter 38 (see 61–62). Since pleasure is wrapped up in perception of our own freedom, are we masters of ourselves, or does pleasure master us? The disposition toward excess to Rica seems a fundamental divide between the East and the West. The gallant philosopher contends that "the empire of beauty is universal." Rica's interlocutor, the gallant philosopher, intrigues Rica with the possibility that who is master and who is slave is much more mysterious than Rica thought at first.

19. Rhédi is his friend living in Venice and is very aware of how out of place and time he is. He seems to speak from an ancient perspective reviewing the modern world around him. He has been written to more times than any other recipient save Usbek, and yet has written only four letters. Each of these letters engender a response except for the last one (PL 131), which is to Rica. Rica has what appear to be non sequitur letters that come after, whose recipients are not included. One is left to wonder if these, while not naratologically a response, are still philosophical responses to letter 131. Letter 131 is about the artificial character of Venice and how the arts and sciences both overcome nature and are full of unholy activities. Usbek's response is that secular policies have the same effect on continence as the religious prescriptions, perhaps superior. Usbek thus treats the soul as an artifact of the disposition of the body, given it responds like Alice does to food and drink in Wonderland. In letter 105 Rhédi asks if technological progress brings more grief than joy. At times technological progress is utilized to perfect war, and other times it is devoted to vain pursuits. Usbek's response is that technological arts are a good; even the bourgeois arts lead to energy and industriousness. In cultivating one's craft, one brings home necessities, ignoring the venality, obsequiousness, and erratic character of the arts. Rhédi's last letter to Usbek asks him, "How has nature lost its prodigious fecundity of the earliest times?" (PL 112, 180). Usbek's response is rather extended (PL 113–22). His general claim is dark, as Warner remarks, pointing to the financial ruin rot by the economic

"science" of John Law. These letters represent Usbek's tragic view of human life in full flower: "Men are like plants, which never grow successfully if they are not well cultivated [and] among miserable people." Considering France, whose past was troubled out of fear that war and poverty would destroy their children, the friend came up with a clever plan. They "forced them to marry," and now "from so many marriages, many children were born, . . . who misery, famine, and maladies have disappeared." It is Usbek's view that if you seek happiness in this world, all the clever schemes are for naught.

20. Compare to letter 38. The wisdom of the gallant philosopher who Warner conjectures is Montesquieu, "The empire of beauty is universal" (Warner's note, 61–62, PL 38). This is in the context of whether or not men should rule over women. The gallant philosopher thought there was no law of nature that men should rule over women (61–62, PL 38). That is, one might suppose that it is Montesquieu's position that the empire of beauty liberates us from the necessity of the sort of despotic rule that is found in Usbek's seraglio. This gallant philosopher's comment ties power, education, and the relation of the sexes to the fundamental expression of right. Entertaining the idea that he is Montesquieu, we must consider how this political philosophy comports to the presentation of the philosophy he expresses in his own name in this work. To put it another way, is his gallantry an affectation or an effect of his philosophy?

21. Plato, *The Republic of Plato*, ed. Adam Kirsch, trans. Allan Bloom (New York Basic Books, 2016), 474c–d.

22. Plato, *Republic*, 154–55.

23. While this discussion is narrowly focused on the laws prohibiting suicide, the discussion of consent could be applicable to all laws. Specifically, these laws may be especially galling to Usbek because unique among the laws, there can be no consequence for disobedience in this world. There is a tension in the principle of consent. Free laws find their legitimacy in our agreement to those laws. Usbek indicates two sources of our agreement: either in our being party to the formation (explicit) or in the advantage we gain from those laws (tacit). This is not altogether dissimilar to Locke's understanding of consent. Locke is more sanguine about human rationality and its ability to attend to our needs and our advantage. Laws are legitimate when those under the laws participated in their formation. He did not consent to these laws because he is a foreigner. If this is both the necessary and sufficient conditions, then all laws are legitimate so long as one agreed to it, but one can agree to things under false pretenses. Usbek's second principle of consent may seem to be corrective to this problem. All laws are legitimate if I have some advantage under them; that is, if one has complete or at least best possible knowledge, they are laws I would agree to because they are beneficial to me. This would seem not just to correct but to ignore the first principle. Free laws are in our best interests regardless who writes them. His foreignness does not matter if we are concerned with his best interest. This means his perceived advantage that one always seeks may not be advantageous in reality. The laws are limits on us, limits that keep one from seeking one's perceived best interest for the sake of one's true interests. Yet, arguments for legitimacy are made so that the criminal admit, "It's a fair cop; I will come quietly." This means that legitimacy is of importance when one's perceived interest contradicts the law. One does not need a

law to tell one to do what one perceives as advantageous. Under this second principle of consent, either there is no need for law or it is not a principle by which we can know for certain we have consented to any law. The pessimism that leads Usbek to think the prohibition of suicide is disadvantageous is one about human capacity to know. Usbek plays no part in the formulation of laws in Europe or of any laws in this world. For Usbek, any question of true advantage must remain a question until we have complete knowledge.

24. Jaron to the first Eunuch a letter added in 1758 edition. He has been sent back because as he travels further from the seraglio, Usbek finds his concern for his "sacred women" less and less tolerable. (See "Some Reflections." The second thread in the narratological chain is a formal ratio of Usbek's jealousy and his proximity to the seraglio.)

25. There are several contrasts that are expressed.

26. Montesquieu's notion of the proper reader of his work is important to examine. There is an initial tension pointed out in the preface between how the work is meant to be good, and "not to be read," on one hand, and his willingness to reorder the letters for taste but unwillingness to extol the work's utility and excellence, on the other. It would seem to belie his contention that he is not interested in it being appealing over its goodness. Montesquieu proposes a comical version of Euthyphro's dilemma. He is indifferent to whether his book is read. He only wishes it to be read if it is good. What, then, does he mean by good? It cannot be the fact that it is appealing, for if "appealing" was his standard of goodness, it would be good if it is read. Perhaps it is good to reveal something true or something good to know. Not all readers, however, will be astute enough to notice, nor can everything be said publicly, for some will say it is distasteful and others will say it is unworthy, perhaps laughable. Still, there remains the question, how is it good? He refuses to "extol its usefulness, merit, and its excellence." His refusal points to necessity, right to rule, and virtue. In Montesquieu's silence, he is being gallant, either brave or a flirt, either teasing readers with the fruits of a careful read or seducing readers to believe they are capable of learning those fruits.

27. The preface denies readers what might be their main expectation. The broad expectation of the work is that it will contrast the Persian and the European worlds (compare with "Some Reflections" on expectations of readers). Perhaps revelation will settle Montesquieu's epistemic question, but Montesquieu takes pains to remove the sublime from the letters so as not to move the reader "upward." Such language would distort a reader's perspective. In this way, he remains neutral or agnostic about the spiritual differences in the worldviews. He does explicitly point to morals, but these are not universal morals. They are something that can be appealed to as taste by removing hyperbole and expansiveness. Moreover, he does not point out the differences in laws among men, but to what degree they are hidden and to what degree they are revealed. Does this imply secretly humanity's roles in the cosmos and in the city are universal, but exhibit themselves as particulars? Like the epistemological question of nature, nature's expectations may also be unknowable. Montesquieu makes this conjecture by way of a joke at the expense of the Germans, who never come to

understand the French even though they have an exhibitionist nature. Even if there are truths displayed nakedly before us, we may not be able to see them.

28. Consider the additions of Jaron which also happened with the new edition: letters 15 and 22. Letter 15 follows the "Troglodyte vignette." They begin with a question about whether men are happy due to pleasure and the satisfaction of the senses or to the practice of virtue. Usbek is frustrated with his friend. To answer the question, Usbek explains that when reason fails, one must feel certain truths. The reasoning of the tale pushes toward the practice of virtue, but considering the vignette of the wives and the strange degeneration of the republic of Troglodytes, some readers might feel a different and more complicated truth from this tale. Letter 22 letter is from Jaron. It comes after an exchange where Usbek chastises Zachi and the white eunuch for falling short of their virtue. In this case, happiness is not "on offer" for virtue, only unhappiness for vice. Even if unstated, there is tenderness on offer to his wives. It will be divided in exact proportions among them, as if beauty and love can be divided in exact quanta. There is a tragic tension that exists both for Usbek and Jaron: Happiness and a rational life.

29. Montesquieu, *The Spirit of the Laws*, xliv, emphasis added.

BIBLIOGRAPHY

Aristotle. *Aristotle's Nicomachean Ethics.* Translated by Robert C. Bartlett and Susan D. Collins. Chicago: University of Chicago Press, 2011.

Locke, John. *Two Treatises of Government.* Edited by Lee Ward. Indianapolis: Hackett Publishing Company, 2016.

Montesquieu, Charles. *Persian Letters.* Translated by Stuart D. Warner and Stéphane Douard. South Bend, IN: St. Augustine's Press, 2017.

———. *The Spirit of the Laws.* Translated by Anne M. Cohler, Basia C. Miller, and Harold S. Stone. Cambridge: Cambridge University Press, 1989.

Plato. *The Republic of Plato.* Edited by Adam Kirsch. Translated by Allan David Bloom. New York: Basic Books, 2016.

Strauss, Leo, and Alexandre Kojève. *On Tyranny: Including the Strauss-Kojève Correspondence.* Edited by Michael S. Roth and Victor Gourevitch. Chicago: University of Chicago Press, 2013.

Walsh, Jonathan. "A Cultural Numismatics: The 'Chain' of Economics in Montesquieu's Lettres Persanes." *Australian Journal of French Studies* 46, no. 1–2 (January 2009): 139–54.

Warner, Stuart D. "Montesquieu's Literary Art." In *Persian Letters*, translated by Stuart D. Warner and Douard Stéphane. South Bend, IN: St. Augustine's Press, 2017.

Index

absence, of love, 87–92
absolutist monarchy, 206
abstract ideals, 45–46
abstracts, 183–84
Adorno, Theodor, 29, 33
alchemy, 133–34
alcohol, 239–40, 257n3
altruism, 91
Americas, 33, 105, 118, 130
amour propre (proper love), 94, 152
anarchism, 29–30
anthropology, 84
Arab tales, 25
Arendt, Hannah, 27–28, 29
aristocracies, 85, 129
Aristotle, 65, 81
ascetics, 7, 9
Asia, 50, 69, 243
astrology, 114
austerity, 69, 91, 97, 137n14,
    140–41, 155n5
authority: in Catholicism, 146–47;
    dogma from, 184–85; in the
    Enlightenment, 37; over eunuchs,
    212–13; honor in, 68; in monarchy,
    177–78; in Ottoman Empire, 73–74;
    paternal, 66; political, 218–19;
    politics of, 29–31, 114; power of,
    55; psychology of, 74–75; rational

autonomy in, 185–86; rebellion
    against, 77, 179; traditional, 176–77;
    in Western culture, 177; over wives,
    220, 233–34
avarice, 108–10

Bacon, Francis, 225
banking, 86–87
Before the Deluge (Sonenscher), 110
Berman, Marshall, 28–29, 36–37
Bibby, Andrew, 105–6, 116–17
Bodin, Jean: criticism of, 76; monarchy
    to, 65–67, 65–68, 71; Montesquieu
    and, viii; on political community,
    75; reputation of, 63; scholarship on,
    77n1; typology of, 64; tyranny to, 74
Boétie, Étienne de la, 81
Bourbon Crown, 117–18, 120,
    140, 146, 150
Braun, Theodore, 207
Brennan, Timothy, 136n11
Britain: commerce in, 106; culture of,
    35, 71–72; in literature, 195–96;
    money in, 91–92; oppression in, 31;
    Persia and, 21–22; Russia and, 196;
    society of, 94
Brooke, Christopher, 94

Calvinism, 150

About the Contributors

EDITORS

Jeffrey Church is professor of political science at the University of Houston. His research area is the history of modern political thought, with particular interest in Continental thought from Jean-Jacques Rousseau through Friedrich Nietzsche. His work examines the reflections of past philosophers on freedom, individuality, education, and culture, and shows how these reflections can inform contemporary liberal and democratic theory.

Alin Fumurescu received his PhD from Indiana University, Bloomington. His dissertation, *Compromise and Representation—A Split History of Early Modernity*, received the 2013 American Political Science Association's Leo Strauss Award for the best doctoral dissertation in the field of political philosophy. Currently, he is associate professor of political science at the University of Houston. Aside articles and book chapters, he has published *Compromise: A Political and Philosophical History* (Cambridge University Press, 2013, 2014), *Compromise and the American Founding: The Quest for the People's Two Bodies* (Cambridge University Press, 2019, 2021), and, with Anna Marisa Schoen, *Foundations of American Political Thought: Readings and Commentary* (Cambridge University Press, 2021).

Constantine Christos Vassiliou is a visiting assistant professor in political science at the University of Houston. He is a political theorist and historian of ideas specializing in Enlightenment political thought. His forthcoming book *Moderate Liberalism and the Scottish Enlightenment: Montesquieu, Hume, Smith, and Ferguson* (Edinburgh University Press, forthcoming 2023) unearths a moderate strand in foundational liberal thought, which emphasizes the critical importance of honor. Vassiliou has contributed to and coedited *Liberal Education and Citizenship in a Free Society* (University of Missouri Press, forthcoming 2023) and *Emotions, Community, and Citizenship:*

Cross-Disciplinary Perspectives (University of Toronto Press, 2017). His next book project, *Cross-Atlantic Connections: Commerce, Liberty, and the Birth of Liberal Democracy*, examines how Augustan-era political debates over questions concerning commerce, liberty, and the role of religion in market society shaped the formation of institutional life in pre-Revolutionary America.

CHAPTER CONTRIBUTORS

Megan Gallagher is an assistant professor in the Department of Gender and Race Studies at the University of Alabama, where she teaches classes on contemporary feminist theory and sex and gender in the history of political thought. The author of essays on Montesquieu, Rousseau, and Wollstonecraft, her work has appeared in *Eighteenth-Century Fiction, Law, Culture and the Humanities* and *Polity*, among other places. She is currently completing her first book manuscript, *Beyond Sacrifice: Civic Virtue and Emotional Practices*.

Ryan Patrick Hanley is professor of political science at Boston College. Prior to joining the faculty at Boston College, he was the Mellon Distinguished Professor of Political Science at Marquette University and held visiting appointments or fellowships at Yale, Harvard, and the University of Chicago. A specialist on the political philosophy of the Enlightenment period, he is the author of *Adam Smith and the Character of Virtue* (Cambridge University Press, 2009), *Love's Enlightenment: Rethinking Charity in Modernity* (Cambridge University Press, 2017), and *Our Great Purpose: Adam Smith on Living a Better Life* (Princeton University Press, 2019). His most recent books are *The Political Philosophy of Fénelon* and a companion translation volume, *Fénelon: Moral and Political Writings*, both published by Oxford University Press in 2020.

Rebecca Kingston is professor of political science at the University of Toronto. She is author of three monographs, the most recent being *Plutarch's Prism: Classical Reception and Public Humanism in France and England 1500–1800* (Cambridge University Press, 2022). Her research interests are largely within the history of political thought of the early modern and Enlightenment periods, including the thought of Montesquieu. She has been awarded research fellowships at Clare Hall, Cambridge, the Bodleian Library Centre for the Study of the Book, and the Jackman Humanities Institute of the University of Toronto. She is currently doing research on political motifs in material culture.

Dr. Pauline Kra is professor emerita at Yeshiva University. She collaborated on the definitive critical edition of the *Lettres persanes* published by Oxford University. She wrote numerous publications including "The Invisible Chain of the *Lettres persanes*," "Religion in Montesquieu's *Lettres persanes*," "The Role of the Harem in Imitations of the *Lettres persanes*," "Multiplicity of Voices in the *Lettres persanes*." She explored "The Concept of National Character in Eighteenth Century France" and Rousseau's idea of nation. She edited several works of Voltaire. At Columbia University she wrote the Genie software for automatic extraction of information on interactions between biological entities from natural language text data.

Peter Lund began his academic career at Hiram College in Ohio. He has two master's degrees, one from St. John's College in Annapolis and the other from Baylor University. He has studied classics and philosophy at Kent State University. He also taught Latin and English for seven years. Currently, he is a graduate student in the University of Houston's Political Science PhD program.

Michael Mosher recently contributed a chapter entitles "Internationalism, Cosmopolitanism, and Empires" to *The Cambridge Companion to Montesquieu*, edited by Keegan Callan and Sharon R. Krause (Cambridge University Press, forthcoming 2022); a piece in a Festschrift for Glen Newey, "Brief Against Comprehensive Justification," *Biblioteca della Liberta* 14, nos. 225–26 (May-December 2019); and, with Anna Plassart, the volume on enlightenment in *A Cultural History of Democracy*, edited by Eugenio Biagini (Bloomsbury Press, 2021). As the chapter in the present book comments on biographical themes, this note will suffice except to mention that he continues to teach political science at the University of Tulsa.

Emily Nacol (PhD 2007, University of Chicago) is associate professor of political science at the University of Toronto and author of *An Age of Risk: Politics and Economy in Early Modern Britain* (Princeton University Press, 2016). As a political theorist who specializes in the history of early modern political thought and political economy, she studies how early modern people coped with the problems of risk and uncertainty in political, social, and economic life. Her current work explores shifting attitudes toward labor and risk in Britain in the long eighteenth century, with special attention to how Britons conceptualized and singled out certain types of workers as particularly risky and undesirable (e.g., prostitutes, new finance workers, and the laboring poor). Nacol has held fellowships at Brown University's Political Theory Project and Cornell University's Society for the Humanities.

Andrea Radasanu received her BA, MA, and PhD at the University of Toronto. She is associate professor of political science at Northern Illinois University, specializing in early liberal thought and the political theory of empire. She has published articles and book chapters on Montesquieu, Burke, Rousseau, and Flaubert and is the editor of *The Pious Sex: Essays in the History of Political Thought* (2010) and *In Search of Humanity: Essays in Honor of Clifford Orwin* (2015). She also serves as the director for Northern Illinois University's Honors Program and has published several articles and book chapters on honors pedagogy and administration.

Helena Rosenblatt is professor of history, political science, and French at the Graduate Center of the City University of New York. Her most recent book is *A Lost History of Liberalism from Ancient Rome to the Twenty-First Century* (Princeton University Press, 2018). She is also the author of *Rousseau and Geneva from the* First Discourse *to the* Social Contract (Cambridge University Press, 1997), and *Liberal Values: Benjamin Constant and the Politics of Religion* (Cambridge University Press, 2008). Her present project, for which she was awarded a John Simon Guggenheim Fellowship, is an intellectual biography of Madame de Staël.

John T. Scott is professor of political science at the University of California, Davis. He received his PhD from the University of Chicago in 1992. Most of his research is on the thought of Jean-Jacques Rousseau, and he is past president of the Rousseau Association. He is the author of *Rousseau's God: Theology, Religion, and the Natural Goodness of Man* (University of Chicago Press, 2023), *Rousseau's Reader: Strategies of Persuasion and Education* (University of Chicago Press, 2020), *The Philosophers' Quarrel: Rousseau, Hume, and the Limits of Human Understanding* (Yale University Press, 2009), and *The Routledge Guide to Machiavelli's "The Prince"* (Routledge, 2016). He is the editor of *Jean-Jacques Rousseau: Critical Assessments* (Routledge, 2006) and *Rousseau and l'Infâme* (Rodopi, 2009). He has translated and edited the *Essay on the Origin of Languages and Writings Related to Music* (University Press of New England, 1998) and *Jean-Jacques Rousseau: Major Political Writings* (University of Chicago Press, 2012), in addition to numerous articles in leading journals and chapters in edited volumes.

Robert Sparling is an associate professor of political studies at the University of Ottawa. He is the author of *Johann Georg Hamann and the Enlightenment Project* (University of Toronto Press, 2011) and *Political Corruption: The Underside of Civic Morality* (University of Pennsylvania Press, 2019).

Céline Spector is professor at the philosophy department of Sorbonne University. Her work is devoted to modern and contemporary political philosophy, to the history of philosophy from the eighteenth century (Montesquieu, Rousseau) to the present day, to theories of justice, and to liberalism and its critiques. In the wake of a reflection on the legacy of the Enlightenment, she has been engaged for several years in an analysis of European democracy and sovereignty. Her latest publications are *Eloges de l'injustice. La philosophie face à la déraison* (Seuil, 2016); *Rousseau et la critique de l'économie politique* (Presses Universitaires de Bordeaux, 2017); *Rousseau* (Polity Press, 2019); *No demos? Souveraineté et démocratie à l'épreuve de l'Europe* (Seuil, 2021); *Europe philosophique, Europe politique. L'héritage des Lumières*, edited with T. Coignard (Classiques Garnier, 2022); *Rousseau et Locke. Dialogues critiques*, edited with J. Lenne-Cornuez (Oxford University Studies on the Enlightenment, Liverpool University Press, 2022). She coedits the series "L'esprit des lois" for the Librairie Vrin.

Vickie B. Sullivan is the Cornelia M. Jackson Professor of Political Science at Tufts University. She is the author of three books: *Montesquieu and the Despotic Ideas of Europe: An Interpretation of "Spirit of the Laws"* (University of Chicago Press, 2017), *Machiavelli, Hobbes, and the Formation of a Liberal Republicanism in England* (Cambridge University Press, 2004), and *Machiavelli's Three Romes: Religion, Human Liberty, and Politics Reformed* (Northern Illinois University Press, 1996; reissued Cornell University Press, 2020). She has also edited two volumes: *The Comedy and Tragedy of Machiavelli: Essays on the Literary Works* (Yale University Press, 2000) and *Shakespeare's Political Pageant: Essays in Politics and Literature*, with Joseph Alulis (Rowman and Littlefield, 1996). She is a contributor to the *Cambridge Companion to Montesquieu*, edited by Keegan Callanan and Sharon R. Krause (forthcoming). Her articles have appeared in the *American Political Science Review*, *History of European Ideas*, *History of Political Thought*, *Political Theory*, *Polity*, and *Review of Politics*.

Lee Ward is professor of political science at Baylor University. He has published widely in the areas of political theory and American political thought. His books include *The Politics of Liberty in England and Revolutionary America* (Cambridge University Press, 2004), *John Locke and Modern Life* (Cambridge University Press, 2010), *Modern Democracy and the Theological-Political Problem in Spinoza, Rousseau and Jefferson* (Palgrave McMillan, 2014), and *Recovering Classical Liberal Political Economy: Natural Rights and the Harmony of Interests* (Edinburgh University Press, 2022). He is editor of John Locke's *Two Treatises of Government* (Hackett, 2016). He has also published articles on John Locke, Thomas Hobbes, Aristotle, Montesquieu,

Algernon Sidney, Plato, Baruch Spinoza, Jean-Jacques Rousseau, Tom Paine, Irish republicanism, John Rawls, and Jürgen Habermas that have appeared in several leading academic journals.

Stuart D. Warner is professor of philosophy and founding director of the Montesquieu Forum at Roosevelt University. He has translated Montesquieu's *Persian Letters* and La Rochefoucauld's *Maxims* (bilingual); edited the writings of Hume, James Fitzjames Stephens, and Michael Polanyi; and authored essays on Herodotus, Montaigne, Descartes, Hobbes, Spinoza, Locke, Montesquieu, Hume, Adam Smith, and Hegel.